What's Your F***ing Opinion?

How to Have Political Conversations
Without Deleting, Defriending, or Decapitating Family and Friends

Michael Charming

What's Your F***ing Opinion?
How to Have Political Conversations Without Deleting, Defriending, or
Decapitating Family and Friends

First printed in the United Kingdom, 2021

ISBN: 978-1-80049-390-2

Published by
Michael Charming
Kemp House, 152 City Road
London EC1V 2NX

Book Layout © 2017 BookDesignTemplates.com

DEDICATION

I dedicate this book to:

All the people in the world who …
>work towards bringing a change in society for the betterment of humankind, other species, and our planet.

All the people who have …
>found themselves at crossroads, just at a mere expression of their opinions or supporting a certain leader, a policy, or an organization and are now considered a foe by their friends, family, those near and dear, or even strangers.

Every leader who…
>doesn't give up and continues to fight for his/her followers no matter the backlash, defamation, blame, or personal attacks faced by virtue of holding that position.

Every single voter who desires…
>to live in a society filled with love, care, respect, and mutual understanding.

And, as always, *Dad, Mom, Brother, Sister-in-law, Friends, and Well-wishers…*

Thank you, hugs, and love.

EPIGRAPH

COMING TOGETHER

A wish, a desire, a need, or an even deeper longing by many
for us to come together as a family, a society, a nation, or even as humanity.
A beautiful wish and a great goal to strive for....
...but do our actions speak louder than our words?

At the slightest difference of opinion or the mere sight of a social media status
we don't want to read,
we respond with
'stupid', 'idiot', 'asshole', 'fucking cunt', 'don't talk to me ever again',
'defriend me right now', 'goodbye, I hope never to see you again',
or 'may Satan eat you alive',
because we are angry, hurt, and offended.

Can someone tell me how this type of communication is meant to bring everyone
together,
how it aims to educate the uneducated, love the unloved, or serve the unserved?

*If we are to **Come Together**, shouldn't we be displaying the opposite?*
What happened to the wise old teachings of our parents; 'when others go low,
we go high',
'although I am not with you, I hear you and am willing to see and understand
your perspective',
'I disagree with you, our life experiences differ, but we don't have to kill each
other'?

Child prostitution is happening in a distant country; let's blame our government.
The rich get richer; life gets tougher; winters become colder; let's blame our
government.
A pandemic is in our cities because of some fucking virus; let's blame our gov-
ernment.
There's too much spice in my food; my partner left me; let's blame our govern-
ment.

Do we ever look inwardly and reflect on our actions, behaviors, and responses?
Everywhere we see a lack of integrity, exaggeration, and double, triple, or even
quadruple standards.

We may find painful memories, emotional blockages, grief, anger, and hurt from
our past is rooted within our DNA.
That causes many to see our worst when we disagree, spewing our brand of ven-
om,
ready to annihilate, ready for fist blows and bloodshed...
...because somebody dares to offer a different opinion...
....even though just a second ago, this person was very dear to us.

What happened, what shifted, what fell from the sky all of a sudden?
This person doesn't make legislation or run the country,
neither does this person have more voting rights than you,
nor does this person have more mouths, more hands, or two asses to show or
twerk around.
So, why bother?
Why lose a great friend or family member because of something over which one
has minimal control?

When we realize this, when we begin to utter compassion after hearing the
fucktard words,
when we open our arms towards others, no matter how closed they might be,
and when we stop blaming governments for all the miseries in our lives,
only then can we start taking the first steps towards the dream we all aspire to.

Perhaps then, a wish, a desire, a need, or an even deeper longing by many
will no longer remain a distant dream; maybe then we all can proudly say, shout
and sing that

We are All Finally Coming Together!!!

CONTENTS

PREFACE

Mentioning that I am an orgasm coach and bodyworker brings mixed reactions; some joke about it, others are surprised, most are shocked yet curious, and some just run away. I have discovered that the majority have an immense curiosity to learn more about orgasm, relationships, and sex. Still, they don't want to discuss the topic in public or in private. Many are open to discussing the relationship aspect but draw the line and scream NO when asked about sex and orgasm. Yet, I have felt their huge desire to discuss these forbidden topics. The aversion to having these discussions seems to be multiplied when the professional is a man.

In my field, both women and men generally prefer to work with women, though covertly, some men work with women for very different reasons. When dealing with issues relating to sexuality and orgasm, few seem comfortable working with a man. Suppose a person working in this field, like me, tends to share political views openly, especially those involving taking a particular stance, does not help in any way. Working in an area already very judgmental of men's inclusion, he may find himself being out-grouped by coaches, transformational leaders, and clients alike. Perhaps their dislike for the political leaders I support and the views that I hold cause them to project their beliefs about those leaders or issues onto me, creating a perception based on the collectives' misguided and manipulated views and opinions. I have never out-grouped anyone based on their opinions or political support. I find it hurtful to receive this treatment when I am open and welcoming to others, especially transformational coaches.

In 2015, I started sharing my political opinion, openly and widely, on social media. I was bombarded with private messages from many, including my then partner, suggesting I avoid sharing these views online. There was a backlash of name-calling, labeling, ghosting, scapegoating, and backbiting from transformation coaches and close friends. It was heartbreaking to be at the receiving end. Back then, it was frowned upon to talk about your political beliefs openly, as many found this upsetting. In the early days, my posts regarding specific leaders or policies would result in hundreds of Facebook connections disconnecting immediately. Over time, this disconnection with friends, based on my posting political opinions, became a regular occurrence that I got used to.

After my first political post, an experienced coach and good friend warned me of the negative consequences of mixing politics and business. I had pondered the potential negative consequences before posting because of the way politics was viewed then. Being a coach and working on sensitive topics like sexuality and orgasm, but simultaneously reflecting political opinions that may not bode well with spiritual and sexually liberated communities whose members' esoteric views are far from being broad enough to cope with my more realistic perspective. Based on this, I tried to resist sharing my views relating to the goings-on in the political arena, but it felt suffocating. To liberate myself from this suffocating feeling, I chose to accept the consequences of expressing my opinions, no matter if they differed from others. My quest to gain emotional, mental and physical strength began, as I needed to face the regular setbacks and disappointments of being side-lined and out-grouped by many. These times were challenging, but I learned and grew at tremendous speed.

I was born in India. Being part of a Hindu family, spirituality was part of life during childhood and teenage years. Studying in India is never easy, and being top of my class during my school years shows my intelligence level. In college, I won an election, giving me a good understanding of what it takes to win an election, something many lack. Leaving India's warm, friendly, and fun-loving culture to study and work in the cold and conservative UK culture, and being a minority group, gave me the experience to be a member of an out-group. After the UK, I moved to the US, then Singapore, before coming back to the UK in 2010. During this time, I traveled to 45+ countries globally. These experiences gave me an understanding of different cultures, economies, and human behaviors. It allowed me to see and understand the world in a manner that few get to experience. There is a saying, '*one cannot buy maturity; it only comes with experience.*'

With my many years of experience and personal growth relating to sexual mastery, I found dealing with political conversations, in a non-offensive way, a whole new ball game. Still, I was determined to work through this minefield. It wasn't easy, but I knew that it would improve with practice, which is what happened. Fast forward a few years, I began to receive private messages from friends, thanking me for the opinions I shared. Some said that conversations about politics or views and comments read on other people's feeds spoiled their mood, as they were generally nasty or filled with hate and personal attacks towards one another. My views were found to be very different, often unique, offering the reader another perspective. It was said that while they may disagree with my opinions, they do eagerly wait for me to share them. Often, friends who held opposite views stayed at my place. We had lengthy political conversations in a friendlier manner without losing any sleep. These changes felt good and provided an excellent reason to continue in terms of my personal growth. It was tough, but seeing the results gave me the energy I needed to continue.

On a warm summer Saturday in 2017, the idea of writing a book on this subject crossed my mind. 'Someday, for sure' was my immediate response, and I left it there. A year later, in 2018, the idea crossed my mind again, but I decided to work towards it this time. After thinking about it for a few months, I finally began to lay the book's foundation. By the end of 2018, I had drafted the bullet points relating to all the chapters. I continued my work on sexuality, running workshops, giving coaching, and exploring more about orgasms and bodywork. In March 2019, I decided to finish the book on orgasm, the structure of which was also laid down in 2018. After six months of arduous work, my first book, *Amplify Your Orgasm,* was published in November 2019. I loved the feeling to be the author of a book on orgasm, a topic many dread, many frown upon, and seldom, if ever, discuss. Science shows that orgasms offer several benefits, but it really perplexes me that we run after external things for our well-being but ignore the most potent, powerful, and healing sexual and orgasmic energy present within us. We try to derive pleasure through sex toys, robots, watching porn, and objectification. Still, we hardly get to even scratch the surface of these hidden but deeply nourishing orgasmic energies.

As soon as that book was published, I knew that my next project was to complete the incomplete work relating to another sensitive but confrontational topic, politics. Since March 2020, this book had been my focus, and I am delighted that it has finally reached the stage that I can present to you.

My wish is that you will find this book useful and transformative. If so, please drop me an email to let me know how it helped you. I hope you will find some nuggets that will help you deepen your relationship when having political conversations with others. If you notice anything incorrect or that may add value in the next edition, please feel free to provide feedback. I strive to learn from those I aim to 'teach' and will always continue on that path.

I look forward to connecting with you, in one way or the other. I am sending you lots of love, hugs, and best wishes on your political triggering but worthwhile journey. Have an exploratory, transformative, and safe journey, without any bloodshed. Inwards and Outwards, Micro and Macro. Over to you now 😊.

Michael Charming

Email: *coach@michaelcharming.com,*
Website: *michaelcharming.com*

ACKNOWLEDGEMENTS

First and foremost, I would like to thank the Universe for showering me with blessings and gracing me with the courage and wisdom to continue working towards my destiny. This book is a crucial step towards my goal of bringing togetherness, helping individuals rise to their optimum human potential, and support each other with more love, compassion, understanding, and empathy, in our society.

I am incredibly grateful to my mom and dad and my brother and his wife for their prayers and continuous support throughout my life, particularly while writing this book. Without their sacrifices, love, and care, it would not have been possible to finish my second book.

I would like to thank my friends, who knowingly or unknowingly contributed to this book by exchanging their views, agreements and disagreements, resentments, anger, upsets, and passive aggression on various political posts I shared on social media platforms.

I would like to think my teachers, colleagues, and community members, whom I met during my journey of Orgasm, which allowed me to get to know and access deeper parts of myself and helped me understand human behavior. Though those experiences and understandings were mostly in terms of sexuality and relationships, the experiences and knowledge gained allowed me to relate the behaviors often portrayed by people during political conversations.

I would like to thank all my friends who disengaged and defriended me due to my political opinions. Their actions and simultaneous disconnection without even saying goodbye gave me the emotional ammunition needed to think and lay the foundations for this book.

I would like to express my sincere and heartfelt thanks to all my lovers, especially those I have had a chance to share and discuss political opinions. I am extremely grateful for the love, support, and care that each of you offered me during our relationship. Thank you for coming into my life, for allowing us to spend some precious moments together, and for being yourself. I wouldn't be who I am today without the experiences we shared. I wish each of you happiness, positivity, and lots of love.

I would like to express my sincere warmth and gratitude to Cordelia Zafiropulo. She has always been willing to help, support, and guide me throughout this book journey. I am deeply grateful to learn from her depth of insight, wisdom, life experiences, and profound knowledge.

I would like to thank my PA and rest of the staff for their continuous support and for often going beyond expectations of their job requirements to help me achieve my goals.

I would also like to thank my editor, Tracy Cockcroft, for her expertise and willingness to participate in this project. From the get-go, her expertise assured the book would be in the right hands as far as the final editorial aspect was concerned.

I would like to thank everyone else who helped me in any shape or form to bring my book to completion.

Finally, I would like to thank the readers who decided to buy and give this book a chance. I hope you will find the information deeply valuable.

Regards, Hugs, and Love.
MC

INTRODUCTION

Why, starting in 2015, give or take, politics became ugly, divisive, and polarizing. In the US, in the UK, and frankly in many other places globally. Most seem to reverberate what was happening in the US and the UK?

It is an interesting question and, to no small extent, the motivation and basis for this book.

It is time for you to be honest. Think carefully, how many people did you 'defriend' either during the 2016 US election, during the UK Brexit vote, or since then? Okay, now think again, how many people did you simply AVOID seeing or talking to during these two campaigns? Did you include NOT attending family or close friend functions while thinking, "that damn Uncle, I am NEVER going to sit with him again, imagine, he actually thinks Hillary is honest! Jerk?"

And the other question puts this into perspective for me. Why didn't Obama vs. Romney, May vs. Corbyn, or Modi vs. R. Gandhi, for that matter, elicit the kind of visceral, death threat, vitriolic outpourings that the 2016 UK and US elections demanded? Yes, I said demanded because you HAD to take a side; you HAD to make a stand as though your life depended on it. Many commentators even told you it was that serious, critical, and fatal.

If hating a black candidate made you a racist, then what did hating a Mormon make you? The media and the wingers, both left and right, couldn't even come up with a word to describe hating a Mormon. My word for this is "stupid." Was that perhaps holding back unseen and unknown hatreds?

As we will discover by taking a trip through pretty much all the human options, it is a human thing and not a political thing. You know, we weren't born with an R or D, or C or L, sticker pasted on our newborn heads. So, if politics is not entirely a DNA thing, not a hereditary thing, then the human issue must be the answer, and not so much the political one that seems obvious. We have traits we carry as members

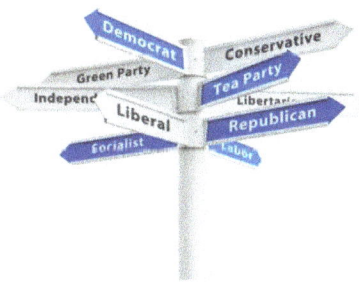

Figure 1: Several political parties exist in every country, each with their own manifesto and principles.

of tribes (families), larger groups (political parties), our country and the world itself. Yet, even when a virus threatens the world as a whole, many countries continue their nationalistic posturing until the very last second before their entire population is wiped out.

While the pattern of sides disliking one another during elections is nothing new, over the last four years, it has borne out that THIS time and THIS space has had the worst of it from Trump vs. Clinton to the UK's Brexit. Both resolutions appeared to be a vote for nationalism, in one form or another, which then sparked nationalistic leaders, and elections for leaders to tilt that way, world-wide, ever since.

History tells us that this is nothing new. In the early 1800s, politicians called each other liars and scum, even declaring that some were unfit for any office. Now, society is louder and has many more ways to express their upset, anger, views, polarization, disdain, and dismissal of the 'other side.' Each side has their own TV networks, social media channels, websites, and print media. Suppose we NEVER want to hear or see even one word from the 'other side.' In that case, we can completely insulate ourselves rather quickly and completely.

We will examine the many reasons for this trend. Some have skipped the 'trend' designation and suggested we have driven straight off the cliff edge without hope of recovery. We will examine that, too.

We will look at all of this, not so much as a political phenomenon, but more as a psychological, sociological, group dynamic, world dynamic, and all the way down to the personal level of the human makeup, love and the phenomena of making connections or disconnecting.

Since self-reflection is almost a lost art, let us again take a moment and ask ourselves, "Did we really, really listen during conversations with someone from the 'other side'? Or were we just being polite, waiting for our turn to blast that bastard into the next century along with his idiotic ideas? While listening, did your thoughts wander to how could a sophisticated Londoner be so damn stupid? Or maybe, just what you would expect from a WOMAN to support Hillary even though she is a first-class prevaricator.

One more question; can you honestly recall how many political conversations you have had with someone from the 'other side' that were civil, lasted more than a minute, contained no swear words or insults, and resulted in you shaking hands, smiling, or hugging (pre-Covid) the other person afterward? This is a tough one, so I will give you another minute to strain your brain.

For me, politics, sex, and relationships are the most confrontational topics of conversation. But, they are, without any doubt, the most exciting. Being an orgasm coach, I have taken an in-depth look at orgasm in my book *Amplify Your Orgasm*. In my upcoming book, I will be looking at relationships. Being able to have non-confrontational discussions around these topics is something everyone needs. Imagine for a moment how wonderful your life would be if you had a nourishing relationship and deep sexual connection with your partner?

Then, imagine a society if everyone could discuss things even with strongly held opinions that differ. Despite these differences in opinion, we all talked things through without dismissing or building resentment against one another?

It is time for us to understand how we act, what we do, and most of all, WHY we act the way we do. This understanding can rapidly change our behaviors to stop us from losing connections, family, friends and bringing an end to social discourse. Correct me if I am wrong, but I believe that saying "I am right because you are a f***ing idiot" is not exactly a debate or a dialog response to any question asked by someone with whom you disagree politically.

Read and USE this book to improve yourself. Yes! You really do need to improve yourself. It is based not only on political issues but also on social, personal, and family issues. These will also be easier to navigate using what you will learn in this book.

How to use this book

This book's concepts are cumulative; therefore, I suggest that you read from beginning to end rather than jumping to pieces that may seem the most interesting. As you progress, you will notice tips referring to various chapters. I encourage you to stop and see which of these you can implement, set the reminders and have accountability buddies so that you can integrate these into your life, your behaviour, and conversations with your family, friends and even strangers.

I encourage my readers to use my "Feeling Over Doing Formula." Instead of being goal-oriented with any of the tips, exercises or practices or aiming to finish the book as fast as you can, that you rather listen to your body (on all levels) and let it be your guide. If anything feels overwhelming, it is okay to back off and come back to it when you feel more open and receptive. Respect your boundaries and limitations and approach this topic with a mindset of curiosity and exploration. If you are already aware of any aspect, explore it further rather than forcing a particular goal or dismissing it from the outset. Allow reading and implementing tips from this book to be a journey. Politics is a sensitive, important and very confrontational topic. As you read, it may trigger a few sensitive spots within you or bring back memories. If this happens, pause and reflect on what happened. Pay special attention to how you and the other person interacted before considering what you could do differently in similar scenarios.

My suggestions are guidelines and should be practised with caution. Before trying any of the book's exercises, please consult relevant specialists if you are unsure. The book will also help you transform at a personal level. Transformation is the process of old patterns and behaviors begin shifted when a new identity begins to form, and new experiences and new parts of your being begin to emerge. This can feel exciting, adventurous, and uncomfortable all at once. Feeling like this lets you know that you are definitely on the right track. Just like any other path, we need to feel our way into the process of change rather than trying to jump over the parts we don't like.

I invite you to quieten your mind and drop into your body, feelings, and desires, letting them emerge and see what they would like to do. After all, the journey towards creating a positive, connected and vibrant society who care for one another's needs and empathize with each other is an exceptionally challenging yet very desirable goal.

Are you ready to bring transformation to our society?

Although I have aimed to cover the essential topics; this is by no means an exhaustive list. What I have offered should give you a solid framework to convert any hostile or disparaging conversations to those of love, in the hope of assisting to save the relationships that you desire. I wish you success in getting through the book from start to finish in your own time. If you need any help in further growth or need to discuss anything, please reach out to us; we are here to help. I hope with your open mind, and curious mindset, you will take to this opportunity to learn more about yourself, others, and the world around you. Ready? Let's go!

CHAPTER ONE

CONFRONTATIONS

Many either confront or avoid, but do so at the wrong time. Confronting when not needed or avoiding when needed. Let's do both parties a favor by confronting at the right time and in the right way.

Michael Charming

Introduction

We are currently bombarded with news relating to confrontation between various political leaders, organizations, groups, or countries. What does it mean to actually confront someone? Why do we feel the need to confront anyone?

Why do leaders respond to confrontations differently? What does this tell us about their leadership style, impact on society, inter-country relationships, and different political parties? Most importantly, what effect does this have on those at the receiving end, the ones who are digesting this news and trying to make sense of it?

They used the most advanced methods to solve their conflicts

Figure 2-3: Do all confrontations have to escalate to the extent that resolution can only be found in the boxing ring or on the field, figuratively speaking?

Some of us panic and start feeling fearful; we get concerned about what might come next, while for others, life goes on as if nothing happened. Why do our friends react differently to the same news that makes us concerned?

In our own world, we confront our friends, loving relatives, even partners, creating animosity on levels never before seen. Why? Was it worth it? And it has continued for four years already. We don't forget! We don't forgive!

But what is it we should be forgiving and forgetting? Our friends and relatives don't make bad government policy, nor do they lie to us, cheat us or run over our fundamental rights with a steamroller. They did not take us out of the EU, so why do we blame them and blame them in very aggressive ways?

Suppose we learn how to disagree while being respectful and civil, disagree without being disagreeable and learn how to keep our relationships while retaining our self-respect and philosophical positions. In that case, the very first thing we have to understand is confrontation. We are currently confronting instead of conversing, confronting instead of arguing our case without being argumentative, confronting with judgments instead of being non-judgmental, and confronting with resentments and grudges being held rather than not.

Confrontation – embarrassment or necessity?

* *Jeremy Corbyn confronted with Donald Trump over the NHS and now he is kept apart from the President - who said he would NOT want the health service even on a silver platter*
* *Britain risks being dragged into wider confrontation against Iran as highest-level security alert issued*
* *India confrontation with Pakistan emerges due to escalation of conflict over Kashmir*
* *China and India on brink of armed conflict as hopes of resolution to border dispute fade. Chinese military primed for battle military sources say; Indian troops 'prepared for any eventuality*
* *Confrontation between Iran-Saudi Arabia has engulfed several Middle Eastern countries and many regional and international Islamic organizations, such as the League of Arab States, the Gulf Cooperation Council, and the Organization of Islamic Cooperation (OIC). What impact will this confrontation result on the OIC?*
* *Trump confronts 'questioning' governors, asking for more supplies, calls them unappreciative*
* *Trump confronts medical community at his rally, and calls coronavirus a 'Democratic hoax'*
* *Most countries having to deal with 'balancing act' of U.S.-China confrontation: UAE foreign minister*

Let's define **confrontation:**

- To face or oppose hostility or defiance
- To present for acknowledgment or contradiction
- To stand face to face (suspect and victim; declaration of war)
- To be in one's way
- To bring together for examination or comparison

Sounds pretty bad. Who wants to confront or be confronted?

Political leaders, apparently, confront each other continuously. Country leaders do it louder and with more venom. Political candidates are the loudest and most vitriolic. Yet, these politicians and their countries manage to handle the confrontation, even when it escalates, and then finally find a way to de-escalate the tension and reduce the level of confrontation from 'potentially globally fatal' to just plain old 'politically inconvenient.'

In the 'macro' sense, we watch leaders deal with confrontation. Sometimes, they must create it for national pride. Other times, from a belief, true or otherwise, that their sovereignty is being trespassed, or economic or treaty foul play. More often than not, politically, because their supporters EXPECT a particular response based on the political party's philosophy. And occasionally, from merely being insulted.

"Aren't you glad we had this meeting to resolve our conflict?"

Figure 4: No matter how well-intended the political conversation starts, it often results in confrontation, aggression, and at times, fistfights.

So, how do leaders handle confrontation?

In most cases, much more carefully than one might assume. There is a specific mathematical matrix of options and values for good and bad outcomes in these cases. This matrix is very skillfully considered based on the assigned values. The most optimal outcomes are highlighted, and with the necessary levelheadedness are likely engaged. Most leaders want to have a country, party, or state to lead when the confrontation is over. Some, apparently, don't care.

Let us consider the example of "small hands, dotard Donald Trump." Then his associate repeated the insult with "the relapse of the dotage of a dotard," as seen by Kim Jong Un, the Leader of North Korea. Kim's response to Trump was to call him "Little Rocket Man" for sending up all those rockets. Things quickly went from bad to worse.

It was bad enough that Trump felt the need to insult his opponent, as he does more often than not. Everyone who disagrees or doesn't do what he wants is an 'opponent.' So, this is where the Little Rocket Man came from. Then, Little Rocket Man threatens to destroy half the world and fires test rockets to prove it.

Headlines are screaming about the potential of nuclear war. Worldwide, people are begging for someone to be the adult in the room and calling for United Nations Security Council meetings.

The matrix is as follows:

Trump can escalate, resulting in Kim either backing off or a nuclear war.

Trump can de-escalate, resulting in no nuclear war, but risking his base seeing him as a weak wimp.

Figure 5: Two babies with access to nuclear weapons.

Trump can thread the needle, enough to placate, but with sufficient bravado to keep his base proud of his strength. But this risks an escalation from Kim.

This demonstrates that leaders must study confrontation carefully, do the matrix, weigh up all options, make a decision, and hope their 'math' was right.

Whenever results fall out of the matrix (or perhaps were part of the matrix), various government ministers are sent to deal with these confrontations. Suppose the vice presidents of two countries have resulted in an escalation of a conflict. A phone call between the Presidents will be arranged. They will tread water very carefully, knowing this is their last political move to de-escalate the situation. Similarly, suppose Presidents confront (as seen in the case of US-China between Trump and Xi). In that case, various foreign and finance ministers will aim at opening the dialog to de-escalate. Finally, there is the option of bringing a third party (leaders from other countries or world organizations) to diffuse. China was requested to speak to Kim Jong-Un when the confrontation between North Korea

Figure 6: From a nobody to Prime Minister, then President, and back to PM before becoming President again. Putin grew himself to be Russian's National Hero, even though the rest of the world had condemned Russian aggression time and again.

and the US was at its peak.

Before we move on to the types of confrontation and how to handle these on a more personal, 'micro' level, and the personality types that both create and deal with confrontation, let us take one more look at how countries and leaders get into confrontations and how they deal with them.

- A need to create confrontation from a sense of nationalistic pride.
- In Spain, the Basques would not allow the national government to usurp their regional laws and rules. When this started, the Spanish government 'took over,' which elicited pushback from the Basques. The situation continued to escalate until both inside and outside forces finally brought the tension level down to tolerable before (somewhat) jointly accepting interim rules.
- From a belief, true or otherwise, that their sovereignty is being trespassed.
- Russia decides to simply walk in and take Crimea from Ukraine. Since the US did not step in, for whatever reason, Ukraine had no choice but to go to war with the Russian forces still remaining outside Crimea but inside Ukraine. While no one locally would call the thousands of dead soldiers and civilians a skirmish, Russia 'seems' happy with its spoils. They aren't pushing their enormous advantage but believe they will be back for the rest of the country.
- From economic or treaty foul play.
- When it comes to trade with China, Trump feels that they have taken advantage of the treaties and agreements with the US. both legally and illegally. He imposed tariffs and threats, but China responded with tariffs and more threats. The matrix was crumpled up and tossed into the Rose Garden. Thinking it was a rogue golf ball, Trump hit it with a Three Wood and knocked it out onto Pennsylvania Avenue. He then added more products to the tariff list. The Chinese matched his bet and raised him a few additional products.
- Sidebar: Until today, Trump still tells his base that China is paying these tariffs. He needs to believe he is in a strong position, to hang on for a while to win since his objective is winning. The reality is that American importers are paying the tariffs, which hurt American companies as much as the Chinese. Trump, declaring himself the great negotiator, cut a deal for both sides to reduce tariffs, with some good and bad add-ons, allowing him to (wrongly) claim a win.
- Politically, because their supporters EXPECT a specific response based on the political party's philosophy.
- A solid example was Boris Johnson's campaign 'Get Brexit Done' to get out of the EU by a specific date, come hell or high water. He won, and the jury is still out on how badly this decision may turn out. But he did what his party and his supporters demanded, right or wrong.
- From simply being insulted.
- See Trump vs. Kim.

Let us finally answer the question as to how leaders actually handle confrontation. There are generally three types of leaders, Despotic, Autocratic, and Democratic (more on Leadership in Chapter Ten). They will manage their issues similarly within their category, but each category will manage their issues differently.

Despotic – Good luck figuring this one out. Egotistical, self-important, self-preservation instincts. Will bully until a bigger bully steps on them. Confrontation is handled viscerally, often militarily.

Autocratic – This type of leader realizes that they can be removed if the effort is great enough. (for example, see Arab Spring). This leader is egotistical and self-important, but their bullying tactic is usually more domestic than international. They really don't want a bully from the outside telling them what to do. They like sticking to domestic confrontation, resulting in softer but equally effective bullying like removing competing political parties, arrests, and constant public shaming of opponents.

Democratic - Democratic leaders realize, like company CEOs, they are only around for as long as the people want them. Thus handling confrontation is most likely done through the lens of the matrix described above. The political fallout, the public perception, and the group of supporters to whom they must kowtow are always kept in mind.

Now, to make it interesting, let us bring this 'macro' view down to you and me. Find out why we confront and how to do it without an individual level of nuclear war.

> ❖ *Man fatally shot during confrontation with police*
> ❖ *Cops use gas in confrontation with protesters*
> ❖ *72-year-old vet's jaw broken after confronting man about masks, Washington police say*
> ❖ *Woman shot 8 times after confronting neighbor over fireworks, New York cops say*
> ❖ *Couple apologizes after confronting man over 'Black Lives Matter' chalk in front of his home*
> ❖ *The real midlife crisis confronting many Americans*
> ❖ *Woman confronting vandals covered in paint during renewed Portland protests*
> ❖ *Gun violence kills 160 as holiday weekend exposes tale of 'two Americas'*
> ❖ *Buffalo Cop Suspended After Calling Bystander A 'F**king C**t.'*
> ❖ *Protestors try to topple president's statue outside White House*

What causes confrontation at the human body level?

Confrontations exist because, at the body level, our brain's primary responsibility is to protect the body. When we feel attacked, which is often the case with political conversations, our brain deploys the same defenses for protecting the body. A study found that when people are challenged on their firm beliefs, which is often the case with political conversations, more activation is triggered in the brain's area that corresponds with self-identity and negative emotions.[1,2] In the same study, through MRI scans found that political arguments result in increased activation of brain structures, called the 'default mode network,' structures responsible for mind-wandering, memory, and thinking about oneself and one's identity.

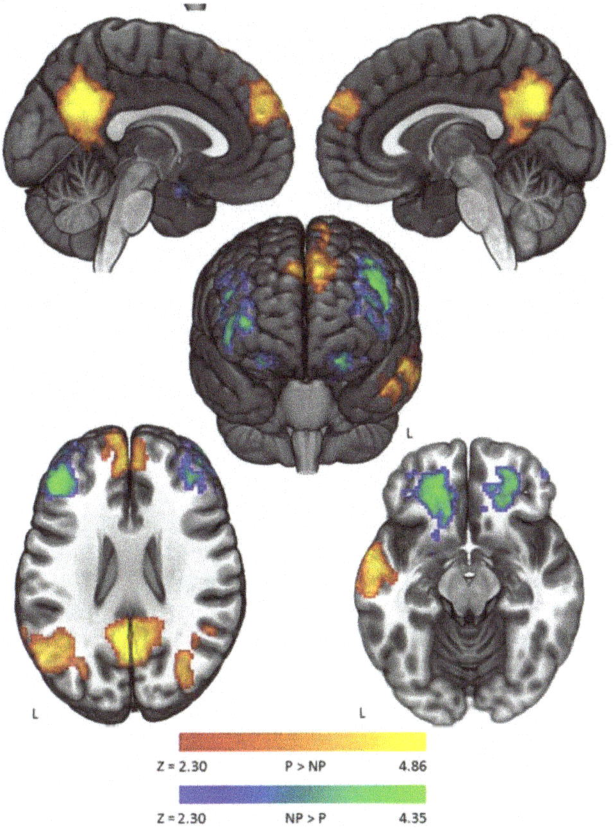

Figure 7: Brain activation during challenges to political vs. non-political beliefs. In red/yellow, brain regions that showed increased signal while processing challenges to political beliefs (P > NP). In blue/green, brain regions showed increased signal.[2]

As per researcher John Hibbing, it is difficult to change someone's mind about political issues because their reactions are rooted in their physiology.[3] "If people spend most of their lives focusing on negative rather than positive, they're probably going to have a different way of experiencing the world than those who do the opposite," says Hibbing. Arguments that seem rational to one side will seem irrational to the other.

When conflict happens, we tend to respond by accommodating, avoiding, or confronting. While the first two are passive approaches, the latter is more aggressive. We must accept that confrontation can occur anytime that there are two or more people with differing views. This will likely result in confrontation at some point, so admit, it can't really be avoided. Surprisingly, confrontations are important for the growth, success, and advancement of our society.

Let us repeat that again for those waiting for their turn to bitch about what we are saying and missed the point: **we must accept that confrontation can occur anytime that there are two or more people with differing views. This will likely result in confrontation at some point, so admit, it can't really be avoided. Surprisingly, confrontations are important for the growth, success, and advancement of our society**.

With our abilities to find resolution relating to complex issues, individuals will be able to do so when permitted. The actual issue is not really the confrontation, but rather how we deal with it. This means we can choose a productive manner that allows acceptance of diversity of thoughts, clearly defined boundaries, and everyone engaged is conscious of their and others' bodily feelings, emotions, and perspectives. Or we can choose a negative manner where we blame, shame, demean others, exercise judgment, stay narrow-minded, and fixed to our beliefs without allowing the space for the expression of others' thoughts.

The answer is simple. We will have confrontations, and just like the weather, we cannot change this. (Could this explain why London has an abundance of gloomy weather?) We need to understand, since we are going to have disagreements, the question is: do we want to be the adults in the room or act like spoiled five-year-olds who just had their cell phones taken away?

Why confrontations exist:

Now that we know we are going to have confrontations, there seem to be several basic categories as to WHY we have them:

Giving opinions rather than facts: People often have the tendency to share opinions rather than present the facts. More importantly, if the other person disagrees, they habitually categorize them. For example: all Republicans are sexist, all Democrats are socialist, all Labour are after free money, all Conservatives are capitalists. If you want to give an opinion, the best way is to present the facts before offering your opinion and clarifying the two. Or, better yet, make a clear CONNECTION between the facts and your opinion.

According to the Congressional Budget Office and the Government Accounting Office, Trump's tax cut gave 88% of the benefits to people and companies earning over $1,000,000. Do you think he gives a damn about the middle class and poor like he keeps yapping about day after day? When the pedal hits the metal, it hits the rich, not the middle class and poor.

Disagreeing disrespectfully: Sometimes, when people disagree, many tend to shake their head in disgust, roll their eyes, and generally disrespect the other person. (Sometimes? Really? Not me!) Quite often, we are not even aware of doing this. We are not aware of our underlying emotions. We have to remember that there are two sides, or even three or four sides (known as perspectives, more on this in Chapter Five), to every story, and yours is just one of them, which may only be right in your

Figure 8: Need I say more? Oh, and thank you for listening and for your respect.

mind. Think of your disagreements. Do you get personal and say things like, 'you are wrong.' We need to learn to agree to disagree, which is a skill discussed in Chapter Twelve (communication).

In short, what we are saying is, "You stupid idiot," which is NOT a respectful comment to make. Neither is "You are dumber than a bag of hammers, and that disrespects a bag of craftsman hammers." Try closing your mouth and engaging your brain before responding. It works wonders!

Not willing to see the perspective of others': There is no wrong or right side, only our perspective. We should be willing to see the other person's perspective. Only when we do this can we relate to where they are coming from, and when this happens, statements like, 'I didn't see it from this side. You are right,' should be the next words you utter. Really! You are not agreeing with them; you are only acknowledging where they are coming from.

Taking it personally: The other person does not disagree with who you are as a person; they only disagree with your opinion. There is a difference. If you asked your friend whether they would like a coffee and they said no, would you take it to heart? If you do, you really need to work on how not to get offended or simply stay out of social situations for the rest of your life.

And if you don't get offended, then people having disagreements is nothing more than saying no to your coffee offer. If you and your pals or in-laws once disagreed over how President Barack Obama had handled the economy or whether Mitt Romney really understood the middle class. Who cares? If your feelings and ego are being hurt, it is better to work on THAT than make your friends or others responsible for it.

Speaking for the sake of speaking: In social circles, we often have the habit of speaking for the sake of filling the vacuum or to let others know we are listening. But, if you don't have anything to contribute, it is better to say nothing. Suppose you have no understanding of the topic being discussed. In that case, it is better to stay quiet, listen, and gather information this time around. And if you are asked to contribute, you can say, 'Sorry, I don't know much about this, but I am listening and learning.'

Remember what Abraham Lincoln said, "It is better to remain silent and be thought a fool than to speak and remove all doubt."

Adding our judgments: More often than stating the facts, we have conversations filled with inferences, judgments, or assumptions. Inferences are conclusions we draw from our observations. 'So, you don't think this is important?' 'Why don't you care about this?' 'You think the economic benefit is worth the lives that will be lost?' 'If you could see things clearly.' These lines contain assumptions, guesses that we don't know for sure, and speculations that may or may not be correct. The statements should instead be, 'between people dying and economic benefit, which one would you prefer and why?' The confronter acts as an authority, but we forget that these sentences imply that the other person is wrong.

And the reality of this exercise is that the other person isn't wrong, just misguided, in our opinion (or fact). We need to find a gentle but effective way to 'bring them around.' And that isn't by insulting them.

Many more reasons can be bundled into the phrase "I know what I believe is right and nothing you can say will change it." This includes the 'Blocked Listening' program where you simply aren't listening from the moment you hear a 'trip word or phrase.' 'Democratic hoax' is one that comes to mind. 'Fixed Belief System' is another that pretty much refers to the same thing. Both create the 'Unwillingness to Engage' because who the hell wants to listen to an idiot?

Figure 9: It looks like a great conversation. Good luck with further discussion and resolution, or should I say, better luck next time!

There are also a few more esoteric reasons for confrontation.

Sarcasm is undoubtedly one of them. While it may be an appropriate tactic for Rachel Maddow or Sean Hannity, it won't score the first point in a more private discussion.

Distorting what the other person is saying, whether by accident or deliberate, will get you nowhere. "So, what you're saying is that the UK can afford a 10% unemployment rate as a small consequence of Brexit," when the other person actually said, "a small increase in the unemployment rate."

And finally, the killer of all confrontational stances, "Emotional Intensity." You know the person who can't help but get so emotionally involved and defensive in their position that it becomes a screaming match. Personally, I have a great line for this: "Just so you know, I divorced the last person who screamed at me."

Figure 10: What is worse – facing confrontation happening outside or dealing with suffocation & turbulence happening inside?

Some advice from President Ronald Reagan. When he and Mikhail Gorbachev were negotiating the nuclear treaties, Reagan was often asked how he handled these very delicate negotiations. Could he trust the word of the Russian leader? Many Americans were up in arms (pun intended) and didn't trust any Russian for any reason and had almost forty years of reasons not to.

Being very careful, yet desperately wanting to stop the growth of nuclear weapons and seeing Gorbachev as a partner in this pursuit, Reagan used a phrase that became ubiquitous, representing this period in the US - Russia relationship.

He said, "*Trust and Verify*." Meaning, trust what the other side is promising, but verify that the result is as promised. It was used so often that, at one point, Gorbachev was asked a similar question, and he replied to the journalist in front of Reagan, "I believe the answer is Trust and Verify."

The advice to draw from is when you hear something that might not seem correct, don't run off at the mouth about how the other guy is making things up. Simply accept what is said as fact and then verify it. If they are right, you look like a civilized friend, associate, or conversationalist. If they are not correct, you have ammunition for your next confrontation!

Why people avoid confrontation

Many people dread confrontation and avoid it in every way possible. Some of the reasons are:

- Memories of past confrontations resurfacing, which might have been challenging, hurtful, and painful.
- Errors of omission and commission are equally destructive. Adding opinions, puffery, or outright fabrication to strengthen your argument is simply wrong. And, by the way, in most cases, unnecessary. Leaving out important facts is just as damaging. Once your 'opponent' discovers your zigzag tactic, your future arguments will ALL be suspect. Frankly, you will have lost face in the eyes of this person. By the way, in most cases, it is unnecessary. Because if you can't make your argument stand on its own without adding or deleting the truth, you don't have an argument at all. So, why are you having a confrontation if you have nothing legitimate to use? Watch Maddow or Hannity and brush up on your side's current grievances!
- Fear of being considered or taken wrongly and your views not being heard correctly. I am not sure about this one. I don't ever worry about being misquoted. I am more concerned about not being quoted at all.
- Fear of losing a friendship, relationship, and other insecurities cropping up. I have to admit this one has reared its head more than once. When my partner and I are in the company of opposing supporters, we tend to do our best to make quiet and cogent arguments about whatever the subject du jour is. I am very careful not to let the conversation turn into a confrontation because there is little to be gained trying to sell ice to First Nations. Still, there is much to be lost AFTER the confrontation is over.
- Finding it difficult to deal with emotions that can be triggered as a result of confrontation. This is a big one. Screaming and throwing things doesn't endear you to hosts of parties in the future. Actually, hitting someone with something is a whole new level of trouble. Avoiding it isn't a bad thing.

- Having difficulty in asserting ourselves can be frustrating and challenging to contain. See some of the above commentaries for backup on this point.
- Fear of being misjudged, having our motives questioned, conclusions being deduced based on their perception rather than ours, or selective listening. Selective listening is the other side's counterpoint to selective deafness. While this is another of those unfounded fears, it is understandable that being misquoted is undoubtedly not a good thing; being misquoted before a larger group can be mortifying.
- Thinking that things will get resolved over time or magically. If I wanted to be mean, I would call this Trump's pixie dust disease. He tried sprinkling it on the virus, but that didn't work very well.
- Despite doing everything to ensure a positive outcome, we might still make the relationship worse than when the confrontation started. This is a common and real problem. Often, since the other side (and sometimes us) is intractable, what is the point of even trying? It will cause unnecessary upset, damaging the relationship.
- When confronted, our feelings and emotions start surfacing, even if we do not intend to show them. We might believe that others do not know how to deal with them harmoniously. Meaning, the other side will treat us even worse than we would treat them in an ugly confrontation, and frankly, who needs that?

Do you identify with any of the above reasons why you avoid political discussions? **What if I were to tell you that confronting someone or being confronted is a place of growth for everyone? Well, it is. The greater the confrontation, the greater the benefits one can have in the sense of growth, whether expanding knowledge, awareness, expressing emotions, or, most importantly, deepening friendships.** Another essential point to note is that the greater the relationship's importance, the more meaningful the confrontation would be.

Translation. Suppose you really, really like the other person. In that case, you will work like hell to explain your position, and listen to theirs, and hope to God, you can come to a reasonable agreement to disagree and continue the relationship. It strikes me that many couples have found ways to either ignore or embrace the confrontation to keep their relationship going. If permitted to be, this kind of tribal polarization can destroy even the best personal relationships.

And the wildest personification of this point is that, during and after the 2016 US election, dating sites had filters for Trumpers and Never Trumpers, so you couldn't accidentally date someone who may hurt you in the middle of the night.

You can say negative things about another person and have them taken in a positive and supportive way. Funny, you should ask. Since 2015, there have been studies and workshops to address this specific point. It turns out that when you ask permission of the other person to tell them two or three things they could do to improve themselves (not political but more personality or personal), and they give you permission, the results were that the recipient was very positive in listening and understanding what was being suggested.

Should we confront or should we avoid?

Once we are aware that a discussion is moving towards a confrontation, the next question is should we confront or should we avoid. The answer to this would lie in the following questions:

+ How much do you value that relationship?
+ For example, do you value the relationship status quo, or do you want either of the parties to grow? Are you okay with the relationship as it is, despite strong unhealthy behaviors and patterns, or would you want to challenge your friend for their own growth?
+ What is the impact on you when you confront vs. when you don't?
+ How upset do you get with yourself when you "let a comment go." Not only on a personal level, what does it do to your philosophical and political psyche?
+ How will the other party react to being or not being confronted?
+ If the other person is generally open to a civilized discussion and 'plays by the rules' when arguing, this might work. But, if you already know that they are bull headed, bullshitted, jerk, Labour, Trumpsters, Libertarian, or Democrat. There might not be much upside to further pursuit of these discussions.
+ Consider your physical, emotional, energetic, mental, and spiritual make of the so-called human body.
+ Suppose the other party has less tolerance or higher anxiety. In that case, we know confronting them too much will not be good for their overall well-being, at least in the shorter time frame. In such a case, it would be better to work by building the communication level slowly and gradually (more on this in Chapters Three and Twelve).
+ What is your personality type? Analytical (like to debate, discuss, use mental cognition). Passive (don't necessarily mean good or bad for others and don't want to get into heated debates or upset anyone). Fixed (value peace, prefer routine, status quo, choosing to know everything well in advance). Open-minded (like to see both or all sides of disagreements, but will not take sides). Emotional (gets overwhelmed very quickly).

When two people express their views openly and honestly, especially on matters like politics, it is likely to result in aggravation due to the complex and emotive nature of the subject. I know how this works in terms of Relationships and Sexual Issues, as they are my professional specialties. I dealt with both in my last book and my next book due for publication next year. But neither explains how to deal with confrontation of a political nature.

We are not taught to engage with someone who is hurtful or whose behavior is unacceptable. We then struggle to find a way to defuse the situation without silencing or dismissing the other person, thus disconnecting from the situation rather than the individual.

Imagine the conversations if we could to speak in well thought out ideas and views, by fully acknowledging all of our emotions calmly. Being allowed to speak our mind without fear of any backlash for being found contrary to others' positions. We could hold the space for others when we see and feel them being overwhelmed by such conversations. If this was the case, do you think our family members, friends, and strangers would still feel defensive, intolerant, and decide to defriend us? Or would they be willing to invite us to engage in such conversations even more, which, in turn, would foster and deepen our friendships and relationships?

Meet people where they are, in terms of their mental and emotional needs, rather than where you are (more on this in Chapters Three and Four).

I like healthy and positive confrontations and not the destructive or negative types where someone needs to scream, developing resentment and disconnection, affecting relationships. To enjoy a positive life, it is crucial to effectively engage and deal with confrontation when necessary.

Watch out for those who love confrontations just for fun. Talk about lack of consciousness! The question is not, should you confront, but what do you lose or how do you feel if you don't? Nip the evil in the bud. Say politely, "if we allow this to happen now, in time, it will become a habit which may be difficult to change later."

The questions you can ask yourself are; "is this confrontation necessary?" "How will my life be impacted if I choose to do nothing?" "Can I forgive myself for not confronting even though I knew it was the right thing to do?" Confrontation is not a confrontation if done with curiosity, an open mind, and allow the space for feelings and emotions to be addressed. It is not about resolving the issue but hearing and listening. We will talk more about this in succeeding chapters.

We all know that human behavior can be erratic and unpredictable. Confrontation might not bring the desired positive results one is hoping for, no matter how much effort one might put in. You will see how behavior is impacted by internal and external influences, energetic centers, energy bodies, and should not just be taken as someone shows up at a physical level.

What is the downside of not dealing with confrontation? Confrontation will happen if we live in a family with complete freedom of expression. Why, because as individuals, we are different; our understandings, perceptions, priorities at any point are different? More on this later.

How to confront someone without showing aggression or creating an enemy

+ Do your research: Is the topic important to you? Have you looked at facts, information, and the situation from all sides to understand the broader perspective? Were things perceived with as little bias as possible?

- Decipher the personality type of the person: Different people communicate, interact, understand things in different ways. Spend time analyzing the personality type and behaviors of the person.
- Prepare yourself: Become aware of your mental, emotional, and physical state. Suppose one is mentally restless, emotionally triggered, or physically exhausted. In that case, the interaction with the other person will not be productive and will most likely worsen.
- Set the stage: Create a safe environment for all engaged parties. Set the agenda beforehand and have a mediator to oversee the running of the meeting. Avoid using aggressive language (unless the personality type only understands that kind of language) and use non-violent communication (more on this in the communication chapter).

Figure 11: How not to do conflict resolution.

- Keep it simple, clear, and engage productively: Avoid unnecessarily blabbering or waffling. Instead, stick to facts, emotions, and feelings. Take note of any beliefs that might be clouding perceptions. Be open to compromises that will involve give and take. Manage your emotions, feelings, energy, stay grounded, and check-in with everyone every now and then.
- Bring it to close: Ensure everyone has had their say. Make use of prompts like, 'I've learned …. from this experience', 'I'm leaving here with….', 'This interaction has made me feel……'. If possible, leave with a hug (pre-COVID) and gratitude towards each other.

Conclusion

We now have some understanding of confrontation and what causes it. How it can be minimized to continue our civility to family, friends, and strangers. We need to understand the life experiences of the people we are speaking to (arguing with) to further improve our communication with them.

CHAPTER TWO

LIFE EXPERIENCES

People do the best they can, given their understanding, life experiences, beliefs, upbringing, cultural and societal conditioning. If any of these had been different, they wouldn't be who they are today, and their lives may possibly have followed a different trajectory. We should come with openness and curiosity and a willingness to read the chapters of their lives that they have written as best they could under the given circumstances.

Michael Charming

Introduction

Our life experiences shape who we are. Be willing to look beyond the friend in front of you with a curiosity to inquire further than the judgment in your mind. We are made up from a set of experiences, some parallel with others, some mutually exclusive to ourselves, or so we think. The reality is, there are potentially a few hundred life scenarios, and we fit into a combination of between one to ten of them. It could be drugs, abuse, abandonment, divorce, poverty, crime, or a normal upbringing of proms, cars, travel, good schooling, college, and a great job.

By understanding where another person comes from deep in their life experiences, we can gain insight into why they take the positions they take and respond to us and our positions the way they do.

Our life experiences – did we created these, or did they just happen?

- *8 childhood wounds that emerge when we are adults*
- *Paris Hilton opens up about abuse she endured as a teenager at boarding school: 'I felt like a prisoner'*
- *Women of Color in the DC Universe Talk Casting Backlash and Importance of Representation*
- *Ruby Bridges was 6 when she walked into a segregated school. Now she teaches children to get past racial differences.*
- *Richard Dreyfuss: 'I was a bad guy for a number of years'*
- *11 science-backed ways your parents' behaviors shaped who you are today*
- *The initial distress of the Beirut explosion was enough – but the horrors that followed truly shocked me*
- *Centuries of Racism Have Created a Mental Health Crisis Among Black Americans*
- *Delhi govt creating hype on pollution issue for political reasons*
- *Business lobbying on climate change is 'a murmur and not a message'*

To 'disagree civilly' and 'grow together instead of apart,' we all must understand that those to whom we speak are different from us. And different for more than the obvious reasons of religion, gender, and race.

Our experiences in life define and shape who we are. We become the product of our external realities and the altered internal realities because of our past experiences. As human beings, we constantly evolve, as is the nature of life. Sometimes we evolve because we choose to, and other times because circumstances force us.

Being in motion is one of the principles of the Universe.

Figure 12: In life, each individual has multiple choices every moment. Each choice leads to a different path, bringing a certain personality and different needs.

As you look around, you will see that everything changes with time –be it another human being, your pet, or even a tree that has stood for decades or centuries. Suppose we are aware of such changes and make a conscious choice towards it, we would be more in line with the flow of the surroundings, which will be conducive to our overall personality and life purpose. We will also be more likely to listen to the opinions of others from their life experience perspective.

We can go into the history of civilization to find examples of when humans had to evolve, or change, due to life circumstances, but 20th Century history will be easier. The Second World War is an unfortunate example. Those who lived under Hitler's rule had to adopt new attitudes and beliefs to survive during the war. It was a forced evolution, and fortunately, did not last long enough to make any permanent evolutionary change. The German soldiers, and some citizens, who were 'only following orders' or "we were only citizens, what could we do?" Or a circumstance, even more, life-changing was the Youth Corps of the German public.

Those forced to visit the death camps throughout Europe experienced the ultimate in life-changing situations. They quickly, almost immediately, understood the gravity of their situation and rapidly evolved physically, mentally, and emotionally to likely the most horrific human situation in the history of civilization. They faced death everywhere, from lack of food, one word and you are gone, work till you drop and if you drop, you die, and being used as human experiments. One interesting adaptation to these circumstances were those who directly served their captors as musicians who played in orchestras and actors in plays, doing what they had to, just to survive.

Long after the war, survivors interviewed said that it wasn't the physical, the mental, or the emotional adaption they felt was significant. The major change, the major adaptation, and evolution of this group of people was their ability to survive. Circumstances were literally imposed on them 24/7, and they found ways, some completely ingenious, to survive. They held so tightly onto the belief that they would live and used this belief as their life focus to stay alive.

Many survivors held no anger or contempt for their captors, saying that anger and revenge only served to hold them back from a new life. In a situation like this, anger, revenge, and retribution would be 'normal.' These survivors actually experienced an evolutionary change. They grew and evolved consciously and

Sometimes life will feel like a roller coaster that you will run through it and sometimes it will feel dull and boring that you just sit there on a cold, hard surface counting the days !!

Figure 13: Life situations change constantly, and we should adapt as circumstances require.

23

passed that growth down to the next and subsequent generations in such a way that Israel has not chosen to bomb the hell out of Germany in retribution for what happened only 75 years ago.

The sooner we recognize and are aware that these changes can and do happen, the sooner we realize that growth occurs in any kind of evolutionary process.

As some studies now seem to indicate, our life experiences begin well before we are born.[4] Our parents, the kids we deal with at school, our early work, university if we go or don't, working away from home, partnering, having children, and getting older are all experiences that help form who we are and what we believe. By the way, this also influences how strongly we believe what we believe.

We can also factor in religion, gender, race, how we grew up culturally and ethnically, where we grew up and chose to live, and, finally, what we are doing at any given moment and how that impacts our lives and experiences.

Before the pandemic, we had certain beliefs. For example, we would never be able to work from home, and now, we do. We would never be able to live without our family dinners, and now we do. Even church activities, the cornerstone of our life and community, and now, our religious lives have become virtual. Is that good enough? Our beliefs are only as permanent as our circumstances allow.

Sometimes, we are so lost in the day to day running of our lives, we fail to stop for a second to carefully look at ourselves. We fail to introspect into our behaviors and the patterns that no longer serve us, or the ones that have played a part in making us who we are today. We behave in a certain way without awareness. We support a cause without being cognizant of the life experiences that got us here. With the current pandemic, we have time to be more introspective, thinking and wondering what is next? Finally, with the knowledge that change might be afoot and likely a change we may not like.

So, what are these 'automatic' behaviors, and where do they come from? Before we get into the possibility that some or many are genetic (yes, we are going there shortly), let's suggest something simpler for everyone to understand. They come from our life experiences.

Suppose you were abused as a child; you are more predisposed to support any child or domestic abuse policies. Maybe you belonged to a wealthy family where money, prestige, and bank balance always mattered; you are then more predisposed to supporting policies that protect wealth, reduce taxes, and maximize business profits, irrespective of the social or societal impact of such actions. Your environment taught you to ignore any personal or emotional connection with people and focus on making money.

Coming from a family who always traveled, whether on vacation or by necessity in a caravan, you could grow up thinking life is about seeing the world. Your parents might have believed in helping others, improving the world, and that the highest calling is public service. If you ever got that chance, you are more likely to support policies that cater to people in need. Maybe, as an adult, you have had different experiences that reinforced these beliefs. Your personal hardships and losses have made you acutely aware of what the rest of society goes through every day. It is also possible that growing up in a wealthy family, with parents exerting so much pressure and control on you that you dislike them and money. Here your support for policies against money would be coming from a place of anger and resentment. When was the last time you asked yourself a question? *'I went through this experience, and it has affected my life (whether positively or negatively) in this way, and I've become as such? As a result of this experience, I have gained and learned this'*.

Allow me to digress from the 'maybe this and maybe that' theory and give you a real-world example. Read the two descriptions above again.

The first one is almost a word for word description of Donald Trump. If you have ever watched any documentary on his family, parents, and a few generations before, this description fits him like a custom-made Trump tie.

Interestingly, the second one is almost a word for word description, but of Joe Biden, his 2020 opponent. From a working-class, poor background, he learned that public service is the highest calling. Joe Biden lost a wife and child to an automobile accident when he was a young Congressman, and another son to cancer not very long ago. He has spent almost his entire adult life in public service, including eight years as Vice-President of the United States.

Figure 14: Different upbringing and life experiences result in different personalities that could be completely opposite, offering different perspectives.

In a nutshell, here are two stark, 180-degree opposite examples of life experience who have faced off in 2020 to lead the United States. Now that you can see that current positions are strongly influenced by life experience, you should understand that neither position is 'right' or 'wrong', just different from yours.

It is irrelevant whether the life experiences were painful or pleasing. It is essential to realize that your life teachings, learnings, and experiences shaped you and made you the person you are today. Similarly, the friend in front of you, or the person you are so hotly debating with, have had their own share of life teachings, learnings, and experiences that made them who they are today. And yes, even within the same family, like having it out, policy-wise, of course, with your sister, parent, or cousin, means a different set of life experiences within the same household.

Each of us face numerous situations at every point in our lives. So, our experiences, beliefs, ideologies, and decisions define who we are today. To relate with each other, civilly and graciously, we shouldn't be calling anyone's life experiences 'wrong'. Of course, we may disagree strongly with a position they have taken, but that doesn't make their position wrong unless based on erroneous information. Otherwise, their positions are valid. Not attractive but valid.

Would you agree that at any given time, you do the best you can in facing any circumstances, whether as a father, worker, mother, leader, or caring friend? If you believe you are doing your best, don't you think others are also doing their best at any given point?

Thus, it is important to remember:

"…most of the time, people make decisions the best they can in their capacity at each and every specific time in their life, especially considering who they are at that point."

However, it is also important to consider:

- We should be able to look beyond ourselves.
- At times, we want to hit each other's heads because we are acting from unconscious needs that are not met, and sadly, we are not even conscious that we are behaving in this way. We are defending our positions without even knowing we are doing so (more on this in Chapter Four).

Factors that affect our life experiences

In the rest of this chapter, we will be looking at various factors that affect our life experiences. Starting from an early age, all the way to our current place, so we can start having an awareness of where we came from, how far we have traveled in life, the hurdles and pressures we have faced becoming the person we are, which led us to have the views we currently have.

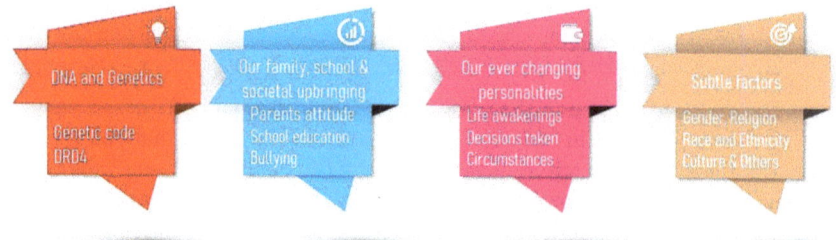

Figure 15: Factors determining who we are and what we become.

Would you agree that if you have this kind of awareness about your friends, you will relate to them differently? Instead of defriending, you will be opening up to more connection through empathetic presence, love, care, or at least a civil understanding that we are all different. In this way, no one is 'right' or 'wrong' (more on this in Chapter Fifteen).

DNA – Genetics impact towards political leanings (also called geno-politics)

❖ *Are Our Political Beliefs Encoded in Our DNA?*
❖ *How much does genetics affect political beliefs?*
❖ *Human genes reflect impact of historical events*
❖ *Struggling to quit smoking? Now you can blame your genes*
❖ *The genes that make us human: Scientists identify dozens of genes that could be key to our species' evolution*
❖ *Duke of Edinburgh 'blessed with James Bond-esque genes'*
❖ *Men's weight affecting sperm genes 'could make children overweight'*
❖ *Depression breakthrough as scientists identify 80 genes linked to condition*
❖ *So-called 'love' hormone can make you FEAR new experiences*

First, what is genopolitics? Genopolitics takes seriously the possibility of some of the differences we see among individuals, such as their propensity to participate in politics or how they respond to different policies, maybe due to genetic variations. I.e., in short, it refers to the study of political behavior and attitudes based on genetics.

If you read the numerous studies, it becomes surprisingly clear that there really is a role for genetics in individual politics. We will cite just a few of these studies and let you sort this one out for yourself.[5-8]

But the conclusions in some aspects such as propensities to vote and political leanings are somewhat clear. A full 50% of our political leanings come from our DNA. As per recent studies, the gene called DRD4, carrying the genetic code for a dopamine receptor, plays a vital role in a person's political views.[9]

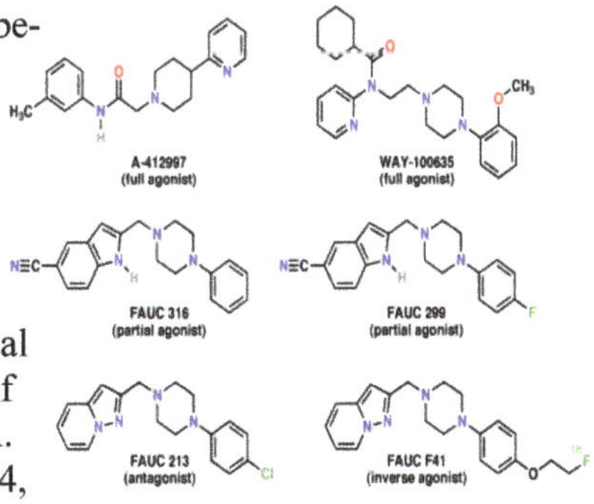

Figure 16: Chemical structures of representative D4 - with ligands (ions or molecules attached to coordinate bonding). Credit: Wikimedia.

Researchers and theorists have considered many factors such as age, gender, education, religion, marital status, and political know-how, but found these exert only a small impact on a voter's behavior.[10] Therefore, deciding whether to vote or not must be something more ingrained in the person's biology. And THAT brings us to genetics.

We know there are variations in the way voters think and behave. Some believe their single vote will not make much difference, but they still continue to vote despite knowing this. Others will continue to vote, no matter what. And then some will just not vote at all. One research concludes that genetics cannot determine people's behavior in terms of their voting selection but can tell whether they are likely to vote or not.[11] The other important factor affecting voters' choice is the environment; here, political leaders play a big part in influencing their decisions (more on this later). The percentage of influence genetics play is debatable?

Studies have shown conflicting results:

- Genes do play a role in decisions relating to an affiliation with any political party.[12]
- Genes do not play a role in a choice relating to a political party.[13] This argument's supporters argued that researchers who believe genes play a role in political attitudes ignore environmental factors and behaviors. One can never find a gene that can identify whether it is Tory, Conservative, Labour, Democratic, or Independent.

In a study, geneticists found that political conservatism was 64.5% heritable in men and 44.7% heritable in women, comparable to most personality traits.[14]

One of the researchers, Phil Spector, quoted, "*We took a bunch of old, rich, white men with entrenched and outdated views on virtually everything, and what we found was that their children had equally disgusting views of the world. As there is no other possible way we could think of by which a parent could transfer their opinions to their children, we concluded that it must be genetic.*"[15]

Parents, family, school, and societal upbringing

❖ *Donald Trump Jr: from childhood struggles to global notoriety*
❖ *Congress has no regard for Northeast region, its traditions: PM Modi*
❖ *Catalan separatist left may push for reversal of austerity policies*
❖ *The politics of language is destroying the language of politics*
❖ *Me and my school photo: Kenneth Clarke remembers getting caned and his introduction to politics*
❖ *Lies. Spin. It's politics as usual...*
❖ *Khomeini's grandson to enter Iranian politics.*

'Let's not talk about politics!'
'We do not want to engage in these kinds of conversations.'
'Can we talk about something more meaningful?'
'Do you want to create conflict between Mom and Dad?'

'I warned you not to start it and now see what you have done.'

'We will be casting our vote and as a family we will give our vote to the same leader.'

'I will vote for whomever your dad will vote for.'

'Don't talk about politics with anyone else as it is dangerous, and you can get killed (yes it does happen a lot in my country).'

These were some of the comments I heard whenever the topic of politics was mentioned in my family. What were political conversations like when you were growing up? Were there healthy discussions taking place? Was there room for having political discussions at all? When conversations did lead to confrontations, how were these resolved? Imagine what growing up would have been like had our parents and schools taught us the art of dealing with confrontation in a much healthier manner. Imagine if your parents would have given you the skills to lay clear boundaries and intentions by creating an environment conducive for such conversations to take place more freely. If that had been the case, would you still resent politics? Would you still avoid dealing with political discussions?

Imagine adult conversations in the home, around the dinner table, particularly if the nuclear family has a single belief. Or conversations with extended family if they also have a singular belief. Imagine if, as a child or young adult, all you hear and all you get to see at home is Fox News or MSNBC on the other side. Among the discussions, the news, and social commentary, you would become quickly inundated and inculcated with a specific viewpoint. Studies show that you will potentially carry these with you into young adulthood.

As a relationship and sexuality coach, I come across many situations where my clients need to confront, especially when dealing with long-established beliefs, ideals, misconceptions, and behaviors. If used correctly, confrontation is actually a powerful tool that opens the inner world of the people involved. When done correctly, with love and open listening, this can become the catalyst for change within a relationship, a fractured family, or a defriended friendship.

The question is, do families exert influence on a person's political leanings? The Bush family makes a solid case for the idea that even when a child strays as an adult, he eventually comes back into the family fold, as George W did after his escapades as a younger, unruly, and apolitical adult. Ron Paul certainly had the parental influence to provide his son Rand a solid Libertarian grounding. (Unfortunately, Rand has taken a bit too much of the Trump Kool-Aid and is now under the spell of the Evil One.) In the US., the best example would be the Kennedys, where the fourth generation of political Kennedys are pursuing public office and are still as liberal as the first- and second-generation.

As one tends to grow, external influences begin to shape their political views. *Despite family conflicts and generational gaps, the more active political discussions have been in the family, the more likely one will hold onto parental beliefs.*

Exceptions: Children can rebel if raised with excessive control and are asked to hold onto beliefs more strongly. Parents often want their kids to become a carbon copy of themselves in many aspects and behaviors. 'He behaves like his mom,' 'She is just like her father.'

The really forward-thinking and open-minded parent who wants to raise a fair thinking child into adulthood should be informing them of different ideologies, facts, parties, positions, and then allowing the kids to decide and let them have full freedom from an early age, without pressure. Because parental views are forced on some from an early age, thus curbing and suppressing expression, it leaves no wonder that some kids rebel against their parents, in all aspects, including politics. A study found that children who had political views forced on them tended to abandon these beliefs once they become adults.[16]

Figure 17: Though well intended, strict control and repression often negatively affect children and their relationship with their parents.

Just like kids have their own genetics, it is essential to note that parents' views on politics are also influenced by their own genetics, environment, their parental views, society, and the circumstances they grew up in. For example, parents who lived during and after Nazi Germany would understand the importance of social welfare, basic human rights, racism, and empathy than those who did not live in Europe and are more likely to favor socialism without understanding nationalism. Similarly, a father who had to work hard and realized that money is the way one feels self-esteem is most likely to favor Conservatives and Republicans.

We have the habit of manipulating rather than stating the facts. The question to ask is, how often did your parents manipulate and state opinions rather than facts? Did they discuss current events and issues to create a better understanding for you, or did they simply spew their biased positions? Did they influence you with facts and logic, or feelings, or did they create space for both?

Some parents intentionally never shared their political views with kids, as not to influence them at all. How did that impact you? Did you ever ask your parents what they believe or how they voted? What kind of response did you get? Did you wish things were slightly or mostly different in this arena? Did you feel your relationship with your parents might have been different if there had been conversations about political beliefs?

On a personal note, I find it interesting that many told me that politics was never discussed as a family thing after speaking anecdotally about this choice. Their parents had discussions and sometimes noisy ones, but they were never included as kids or teenagers. As young adults, it seems they were mostly told they didn't have enough 'life experience' to make a serious choice. And for most, it wasn't until they reached their thirties with spouses and children that their opinions were considered legitimate, or considered at all.

How did your society and school impact you during the early years?

School civics, geography, and history lessons. Were we interested; did we pay enough attention to really know about them? What makes the Magna Carta relevant to our current political system? How does an idea or the policy of one party or another become a new law? If you want to support a position, at what point do you need to get involved? How exactly do you get involved? Do you even know who your local and national representatives are?

Every year, Princeton University (top-shelf US college) does an interesting survey with freshmen in Political Science, and one assumes they have a bit more political information than, say, Drama students. They have done this for many years, with just three questions, but the results are beyond disappointing. The first question is, who is the Vice President? Fortunately, roughly 75% of the students answer that correctly. But then again, only 75%! The second question is, Name one of the two Senators from your home state. Now we go down to under 50%. And the final question is, Name two Supreme Court justices? Up until the recent Kavanaugh hearings, only 25% could name two. Really?

Ask an American what the protocol is before a President can really 'press the nuclear button'? If we remembered our schooling, this wouldn't be such a scary concept.

Bullying in school has existed for decades and is increasing. Did this impact your political beliefs, and if so, how? During our studies of subjects like civics, history, and political science, more focus is given to the theory and concepts that are important. Still, hardly any focus is given to subtler things like dealing with confrontations, as mentioned in Chapter One. How much awareness do you have that political conversations are more than just discussing headlines, articles, two-minute soundbites, and the like?

Teachers might have created debates around political topics, but then:

They generally tend to avoid for fear of escalation and conflict.

Not many people participate in such discussions. Hence, we end up creating an army of students who avoid politics from the get-go.

It is not difficult to imagine that we might avoid this for obvious reasons when we grow up.

Did you have healthy dialogues in class or at school? Did you participate, or did you always avoid? What were your reasons for avoidance?

Had we been more involved in understanding politics, at the stage when we were open to learning, imagine what we could have become, but we didn't, so we haven't.

Our ever-changing and evolving personalities

❖ *Obama reveals experiences with racism - magazine interview*
❖ *Positive childhood experiences tied to better adult mental health*
❖ *I Was Desperate to Find A Roommate. Now, I'm Marrying Him During A Pandemic.*
❖ *Maisie Williams Says She 'Couldn't Be Happier' with Game of Thrones' Ending: 'I Was Thrilled.'*
❖ *She started making almond butter at home. Now it's sold at Walmart across the country.*
❖ *Kim Kardashian Slammed for Looking Unrecognizable in New Photo*
❖ *Traumatic experiences as a child can shorten your life: Stressful events speed up the body's aging process*

Once children become young adults, parental influence begins to wane. Whether they instill new beliefs and become rebellious or continue developing their parents' beliefs depends on parental values, communication, and personal values. Their direction will depend on which side they adopt; right or left, trust or distrust, shy away from politics for the sake of a cordial relationship with parents, or risk it favoring their views more than that relationship.

Strong awakenings in life (personality, life, political), and further enhanced learning will determine whether children will stick to their parents' same opinions or diverge from them.

Parent-kid conflicts are bound to become more prominent during this time. We need to realize that our parents grew up with different realities, in different circumstances, with different life experiences; hence, their views will be based on different perceptions. Instead of having conflicts about them not being right, we need to adopt a more understanding approach of where they are coming from (more on this in the communication chapter). Similarly, parents need to understand that their kids have different realities than theirs.

Not being political doesn't necessarily mean one is disengaged from the world. It just means not having any strong moral, social, and cultural views. Interestingly, I have found that many who do not want to engage in political conversations (signifying that politics is not for them) would always be the first to form a political opinion about a particular leader.

Constrained views bring a limited perspective.

A study concluded that the older we get, the more important our political environment becomes. Participants' opinions were analyzed at different ages 18, 35, and 50.[17] At the age of 18, the participant's political stance was closely tied to their parents' political beliefs. At the age of 35, the country's and their spouse's politics were two and three times more influential than parental beliefs. At the age of 50, a spouse's political beliefs were most influential, followed by their country and then their parents (mostly fathers). The study also concluded that people strongly influenced by their spouse's political beliefs were more likely to remain married at 50.

Subtle factors influence our political decisions

While many of the following factors don't seem so subtle, they take a back seat compared to the ones we have already examined. Issues like religion get top billing, but if you are in the US, issues like abortion are critical for some. Many votes are 'one-issue voters' on this specific issue. But overall, these are secondary factors to life experiences.

Gender

- *Elizabeth Warren was the ideal candidate, but there was only one problem... she was a woman*
- *'Kickass women win': Warren makes case to Iowans*
- *Justin Trudeau: Gender Diversity in Politics Is 'Fundamental to Governing Well'*
- *Bill aims for more women in Indian politics amid poor representation*
- *Iceland Blows the US Away When It Comes to Women in Politics*
- *Make this the century of women's equality: UN chief*
- *The UK Is Now Run by A Woman, But Feminists Aren't Celebrating Yet*

The role of gender has changed in making political decisions, especially in times of women's empowerment. If this specific issue changes within a 'party', many women will change 'party' with it. Most women in the US vote Democrat due to their focus on equality of pay, gender, and legal rights. Yet, it is important to note that 'spousal influence' may have given Trump an abnormally high female vote despite his misogynistic statements and history.

Woman's votes will depend on which of these issues matters more. Abortion may overrule women's rights in some female voters' minds. Voting Democrat on these issues doesn't mean women are likely to vote for female candidates. However, the data from the 2018 midterm elections are beginning to change this data fact.

Figure 18: People often support a particular leader due to gender rather than accomplishments or credibility.

Religion

It would be insightful and interesting for us to take the time to study religions and determine what each has to say about engaging people with different political opinions, especially considering the political framework existing in those times. Religious beliefs, for those of firm religious convictions, control the way people vote. The abortion issue is likely the strongest example of this, particularly in US politics. Other Western (progressive) countries do not have this issue with the same intensity and vitriol. While many Jews vote for candidates who support pro-Israeli politics and policies, data suggests that policies closer to home take precedence for the less fervent religious Jews.

Before having conversations with friends, we should know which religion they favor since religion has sentimental and family values and strong beliefs. For example, in general, Catholics support economic issues (minimum wage, taxes) rather than social issues (abortion, divorce). Affiliation to different religions influences political attitudes and behavior. A party supporting prayer, abortion, anti-divorce more than economic issues or foreign affairs is likely to get a vocal and robust base. However, it will be much smaller than a base that supports the more "social issues" of income equality, race, homelessness, and social justice.

Race and Ethnicity

Despite living in the 20th century, talking about flying cars and AI technology, race and ethnicity continue to ignite masses, tilting their vote towards a particular leader.

Depending on how well and settled they are, different nationalities will vote and have beliefs often en masse because of similar life experiences. Even within Latinos, there are varying voting patterns, such as Cuban Americans for Republicans vs. Mexicans for Democrats. Asian Americans generally tend to be Conservatives.

In the UK and Europe, Polish people would vote Labour, and Germans would vote Conservative, at a race and ethnicity level. At an individual level, the needs and priorities will determine the actual vote. Before I became a UK citizen, I would only vote for the party with a positive immigration approach, no matter how terrible the other policies might have been. For me, getting UK citizenship was the number one priority in my life. But after becoming a UK citizen, different political parties' stances on immigration were low on my priority list. Hence, I was a one-issue voter at that time. My British friend, who had just graduated and looking for employment, was concerned about immigrants taking their jobs; he favored parties with the most hostile immigration policies.

Culture

- *China must 'pay big time' for coronavirus response, Lindsey Graham says*
- *Trump claims he'll 'end the AIDS epidemic,' 'cure childhood cancer' at rally*
- *Warren and Sanders: Amazon must end culture that puts profit over people*
- *Brazil's Top Culture Official Fired Over Speech Evoking Nazi Propaganda*
- *Class politics is rising in America. Trump hopes a culture war might stop it*

How do different cultures influence decisions?

Resistance to change is immense, and even a tiny shift may take many generations. Think about the American attitude towards Gay Marriage, which took 50 years. Think about the smallest token advances that Saudi Arabian women are making. How many such behaviors do you identify when making your view about a specific decision impacting a country? Realize that culture is deeply rooted. Consider the Southern US attitudes towards Blacks, and it has been over 150 years.

"We're not hibernating this year.
Too much cultural change to keep up with."

*Figure 19: Culture is ingrained from childhood.
Unless we actively integrate into other cultures
and open our culture for others or begin to develop more understanding and tolerance
towards each other, our society will continue to
remain disconnected.*

Looking at this specific issue isn't always something you can see, but it is there. The place's culture is exhibited in a thousand ways and through signals that outsiders don't see but locals understand. That defines culture.

Another example is the Hasidic Jewish community, which in almost every country outside Israel insists on separation and social seclusion. Most of the time, they stay separate, keep separate, and are generally not overly nice to locals except when they need something.

We often view another country's political decisions based on our culture rather than understanding theirs, which creates many prejudices about other places globally.

Region

- ❖ *Congress has no regard for Northeast region, its traditions: PM Modi*
- ❖ *Regions demand Brexit compensation from EU budget*
- ❖ *UK could save £4bn a year on EU regional aid*
- ❖ *Catalan separatist left may push for reversal of austerity policies*
- ❖ *Regional co-operation can drive defense policy*

In the US, there are red states, blue states, and purple states. In the UK, there is working-class housing and horsey-set estates. How the region is defined presupposes how it will vote on various issues. Regions do influence political decision making. The US states are conservative or liberal, red or blue, or in between, purple. They vote this way because birds of a feather... The horsey-set lives in a specific part of the country (conducive to horsey activities). Thus, this area becomes relatively homogenous in its attitudes and voting preferences. In simple terms, history seems to be the primary factor in why this type of life experience continues.

More subtle factors

More subtle than those listed above are some that you may not even consider factors. These are more of what a person is feeling at a given moment, still, factors, nonetheless. Without too much depth, I will just list them for now, and we will explore them elsewhere.

Having an open vs. closed mind.

Having a curious mind vs. a judgmental mind full of assumptions.

The way we feel at any given moment, emotionally, mentally, physically, energetically, and spiritually. This is a significant factor, as a person who is extremely focused on enjoying life is much easier to deal with than one whose life is in turmoil.

Impact of our immediate timeline on how our day has been or what challenges we face in our life (pregnant, being fired, going through a relationship breakup, death of a family member). This is very similar to the point above but much more experiential than personal.

Conclusion

Several other factors play a part in arriving at political decision making. Can you think of three or four more factors? Of course, you can, or we wouldn't ask the question! Despite the above factors, exceptions will be found, which we discuss in succeeding chapters. There are many factors at play on the election day itself, e.g., national issues, worldwide issues, crises, personal issues like unemployment, and what the candidates have said in the days running up to the vote. When we understand what the other person has been through, it is easier for us to relate to them and their views. We get to develop an empathetic response of what it could be like to be them. Or, more simply put, "But for the grace of God go I." We all need a bit more of this attitude in our lives.

CHAPTER THREE

GETTING TO KNOW OURSELVES

Human is more than just the physical being we see or hear. To deeply understand and relate with someone, we must be willing to go beyond what is shown or spoken. We must be open to discover their inner world and belief systems, decipher their emotional, mental, energetic, physical, and spiritual states, and learn to manage our own states when interacting with them.

Michael Charming

Introduction

"Do NOT discuss politics or religion!" In my youth, I heard this countless times. No explanation, merely a command. Why? Politics is seen as one of those incendiary subjects. Open your mouth, and the room will catch fire, or worse. In Chapter One, we covered many reasons why people avoid this discussion and ignore it in their daily lives.

If politics affects everyone, shouldn't we pay more attention to it rather than ignoring it? Shouldn't we create more dialogs and discussions and become more aware, understanding, and informed? Simply voting on the day is not enough, and many people don't even do that. Not having accurate information, a good understanding of policies, programs, and future challenges, issues, and resolutions is merely detrimental to society in general.

Politics means different things to different people based on where they are in their lives and who they are as people. What is the makeup of their human body composition? We talk about the latter in this chapter, leaving the discussion about the former for Chapter Five, Perspectives.

Once we know who we are as individuals, it becomes much easier to understand how each of us operates. That gives us tools, clues, and the awareness of knowing where any one of us is in a human sense. How we got here is something we covered in the previous chapter.

When I talk about human composition, I see the five different layers: emotional, mental, physical, energetic, and spiritual. In my book, Amplify Your Orgasm, I shared in detail each of these bodies and their part in our experience of orgasms. Now we are looking at the same person, just in the light of politics instead of orgasms. Now THERE is a jump! It makes sense that we talk about this to gain a deeper understanding of this human body, whether ours, friends, or any leader in the world. This chapter discusses the emotional layer in the first half and the other layers in the second half.

Perhaps one of the starting questions should be, 'How well do you know yourself?' Margaret Thatcher had a 'tough as nails' personality. Jimmy Carter had a 'soft, down-home personality.' The religious leader in Iran has a religious fanatic personality. What does this mean? Why do two friends and two leaders with similar personalities differ in many views, ideas, and policies? While previous chapters have thrown light on the reasons for the differences, this chapter will throw even more light because we look at things that make up the human body internally.

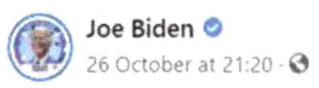

Joe Biden ✓
26 October at 21:20 · 🌐 · · ·

No president whose lies and failures have cost 225,000 American lives should keep his job. Period.

 107K   15K comments 6.9K shares

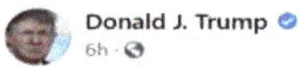

Donald J. Trump ✓
6h · 🌐 · · ·

Covid, Covid, Covid is the unified chant of the Fake News Lamestream Media. They will talk about nothing else until November 4th., when the Election will be (hopefully!) over. Then the talk will be how low the death rate is, plenty of hospital rooms, & many tests of young people.

 134K   25K comments 9.2K shares

Kamala Harris was live.
23 October at 19:53 · 🌐 · · ·

More than 223,000 people have died from coronavirus and Trump still doesn't have a plan. We need a real leader in the White House who will listen to the scientists and protect Americans—that's Joe Biden.

Figure 20: A snap of how COVID-19 was used as an issue to woo the voters. There is no guarantee that Biden would have handled it any better. Many voters fail to realize that control over COVID-19 depends on several factors and not just leadership. E.g. technological advancement and integration (test and trace), opposition faced by the leader, attitude of citizens (pro or against, protest or no protest, emergence and participation in conspiracy theories), demographics and size of the population, ability of medical facilities and hospitals to cope, advice of medical experts, and time of the year and climate). Image source: Facebook.

If we are to 'come together,' we should fully understand the human makeup and what makes us who we are inside. In this chapter, we will get to know ourselves because the better we know ourselves, the more we will know the factors and influences that affect us in how we behave in relating to others.

In politics, the emotional states of a being are given priority over logical thought, particularly on voting day. Imagine the US having an election in the middle of the virus pandemic. Trump will give very emotional speeches about stopping the Chinese from coming in, stopping immigration, stopping everything else, and taking credit for giving YOU $1,200! These speeches will ALL be emotional. The successes he has achieved throughout his term can't be brought home now because all economic gains he has touted for 3½ years have been wiped out in three months.

Trump's opponent, Joe Biden, has a great deal more experience as a policy-maker and politician, just about an entire lifetime. His speeches are likely to be just as emotional but putting tens of thousands of deaths at Trump's desk. Nothing could be more emotional. If you lost someone during the pandemic, you are very likely to emotionalize your vote and blame Trump. Also, it has been said that he knew more than he admitted in the beginning, thus making it far worse than it needed to be for the US. On the other hand, if you got $1,200 gift checks and your small business got a pile of money to keep you employed, you will be likely to emotionally vote for Trump. Let us forget for a moment that all politicians lie 28% of the time; Trump has taken it to an art form at roughly 82%.

In Amplify Your Orgasm, I divide the human body into five 'bodies or states':

- Emotional body or state or layer
  - Emotions and feelings, emotional sensitive spots, expressions, and sensations.
- Mental body or state or layer
  - Brain, mind, open mind, belief, social scripts, mental health. In the book, I shared five keys to orgasm: presence, awareness, intention, and consciousness, also crucial for sensible and mature political conversations.
- Energetic body or state or layer
  - Energy centers and energy levels.
- Physical body or state or layer
  - Sensations in the different body systems: muscular system, nervous system, endocrine system, etc.
- Spiritual body or state or layer
  - Desire and fear.
- Our personality is composed of all these bodies; separately and combined, they make up the human individual.

Emotional body or state or layer

❖ *As families grieve over New Year's Eve stampede that killed 36 people, China manages public emotions*
❖ *Polish official understands emotions behind far-right attack on anti-government protester*
❖ *Survivors of fire struggle with emotions as probe continues*
❖ *Returning to Pakistan, Malala is overwhelmed by her emotions*
❖ *Researchers criticize A.I. software that predicts emotions*
❖ *It's just emotion: Conservative leader says to the PM*

Most people are so caught up in the rat race and being lost in the process of 'living'; they ignore their emotions and feelings. This same behavior takes place during political conversations with friends or strangers. Many use these terms interchangeably or are entirely unaware of their emotions and feelings.

What is your understanding of the words, emotions, and feelings? Why do you think it is essential to know the different emotions and feelings that everyone in the conversation is having or expressing? Why does issue 'A' trigger three people in different ways during a conversation, but issue 'B' triggers them in the same way, or interest-

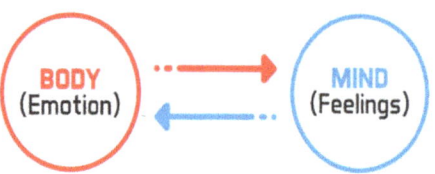

Figure 21: Emotions are rooted in the body; feelings are rooted in the mind.

ingly, might not trigger some of them at all? Are you aware of your and your friends' emotional and mental triggers and sensitive spots? How often during the conversation do you ask your friends how they are feeling? And if you do, what kind of response do you generally get?

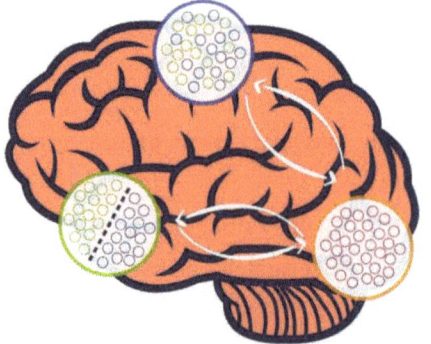

Figure 22-23: (Left image) Brain processing and responding to triggers through neurotransmitters. (Right image) Transmitters and receptors working along a neural pathway to generate an emotion.

In my book, Amplify Your Orgasm, I've shared that emotions are rooted in the body, and feelings are rooted in the mind. Politically, most of us have emotional sensitive spots. It could be immigration, economics, taxes, welfare, military spending, childcare, or any number of sensitive spots.

Emotions are the body's way of responding to stimuli (called emotional triggers) at the biological level. These include physical processes, such as communication between transmitters and receptors along neural pathways, the release of endorphins throughout the body, and various processes in the central and peripheral nervous systems.

Another way to think of emotion is energy in motion within the body. This energy moves or gets stuck depending on flow or blockages. These ancient ways of knowing offer important tools for learning how to observe and use the energy flow within the body.

Figure 24-25: Emotion is energy in motion like electric energy (left image) or soft energy (right image).

Psychological research led by Paul Ekman led him to classify six basic and universally recognized emotions: sadness, anger, fear, tenderness, excitement, and happiness.[18] You can probably identify with having experienced each of these during political conversations. However, you may not be used to thinking about them as recognizable states that generate specific physical (and energetic) states within your body, causing you to react when conversations are edgy or catch you off-guard.

Emotional states in the body are the same for everyone. E.g., anger is characterized by the same physical state within the body, the same endorphins, and the same basic energy, regardless of who is experiencing the emotion. However, what makes us unique when it comes to emotion is that some are more sensitive to some energy states than others.

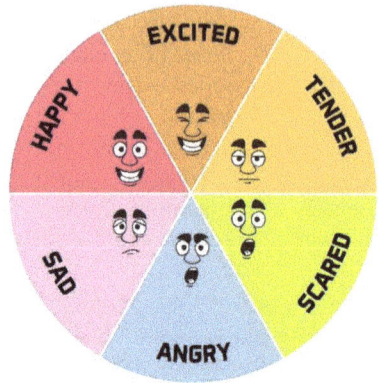

In this book, I will refer to this phenomenon as emotional sensitive spots or emotional triggers. If anger is our emotional sensitive spot, we will get angry very quickly, likely in response to various triggers. E.g., immigration issues will not make everyone angry. The questions to ask those who are feeling angry: What is it about immigration making you feel angry? Do you believe immigration will change the social dynamic, giving rise to feelings of uncertainty?

Using the example of climate change, do you feel threatened or fear for your life? Or the example of cutting social welfare, do you feel you would not have enough money to take care of your family? Do you feel the government is lacking in the responsibility of fulfilling its duty towards society? In each of the above examples, the issues remain politically similar. The triggers for each of these issues are different resulting in various emotional states.

Our emotional sensitive spots are deeply influenced by our individual life experiences. Some are more inclined towards sadness and fear than the other emotional states. Imagine for a moment someone who has been a victim of physical abuse. They may have experienced a great deal of trauma from an intimate partner. Because conflict has preceded violence against them in their past, any conflict will trigger fear.

On the other hand, someone with the experience of successfully intimidating others with outbursts of anger may be more inclined to default to an angry emotional state in response to any conflict. These different responses to the same trigger, namely conflict, demonstrate different sensitive spots. It is vital to be aware of one another's sensitive spots in a healthy relationship. Empathy and understanding for our partner's emotions and the past experiences that have created their sensitive spots, are among the foundations of intimate bonds. Suppose a person has always relied on social welfare without ever being told this will be temporary. In that case, they will likely have a negative reaction when the welfare is stopped.

Likewise, in the case of immigration, if someone has grown up among people of their own ethnicity, with no family or schooling that emphasized tolerance of inviting nationals from another country into their physical and mental space, they would most likely have an emotional reaction often misconstrued as hatred. In contrast, a person who has traveled or grew up in a town or city with multiethnicity would be more open-minded and tolerant towards nationals from other countries. Someone with parents who fostered tolerance and empathy towards human beings from all cultures and races would be more compassionate towards nationals from other countries. On the other side of this example is someone who

has traveled or lived in different countries and experienced hatred towards them; they would have two choices:
a) Either to let that feeling of hate develop within and take revenge on these countries' nationals and continue to have hatred towards them.
b) Realizing hate as an unwanted emotional spot and choosing to work on this to not portray the same to others, knowing how it felt on the receiving end.
These are called conditioned emotional responses.

Sensations: Expressing feelings is enhanced by the physical sensations happening within our body, such as pulsating inside the lips, hot liquid warmth in the belly, or a tingling sensation in the genitals. When we feel happy, our heart (and even body) feels lighter. When we are sad, our heart feels contracted or suffocated, and our body feels heavier. When we express sensations, it allows us to associate and relate to what the other person and we might be experiencing in the body. Having this awareness can impact the way we feel and relate to others. More on this later under the heading 'physical body'.

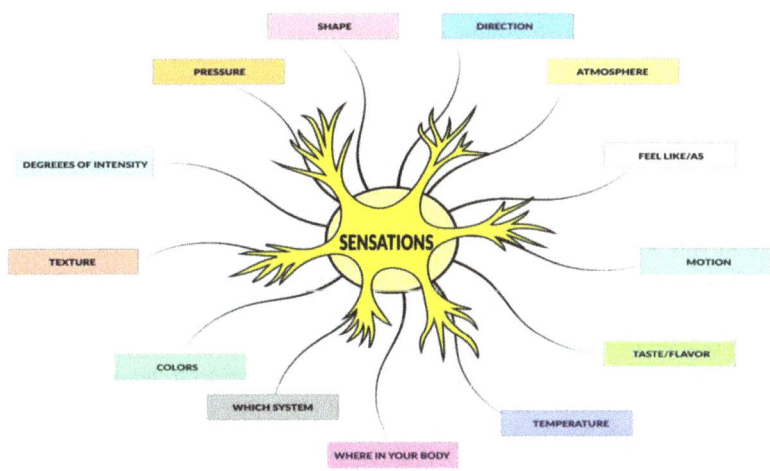

Figure 27: Qualities of sensations.

Points relating to emotions and feelings

- To understand the importance emotions play in politics, it is essential to understand these emotions at an individual level and how we are being played by leaders, media, and political parties.
- In conversations, people often project their feelings onto others because of different associations based on their life experiences. They do so either consciously or unconsciously (but mostly unconsciously). The others can evoke those feelings within us, but they do not have the same feelings (triggers and sensitive spots).
- People patronize their and other people's feelings.
- Feelings are never wrong for that person.
- We are not connected with our feelings, generally speaking.
- If we are connected, we do not express them to others or allow others to express theirs to us.
- Our feelings are affected by our body responses, which in turn depends on our past experiences.
- Our physiological and emotional responses affect how we feel about certain situations.

How leaders, campaigns, and candidates use emotions to win votes

- Common emotions used by leaders are anger, fear, anxiety, hope, and enthusiasm.
- In 2016 and 2020, Trump uses anger and pride. While we don't have numbers, just recounting his rallies and speeches, he is angry about everything from Obama to Democrats and immigrants to anyone who disagrees with him. And then he uses pride, saying, "Make America Great Again" or "Keep America Great Again." Even when he strays from the truth, he uses his own version of facts to instill pride. A good example is his boasting about bringing coal jobs back. Since he has been elected, the net LOSS of coal jobs is 27,000, yet he boasts about coal jobs coming back, and miners should be proud and support him.
- The use of flags at rallies invokes emotions of pride.
- Emotional appeals using visuals, music, songs, and narrations are used continuously. Black and white film ads are ten times more likely to evoke fear or anger than pride or enthusiasm. In contrast, bright colors evoke uplifting, patriotic, and positive emotions. All viewers will not experience the same emotion because of different triggers and emotional sensitive spots. An advertisement might trigger anxiety or fear among Democrats, but calmness, positivity, and enthusiasm among Republicans.

When emotions are triggered, most people will behave through emotional response rather than the norm. When rapid response is required, bodily instinct comes to the fore, and what is stored will come out. If fear is stored, their minds and bodies will be operating in flight or fight mode at the subconscious level.

These are sometimes deliberate and sometimes because of an event. E.g., in a terrorist attack or fake news of an attack, the fear is so prevalent with events and movements happening rapidly that the emotion of fear is riding high. The mind starts creating stories and associations that have nothing to do with the current reality. This is where the emotional detox bodywork is such a great tool to keep the body clear.

Many of my clients generally appear very positive, inspiring, calm, and loving on the surface; during emotional detox sessions, they initially find themselves full of rage, anger, pain, and hurt. This happens because we are working on what is stored in the body. Once this is released, the clients experience happiness, pleasure, bliss, and contentment in a way never experienced before. After a couple of sessions, no matter how much their emotional buttons are pressed, that rage, anger, bickering, and belittling, doesn't raise its head because most emotions held beneath the surface have been cleared. Their parasympathetic and sympathetic nervous systems, mind, body, and energetic bodies are now more aligned, more in control, making them feel grounded and less triggered.

We often find ourselves telling others, don't be angry, don't be emotional, don't sob, why are you feeling hurt? I'm sorry, but emotions don't work this way. Telling people to keep their emotions repressed isn't the best or even a good way to deal with this. Neither should people be required to be told to keep their emotions in check. They should be able to do this themselves, allowing the leader to focus on the issues and tasks at hand. How much responsibility do we take for our actions to make it easier for any leader to do their job?

Protests are an excellent example of emotions out of control. How often do we hear of a protest turning violent? A protest that was meant to be peaceful, like Charlottesville in the US a few years back, (at least that is what the organizers said, but the night before when thousands turned out with torches, chanting racial and ethnic epithets for hours … not so sure), turned violent and full of rage. In this case, rage pushed one member to drive a car into the crowd, killing a young woman. Shouldn't people learn to have self-control? But, maybe, in some cases, the fever pitch is DESIGNED to create chaos and the ensuing violence.

If we had worked on not getting triggered because of stored past emotions, then we would not be easily provoked. For this reason, I am generally not provoked by the leaders I listen to, irrespective of whether I like them or not. For years I have worked on this aspect. Consciously working on self, which often felt uncomfortable and required much commitment, but I reminded myself of its worth, not only for my own well-being but for showing up in society and my friendships. I now teach others to do the same through various in-person and online emotional detox and full-body de-armoring sessions and courses. What would your life be like if you were to find a way to not get triggered, no matter the situation? The ability to think and reflect calmly, with full presence and awareness before responding, instead of reacting. My clients find this fascinating, but it does take emotional work. I can now watch the news without my blood pressure rising.

Leaders say what the crowd wants to hear, truth or otherwise. If they did the opposite, would the crowd still attend? A tiny minority of attendees would like to listen to the other side of the story. People should visit the rallies of the opposition and not only the ones they already support. They should watch the news and read the papers relating to leaders and parties they don't support to get as much information as possible before deciding. It wasn't easy taking it all in, both the quantity of data and information and the feelings that would get triggered. Both have become easier because of emotional and mental clearance due to emotional detox sessions and multi-orgasmic states.

Mental body or state or layer

- *Children's mental services attacked and considered as 'not fit for purpose.'*
- *The mind-boggling numbers behind India's election, the world's biggest democracy*
- *Congress's bankrupt state of mind*
- *Rouhani: Beliefs stop Iran from pursuing nukes*
- *Man arrested in French car attack had radical beliefs*
- *Bible vs indigenous beliefs at issue in Bolivia*
- *In battle of beliefs, Nigeria targets Boko Haram's top brass*
- *Black Americans under-treated for pain due to false beliefs: study*

The brain is part of our body's central nervous system playing a massive role in our feelings of anger, hurt, happiness, pain, and resentment. Different parts of the brain serve different functions: frontal lobes (control cognitive functions), parietal lobes (interpret sensory information), occipital lobes (process images from eyes), and temporal lobes (process information from our senses of smell, taste, and sound). There are other important parts like the brainstem, thalamus, hypothalamus, pituitary, hippocampus, and cerebellum. When we talk about associations, the two of the most important parts we should know are the limbic system (controls emotions and memories) and amygdala (acts as a hub in the limbic system), which becomes hypervigilant if not feeling safe.

When resonating with someone regularly, the limbic system releases neuro-chemicals that are important for one's well-being. If a person doesn't have a

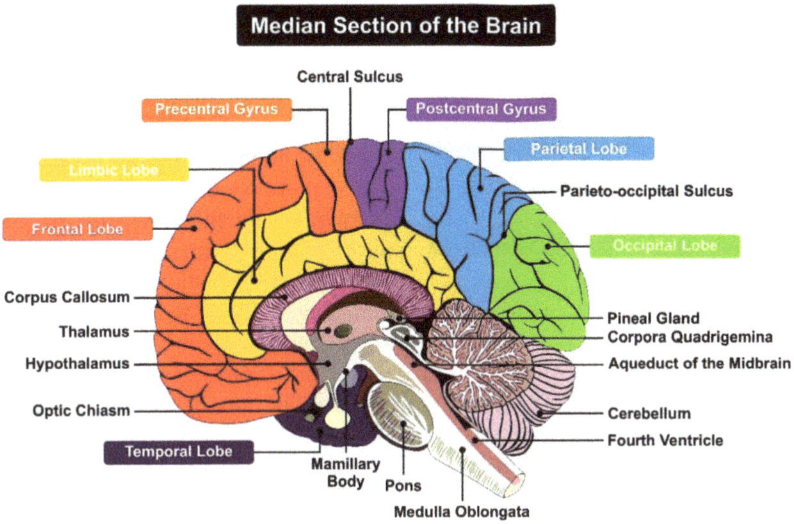

Median Section of the Brain

Central Sulcus

Precentral Gyrus

Postcentral Gyrus

Parietal Lobe

Limbic Lobe

Parieto-occipital Sulcus

Frontal Lobe

Occipital Lobe

Corpus Callosum

Pineal Gland

Thalamus

Corpora Quadrigemina

Hypothalamus

Aqueduct of the Midbrain

Optic Chiasm

Cerebellum

Fourth Ventricle

Temporal Lobe

Mamillary Body

Pons

Medulla Oblongata

Figure 28: Anatomy of the brain: the limbic system and brain stem.

limbic resonance with others, then our brains and well-being tend to suffer over time. People who lack loving and caring interactions, those who are lonely, or those who have had experiences of being taken away from maternal touch during birth or infancy are often prone to depression and anxiety.[19,20] Likewise, if conversations get intense, causing one to feel unsafe, most likely the amygdala has become hypervigilant for that person, even though others might be completely unaffected by the same conversation.

You will notice that people are generally creatures of habit. Suppose a friend has supported a particular view in the past. Assuming other things remain constant, they will continue to support the same view, same policy, react in the same way and exert similar behavior year after year due to conditioning on the brain. When we repeat specific thoughts, feelings, or actions, these repetitions strengthen neural pathways. A neural pathway is a connection formed between neurons, enabling a signal to be sent from one region of the nervous system to another.[21]

One way to think of a neural pathway is like a road that connects one town to another. Imagine a dirt path with only one person traveling on this road each day. It is not very wide, and the weeds on either side threaten to

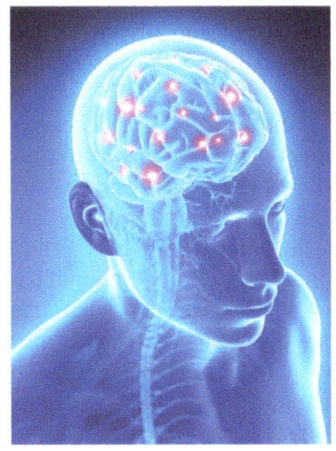

Figure 29: Neurons in the brain firing together through neural pathways.

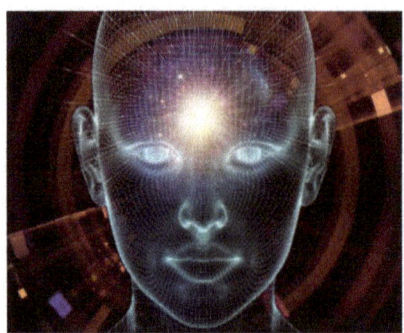

Figure 30: Our mind, though separate from the brain, is shaped by it.

bury it. On the other hand, imagine a major highway in a modern city, carrying hundreds of thousands along its path each day. Which is stronger? Bigger? Faster? Offering more efficient travel? The highway, of course. Similarly, neural pathways are influenced by our behaviors, beliefs, and environment.

The more we use a pathway, the easier travel along that route becomes. In psychological terms, this process is known as 'conditioning'. The associated strengthened neural pathways have been called 'neural superhighways' by brain researchers. So, instead of getting frustrated about friends showing a particular behavior, view this from a place of awareness about how habits are formed and understanding that it is not easy to change habits. We would then realize they are acting according to what has been deeply instilled in their human system. We do the same things repeatedly because we are wired to follow the path of least resistance. Repeated behaviors become habits that can be healthy or unhealthy. The good news is that habits can be changed.

If you really want to change a habit effectively and quickly. In that case, you need a professional bodyworker to assist you in this quest. My work with clients involves changing hard-wired habits, dismantling patterns of being in unhealthy relationships, being inauthentic, and many other kinds of addictions.

When having political conversations, we need to ensure that excessive stress is not caused for any of the participants, leading to anxiety, nervous breakdowns, or even mental health issues. As we, or those of us in the US., saw in 2016, tens of thousands of Hillary supporters required mental health interventions after the election. Anecdotally, every counselor to whom I spoke in the US and UK at that time had gotten 50% busier with Hillary supporters unable to deal with the outcome.

Now that we understand a little about the brain, it is time to focus on the mind. The transcendent world of thoughts, feelings, attitudes, and beliefs are the mind's products. The brain is responsible for providing the structure and mechanisms to keep our bodies operational and the canvas upon which the mind is painted through subjective and intersubjective experiences. The mind is the awareness of consciousness, the ability to control what we do, why we do it, and how we do it. It is the reasoning, the know-how, and the ability to understand. The mind is largely involun-

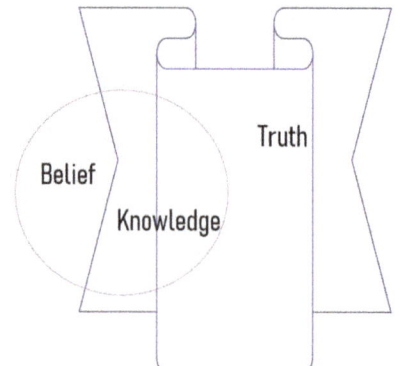

Figure 31: Beliefs are subjective and form a small part of the overall truth.

50

tary, which means if people are not engaging in mindful activities like yoga or meditation, they will most likely wander on hearing different kinds of news depending on their stories, associations, and beliefs, and project what might be very different from reality. 'Belief' is the attitude when we take something at face value and regard it as fact.

It is one of the reasons that Trump has so many followers. With the support of Fox News and the Wall Street Journal, he has managed to state a 'fact', real or fake, and have Fox repeat it, WSJ repeats it, and he repeats it. His supporters then accept it as fact and at face value, regardless of the insanity of the assertion. Why many of his supporters specifically do not do any research is unusual. Still, emotions, anger, pride all combine for a soup of reasons.

Try just a few:

"There is a caravan of tens of thousands coming from Central America to get into our country." (When the final count was closer to 2,000).

Figure 32: Generally, Trump's 'stories' come back to whack him.

"The virus is a Democratic hoax. They couldn't impeach me, so now they are using this." (At the book's writing, the death toll in the US was at 220,000 people.)

"I have no illegal immigrants working at any Trump property." (NYT followed that up with a story of dozens at one facility alone.)

- Beliefs help us understand and navigate this world. They are the internal commands to the brain relating to how we represent ourselves and perceive what is happening around us when we believe something to be a fact.
- Some beliefs keep us safe, so we try to preserve them once they are formed and guard them carefully.
- Beliefs play an important role in serving our subconscious mind. We often take them for granted, assuming them to be factual, without ever really checking if they are true or not.
- It is our beliefs that determine whether anything is good or bad, sexy or not sexy, desirable or undesirable, worthy or unworthy, acceptable or unacceptable, achievable, or impossible.

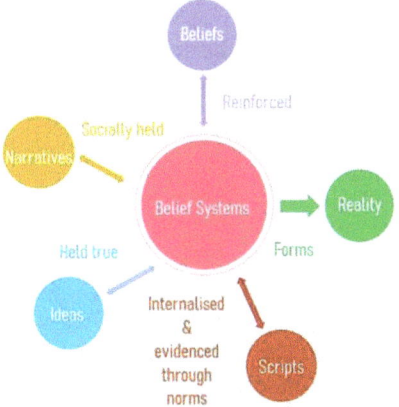

Figure 33: Formation of reality through belief systems

- When a set of beliefs is stored in our subconscious mind, our belief system emerges. These belief systems are often passed around on a social level.

- When they are, they are known as narratives or social scripts by researchers in the social sciences.

- Narratives or scripts become like stories that we believe about the world, ourselves, and others.

- These narratives are something individuals hold (beliefs); we pass these stories back and forth, creating social narratives that reinforce or challenge current norms and values.

- Beliefs are formed throughout our lives, but those formed during our childhood are so deeply rooted that by the time we are adults, some of our beliefs are ingrained so deeply

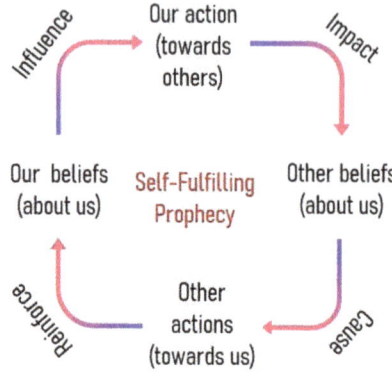

Figure 34: The cycle of the self-fulfilling prophecy

it feels like they are part of our core. They are part of our body, living inside the marrow of our bones, living inside our soul, and are met with huge resistance when challenged. Because they are intertwined, challenging one belief can begin to unravel our entire belief system.

- Beliefs are ideas that individuals hold to be true. Belief systems are constellations of individual beliefs that reinforce each other in the mind of an individual. Narratives are socially held beliefs that are passed continuously around through culture, media, and personal interactions.

- Social scripts offer insight into how cultural norms are first in the collective mind and then manifest in the world as individuals internalize these stories and comply for fear of social rejection and punishment.

We become the social scripts of our culture. We look around and see compliance with these norms because this way of being is "natural," thus "true". This kind of circular reasoning then feeds into a self-fulfilling prophecy. *The world is this way, the world should be this way, the world can only be this way.*

Close Mind vs. Open Mind

What do the concepts of "open-minded" and "close-minded" mean to you? How often do you find yourself closed off to other people's views? How openly do you share yourself with others who are open to hearing your views? When we are open-minded, we open ourselves to developing a greater perception of our own feelings, thoughts, and sensations. We are opening ourselves to new levels of attention, awareness, intention, presence, and consciousness that come with an open mind. Having an open mind doesn't mean accepting other people's views, but instead being willing and having the ability to listen to their views no matter how opposing they might sound.

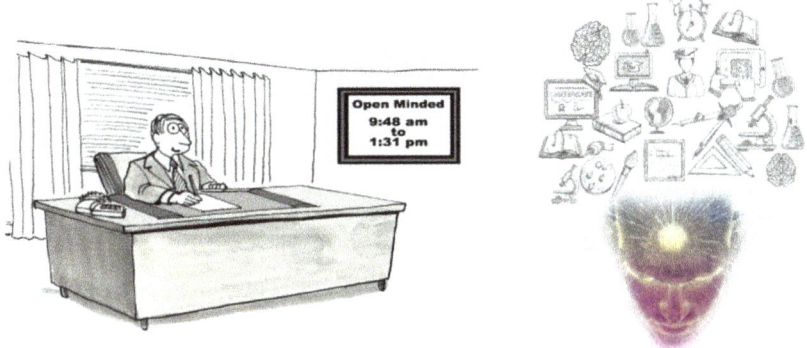

Figure 35-36: (Left) People often say they are open-minded, but their behavior depicts something else. (Right) An open mind is key in learning, self-improvement, and creating togetherness.

Attention – to give or not to give?

The millions of stimuli our brain receives every minute pass through a filtering mechanism. Some are selected, whether consciously or subconsciously, while others are partially or completely ignored. Attention is the act of directing the mind to focus on an object or phenomenon. This process happens across all the bodies, not just the physical. Are you aware of this process? Do you know that you are selectively ignoring thousands of pieces of information coming at you?

Political 'talk' is a prime example. If YOUR candidate is speaking, you tend to listen to everything and discard what is irrelevant to your particular situation. Maybe you don't care about immigration or income tax. But, if the opposing candidate is speaking, one of two things happens. Either you listen carefully and discard 90% of what is said, or you don't listen to 90% of what is said.

A great sports example is soccer. Soccer is a complex game with 22 people on the pitch at one time. You cannot focus on all 22, so you choose to accept information on some and ignore information on others. If you have a favorite player, you will likely focus there and ignore thousands of inputs from other players and situations. With two minutes of play and a tie game, you probably focus on all the activity close to

Figure 37: When there is chaos, if our mind is clear and we are grounded, we can still pay attention.

53

your opponent's net.

We all know that each of us has a limited attention span, so the question is, where are you putting your attention? Which topic and why? Why are other topics being ignored? When we focus our attention on a specific topic, it is not just our attention. The topic will consume our emotional, mental, physical, and energetic space. The more a particular topic consumes the space in our bodies, the less available to digest other topics. Have you ever found yourself being consumed for hours by a certain topic on social media? Why is that? In my book Amplify Your Orgasm, I share characteristics of attention, one of which is that selection of one thing implies de-selecting everything else. Inattentiveness and attentiveness go hand in hand because if someone is inattentive to something, they are attentive to something else, and vice versa. Inattentiveness on important things is attentiveness on unimportant things.

In later chapters, you will understand the different complexities of the world, the millions of issues surrounding a nation, the diverse demographics of voters with their non-finite choices, and the thousands of hurdles and decisions a leader faces. Do you think you have enough attention or put enough attention on all the topics if such complexities exist? If not, why not? Do you even allow yourself to look at different aspects or as many aspects as possible? A newspaper or online news portal has different sections; which do you attend to most and which do you disregard?

Awareness – the key to end ignorance and start connecting and transforming

What does it mean to be aware of something or of someone's emotions and feelings? Why does having profound awareness matter for a deeper connection with your friends? To be aware means to have the knowledge or perception of a situation, a fact or a state, and of ourselves and our friends in relation to it. In the context of the different layers of the body, awareness refers to having knowledge or perception across these different domains, often more than one at any time. Examples include:

Physical: I'm aware that I have not been taking good care of myself. I'm aware that my body goes into defense mode whenever immigration is brought up and that my friend goes into withdrawal or hiding mode.

Mental: I'm aware that I've not allowed my mind to rest for a minute. I am aware that issues surrounding child trafficking or social welfare cuts make my mind restless. I am aware that what Congress is doing with budgets will fiscally bankrupt all citizens, and I worry about my money and savings.

Energetic: I'm aware that my energy has been low since I stopped attending my yoga class. When I have a political conversation with a friend, I am aware that my energy drains and my body weakens.

Emotional: I am aware that conversations around the new world order, the establishment, the elite, and terrorism instill great fear within me. I am aware that conversations around women's rights and abortion bring emotions relating to anger and hurt due to past experiences.

Spiritual: I'm aware that I should be doing meditation and my daily practices for spiritual growth. I am aware that corporate greed and a capitalist society are not in line with my spiritual values. I am aware that many Christians consider Donald Trump a new messiah sent by God to protect America and us.

Other points relating to mind:
- It is surprisingly easy to change someone's political views depending on their flexibility.
- Group belonging and identities shape our political world (more on group dynamics in Chapter Seven). We find it easier to argue our views and are motivated to pursue these arguments because of our ingrained beliefs.
- Phenomenon of choice blindness. If a person is comfortable in false-feedback, they don't feel the need to argue as hard, or at all, to defend a point.
- Role of our beliefs. How social scripts get written. By having a better understanding of our beliefs, we can reduce aggression when defending them.

Energetic body or state or layer

We know that everything moves based on energy. Even our own existence is based on the energy within our bodies. We are continually being influenced by energy, externally by radiation, sunshine, other people's emotions and thoughts, and internally by chemical and neurochemical processes and energies from different energetic centers and energy meridians.

Most of us are familiar with the forms mentioned above. This section will focus on what many are not familiar with, the energy from the energy centers. Would you agree when you have a conversation with someone that resonates, you feel connected, loving, and in alignment with that person? And the opposite will also hold true. When you have a non-resonating conversation, you feel disconnected, distant, and unfriendlier, even though perhaps a minute before starting the conversation, you were feeling connected and possibly caring toward the same person.

What has changed? Yes, there could be mental disagreement, and yes, there could be emotional triggers. What if I were to tell you that despite disagreements, despite the strongest of the strongest emotional triggers, there is a way you can still feel loving and caring toward the other person? Would you be interested to know how? Do you think it will encourage you to have more political discussions with the friends you disagree with because you know that your love towards them will not change?

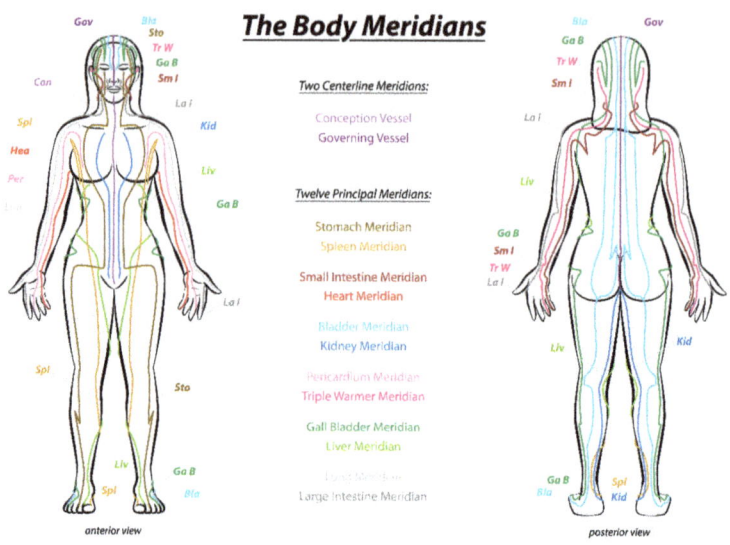

The Body Meridians

Two Centerline Meridians:

Conception Vessel
Governing Vessel

Twelve Principal Meridians:

Stomach Meridian
Spleen Meridian

Small Intestine Meridian
Heart Meridian

Bladder Meridian
Kidney Meridian

Pericardium Meridian
Triple Warmer Meridian

Gall Bladder Meridian
Liver Meridian

Large Intestine Meridian

anterior view   *posterior view*

Figure 38: Meridians, or energy highways, that exist in our bodies

Energy goes by many names based on the discipline; Aura (Hindu), Qi (Chinese), Prana (India), Ki (Japanese), Barraka (Islam). This vital life energy comprises the non-physical aspect of our energy system. Like blood flowing through our blood vessels, our vital life energy flows through our energy vessels called meridians. Just as we have various nerves that branch off in different parts of the body as part of the nervous system, we also have large and small meridians that branch off to carry energy throughout the body. The meridians flow throughout the body, and the seven energy centers correlate with various meridian points.

We associate specific places in our bodies with certain emotions and sensations. E.g., we feel love in our hearts, not in our toes. Energy centers help us make sense of why and how these different body areas seem to contain the capacity for certain types of emotions and feelings. Besides, understanding energy in this way allows us to make sense that sometimes we may be blocked from fully experiencing certain feelings.

The Law of Conservation of Energy, a foundational idea in physics, states that energy cannot be created nor destroyed; however, it can be transformed. Hence, it is important to keep this law in mind when talking about these energy centers.

SAHASRARA
CROWN CHAKRA

VISHUDDHA
THIRD EYE CHAKRA

AJNA
THROAT CHAKRA

ANAHATA
HEART CHAKRA

MANIPURA
SOLAR PLEXUS CHAKRA

SWADHISTHANA
SACRAL CHAKRA

MULADHARA
ROOT CHAKRA

SPIRITUALITY

AWARENESS

COMMUNICATION

LOVE HEALING

WISDOM POWER

SEXUALITY
CREATIVITY

BASIC
TRUST

CHAKRA SYSTEM

Figure 39: Seven primary energy centers in the body

We can always choose to use energy to fight with each other, create dishar-mony, or align ourselves with remaining in harmony with ourselves and those around us. Hence, our bodies' energy can be used for constructive, positive, and supporting purposes, rather than destructive, draining, and counterproductive purposes. Specific qualities and vibrations are associated with each of these en-ergy centers. The lower energy centers have lower, thicker, and denser vibrations that fulfill the base-level materialistic self-identity, fundamental emotions, and basic needs. In comparison, higher energy centers have higher, lighter, and thin-ner vibrations that fulfill our higher selves, our sense of purpose, and spiritual-related identities. Because they bring more awareness to our consciousness and are important and essential parts of us, it is vital to pay good attention to each of these. Understanding them can align them all into a unified field of brilliance.

The interaction between the physical body and the energy field occurs through a flow of energy via consciousness and various physical body parts, such as the endocrine and nervous systems. The tension or contraction in con-sciousness and each of these systems will impact each of the energy centers and auras associated with them.

Physical body or state or layer

❖ *Trump's body language during debate raises social media eyebrows*
❖ *China denies 'flexing muscles' in military parade*
❖ *PM 'nervous' as referendum looms*
❖ *Iraq-Kurdistan crisis makes oil market nervous*
❖ *Why does coronavirus cause digestive symptoms?*
❖ *Duterte, President of the Philippines, slammed over threat to shoot rebels in the genitals*
❖ *Somaliland leaders want female genitals to be cut*
❖ *Nipples stimulate the same area of the female brain as genitals do*
❖ *Australia faces heart failure epidemic as 1 in 20 people estimated to have the heart condition*

In high school, maybe you learned about the body's eleven different systems: the skeletal system, nervous system, circulatory system, respiratory system, etc. Chances are good that your teacher did not spend much time (probably none) on the relationship between these systems and how you feel within your body. We will share a few examples without going through each system.

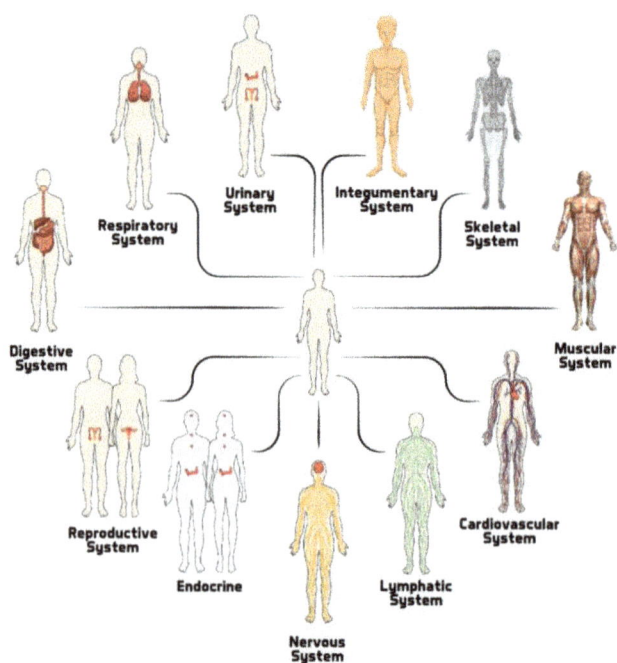

Figure 40: The eleven systems of the human body

58

Skeletal system: This system includes the body's rigid framework of 206 bones that support and protect the human body's muscles and organs. Our skeleton system provides the structure to the body, and its growth depends on genetics, parents, calcium, etc. Do you think it does any good making fun of someone based on their looks?

Muscular system: This system comprises muscle and its attachment tissues, tendons and fascia. Earlier, we learned that emotion is associated with three things: energy, movement, and feelings. Tensed and contracted muscles can hold back the emotional energy affecting the tissues surrounding those muscles, the circulation, and nerves, ultimately stopping the flow of emotional and orgasmic energy.

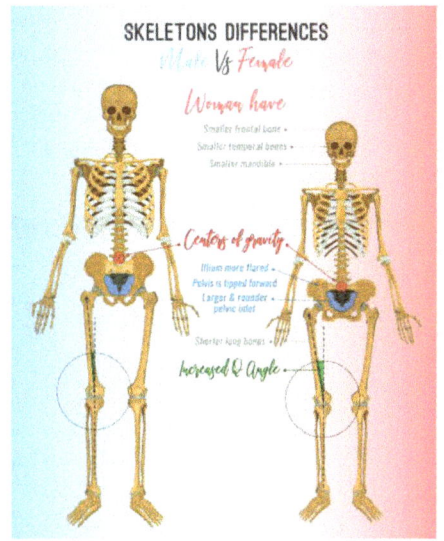

Figure 41: Women and men have different skeletal systems, as shown in the diagram above.

Suppose our muscles are tensed or contracted during conversations. In that case, it is important to note we are likely to get fatigued (and often irritated) much quicker, irrespective of the topic of conversation.

Lymphatic system: This system includes the body's complex network of tissues and organs that eliminate waste and toxins while delivering white blood cells to various parts of the body to fight infection. Those not engaging in physical exercises have systems that are not cleansed, meaning a blockage in the flow of ideas, well-being, etc. When we lack good health and well-being, our attitude towards life will generally be negative instead of positive.

Nervous system: This communication and instruction network is categorized into two parts: the central nervous system (CNS, which consists of the brain and spinal cord) and the peripheral nervous system (PNS, which consists of the nerves throughout the body). The brain is the central unit, connected to the rest of the body by nerve cells that function as messengers, carrying information to and from the brain. Feelings of stress are generally due to activation of the sympathetic nervous system. At the same time, relaxation is due to

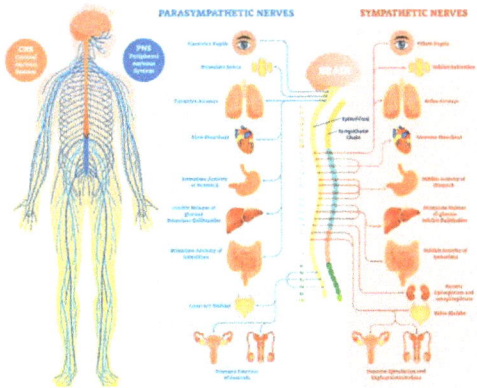

Figure 42: The nervous system is responsible for signaling sensations of pain or pleasure.

activation of the parasympathetic nervous system. Hence, if you feel fight or flight mode or stress during conversations, you can easily manage your emotional state by focusing on different systems' activation.

The more we are aware of our different body systems and the more we can check-in with each other, the more we will enjoy having intense conversations and taking our friendships and relationships to a deeper level.

Spiritual body or state or layer

❖ *Bangladesh arrests cafe attackers' 'spiritual leader'*
❖ *Bali bombers' spiritual leader hospitalized in Indonesia*
❖ *China, Vietnam affirm 'desire' to solve problems*
❖ *Israel, Palestinians show desire to continue talks*
❖ *Iran awaits Lebanese "desire" to accept its military aid-FM*

"If you light a lamp for somebody, it will also brighten your path." Buddha

Figure 43: Religions contain amazing philosophies and teachings, but we need to focus on learning and implementing them rather than fighting over which religion is best. Why not adopt the best of each?

When it comes to our connection with the divine, there are many paths and languages to make sense of a spiritual journey. Christianity, Hinduism, Buddhism, Judaism, Islam, Shintoism are but a few of the ways to understand and connect to something larger than ourselves, a force beyond our immediate control that drives the creation of all that is beautiful in our world. Our spiritual journey is a highly personal one and is often deeply shaped by our cultural heritage and life experiences.

When choosing how to teach my clients and students about the spiritual body, I have found it critical to respect these different paths to connect with the divine, without proposing that one is more valid than another. However, as individual human beings, I believe that a connection with a higher power, a force greater than ourselves, is essential for our overall health and well-being. I do believe that connecting with our higher life purpose is central to a spiritual journey.

60

It may be the reason we are taught that 'religion and politics' are off-limit subjects. The depth of our needs, feelings, and beliefs in spiritual issues is even deeper than our political beliefs. When speaking of either, one must tread carefully and understand that our counterpart in conversation may be a bit spiritual or 'all in' spiritually.

Over the years, in my work with clients and students, I have found that regardless of the specific religion, faith, or language used to describe a connection to something greater than ourselves, two key concepts pop up over and over in terms of the spiritual body: desire and fear. In discussing the spiritual body, I have chosen to focus on these concepts because they require no specific faith. Yet, they are universal to developing greater spiritual health. Desire and fear are by no means the be-all and end-all of the spiritual body. There are many more aspects, such as the role relationships, practices, values, and transcendental lovemaking play in developing and nurturing the spiritual body.

Figure 44: Religion and politics are the two most dreaded topics.

Fear is what plays a big part when it comes to politics. We have covered this already in previous chapters and will be covering it many more times.

Desire, at its core, is about the spiritual body trying to show us how to fulfill our life's higher purpose. We will see that correctly identifying and connecting with your true desires is complicated in our modern world full of conveniences, addictions, and distractions. Still, only by allowing our true desires to become our guide can we connect with our higher life's purpose. We will be talking about desire in the next chapter.

On the other hand, fear is also common to the human experience, regardless of the faith we practice. Fear has an extraordinary relationship with desire. Where true desires emerge, so too will fear, always trying to block us on our path of spiritual growth. Identifying, facing, processing, and releasing fear is central in learning to trust and strengthen our spiritual body. Again, this is regardless of the specific religious tradition we use to make sense of our connection to the divine.

Conclusion

Now you know a great deal more about how the various layers of the human body, from physical to spiritual, play roles in how we interact, what we believe, and how best to cope with others in difficult discussions. We are used to relating with people at face value, taking what they say rather than understanding their intention or where they are coming from. Going beyond this first layer of physical appearance and words won't be easy, as we are breaking away from habitual patterns and dealing with our ego being challenged without having a defense mechanism from the outset. Once we can do that, we save our relationship, friendship, and even develop new friendships with strangers. This can often provide insights into the other person's unwanted habitual patterns, helping them with their own personal growth. As a word of caution, don't expect to get any credit for that. Why? Because friendships and relationships are often taken for granted. Hey! This is where we need to develop boundaries (more on this in Chapter Twelve).

CHAPTER FOUR

NEEDS

Wants, though sometimes necessary, are superficial. Though essential for well-being are not essential for survival, core needs are often dismissed, not expressed, or remain unmet. Desires, when fulfilled, provide us immense satisfaction, nourishment, and happiness, but often remain unmet and are instead repressed, shamed, met with confusion, or unmentioned.

Michael Charming

Introduction

Having covered who we are, what we become, and why we confront, I think we are now ready to dive into the first topic to relate to each other on a deeper level. Understanding why someone makes a particular choice or decision today but could make a completely different choice or decision tomorrow brings us to the topic of needs.

I want a new hairstyle. I need to have a hairstyle. I desire a new hairstyle.
I want to feel safe. I need to feel safe. I desire to feel safe.
I want him to win. I need him to win. I desire him to win.

What is the difference between each of the categories mentioned above? Though, initially, each option looks the same within each category. If you were to take a guess, what do you think the difference is?

We often mistake wants for needs. In this chapter, we will be discussing both and understanding why the difference really matters. We will cover both understanding and honoring the needs of others without dismissing our own.

Everyone has needs. Society, in general, has basic needs such as protection, food, water, and shelter for everyone. Nations need to take care (in whichever way they choose to define "care") of their citizens, government, military, borders, etc. They need to provide safety. Similarly, communities have needs; safe spaces, schools, traffic control, shops to buy food, space to play, etc.

Organizations have needs; to serve their members, do the work required of them, and enforce their policies.

Groups fill a common need, whether bowling, soccer, book clubs, hiking, political discussion, terrorism, protests, or playgroups. Groups are less structured than organizations or communities.

What are needs?

❖ *David Cameron needs to shake up his inner circle*
❖ *The Voters Trump Needs Most Right Now*
❖ *India's economy needs PM Modi to reinvent himself — again*
❖ *US Needs China More Than China Needs the US*
❖ *Here's what needs to happen for America to return to "normal"*
❖ *The world needs political leadership from its democracies*
❖ *Over 500,000 children in Libya need aid; UNICEF urges political solution to years-long crisis*
❖ *Boris Johnson's intention is clear: he wants a 'people v parliament' election*
❖ *David Cameron wants to return to politics. It's a shame he has so little to offer*
❖ *Why the World Wants Democracy but Not Necessarily the American Version*

Here are a few definitions (courtesy dictionary.com):
- A requirement, necessary duty, or obligation
- A lack of something wanted or deemed necessary
- An urgent want, as of something requisite
- A necessity arising from the circumstances of a situation or case
- A situation or time of difficulty; exigency
- A condition marked by the lack of something requisite
- Destitution; extreme poverty

Be aware that different people have different needs. Are you aware of your friends' top three needs, that at this moment, have not been met? How would you feel if your important needs remained unmet for an extended period? These are the kinds of questions I think are vital as we dive deeper into the concept of needs and having political conversations.

Our needs define our core values and propel us to move towards achieving things in life. While sometimes we are familiar with our needs and other times not, we should always be familiar with our core needs. One person may need to express love, while another may need to be loved. Some have the need to fight for gender equality, while others need to feed their children and support social welfare. Some need to have an open society and support immigrants, while others need to feel a sense of belonging and are against immigrants.

As this book is being written, the United States has a huge divergent need that divides the nation. Some need to stay home, sheltered in a safe place, protected from the virus, and others need to be outside, working, going to restaurants, movies, and the beach. So, is the need to protect the economy more important than the need to keep citizens alive?

In the UK, many have the need to belong, and to belong means belonging to the EU, which has worked well for many citizens for decades. Others feel the need for independence from the EU. Their policies were believed to be restrictive and strangling the UK's ability to self-govern.

Peoples' different needs
Needs can be divided into Basic and Non-basic categories.
- Basic needs are food, water, and shelter.
- Non-basic needs are of a higher nature, love, safety, and self-esteem.

Maslow's Hierarchy of Needs

In 1943, psychologist Abraham Maslow developed what is known as the hierarchy of needs, which still remains influential in psychology.[22] As you can see in the pyramid chart below, physical needs are the most primitive level of human needs. Also, to self-actualize and reach our full human potential, our needs should include companionship, freedom, health, self-esteem, and more along the journey.

According to Maslow, human needs can be arranged in a hierarchy. The greatest needs relate directly to our biological survival: food, water, shelter, and health. The next level needs matter once the biological survival needs are met. Maslow referred to them as the basic needs as these are considered essential for human survival. Then comes the social needs, the need for love, a sense of belonging, and self-respect. Maslow terms these as maintenance needs. These all form the base of the pyramid, and at the top are self-actualization needs.

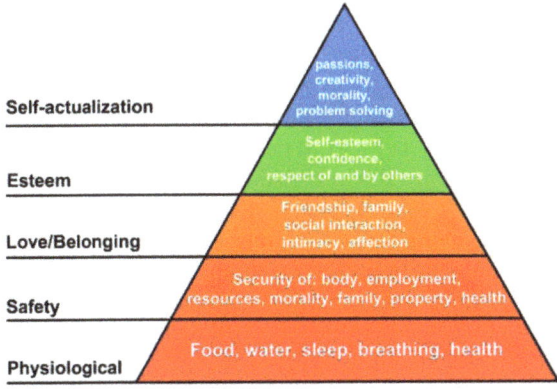

Figure 45: Abraham Maslow's hierarchy of needs

Different researchers have defined needs similar to Maslow's chart, but I define needs in terms of human body layers. In the previous chapter, we studied the human body in different layers, emotional, mental, energetic, physical, and spiritual. Our needs refer to each of the bodies.

Emotional:
I have a need for my leader to understand my emotions and feelings regarding specific policy decisions being made. I like Barack Obama because he can relate and feels the needs of people who do not have money.

Mental:
I have a need to understand the details of this policy's impact to grasp its meaning entirely.

Energetic:
I have a need to create a society where we are aware of each other's sensitivities. I support policies that support organic living; it is in alignment with my body's needs for holistic living and pure energy.

Physical:
I have a physical need to feel safe, a need for order, and structure.

Spiritual:
I have a need to align with my values, principles, religious teachings, and higher beliefs.

We also have needs at the energy center level. Our need is for safety, survival, and vitality at the first energy center. At the third energy center, our need is for love, understanding, intimacy, trust, and compassion. Being balanced in terms of our needs allows for more balance in decision making. The more imbalanced we are, the more likely our decisions will follow the imbalance toward excess or deficiency extremes. These needs, if unmet for an extended period, affect our overall well-being. I refer to them as deep core needs as these are deeply seated within our bodies. When met, these needs tend to bring alignment (or better alignment) of our body layers, drawing our essence to the surface.

In regards to politics, this is how these will play out. E.g., someone whose need for safety and security has not been met is most likely to support political candidates who offer them the feeling of safety and security (survival). Likewise, people who have lacked love in their lives will support policies aimed at community, love, and welfare for everyone.

Many needs are mostly ignored until their lack of fulfillment becomes detrimental to us and shows up in other forms (depression, stress, anxiety, health problems, etc.). Our body has a core need to remain in alignment with nature, but this often remains unfulfilled, resulting in us being imbalanced. When our needs remain unmet for extended periods, we tend to fight with others to secure these. Sometimes, this impacts our usually solid decision-making, resulting in us making decisions that would not normally be in our best interests.

Each level of energetic centers has many needs. It is vital to ensure that at least our deep core needs are fulfilled. To do this, we must have a level of awareness about these needs. Just like we have needs, so does everyone else. As seen in previous chapters, everyone is unique. Their experiences are unique, so two people's needs are likely to be different at any given time. In an ideal scenario, a society should cater to everyone's basic and core needs. Limitations of resources and complexities involved make it impossible to fulfill everyone's needs. (We will study this in detail in later chapters).

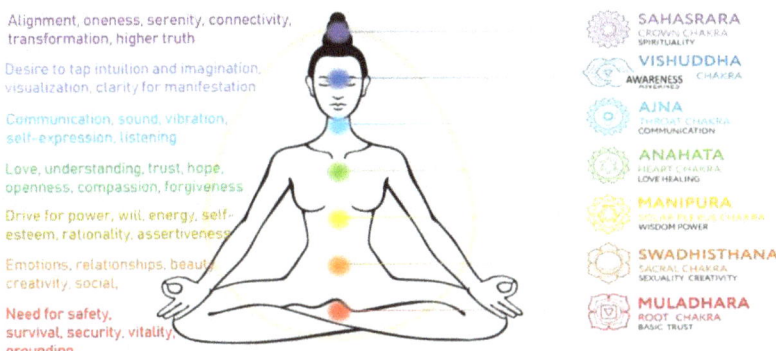

Figure 46: Various needs at the level of energetic centers

If our needs are not fulfilled, we have to ask or work for their fulfillment. **But, the question arises, what happens if two people have conflicting needs?** Whose need is more important, and how do we decide which should be catered to and which should be ignored? To expand this example, suppose one half of the country's population needs government-paid healthcare, and the other half has a need not to have their taxes increased to implement this policy. How do we decide which need is more important? When each of us has this awareness and works towards a civilly harmonious resolution, this can cause a ripple effect. Otherwise, we will continue to live in silos, protecting our own turf and tossing bombs to the other side.

Some important aspects of needs

- Nobody's needs are wrong. Now it can be argued that some needs are a bit outside our societal norms. E.g., for those who wish to kill other people because they are different, we will have to, if necessary, use force to prevent them from exercising their needs. Is killing others really their need, or are they acting out due to some unprocessed trauma (more on this in Chapter Fourteen)?
- Needs can feel superficial, or some may mistake wants and impulses to be their needs, but this is mostly due to a lack of awareness, introspection, and self-reflection.
- When we are deprived of the basic needs, food, clothing, and shelter, our survival instinct rightfully feels challenged. It forces us into demand, protest, or raising hell mode, sometimes even all three. Not being able to survive is

the most basic of needs, and it must be addressed, or people may act selfishly and cruelly.

Political conversations and needs – Why do these matter?

When people talk about political conversation, one of the things to note is most of us (in fact, all of us) operate from a group of deep underlying needs; the need for money, the need for affection, the need for well-being, the need for a sense of belonging, the need to feel safe, the need for care for Mother Earth, the need to take revenge as a result of feeling hurt, the need for Medicare for our parents, the need to lash out when any of these needs appear to be in jeopardy, but the issues are that we are not aware of what is happening beneath our needs not being met, hence the visceral reaction. So, it is vitally important to understand the 'needs assessment' of the person to whom you are speaking, trying to convince, or trying to change BEFORE starting a deep conversation.

Suppose this person has just been laid off, is sick, tired, has had a miscarriage, has missed an entire day's meals, has fought with their partner (this is bigger than you might imagine), or anything else which may result in unmet needs. In that case, your job will be close to impossible to have a reasonable conversation with them at that moment. If you can determine that the issue is a missed dinner, sit down and give them dinner. You are 100% more likely to get your fair hearing, your position accepted, or at least the perspective broadened and possibly a deeper connection. It is often that simple.

Different Concepts of Needs, Wants, and Desires

Our society is more driven by wants than by needs, which is why we are in this messy state, both as individuals and as nations. Should the media be held as the culprit for brainwashing us with the idea of consumerism? Wants are for things we do not have and are mostly generic: I want a car. I want a new branded handbag. I want to travel the world. Wants are subject to change frequently and are often caused by seeing what others have or driven by insecurity. Advertising works on the principle of wants.

It aims to tell you a story about how you are 'less than'… if you have this new gadget or a particular body type, you will feel better, gain respect, or show others how important you are.

Wants are superficial by nature and mostly involve choice. Wants can often be achieved through action, but if not achieved, life goes on. Wants are determined by a person's human composition, upbringing, culture, and mindset. If you pay attention, you will realize when you satisfy one want, the sense of accomplishment is soon replaced by yet another want.

Generally, we don't gain deep satisfaction, happiness, or nourishment from the fulfillment of wants, which is one of the characteristics that separates it from desires. Desire arises from deep within us. It is connected to fulfilling a larger purpose in our lives and is persistent in providing fulfillment. When we are in tune with our true desires, we can use them to help guide our life journey, showing us what we need to learn next, to give us direction in terms of personal growth, spiritual fulfillment, and the achievement of great things.

I want to have children vs. I need to have children vs. I desire to have children.
I want to have freedom of speech vs. I need to express myself vs. I desire to be listened to and be heard.

Do you feel the difference? Ask the person you are having a conversation with now, 'what is one thing you want right now?', then 'what is one thing you need right now?' and finally, 'what is one thing you desire right now?'. You both might be surprised at what unfolds through those responses.

Figure 47: Deciding between wants vs. needs will feel like deciding which road to take.

What makes desires special is that they are tied to our sense of self and are highly individual. If ignored, without us realizing, they cause damage to our well-being. At the societal level, living from desire, though ideal, is not possible, especially given the trauma that humankind has stored within their bodies (more on this in Chapter Fourteen). But, if we can move away from living in the place of want towards having an awareness of each other's needs and possibly making efforts to help each other fulfill our basic and core needs, we have already made substantial progress.

Until we begin to understand each other's needs and wants when having a conversation or coming into association with someone, we will not be able to create a place of harmony, support, and love. Without this, we cannot resolve disagreements of a political, social, or societal nature.

But the dilemma is:

- Helping others without having our own basic and core needs met will be depleting, draining, and unsustainable in the mid to long term.
- Not helping or being able to help those who don't have their basic and core needs met means we continue to create more separation, division, and fragmentation in our society.

Societies and their needs

As a society and as human beings, we should all work together to ensure our basic needs are met. In a society, it should be our duty to ensure everyone's basic needs are met first. But how do we ensure what these basic needs are? Do we simply say, okay, Maslow's first two levels should do it? How many of the policies implemented by the government are aimed at meeting the needs of the people?

In a society where we have gazillions of needs and where many of these needs matter but often conflict, how does one identify a system or process that caters to every individual's needs? Would you agree that it is not realistically possible? E.g., how often do individual family members' needs get fulfilled without clashing with one another in our own home? Mom has the need to rest; Dad is feeling hungry, so he has the bodily need to eat and is waiting for Mom to cook. At the same time, the kids have the need to play with Mom and Dad. Hence, how does one determine whose needs are important, whose are not, and which needs should be given priority?

When government leaders are preparing policies that meet a few or most of the population's needs, others' needs are likely not going to be met. Which side of the equation do you find yourself on at any given time? How does that make you feel? If most of your needs are fulfilled, and you are used to this, are you considering it your birthright? Do you think that we should let go of fulfilling some of our needs so that others' needs can be met? After all, they are part of our family, not immediate family, but of the wider family, which is part of our neighborhood, our society, and contributes to being part of the country as its citizens.

"How about a little water over here?"

Figure 48: With increased awareness and clarity, we can cater to the needs of others more effectively and appropriately.

Societies have created a success culture, focusing on external parameters to determine progress, good grades, a great career, more money, and a better family. This culture creates a sense of 'competition' among individuals. What kind of society would we have if it focused on honoring and fulfilling each other's needs instead? Operating from a mindset of competition, we focus on winning and forget to honor others' needs as we aim to crush them instead. This leads to a 'me-first' philosophy.

While competition can be healthy, shouldn't society be modeled on cooperation rather than competition? Imagine if the class performance was judged on all the students' aggregates as a determining factor. Do you think our attitude towards our classmates would shift? What would happen to those who take the opportunity not to play their part, choosing to be lazy and unfocused instead? The competition, fake life, and images on social media have made us feel more worthless, inadequate, depressed, anxious, and left out.

We place so much importance on happiness, but how does one determine happiness? Happiness is a very subjective feeling that changes rapidly, and individuals need different things to be happy. But is happiness really that important? Children in poor developing countries can be happy by having food on their table. Children in developed countries need more than fine weather, the latest gadgets, and good cuisine to be happy.

After considering what matters most to people, our policies should be designed around family, culture, and education. How do you determine what matters in a multi-ethnic society, where everyone has their individual experiences and personalities? The goal is to make the individuals within the society more connected.

Each individual needs to step up, to do more than just living every day. Everyone should genuinely contribute to society continuously in a way that supports the fulfillment of someone's basic or/and core needs.

When we focus on going beyond our own society, we will realize each society has different needs. In fact, different sections and different groups of the same society have different needs. We will discuss society and groups in detail in Chapter Seven. **Different societies emerged during different periods in history and are at different paths of evolution, thereby having their own unique needs.**

In Indian society, mutual harmony between religious groups, especially Hindus and Muslims, is a critical need; failing here could lead to country-wide genocide. Whereas, in a country like China, where religious groups apart from Christians are minorities, the mutual harmony between religious groups might not be the most immediate need of their society. Their immediate need might be to ensure that they remain alive by toeing the line to the Communist Party and their desire to maintain strict citizenry mind control. Thus religion is put into third or fourth place.

Countries like Somalia, South Sudan, and Syria are considered the most corrupted, poorest, and most conflicted countries globally. Their needs might be to have better governance, accountability and develop international trust to prosper on the world stage. Stopping conflict, feeding citizens, and building places to live all seem to be these countries' primary needs.

Besides safety, peace, and cooperation, one of the most common needs of each society is change or the ability to face change effectively. This cannot happen unless we are ready for that change. Hence, the perception of change determines society's success in meeting that change (more on this in Chapter Thirteen).

Conclusion

With a better understanding of needs, wants, desires, and the importance that fulfillment of needs plays in one's overall well-being when interacting and conversing with others, we should always aim to include the fulfilled and unfulfilled aspects of others' needs. By bringing the conversation around needs (more on this in Chapter Twelve), we create a space to allow them to reflect and become aware of their unmet needs. It could be due to them not being familiar with the concept, or having these denied or not being fulfilled due to circumstances. Or fulfilling them in unconscious or unhealthy ways, thereby fulfilling needs which aren't really needs at all. This can also allow us to feel empathy towards each other and create a sense or feeling of togetherness and the desire to support each other or our communities, cities, and societies.

CHAPTER FIVE

PERSPECTIVES, PREFERENCES, AND PRIORITIES

Wants, though sometimes necessary, are superficial. Though essential for well-being are not essential for survival, core needs are often dismissed, not expressed, or remain unmet. Desires, when fulfilled, provide us immense satisfaction, nourishment, and happiness, but often remain unmet and are instead repressed, shamed, met with confusion, or unmentioned.

Michael Charming

Introduction

Our life experiences (discussed in Chapter Two) determine our perspective (discussed in Chapter Three), which develops our personality. The more expanded and in-depth our awareness (both macro and micro), the better our ability to consider an overall perspective (point of view). With a clear human body and an unbiased sense of judgment, we can consider any perspective. Our personality determines our preferences, and our needs determine our priorities.

To come together harmoniously, we need to understand each other's perspective (put ourselves in their shoes) and know their personalities, needs, and priorities.

Perspectives and preferences allow us to form an opinion. Our final decision, however, will be determined by the severity of the impact on our priorities.

How does our perspective shape our preferences? What happens when a situation changes, demanding us to prioritize a decision, even though it might not be our first preference?

What does politics mean?

We have been talking about politics, but we haven't really examined what politics means to different people. Politics is hugely complex, as we know but often don't realize in our conversations filled with emotional outbursts, involving gazillions of variables surrounding individuals, societies, cities, states, countries, continents, and the world. Given the complexity of human beings, with our ever-changing needs, desires, and wants, it should come as no surprise that no two people will have similar perspectives on every issue surrounding politics. Politics means different things to different people. So, take a pause and ask yourself, what does politics mean for you at this very moment? What do you think it means to your friend or group of friends?

Some may feel it means issues in the range of personal, local, societal, national, and international. For some, it is a system to resolve disputes and avoid a chaotic (not that we are not chaotic at the moment, but it could be far worse) society, offering law and order, debates representing various arguments, and administration of the country, taxes, government, and welfare. For some, it might relate to journalism, telling stories of past, present, and future, information about leaders, relaying tales of heroes, famous personalities, class, and culture. For some, politics is about taking on the existing system and standing for change. For some, politics is about advancing society, justice, equality, fairness, freedom, a community, and the values a country represents and a citizen holds. For others, politics is about creating situations and supporting policies that benefit them and their families the most. Imagine life without politics to discuss and different perspectives to share. Can you picture the lack of growth of society?

Politics is fascinating. Imagine being able to comfortably talk through the complexities on several issues, have agreements and disagreements, and still live on the same boat, in the same society, in the same country, day in and day out.

Having a point of view is similar to a multi-dimensional chess game where every player needs to consider the consequences three, four, or five moves ahead. By understanding the implications in a broader context and grasping the situation's complexity, we are more likely to consider an overall rounded judgment. Our perspectives are limited by our perceptions and experiences and our ability to see things as far and as clearly as possible. If we are rigid on a particular decision, it becomes difficult to remain adaptable. Sharing perspectives involves having a flexible and open mind to be aware and willing to change our stance if something resonates.

Figure 49: When zooming out of a situation, you will gain a different perspective.

Being rigid will make it difficult to develop deeper friendships or create a society that caters to everyone's basic needs. Politics tend to be egocentric because people are generally egocentric.

Perspective – Yours or Mine?

'No, but I think you are wrong,' 'they're an idiot,' 'I don't understand how an intelligent person like you is not able to see this point of view,' 'and you believe you are right.' 'I don't understand how a liberal thinker can be so narrow-minded on some subjects.' 'How can you support a crook?'

Our view of the world plays a large part in determining our perspective. Given a particular situation, some people can see and relate with us, while others simply can't, even when they try.

After reading the previous chapters, I guess it should come as no surprise as to why this happens. When this happens, what do you do? Do you keep bombarding them with countless messages whenever you have a point to make, or perhaps engage in resentful conversations every time you see them? Do you continue sharing, hoping that someday they may see this from your perspective?

Just like you have your perspective, they have theirs too. In such scenarios, whose view is of more significance, or at least more relevant? It is not easy to shift a person's perspective. As an Orgasm Coach, you can imagine how much resistance and conditioning I face when I meet someone who I sincerely believe will benefit from my services and feel they should be willing to try and explore. It is a no brainer to realize I am often met with avoidance and a big NO, even though it is for their own benefit.

In some cases, it even takes a client years to start listening to me and consider or finally say 'yes' to what I have to offer. From the moment we first interacted, my role through the years of no communication, and then finally to have a conversation, is simply to remain

open, loving, and continue doing what I need to do. You might ask the question, 'What makes that shift?' That's precisely what we will be going through in this section.

For someone who has motivated reasoning, confirmation bias, or even cognitive dissonance, no matter how many facts they are shown, they will not change their

Figure 50: Sometimes it's good to get a different perspective.

minds. This is referred to as 'The Affect Heuristic'; using the information to draw judgments, views, and conclusions through subconscious processes that use feelings, life experiences, gut instincts, surroundings, and circumstances.[23,24] This forms the basis of their perspective (likewise ours too).

A few points to note about perspectives

- Perspective is different from perception. Perspective is a point of view, the lens with which we see the world, ourselves, others, and everything around us. Perception is about collation, understanding, and interpretation of different ideas, values, people, behaviors, experiences, and the world around you. The way we perceive something determines our behavior and how we react and respond towards it. We experience external realities in conjunction with our internal realities (more on this in Chapter Twelve). Our beliefs, judgments, life experiences, preferences, biases, and filters are how we experience reality. Being caught up or trapped by these will distort the actual reality that fits social narratives. Two people can have similar perspectives, but their perceptions about these could be totally different. One can have a 'conservative' perspective yet perceive the issue of immigration differently than other Conservatives.
- As per modern psychology, seven major perspectives can help determine how people think, feel, and behave. Discussion of these is out of this book's scope. Still, the invitation is to understand and then observe how these play out in the person with whom you are having a conversation.
- The goal is to identify the good and bad that exists in all perspectives. Every perspective will have strengths and weaknesses that an open mind will quickly recognize.
- It is important to note how much tenacity and rigidity we have in holding onto our own perspective (point of view).

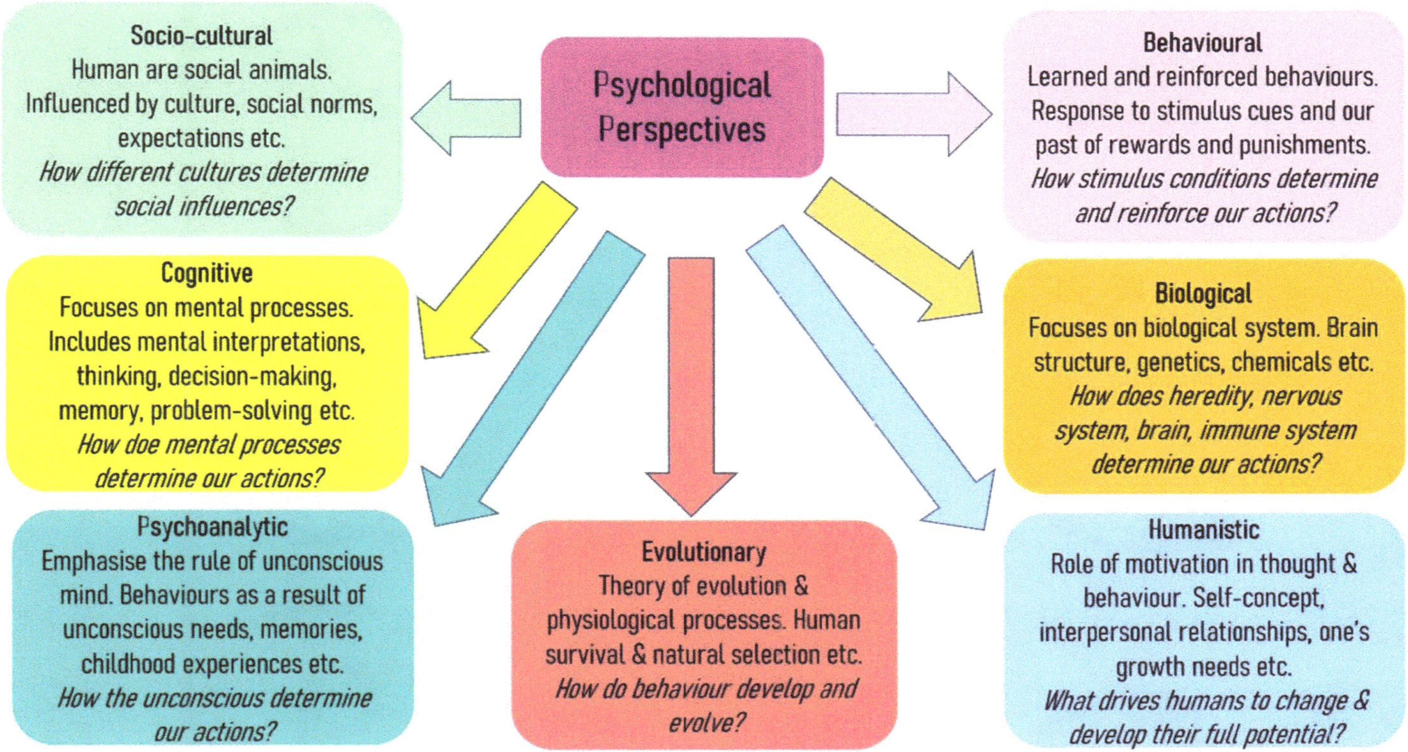

Socio-cultural
Human are social animals. Influenced by culture, social norms, expectations etc.
How different cultures determine social influences?

Cognitive
Focuses on mental processes. Includes mental interpretations, thinking, decision-making, memory, problem-solving etc.
How doe mental processes determine our actions?

Psychoanalytic
Emphasise the rule of unconscious mind. Behaviours as a result of unconscious needs, memories, childhood experiences etc.
How the unconscious determine our actions?

Psychological Perspectives

Evolutionary
Theory of evolution & physiological processes. Human survival & natural selection etc.
How do behaviour develop and evolve?

Behavioural
Learned and reinforced behaviours. Response to stimulus cues and our past of rewards and punishments. *How stimulus conditions determine and reinforce our actions?*

Biological
Focuses on biological system. Brain structure, genetics, chemicals etc.
How does heredity, nervous system, brain, immune system determine our actions?

Humanistic
Role of motivation in thought & behaviour. Self-concept, interpersonal relationships, one's growth needs etc.
What drives humans to change & develop their full potential!?

Figure 51: Perspectives per psychology that can help determine human behavior.

- Our perspectives shape how we act or react in a given situation or support or oppose policy decision making.
- Putting yourself into someone else's perspective might help you broaden your perspective, but where do our perspectives come from? In fact, they come from our perceptions.

Figure 52: Who is right, and who is wrong? In our lives, this scenario plays out daily, but we still do not get it. We may understand it conceptually but don't integrate it into our responses and conversations with others. The question remains, "how can we help one another to see each other's perspective?"

- Our perception of reality determines our perspective on life. When we change our perception, it helps change our perspective. Suppose we have to change someone else's perspective. In that case, we have to be willing to re-main curious and ask ourselves, 'what is the makeup of their internal realities?' 'What makes them feel and see things the way they do?' Once we have this understanding, we can then validate their perspective by acknowl-edging what exists for them, share their reality with them (as sometimes many are not in touch with their own realities), ask them if they would be in-terested in hearing your perspective, and then share with them. When acknowledging what exists for them, ensure that you are not biased or cloud-ed with your own perception about them, their beliefs, or their inner realities.
- Our perception is subconscious, and unconsciously we filter out what does not fit into our world view. Choice happens in our subconscious. Hence, there is a level where we do not access conscious choice, as it occurs uncon-

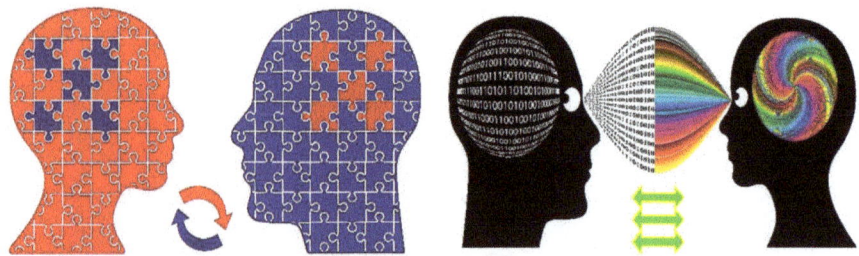

Figure 53-54: (Left image) Shows how subjective perception plays out. (Right image) Shows that when we are willing to exchange, listen, and hear each other's perception, it leaves an imprint in our mind, which gradually will shift perception and perspectives.

sciously, cutting and editing according to what fits into the world's view and what is too threatening to accept. In conversational topics like politics, which is vast, complex, and not talked about enough, it is normal for us to have subjective perceptions and distorted reality. Our goal should be to move away from this to a deeper understanding of others' perspectives and how they form their realities.

Whose perspective is important

I believe the person who has a broader perspective and an in-depth view should make much better decisions given their overall (macro and micro) perspective. In the previous chapter, we discussed awareness. The more awareness we have of our body states, the more we will hear someone else's perspective. Likewise, the more awareness we have of an issue and its overall consequence, the more we will form a view based on a broader perspective.

Unknowingly we have a deceptive illusion of 'my perspective is the only reality.' We don't realize that "my reality" is possibly not the most accepted reality of our society. Hence, it is always recommended to be aware of how far our reality deviates from society. It doesn't mean we have to disregard our reality in favor of society; it merely means that we need to have awareness, giving us an idea of how often we will clash and with whom.

Perspective-taking allows us to put ourselves in others' shoes, giving us the ability to empathize with their experiences (more in the final chapter). We do this every day and have done this repeatedly, so much that we are actually experts in taking perspectives. When crossing a road or driving, we anticipate how the person or driver in front of us will behave by taking their perspective into account. We can become experts in doing the same when having political conversations. For that, we will need willingness (and make an effort) to go beyond seeing our perspective as the only reality. Before we disconnect, disengage, or unfriend someone, we should put ourselves in their shoes to see where they are coming from. Only then should we decide on disconnecting. **If we really understand where someone is coming from, we wouldn't want to unfriend them unless they support a policy or leader aiming to create genocide, dictatorship, or totalitarianism.**

It is important to understand another person's experiences and see their point of view to relate and empathize. Neurons and hormones produced due to the brain region's activation when we focus on our point of view also get activated when considering another person's point of view. Hence, attributes like compassion, love, sympathy, and empathy become easier (more on this in Chapter Fifteen). Research shows that we reflect on ourselves in two different ways:

- Intellectual self-attentiveness, out of curiosity and wanting to know more about our body composition that reacts, responds, and makes us tick.

- Contemplating our experiences, mostly driven by anxiety, fear, and loss.

Positive self-reflection results in a willingness to consider another's perspective, but contemplating due to unwanted emotions, makes us less willing. Unwanted emotions can make us fixated on negative experiences, increasing the likelihood of being less inclined to connect with others.

Everyone's experiences are different, making their views different; therefore, it might not be possible to see each other's like for like perspective. We may never fully understand others, but we can develop the ability to relate to where they are coming from. We can become more empathetic towards ourselves and others, more willing to consider each other's needs, and be willing to compromise.

The Complex Political perspective

Our society is like a giant puzzle; complex, integrated, and inter-woven (more on this in Chapter Seven). To understand, expand, and find healthy solutions to complex issues, we need to broaden our perspectives. We should stop seeing politics as 'just an expression of views,' or 'something that happens mostly during election time only to be repeated five years later.' We need to view politics as a relationship that we build with others based on our own perspectives. We need to decode the destructive relationship patterns, the unspoken communication of each other's inner realities, the non-monetary legacy passed onto us in the form of trauma, and amplify the deep love we have for ourselves and others.

"It ain't' what you don't know that gets you into trouble; it's what you know for sure, that just ain't so." – **Anonymous**

Figure 55: Zoom out for an aerial (macro) view of issues, clearly showing how everything fits together; then zoom in and understand the driver's issues (micro).

How to work with each other's perspectives

✦ Invite others to share their perspectives and see what you can learn about the person, their history, and their human makeup.
✦ Ask them to list the consequences (both positive and negative) based on their perspective.
✦ Ensure that they are listing both the micro and macro consequences.
✦ Ask them to think out loud and list other realities that exist but not within the realms of their realities or perspectives. If they can name some, it will show that they have broader perspectives, and if they struggle, then their lens view is limited. See if you can help them to widen their views by showing them other realities.
✦ Communicate with them in their words, so they feel heard and understood.
✦ Ask them if they would be open to hearing your perspective. If so, repeat the above process, this time putting yourself as the person sharing.
✦ Share what each of you has learned and discovered through this exchange.
✦ Acknowledge the relevant points and thank each other for engaging in this way.

Preferences – we have more than we realize

❖ *Trump: I prefer not saying 'Muslim'*
❖ *Poll: Voters prefer popular vote over Electoral College*
❖ *Poll: Americans prefer China to Japan on economic ties*
❖ *Leaders clash on preferences, debates*
❖ *Voter preferences ahead of Japanese election denote landslide victory for PM*
❖ *Trump ends Hong Kong trade preferences, backs banking sanctions*
❖ *EU may give Syrian refugee host countries trade preferences -Merkel*
❖ *Does the brain's 'happy chemical' influence our sexuality? Researchers find blocking serotonin can reverse preferences*
❖ *Schools face difficult balancing act over cultural preferences: Ofsted head*

Our life experiences determine our perspectives and personality; each plays a part in determining our political preferences. We have looked at perspective, and now we look at personality. There are many ways to determine personality, some of which are listed below.

1. Being aware of human composition and life experiences (as discussed in Chapters Two and Three) is essential for conversations. If someone has been

brought up with a strong religious background, they may tend to show bias in this regard. Christians will favor Christian candidates over Muslims and vice-versa. Suppose one has worked on becoming open-minded. In that case, the candidate's religion may not be one of the most important determining factors. If a woman has suffered abuse from men in her life, she may be inclined to support female candidates. Likewise, if a man has a manly ego, he would be more inclined to support male candidates than females.

2. The Myers-Briggs and Big Five

"The individual's pattern of thought reflects his personality and is not merely an aggregate of opinions picked up helter-skelter from the ideological environment."   *--- Adorno1*

As per research, our social environment impacts far less on our political views than we might think.[25] Myers-Briggs or Big Five can help predict much about our political preferences. Discussion on each of these is beyond this book's scope. Still, the invitation is to understand each of these through numerous texts available elsewhere and then apply this enhanced knowledge during political conversations to gain an insight into someone's personality. In short, the Myers-Briggs personality framework is based on four dichotomous pairs.

- Extraversion and Introversion
- Sensing and Intuition
- Thinking and Feeling
- Judging and Perceiving

The Big Five personalities are extroversion, agreeableness, openness, conscientiousness, and neuroticism. Each attribute represents a scale, and every person can fall anywhere on the scale of each attribute. These are determined by both genes and environment.

Myers-Briggs	The Big Five*
Introversion (I) - Extraversion (E)	Extraversion (correlates with E)
Sensing (S) - Intuition (N)	Openness (corr. with N)
Thinking (T) - Feeling (F)	Agreeableness (corr. with F)
Judging (J) - Perceiving (P)	Conscientiousness (corr. with J)
The final Big Five factor, Neuroticism, is not applicable here	

Figure 56: The many similarities between Big Five and the Myers-Briggs. Credit: Dr. A.J. Drenth. Website:https://personalityjunkie.com/09/openness-myers-briggs-mbti-intuition-big-five-iq-correlations/.

While important to be aware of the different attributes, use these personality types as depicted by this framework as a guideline. We should not take these as biblical; simply note and make room for the following:

- People are more than just attributes that can be exhaustively put into lists and categorized. Hence, get a sense using these personality types but avoid putting people into boxes for long or taking these types as biblical words (more on labeling in the next chapter).

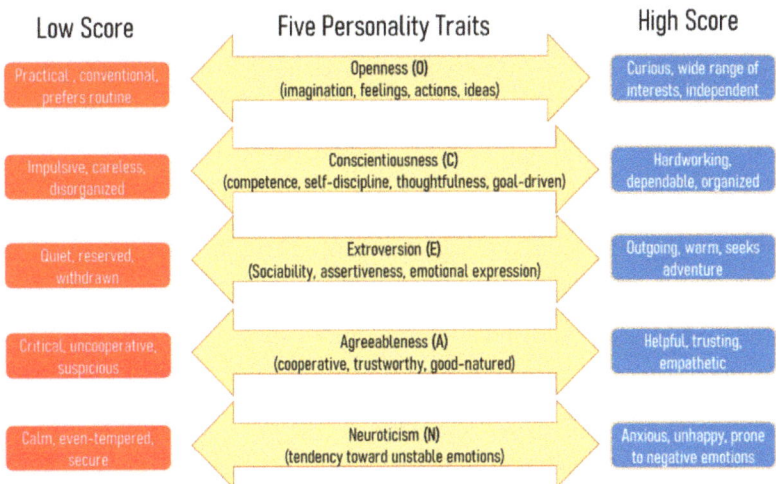

Low Score	Five Personality Traits	High Score
Practical, conventional, prefers routine	Openness (O) (imagination, feelings, actions, ideas)	Curious, wide range of interests, independent
Impulsive, careless, disorganized	Conscientiousness (C) (competence, self-discipline, thoughtfulness, goal-driven)	Hardworking, dependable, organized
Quiet, reserved, withdrawn	Extroversion (E) (Sociability, assertiveness, emotional expression)	Outgoing, warm, seeks adventure
Critical, uncooperative, suspicious	Agreeableness (A) (cooperative, trustworthy, good-natured)	Helpful, trusting, empathetic
Calm, even-tempered, secure	Neuroticism (N) (tendency toward unstable emotions)	Anxious, unhappy, prone to negative emotions

Figure 57: The Big Five Personality Traits. Credit: Goldberg (1990, 1992, 1993).

- Our human composition, especially emotions, feelings, and logic, determines most of our behavior. A change in any of these will bring variations in our personalities at different times. When we are with friends, we generally tend to be jovial, friendly, with a positive attitude towards life. But alone, we might be the most pessimistic person on the planet. Under each of these circumstances, our attitude towards politics and candidates may differ.
- As we go through different life experiences, our human composition will change, bringing a change in our personalities. E.g., I was a very shy boy, and talking about sex would make me feel shameful. Fast forward eighteen years, I am now an Orgasm Coach needing to discover the aspects of life where I would potentially feel shy and shame. Likewise, your friend may have a belief, opinion, or view; it is essential to note that it doesn't mean that it will be held forever, more likely not. Research has shown that many have changed their political affiliations and views over the last decade or so.

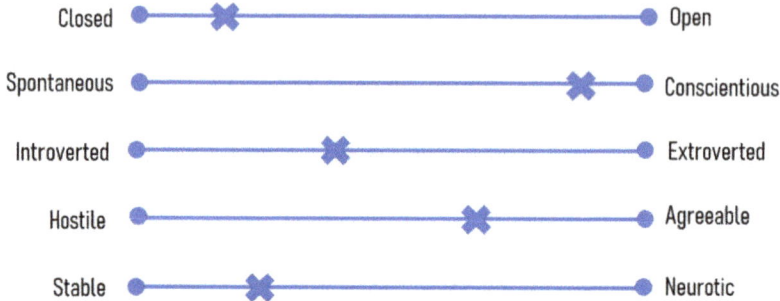

Figure 58: Big Five attribute scale; individuals are ranked between the two extremes of each personality attribute. Image credit: Annabelle G. Y. Lim, published June 15, 2020. https://www.simplypsychology.org/big-five-personality.html.

Priorities – as long as we have these, they matter

❖ *POLITICO-Harvard Poll: Health care costs are top priority heading into elections*
❖ *Priorities USA begins $6 million blitz of anti-Trump coronavirus ads*
❖ *Infrastructure Australia's high priorities*
❖ *Mexican president-elect outlines legislative priorities*
❖ *U.S. outlines priorities for NAFTA negotiations*
❖ *CIA director outlines priorities for the agency*
❖ *Germany and France set joint priorities ahead of EU summit*

Priorities are determined by:

- Knowing where people are in their life cycle graph, situations, and present circumstances is essential when having conversations. Women who have recently become mothers will have different priorities than before this life-changing event, which will determine their needs. Likewise, teenagers will have different experiences than middle-aged adults. Their priorities will be university education, course fees, traveling, nights out, and gap year plans. Similarly, a married person

Figure 59: Do you recall the different stages of your life and how your priorities shifted between those stages?

with kids will prioritize spending time with kids, having money to meet their needs. At the same time, an elderly person will be more concerned about pension savings, insurance,-and care support.

- We should categorize our priorities into critical, high, medium, and low. Critical priorities need immediate attention, while low priorities, if not considered now, will not cause substantial concern.
- For priorities to be categorized as such, we use the impact each decision or policy creates based on:
  severity - critical, high, medium, and low
  causes, consequences, and solutions;
  comparing and choosing the ones most viable and beneficial.

Conclusion

The COVID-19 pandemic is taking priority as health is now considered of paramount importance. The best way to engage in conversations with anyone concerning need preferences and priorities would be:

- Become aware of their needs, including determining their deep core and unfulfilled needs.
- Become aware of their preferences and their reasons for having them. While our basic needs are ideally the same, our preferences tend to vary, change drastically, and can remain unclear at times.
- Get to know their key priorities in life and their reason for having them.
- Consider whether your priorities would shift if you were to put yourself in their shoes.
- Reflect on these perspectives, using both micro and macro views and noticing what impact these create on your perception.
- Share your observations and see how you can both reach middle ground or offer support to each other if possible.

CHAPTER SIX

LABELING

The leftists, the loonies, the snowflakes, the rightists, the eccentrics, the center-lefts, the undecideds, the irresponsibles, and the list goes on. Apparently, if we cannot label it, we cannot fit it into our perception of the world. It is most unfortunate but true.

Michael Charming

Introduction

Labeling happens, whether consciously, unconsciously, or from a default pattern. It has been ingrained in us since childhood, at home, and at school, labeling some good boys and some bad boys. There are many reasons that labeling exists, social construct, sense of identity, and psychological reasoning. The mind feels safe when it has familiarity with associations. It is easy to remember when you give a point of reference. Labeling can be positive when used to empower or boost morale and negative when detrimental to one's confidence and well-being. Labeling is unavoidable. So is the 'Us and Them' mentality, which can be positive, especially with polarizing views when decisions are needed.

It is important not to get lost in labels; to know that every human is more than their label. Likewise, all political parties have ideologies, but labeling them according to specific ideologies is bad because their goals, objectives, and manifestos change. It is good to get various reference points before deciding but try doing this without getting lost in the labels. We also share a few tips on how to avoid labeling.

What is labeling?

❖ *Salvini eyes win in Italian leftist bastion*
❖ *De Wever 'getting close' to forming centre-right coalition*

Labels are the tags we attach about others as part of the reference to how we perceive them. Labels are also what others call you, but less critical to your overall self-concept.

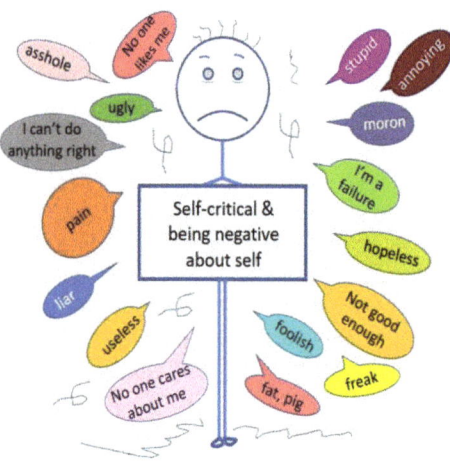

Figure 60: The list is endless

A successful businessman, a super mom, a fatty, a loser, a whiner, a one-man show, an asshole, and an all talk no action. Quite often, we attach labels in our minds and thoughts, and they sprout out when triggered, without us knowing what we are saying. We link someone to a fixed and possibly unrealistic identity we have created about them in our minds, perhaps based on their views, tweets, message exchanges, or even a glimpse of their self-portrayed image on social media. These labels could be positive or negative. Though positive labels are less detrimental and could be uplifting; words, thoughts, names, identity, and labels have power that could hurt, cause harm, or heal. They define us, just as we define others, more often than we realize.

Kinds of labeling that exist

A few categories and examples of labeling:
- Voters (left, right, center-right, based on ideologies; the loonies, the snowflakes);
- Parties (Conservatives, Labour, Democrats, Green, Independents);
- Government (capitalism, socialism, democratic, autocratic, despotism;
- Economic systems (traditional, command, market, mixed, state-controlled);
- Market structure (perfect, monopolistic, oligopoly);

- Leadership styles (democratic, autocratic, Laissez-Faire, strategic, transformational, transactional, coach-style, bureaucratic).

Political labels

Political parties, their ideologies, and voters can be stereotypically summed up using a label, irrespective of who they are as individuals, but we should avoid getting lost in them. E.g., it is a generally accepted notion in the US that 'Conservatives' are business-oriented, benefitting the rich, investing in arms and ammunition, and less focused on social welfare, climate, and social policy. Likewise, 'leftists', who are further left than Liberals or Democrats, are about helicopter money, social welfare, open borders, one world, all love, anti-war, anti-arms and ammunition spending, Green New Deal, and free medical insurance for all. Libertarians were easily defined in two sentences, but lately, they have been co-opted by even more right-wing nut cases than Trump (yes, another case of labeling), causing many libertarians to have fled for 'Independent' status till things slowly coalesce back to normalcy (if ever). Their original philosophy was: Stay out of my wallet; stay out of my bedroom.

Figure 61: Labels are like badges assigned as part of our identity. A small badge to define all of us, how interesting? Even our name is never associated in this way.

Some points to understand labels:

1. Labels are social constructs.

Ironically, labels are placed by society on each of us, our families, neighborhoods, ethnicity, beliefs, political parties, and anything else society can use to label us, the members of society. When we are told something about ourselves that is consistent, we often tend to incorporate that into our personality, whether we believe it or not. In the same way, labels are social constructs given to us.

Labeling leads to certain expectations. We will often change our behaviors to meet those expectations, be it body image, lifestyle, insecurity, or group behavior. Politically, whether we agree entirely with a philosophical platform or not, we may adopt the entire program. "Well, if I am a leftist, I have to adopt the Green New Deal, even if I think it will bankrupt the country."

2. Labels create a static notion of identity.

When we label someone, we assume that they are not going to easily change their behavior. Trump is labeled, among other things, as a misogynist; thus, with every charge brought against him, this is automatically accepted as his behavior. It is not easy for others to change their opinions quickly. Boris Johnson made light of the virus. Apparently, he had karma issues and has had to reconsider and reverse. But many will always see him in the 'virus is a hoax' category. No matter their action, they will always be viewed with the filter of whatever we remember.

Think about your own behavior. You are introduced to someone and told in advance, they have some annoying habits. As you watch that person, everything they do becomes annoying 'Look at how he peels that banana, so annoying! And why doesn't he put his fork down after each bite, so annoying!' When, in reality, this person is no more 'annoying' than you and me.

Remember, we need to remain curious while also remaining cautious.

Other people's perceptions can be helpful, but we should be cautious in accepting these as our own. It is difficult to change this notion, as I now accept their identity of "an annoying person", instead of just referencing it to someone who did annoying things in the past.

There is a tendency to often associate ourselves and our identities based on labels given by others, especially if these boost our ego; our subconscious brain starts believing that is who we are. It becomes truer if that construction of identity is one that validates us. 'He must be rich,' 'she is brave, independent and seems to have everything sorted in her life,' 'he is so nice, he would never say or think about such a thing,' and then we build our identities accordingly based on what others say about us. Being rich, being independent, and being nice. These look great and sound positive labels can counteract, harm, and be detrimental when one starts acting on them if the reality isn't that way. I.e., false identities are created to support these labels. E.g., acting rich when one is not, acting independent and brave when one actually needs support and help. But suppose we can oust this thought from the beginning. In that case, we might be victorious in not constructing such a false identity.

Personally, I don't really care what others think of me because I know myself too well, so external validation is unnecessary. I really thank God for giving me this in my personality and not having me sabotage myself. But there are millions of people who need that external validation and often criticize themselves because of others' opinions or will not dare to say their truth for fear of dismantling this false identity. Think of all the fake life shown on Instagram, Facebook, and other social media platform. We hear day in, day out about the anxiety, depression, and other sufferings one has to go through to maintain this false persona.

This kind of labeling will create disempowering beliefs about oneself and lead to the formation of a new belief system. Good luck in figuring this out and then working years later on dismantling it. In turn, it will create a self-fulfilling prophecy, as discussed in Chapter Three.

3. Ideologies can be deceptive.

❖ *Entrance polls: Democrats divided by age, ideology*
❖ *Attack on Canada soldier 'linked to terrorist ideology' – official*
❖ *Neo-Nazi murder suspect breaks silence, rejects ideology at trial*
❖ *Hungarian teachers say new school curriculum pushes nationalist ideology*
❖ *Clinton sees Trump ties to "alt-right" dystopian ideology*
❖ *Brazil's new top diplomat shifts focus from ideology to trade*
❖ *China suggests Xi's political ideology to be elevated in party constitution*
❖ *Polish president calls LGBT 'ideology' worse than communism*

An ideology, the term coined by the French philosopher, Destutt de Tracy, is a collection of ideas or beliefs shared by a group of people. It may be a connected set of ideas, a style of thought, or a world view.[26]

Ideologies can be mostly divided into two categories:

- Political ideologies: relates to ideas that narrate as to how a country should be governed.
- Epistemological ideologies: ideas relating to philosophy, behaviors, and the process relating to decision making.

There are many different types of political ideologies, some of which you would be familiar with: capitalism, communism, and socialism. A political ideology is a set of ideals adopted by a political party to create the principles, doctrines, and values to govern, allowing society to maintain social order. These become the blueprint for political parties to develop their strategies, goals, and missions. Voters driven by these ideologies will support the political parties, often blindly because they are blinded by these ideologies. It is essential to highlight that political parties have different strategies based on the demographics of sections of society, which means that a party could have one set of ideologies but various strategies that can be very contradictory.

Left or Right? Function or Dysfunction? In my view, the left ideology that focuses on helicopter money, health care for everyone, taxing the rich, and poverty that is not their fault is completely dysfunctional. For some, the right might be completely dysfunctional, catering to the needs of the 1%. Irrespective of whether it is right or left, how much blame we place on each other, with the left generally blaming the government at every instance, the right blaming the left, say "grow up and take responsibility for your actions"? How often do we end up developing a 'fuck them' kind of attitude?

Some sociologists explain poverty as people's own failure and their dependency on others. In contrast, it is said to be due to an unequal distribution of resources and opportunities within society. Some mention the influence of social class has been declining. Simultaneously, several pieces of research show that class still remains important in stereotyping institutions and stigmatizing individuals.

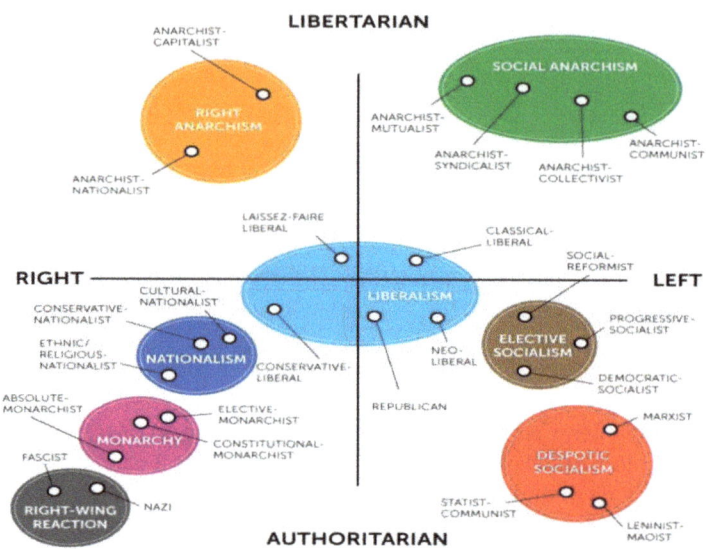

Figure 62: Political Ideology Chart. Where do you see yourself? Where were you five years ago? Where will you be in five to ten years from now? Image credit: Bill Shireman, http://www.transpartisanreview.org/beating/.

4. Psychological reasoning for labels.

Prototypes are definitive versions in our minds, used as quick references to process information and derive meaning. E.g., think of a bird. The one to cross your mind would be one you experience most or the most common birds you may read about and are ingrained in your subconscious memory, like pigeons or sparrows. Likewise, when we think of vaccines, the first person to probably come to mind would be Bill Gates. If we see peacocks in our environment daily, perhaps we might associate a bird with a peacock because our conscious mind is being led and subconscious mind being fed. Likewise, if a wealthy, proactive, public figure talks about vaccines just like Bill Gates, they would face the same brunt that Gates faces from those who consider the pandemic a hoax and Gates having a depopulation agenda. It is worth mentioning, just like Gates, many scientists and leaders, including G.W. Bush and B. Obama. During their era, they had approved policies that aimed at preparing for a pandemic like the one we are facing in the current environment.

5. Labels are a reflection of our self-identity.

Our name is a label, so labeling helps, but we are more than our name. Some names have specific meanings; we are more than our name's meaning in such a case. What is in our name, anyway? It refers to an identity but not encompassing the full characteristics of that identity. Even with our unique identity, others will associate different views about us; their perceptions will vary depending on how well they know us, how well they know themselves, and how clear their body remains to receive unbiased information every time we connect with them.

Figure 63: Our identity is a quick reference to who we are

Labels serve a purpose in identification. Think of the particular brand you buy during shopping, picking one specific milk or vegetable brand, or selecting your next travel destination. We need labels; brand labels, nutritional labels, and travel labels, but self-identity is more than the labels we assign to things or places. Name recognition should only go as far as identifying me when someone wants to communicate with me or refer to me. Self-identity is so much bigger and more in-depth, encompassing everything about me (hint: Chapter Three), which I am not always aware of. I am radical today, but will I continue to be radical tomorrow? Am I liberal today, but will I continue to remain the same tomorrow? Will I also continue to remain poor or employed? Which box should I tick that defines my self-identity? Am I not continually evolving and changing? As you meet people, they form an opinion. Still, because they do not follow your journey and evolution, their opinion will remain the same after you have changed, and therefore be misleading. Don't we do the same with leaders? Think of the identity created relating to David Cameron by associating his act with a pig at a ceremony when he was a student at Oxford University (whether this claim is true or not is questionable). Likewise, Donald Trump said several things when he was part of the American beauty pageant, which he owned from 1996 to 2015. The pageant culture is very different from the White House culture, meaning the words, language, and behaviors would differ widely, often in contrast.

As individuals, we display many identities, often contradicting our own personality. These contradictions are bound to happen depending on the roles we play, issues we discuss, and conversations we have and with whom. We must develop the ability to acknowledge and become aware of each of these roles by fully owning them individually but without getting attached to any of them. We are generally carefree with friends, loving and supportive with family, respectful, responsible, and formal with bosses. These behaviors shift between the situations; hence, the context of things becomes very important if we construct labels based on self-identity.

We label others the way we see ourselves. We might not be aware of how we see ourselves but introspection will surprise you, if not shock you. We need to allow room to receive others more than their labels show.

6. Labels are determined by assumptions and stereotypes.

How do these labels, assumptions, and stereotypes we make about others and others make about us influence identities?

How many times did you categorize someone because they support a particular point of view or a friend said something about them? Have you ever thought about how this person will feel about this? Our unconscious tendency to label people doesn't start with political discussions. That seed was actually sown many years ago when we were in kindergarten or primary school, referring to others as that geek, the nerd, that extrovert, that fat girl, or that rich classmate. The consequences of labeling are profound, both on the one being labeled and on us. For the person being labeled, it affects their motivation and confidence if the labels have negative connotations. For the person labeling, it creates the spirit of putting people in boxes, which subconsciously becomes routine and is applied not just to politics but also to relationships and just about everything else in life. Were you labeled? How has that affected your mental and emotional states while growing up? Think of all the words used to describe you. Positive words would have a positive impact; negative words would have a negative impact.

We must always remind ourselves that human is not just the physical body, there is more to it. Suppose we are to consider what has been mentioned in Chapters Two and Three. Do you really think it is possible to put any two individuals under the same label? At the micro-level, every person is going to be different. Even twins tend to be different in characteristics, despite being called identical.

The labels we use to describe each other are the result of unfounded assumptions and stereotypes:

- Label: words, names, or phrases used to refer to, classify or categorize someone or something; often inaccurate and limited in meaning and essence
- Assumption: not based on real evidence but accepted as the truth; on be conscious or unconscious

- Stereotype: when assumptions are made about all members or items of a particular group, rather than individuals

What do you use to gain your first impression of a person? What kind of assumptions do you make? How long do you hold onto those assumptions? Do you ever ask questions to find out more to see whether your assumptions are even valid?

Let us use Trump as an example. He has had several weddings. Did anyone ever find out why? But they chose to label him as a misogynistic philanderer and sexual lizard. Many celebrities have had several marriages; would you label them the same? If not, why not? How much do you know about those celebrities' lives compared to how much you know about Trump's life? Given what we have shared in previous chapters, do you really believe that you can know about the person within a few hours, a few days, or even a few weeks? Like really? To hell with your assumptions. Are you even aware of them? As a human being, suppose you are not responsible for what you are thinking, how you are thinking, or why you are thinking. Who do you think owns this responsibility – your mom, your local leader, or perhaps your President?

Ignore the political leaders; what assumptions do you make about your partner or friends in scenarios leading to conflict? Have you ever had to correct someone because they held a particular assumption about you? How did that make you feel? Remember, human behavior is more or less the same for everyone. What you are doing, others are doing as well.

7. Labels can be both positive and negative, each creating its own impact.

Throughout our lives, we attach labels based on our perceptions about individuals. Labels influence our identity, whether we like it or not. Labeling has both positive and negative effects, but what makes it dangerous is how we use it and its context. We generally see others based on how we feel.

- **Positive effects** (can act as praise or be useful and empowering): can set great expectations, inspire us, and propel us to move forward. Labels help us to differentiate and associate. If used with good intention or as part of empowerment, labels can be motivating. They can open the door of further connection with the person being labeled. Think of the terms 'friendly', 'hard-working', 'environment and animal lover', 'passionate', 'pro-life', and 'achiever'. If you are labeling, what role do you play, and what role would you really want to play? A contributor to society, a contributor to someone, or a demotivator?
- **Negative effects** (can result in self-criticism and be detrimental): labeling anyone as useless, weak, stupid, or ignorant is mainly due to assumptions and stereotyping. The question to ask yourself is how you feel when you create these negative labels? Perhaps frustrated, unhappy, upset, hurt, or angry? What is happening in your body? Are you tense, contracting, feeling suffocated, or anxious? Suppose we are not feeling good in our bodies. In that case, we will feel bad overall, and, without recognizing this, we will project

the reaction onto others. It's like living in a yucky house. Instead of doing something about it, we transfer our yuckiness, anger, frustration, hurt, and pain onto others. This happens so quickly that we are not even aware of it. Next time you are labeling someone negatively, pay attention to how you feel within your body? It's much more difficult done than said. Criticizing someone is definitely not going to make them want to have a cordial relationship with you or anyone who thinks like you. What if you chose to say the same thing but in a supportive way to initiate the dialog as part of educating someone?

8. Why labeling is dangerous and limiting.

Physical appearance might make someone look black or white or Asian. It is okay to differentiate based on color if we don't know anything else about the person. When distinguishing someone based on color, our intention should not be to demean anyone but only to use it as a point of reference. Our choice should be to always go beyond physical appearance.

Learn to go beyond the physical or the attributes you get to see. In my coaching and workshops, I teach clients to look beyond the physical. If everything was based on the physical, then the Hot and Beautiful woman would continue to be Hot and Beautiful forever, and sex would continue to remain juicy and nourishing. We know that isn't true, and just to be fair, the same goes for the men. If everything was about physical appearance, why does sex start feeling like a tedious chore after a while?

"Labels are devices for saving talkative persons the trouble of thinking." — John Morley

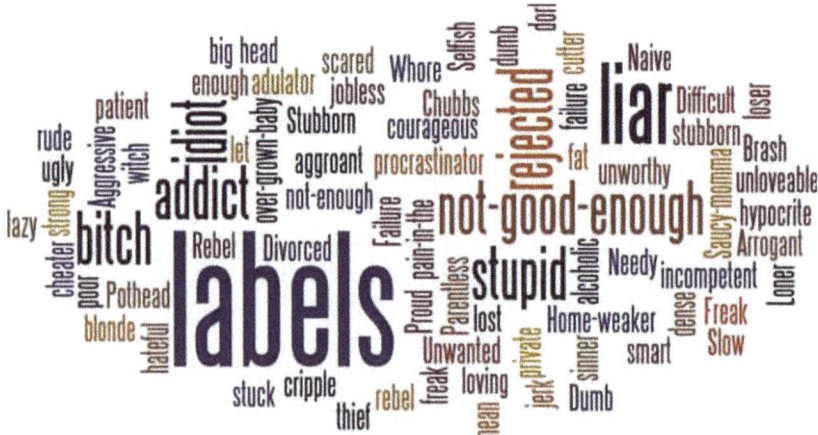

Figure 64: The issue relating to labels doesn't just end in the political arena. Labels constructed in the political arena are nothing compared to other areas of life.

Even though our understanding hopefully increases as we grow, so does the complexity of the world. In our early school days, the human body was identified and categorized as a boy or girl and a man or woman. A few years later, these transcended to hot, beautiful, sexy, big or small boobs, large ass, six-packs, intelligent, idiot, athletic, or fat. Fast forward a few more years, and more words were added to the list; old, young, democrat, sexist, xenophobic, republican, or thugs. I wouldn't want to deny the existence and use of labels in such a chaotic and complex world, but I would like to emphasize that we, as humans, are complex, living in a complex world. By adding political labels, they tend to be more restrictive than descriptive. Look beyond the physical, hear beyond the words, read between the lines, and focus on the underlying intentions. You may be surprised to find that both you and the person you dislike have the same or similar underlying intention but just different ways of achieving them.

Identifying a pro-Brexit voter with 'nationalistic' characteristics may not be at all accurate. Their Brexit leanings may have been caused by other factors. And an anti-Brexit voter could be identified as a 'globalist'. Yet, their understanding of no war in 75 years through the EU could just as easily have identified as a pacifist.

9. 'Us and Them' mentality.

I often see on social media that when views resonate, many express support towards this person with likes or further comments, re-emphasizing what has already been stated. People who disagree join in to question the statement or express their disagreement. A few more exchanges take place. We see labels being assigned before we know it, people colliding, and (unofficial declarative) groups have been formed. Each is now a part of a battalion, racing to rage war with the other side.

They killed our brothers and sisters; we will not ignore this; we will kill their brothers and sisters. They called us stupid and ignorant, but they are the most stupid and ignorant of all

Figure 65: In 'Us vs. Them' both parties view the other through a lens that seems to create mirror opposites.

One of the problems with labels is that it creates an 'us' vs. 'them' mentality, resulting in further division and more disconnection. Each side sees themselves as the victims who then blame and shame the others. Attacks become personal, behavior becomes condescending, and language becomes aggressive. What was supposed to be a mere reflection of someone's view has now become a place for everyone to express their anger, resentment, and grudges towards the other, and become a 'go-to' place to vent with labels attached to others, which may remain so for the rest of their lives—'us vs. them'. From then on, this division always remains stuck in the back of the minds of many people involved.

Our society, and the issues existing in our society, are complex. Fake news and social media sharing add even more to the complexity of situations. It is no longer possible to know what is real and what isn't; whom to believe and whom not to; which issue to support and which not; all of this, while our lives continue to remain complex.

As you can imagine, working in sexuality, I deal with topics, issues, and client's views, which are important and relevant, and very sensitive.

Some of the issues discussed on social media are complex and carry similar or equal levels of sensitivities for many. Hence, it is easy to say something that can offend others, impact their belief systems, and bring emotions from past experiences to the surface. But then, given this limited online space, it is impossible to cater to each person's sensitivity either because it is not easy to go to that depth, create a safe space, and talk about emotions, feelings, and experiences to that level.

Figure 66: Countless times I have heard people saying, "I hate people who have an 'us vs. them' mentality. It is because of them so much division exists in the world." Ironical, isn't it. Another irony is that many spiritual communities exhibit this behavior.

It is very easy to develop this attitude and mentality of 'Us vs. Them'. In my view, there is no harm in having this kind of attitude when we are taking our stance relating to any topic, especially if decisions are required where there is the polarity of views and the complexities of human beings involved. Still, a few things that must be taken into account are mentioned below:

- The 'US vs. Them' stance should always be temporary. This should only happen when supporting or non-supporting a particular stance. Then we should revert to neutrality once the decision has been taken.
- We should not take such support or non-support personally and get offended. If we feel offended, then know that some work needs to be done by us, the person feeling offended.
- When the people within 'Us vs. Them' are part of the same society. All parties', barring certain exceptions, underlying intentions are mostly still the same; love and care of each other, society's progress, more enjoyment of life, and less suffering.
- The people within an 'Us vs. Them' group on one issue could be completely different within an 'Us vs. Them' group on another issue.
- No two widely debated or discussed issues are the same, or their impact would be the same. So, rationale and reasoning applied in one case might not hold true for another. More importantly, the same issues have different implications for different countries due to their culture and demographics.
- We should always be aware of our emotions when in an 'Us vs. Them' mindset. It is too easy for anger, hurt, pain, and even our ego emotions to be triggered. If need be, take a break from discussions, deal with the emotions, and then come back when calmer. Sometimes it is effective to discuss when feelings of anger, hurt, and pain are at the fore, bringing many important and crucial emotions. But there is a fine and thin line of when to do this and when not. The next and most crucial aspect to consider would be: how.

 Every person has strengths and weaknesses, and every attribute has strengths and weaknesses too.

Imagine people who don't do work; their awareness of emotions and feelings is not good. How difficult (if not impossible) would it be for them to recognize and be aware of their feelings, emotions, and communication method? Added to this, the way we communicate could be coming from a place of hurt, ego, or anger. Therefore, we should make every effort to honor each other's feelings, have an open and inviting communication (which I am guilty of many times too), and definitely stay away from the passive-aggressive way of communicating (this will require months of real practice and effort). More on this in Chapter Twelve.

So, let's continue supporting what we believe in but remaining open to each other's views. To continue having an open mind, which does not mean accepting others' views, but rather a willingness to listen, and most importantly, continue to create a place of love, care, and compassion through our communication.

The Politicization of Labels and the problems associated with it

Imagine a political conversation if we didn't label anyone. If conversations came from a place of curiosity, wanting to know the person's views, beliefs, experiences, and all that has led them to support a particular party, leader, or policy. For a better society, while labeling is unavoidable, but we should stop politicizing it. Here are a few more points to consider:

- People associate themselves with political labels because they resonate with certain political parties' ideologies, values, and missions. But it is rarely that straightforward. Each political party's ideologies, values, and missions might change after every election to get more power or appease more voters. Our ideologies change too for various reasons, and there is no guarantee that they would change similarly. At first, the Republican Party didn't support immigration, which they later changed to adopting a friendlier, more accommodating policy. With Trump in office and immigration being one of the most significant issues at the election booth, the stance has again gone back to being anti-immigration.

- Does it add to complexity to determine whether someone is Center-Right, Far-Right, Alt-Right, or Extreme Right (similarly for left)? What about Republicans or Moderate Republicans? Liberals and Progressive Liberals? What about the fact that the term 'liberal' has different meanings in the US, Europe, and Latin America? Suppose a European expresses interest in the US elections. Do we first ask them to clarify which liberal term they are using? What if we have a better way of dealing with this? Would this be of interest to you? Okay, how about changing our narrative to, 'I support XYZ party because of.....', rather than 'I belong to XYZ party because of their ideologies'. Do you think this will be a game-changer, at least in this aspect?

- Political labels can create a feeling of being left out; people supporting independents or Greens might feel left out if the majority of the group are Conservative or Labour. Supporters of two major parties might feel that their opinions matter more. As such, they can exercise dominance over supporters of the minority parties.

- Political labels often create political boundaries in countries—Conservative vs. Labour areas, Red states vs. Blue states. Most focus is placed by media and multi-media on this categorization. While it is understandable that this kind of categorization can help because it is convenient, the problem is that people often get bogged down by these labels rather than focusing on or discussing the issues underpinning each area.

- When we use political labels to define ourselves, it also makes us vulnerable to misunderstandings, exploitation, and abuse. E.g., I may support a particular leader, Mr. Tomato, and I have many friends who despise this leader, but he wins the election. One of the patterns that would emerge as part of my support for him would be to get tagged on and posts, articles, links whenever the media has portrayed (or tried to portray) him and his policy decisions as bad choices. We know that we can find pro and anti-articles just about anything, but since they have been anti-Tomato, only articles that fit their narrative appeal to them. It is my ' friend's' way of demanding an explanation to justify my support of him while silently conveying that I had been wrong in doing so. Likewise, this is the case with the support of political parties.

- People opposing will often pick a few aspects of that party they dislike and demand an explanation. 'How can you support the conservatives when they are against the environment, against social welfare, and against helping the middle and lower class?' If we have to label, shouldn't the question be, 'I understand you associate yourself as a conservative; what aspects do you resonate with?'. When we associate ourselves with a political label, it gives people a free pass to assume beliefs, ideologies, and values about us, which might not have anything to do with the actual ideologies, values, or beliefs we may hold. If you are Conservative, you will be read as the 'right' on the political spectrum, and if you are Labour, you will read on the 'left' of this spectrum.
- Since labeling results in creating assumptions about beliefs, values, and ideologies in others' minds, it creates misunderstandings and incorrect perceptions in their minds. More time is being spent discussing things that were never real issues but have become so because of the assumed beliefs from those labeling and the actual beliefs of those being labeled clashing. I have lost count of the times I have clarified the misunderstandings that others have held about my stance and my supporting a particular party or a leader. The funny thing is that many such people often questioned themselves as to how I could support a certain leader or party when deep down they know that I am not the kind of person who holds the belief that they have now assumed about me because of my association as part of their labeling.
- We have already seen how the 'Us' vs. 'Them' mentality creates further division. The direct impact is that it becomes challenging to alter someone's opinion about you due to this categorization. During discussions (or should I say online banter and war), often the weaknesses or bad policies of the party you support will be brought up time and again as a way for them to find victory over you. And not to forget, you will be excluded and zoned out from all other kinds of political conversations and events they would be having in the future. Did I mention two Battalions fighting a war against each other?

How to avoid labeling

As you have just read, attaching labels has pros and cons. If used in the right context, the benefits far outweigh the demerits. Hopefully, by now, you already have an idea of how to avoid labeling unnecessarily, but here are few tips:

- Observe and note your current beliefs, views, and opinions based on what you have heard, read, or know about the person.
- What kind of label have you used, and what was your motivation to use such a label?
- Compare what you knew about the person before attaching the label vs. what you derive based on the label you chose to attach.

- Are there any discrepancies? Does the information match?
- If it matches:

  get confirmation from others who might have the same information about this person or have more information to offer. Ensure that the person you ask does not hold the same political views as yours. In fact, the more varied, the better. If they have different opinions, ask them the reasons, experiences, assumptions that led them to believe that way.

  Once you have reasonable confirmation, you can then consider having an open and honest dialog with this person, telling them the purpose of the meeting beforehand. See whether you can express positive beliefs about them before any negative, so it doesn't come as critical but rather factual and supportive. When you meet, give enough space and time to share from each side. While you might hold certain beliefs about them, have a dialog with an open and curious mind. Ask them whether they identify themselves with the label that you have attached and to what extent. Take note of what you discover, bring it to a close, and thank them.

- If it doesn't match, then reflect on the beliefs you have formed about them at various stages. Were there were any moments where your own beliefs might have led you to misinterpret the information (and hence project), or was there any exaggeration or deviation from facts at any point? Many times, especially during political conversations, we often get triggered, overwhelmed, and foggy. We end up reacting and lose the sense of knowing what is right and what is wrong. In such a scenario, it is given that any beliefs formed would most likely not be correct.
- If you can figure out the deviations, or find the places where incorrect beliefs were formed, then work on correcting these within your mind so that either

  the new set of beliefs can emerge, or

  the real set of beliefs can be confirmed.
- Once you are clear about the beliefs you have about the other person, repeat the above process starting with getting confirmation from others.
- Take note of what you find out about yourself during this process.

Conclusion

Unlike price tags, which can be removed easily, personal labels can be hard to remove after being attached and ingrained into others' belief systems. Avoid labeling in the first place, and if really needed, ensure that you follow the protocols. Use labels for a certain period, continue to have an open and curious mind, and beware of your communication method. Instead of withdrawing and disconnecting, reach out and create dialog. Remind yourself that just as you label others, others will (or can) label you too. Let's use labels correctly to develop a sense of reference without creating disconnection among us.

CHAPTER SEVEN

GROUPS

We experience so much shit in the world because we run from our own shadows. Pointing one finger at others with four pointing back at self? Shadows may feel like a negative omen, a place of fear and avoidance, and very dark. Still, they can be a powerful teacher helping you unblock yourself from your own mind trap and ending the eternal cycle of suffering. Stop denying that it exists; embrace its existence. Start healing yourself and the world, or should I say, start healing yourself, and then the world might stop feeling so shitty.

Michael Charming

Introduction

In the previous chapters, we focused on individuals, who they are, their behavior, and their composition. Now we move away from individuals, what influences them, and the influences on them, and towards groups. This chapter moves away from being self-centered to more than individuals and groups before discussing societal, national, and international groups in the next chapter. We focus on how different groups are formed, how individuals play out within those groups, the impact groups have on society and general politics, and what awareness we should have when part of a group, no matter the size.

To understand modern politics, we must focus on how people relate to others, especially in groups. Why are groups, political parties, protest groups, climate groups, or women equality groups formed when every voter can just exercise their right via election? What are the elements, norms, and rules needed to ensure a group is functional? Why the rules and the adherence to rules matter? How groups ebb and flow with the number of issues, real or imagined, facing people in a place or country.

We all know that Conservative, Labour, Democrats, Green, and Republican parties exist, but do we know the central core guiding principles that every member must obey to be a member of any party? We are ready to point fingers at leaders for acting or not acting in a particular manner, but do we know the rules, codes of conduct, party whips etc. which serve as their guiding principles and limitations?

E.g., in the US Congress, regardless of how boneheaded another Congressperson acts or speaks, irrespective of the idiocy or pure insanity of their actions (as one might expect in the age of Trump), as another Congressperson, you are not permitted to insult or call out that person, beyond a polite disagreement. Of course, the Trump era has seen all rules tossed in the can, but in Congress, they still attempt to play by the rules and censure any member who steps on or over the line.

The moment we are born, we become part of a group called family. This trend continues through our schooling and into our workplace. We form groups for coffee, lunch, drinks, chit-chat, and dissent towards higher management at work. Why is it that we end up developing these associations, and what purpose do they serve? Why is it that an individual is in an opposing group for one topic, but we may find this same person in our group on another?

Meaning of a Group – a dream team or chaotic bunch?

❖ *Italian group confirms talks with Economist Group*
❖ *Miners' group seeks public inquiry*
❖ *Group of protesters shot at while walking on Lincoln Highway in Pa.; 1 injured: report*
❖ *Former Trump administration officials launch anti-Trump group*
❖ *Local group aims to preserve George Floyd murals*

The simple definition of the word 'group' is – two or more people with shared common meaning and evaluation of themselves who come together to achieve common goals.

Do you believe that the five colleagues you stand with at the coffee machine in the morning have no 'common goals'? Frankly, yes, you do. Whether it is to bond, share work updates, actually accomplish more at work, or bond and share beyond work, it all adds to work satisfaction. This bonding is designed to achieve the goal of bonding or socializing.

Figure 67: Cards playing groups are a leisure and socializing activity for many and a real career for others.

People join groups for various reasons: personal needs, wants, compulsion and desires, social motives, power, personal traits, and many more.

The main reason many JOIN a group is to make or prevent change in your life or the lives of others'. This obviously does not cover groups you may join by accident, by assignment, or without the knowledge that you are a part of a group.

A good example is the 123 Main Street Condo Residents group. You live in a condo at 123 Main Street; thus, you are a group member. Their primary purpose is to prevent any changes to the building or the resident's lifestyle. Suppose the group starts to advocate for more 'house rules', 'gym restrictions', or 'better outside lighting'. In that case, you can decide to continue to belong or drop out.

Of the groups you actually make an effort to join, most will have a primary purpose. Your membership in a church or religious group may support it as it is and prevent any change. Or to propose a change, to perhaps accept married priests or gay members.

Many groups are very similar, thus making it difficult to decide which one to join. This similarity principle stems from many different people wanting to have a say about the group's direction or purpose. The left-handed Gay Fireman's Union protects the rights of the Gay Firemen. So, what is the point of the right-handed Gay Fireman's Union? The split resulted from a disagreement dividing the left and right-handed members, perhaps the fire hoses' grips.

Types of Group

There are four main (but not limited to) types of groups:

- **Primary**: small groups with deep and meaningful relationships. They consider the group to be an essential part of their lives: families, local issue groups, and local ethnic and social groups.
- **Social**: larger groups but not as emotionally connected as primary groups. Supporters of a sports team, co-workers, national service clubs, local political parties, or pressure groups.
- **Collective**: similar actions and outlooks. Often formed spontaneously for a specific purpose. Flash mobs, responses to political and government actions, protesting unfair deaths or policies, or other active reactions.
- **Categories**: a collection of individuals who exhibit similarities based on race, gender, ethnicity, political party, or single issues like abortion, death penalty, and immigration.

Figure 68: We should be mindful of the group we engage in. Different groups will have different members with varying triggers, life experiences, values, and objectives. It is always better to become familiar with the rules, the do's and don'ts, and the group's overall purpose. You can then join to make a contribution while also planning to learn and grow together.

Things to Note About Groups

Can you imagine life without the existence of groups? How will government, political parties, society, or even your own family work, without rules, binding principles, aligned goals and visions, leadership to give a sense of direction, and structure that lists the processes on approaching specific issues or topics? Without rules or norms, groups formed based on emotions lead to chaos and more damage than good for anyone. Consider the MLK riots in 1968, the Occupy Movement, the protestors in Tiananmen Square, and the current issues in Hong Kong.

I heard you hate political parties. Worry no more! We have formed a common interest group to remove them. Cool, yeah?

Figure 69: These days there are groups for just about anything.

Main Elements of Groups

❖ *Trump steamrolls norms with White House convention speech, raising ethics concerns*
❖ *Pope replaces Australian prelate who opposes the sex abuse norm*
❖ *Millions face pension shortfalls on wildly exaggerated official forecasts as 4% growth becomes the norm*
❖ *In the state of pandemic, online classes become the norm*
❖ *Amber Rudd warns workers 'multiple career changes' will become the norm amid concerns over the rise of robots*
❖ *Norway proposes stricter asylum rules*

"Norms" can be defined as the unwritten rules of a group. They are usually determined by the acceptable and unacceptable behaviors within the group, between members and outsiders alike.

Interestingly, members understand these norms and adhere to them just as they would a constitution (written rules). So obvious or hidden, norms keep groups in order.

Thus, "rules" are the (generally) written rules of a group. The behaviors and order of the group to which all members agree to adhere. Often, they come in the form of a constitution or manifesto, notes made on a napkin (for flash mobs), or any other way that everyone reading these knows what is expected of them.

Rules of large groups are often for protecting the group members—no better example than Boris Johnson. At the outset of the pandemic, his personal attitude and thus the country's response were to rebel, not believe scientists, and 'doing as we see fit'. Now, put the man into Intensive Care for a few days, and his "norm" now becomes, 'how the hell do we survive this thing'? This is followed by "rules" about lockdowns to protect the citizens because he understands quite personally the extent of this issue.

It goes without saying that groups, both small and large, substantially influence the individual's behavior. Parents in a family, leaders in a union, and politicians and heads of state in political parties. The group's influence varies; the groups you didn't join (family, living on a specific street, ethnic background) have less sway than those you actively sought to join for whatever reason.

Groups, whether organized or impromptu, go through different stages of group development. Psychologist Bruce Tuckman developed his group development model, highlighting that each stage plays an integral part in building a high-functioning team. If you've been part of any group with a purpose (think of protests, protests against protests, BLM movement, volunteering during election times, raising awareness for days/months, etc.), you may be able to identify with some or all of these.

- Forming: individual's unsure of team's purpose and how they fit in; anxious, excited, curious etc. and are looking for a sense of direction

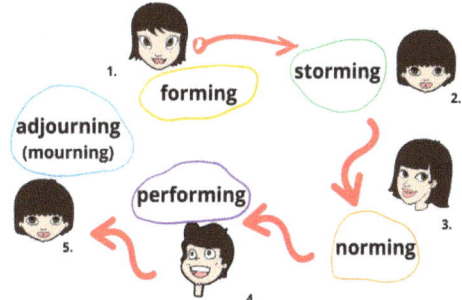

- Storming: individuals may push against established boundaries; conflict, friction, clashes of working styles, frustration are some of the attributes

- Norming: resolution of differences, appreciation of each other's strengths, constructive feedback, commitment toward goals

Figure 70: Psychologist Bruce Tuckman's five stages of group development

- Performing: team is in sync and performing to its full potential; feedback and differences in styles are recognized and used to enhance overall performance
- Adjourning: groups and projects come to an end; hugs, thanks, and tears, depending on the level of personal involvement with project and engagement with each other

Joining a political group

Are you aware of each party's norms, rules, and principles rather than just hearing the rhetoric that Conservatives consist of hard-liners, wealthy individuals with a personal vested interest, and members being subservient to the party's biggest donors? Likewise, for Labour.

The process is pretty simple. You get a copy of the party's rules, constitution, or membership packet. The 'norms' will be trial and error if you decide to get personally involved in the group, but you will learn them. The real thing you want is their principles, even if they have none (most political parties have none, metaphorically speaking). They should also be stated as a 'platform' or 'program' at election time. The day after the election, this platform or program is burned in a ceremony, and things go back to normal, ad nauseam.

Group dynamics – success or failure?

Group dynamics refer to behaviors within a specific group (intragroup dynamics) or between specific groups (intergroup dynamics). It refers to changes, actions, and reactions in the group makeup that impacts the members. Understanding group dynamics is that the group is always larger than all the individuals together.

- **Intragroup dynamics** – referred to as within the group dynamics, are the behaviors that create the set of rules, norms, and common pursuits that identify the specific group. Groups, large and small, include religious, political, co-worker, local and national social and ethnic groups. The group members are interdependent, at least in that their behaviors, norms, and rules are collectively influenced by the other group members.
- **Intergroup dynamics** – referred to as the behavior and relationship between two or more groups. These can be of similar beliefs, ethnicities, positions, or entirely at odds with each other philosophically. Sometimes these groups can work together. Other times, they are unable to even sit in the same building to have a discussion.

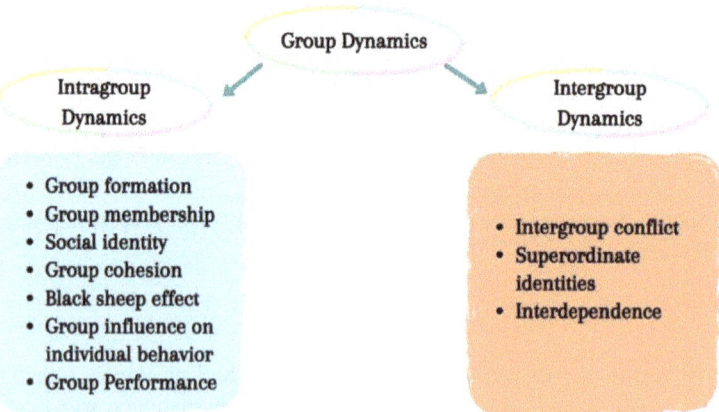

Figure 71: The key concepts of Group Dynamics

Understanding why group dynamics are important

When a political party favors or disfavors a policy, it is because the majority of party members want it or the people of influence within the party are driving the specific decision. People hardly have this in their awareness.

Group dynamics:

- Help to understand decision-making behavior
- Help to understand why parties often get cement feet on specific issues
- Make sense of positions that appear, on the surface, to be in opposition to the wishes of the group

In group dynamic situations, it is crucial not to allow one person or even a very tiny percentage to hijack the group's intent or positions simply because they have a loud and unrelenting voice. Imagine Donald Trump joining the Conservatives and the chaos that would have created in 2010. Likely they would have booted him on day one, but if not, it would have been a very long season dealing with him.

Examples of group dynamics

Generally speaking, gender-based disparities in groups with male dominance means women are likely to remain silent. They won't receive positive feedback or support from men, and will often be dismissed, interrupted, ignored, and will less likely be favored for leadership roles. This seems to be nothing less than repeating the good 'ol boys syndrome or the old white man stranglehold on politics. All this reverses when the gender composition of the group is mostly women, which makes perfect sense.

Okay, so if this is the case, what gave Angela Merkel and Jacinda Ardern, or if history is a better guide, Golda Meir or Indira Gandhi, the power over their entire countries if they were to be disregarded and shunted off to the side as women? And how did the majority of 'new' winners in the 2018 mid-term election in the US wind up being women? The short answer is usually regarded as 'circumstances', but the real answer is different in each case. Working her way into power and being cunning about using it (Markel), living in a very small country and needing the softer 'ruling' touch of a non-political woman (Ardern & Meir) to having the most famous political name in the country (Gandhi). The US example reflects a glacial change in the reality that women can run for office AND win.

Black sheep effect – am I the only one?

Cliques form in every group, formally known as in-groups (groups to which individuals belong and psychologically identify) and out-groups (groups to which individuals do not belong or identify). Members are unknowingly put into either the in-group or the out-group based on how they are perceived by the overall group: Christian vs. Heathen, Muslim vs. Infidel, Jew vs. Goyim. Al-Qaeda militant leader Osama bin Laden once declared, "The world has been divided into two camps. One under the banner of the cross and another under the banner of Islam." One of the most common examples is the multicultural identities that many people have. E.g., I am an Indian who became a British Citizen. When I visit India, locals perceive me as a foreigner. At home, the British don't perceive me as being entirely British. As one might imagine, being placed in the out-group is calling you a black sheep; thus, the process is known as the black sheep effect. If you are in the minority on some votes or decisions, you may be in the out-group. This might make it more difficult to be heard, so consider joining a similar group where you won't be out on the outside or be ready to have a lot of patience and endurance to face the challenge of not being part of an in-group.

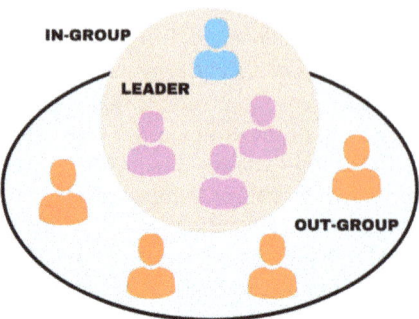

Figure 72: In-group vs. out-group setup.

Figure 73: Black sheep often have the wisdom or ability to see blind spots of others, systems, or cultures that many in the in-group might not see.

Intergroup conflict

And now that we understand the in-group and the out-group, along comes intergroup conflict. This occurs when the in-group determines, for whatever reason, that the out-group should either be eliminated or marginalized. As per Dr. Seuss, "It is a process that is designed to enhance the in-group's 'stars upon thars.'"[27] When this happens, any of the following behaviors will be displayed:

- Obvious favor is shown to the in-group. Have you experienced or done this?
- Highlight and exaggerate the difference between the groups, firmly in favor of the in-group, even going beyond what is honest, if required.
- The in-group will circle the wagons, ensuring no differences the out-group could use to divide them.
- Reinforcing the positive information about the in-group and highlighting the negatives of the out-group. Similar to the US Republicans screaming bloody murder when Democrats are in power and increasing the national debt. During their watches over the last 30 years, they increased it more than the Democrats. Even today, they are still blithely increasing the debt by trillions and not making one sound.

How group dynamics affect decisions

Group dynamics play a major role in how group decisions are made, playing a crucial role in both the quality and creativity of solutions. A group who all believe they individually have power in one form or another is a deadly combination, as they will all fight to hold power. The Military makes very efficient decisions because everything comes from above. These decisions may not be the most creative, but they will be executed quickly and effectively.

The group leader is responsible for diffusing any arguments or friction among members. Interestingly, most groups do NOT select the most knowledgeable person as a leader. Studies indicate that the most charismatic or the loudest person is chosen, as most believe they can dominate the group. Suppose you take the case of Trump, during the Republican primaries and beyond. In that case, it demonstrates that these characteristics are not generally compatible with being a good group leader.

Group dynamics can be positive or negative

- Group dynamics allow jobs to be done faster and more effectively than any individual effort. This capitalizes on various individual strengths.
- When a group has ego issues, style issues, or clashes on ideology between the in-group and out-group, these result in negative dynamics. It becomes increasingly hard to accomplishing anything, including the shape of their discussion table. (A political joke for those who remember). E.g., had the UK reached ANY consensus on Brexit, it would have never happened and saved the pain of the ongoing saga of Brexit vs. Theresa May.

Group dynamics and political examples

The most current example of group dynamics gone bad is Donald Trump. Whether you like him and his odd way of bouncing like a pinball through his work or not. He joined a group, the Republicans, and then slowly took over until he was not only the leader but had eliminated anyone else from a position of power. The apparent issue is now, almost four years later, the Republicans want their party back. They want a more conservative, normal, and ideological state. They fear that Trump may lose the election and take their party down with him. One of the significant risks when one person controls a group. Their worst fear was realized, and they have four years to figure it all out.

Groupthink – what happened to our individual thoughts?

Groupthink is the term developed by social psychologist Irving Janis in 1972 following the roles of group decision-making in historic US foreign policy blunders. He analyzed that in such decision making, people thought not as individuals but as a group because they prioritized conformity over rational thinking. Their ways of working with problems are dealt with by the consensus of a group rather than individuals acting independently. In many such scenarios, faulty or ineffective decisions are made just for the sake of reaching an agreement.

Psychology Today defines it as: "Groupthink occurs when a group of well-intentioned people make irrational or non-optimal decisions that are spurred by the urge to conform or the discouragement of dissent."[28]

In Groupthink, the group will dismiss or shut down alternative viewpoints. The only view that will be valid will be their own; the rest (viewpoints, opinions, or alternative data) would be dismissed. In Groupthink, group consensus matters more than anything else, overriding each member's desire for alternative opinions and facts, especially the unpopular ones. Group identity, perseverance, and team spirit are positive attributes, but they don't facilitate open and honest expression, healthy decision making, and free spirit. Does this description remind you of any Political or Governmental Group?

Figure 74: No egotistical leader ever would ever say this!

Some points about Groupthink

- Groupthink can be quite dangerous (as reflected in our previous examples).
- Groupthink is a suspension of critical thinking and, thus, of rational thinking.
- Groupthink occurs when people's common sense and ability to perform problem-solving, good decision making, and raise unpopular views are overridden by the desire for group consensus.

Real-world Examples

Below are some examples of the Groupthink phenomena:

- North Korea: The perception of their nationals has been manipulated to lead them to believe that their country is a major world superpower. There is a possibility that as a collective, they might make the big mistake of going to war against powerful nations. North Korea and Iran seem to fall into this category. And since there will be zero dissent, whatever decision comes from the top will be implemented. It has

Our ballistic missiles are great success. I now want to sit in them and land on Mars.

Figure 75: A prime example of Groupthink gone wrong.

been good for the world to see that the exchanges between Trump and Kim Jong-un, though very tense, have remained mostly verbal rather than transcending into a real war.

- Pearl Harbor: US naval officers in Hawaii ignored Washington's warnings about a potential attack from the Pacific Ocean. The officers were confident that the Japanese would not have the courage to attack the US. None present challenged the idea and agreed that the US was far too dominant and powerful for the Japanese to even consider an attack.

- Isolated groups are primarily formed due to racial and ethnic background: In such groups, several beliefs could be formed, resulting in distrust with people outside of the group, mostly belonging to other races and ethnicities. Lack of understanding of different races' cultures and beliefs could propel the notion of their group's superiority over others

When does Groupthink occur?

Groupthink tends to occur in scenarios where group members have very similar traits. When an influential leader dominates or a charismatic leader instructs the group. When a group is placed under extreme stress, when moral dilemmas exist, or people regard a particular person to be more knowledgeable or qualified than the rest.

Symptoms of Groupthink

Irving Janis described the eight symptoms of Groupthink:

1. Invulnerability: A misleading illusion of invulnerability is created, resulting in risky behavior, creating excessive optimism and invincibility or immortality—Japan or Germany in WWII and North Korea currently.

2. Rationale: Criticism, negative feedback, warnings, and alternative views are ignored. None want any current assumptions and beliefs challenged and re-considered. The truth is precisely what I say it is. This could relate to numerous countries and leaders today.

MEETING

Figure 76: A Unanimous Agreement?

3. Morality: Ethical and moral consequences are ignored as the in-groups' morale and ethics are followed unquestionably and used as a shield from reality. Many Trump supporters believe that God sent him to protect them. Extreme religious groups and terrorist groups (like ISIS), who believe that their God came and spoke to them, would fall in this category.
4. Stereotypes: Negative or stereotypical views of those they feel belong outside of their group, especially those they dislike, are collated and shared. Maybe we are looking at the "fake news" or the press to discover the "enemy of the people."
5. Pressure: Tactics like pressuring the members directly or from someone of high rank in the group are used to prevent them from expressing their arguments and views if these go against the group. Such techniques are quite prevalent in many cult groups.
6. Self-censorship: Members prevent themselves from going against group consensus, even though they believe it to be damaging and unhealthy, for fear of being reprimanded or thrown out of the group. You often hear from various political party leaders, "We are only following what we have been told to do."
7. Illusion of Unanimity: Members of the group believe that all views, opinions, and judgments are held unanimously. Hence, it must be the best and most appropriate views or action. In reality, it is only in the mind of the leader.

8. Mind Guards: Some group members will either act or be appointed as guardians and spies. They will keep an eye on a few people to hear the gossip and whispers, which will be passed to the leaders to prevent contradictory opinions. This might be analogous to Trump's aides never bringing him information that would upset him, even if factual.

Figure 77: It is not easy to unplug from Groupthink and reflect on all the components that feed each individual's thinking leading towards Groupthink.

Impact of Groupthink (on politics, leadership, and conversations)

Groupthink, at least in 2020 terms, is a dangerous process applied by people who understand its manipulative uses. They drum up, gin up, or whoop up their members and anyone else they can engage to repeatedly speak untrue things. If repeated often enough, particularly within the group, it becomes the full-blown truth, regardless of the factual insanity.

E.g., Fox News continues to repeat debunked conspiracy theories that the Groupthink members (Trumpies) grab onto and continue to believe, often with disastrous consequences. Does anyone remember the guy who shot his way into a pizza shop in Washington DC a few years back, believing Hillary Clinton was human trafficking in the basement? This is a big one belonging to the group QAnon. Or continuing to tout drugs the President touts even though they have been entirely debunked by doctors and studies that have even found these drugs may or may not be dangerous and fatal. This is one of the risks of Groupthink.

To be perfectly balanced, when Senator Al Franken was accused of sexual harassment based on a few photos of him apparently joking around with a woman before and after performances for the troops (about three years ago), he was immediately drummed out of the Democratic Party without so much as an opportunity to defend himself. Unfortunately, Democrats have a Groupthink of 'holier than thou'. Any apparent, obvious, or even smelling of a future violation qualifies the individual for immediate conviction regardless of the facts.

Scapegoating – without it, many may see the truth

- *Businessman in £3.8bn 'fraud' case accuses tech giant of 'scapegoating'*
- *Clinton accuses Trump of scapegoating Muslim soldier's parents*
- *Cries of brutality, scapegoating in 'I can't breathe' death*
- *U.S. Roman Catholic Church accused of scapegoating homosexuals trying to enter priesthood*
- *Beijing accuses Washington of 'slander' and 'scapegoating' after Trump said he wished China 'could have told us earlier' about the killer bug*
- *Angry about Brexit? Don't take it out on grandma, UN says*

The term scapegoating comes from a Biblical reference to the second goat, which was released to carry the sacrificial animal's sins. Today, the term refers to any person or group blamed or punished for others' sins.

As seen above, groups tend to bring people together, connecting their inner worlds and triggering the emotional and other sensitive spots bringing out the worst in people, especially in conversations as confronting and delicate as politics. Narcissistic tendencies, violent communication (more on this in Chapter Twelve), and traumas (more on this in Chapter Fourteen) are played out in groups.

Scapegoating is an incredibly effective way of blaming a specific group for the issues of another group. Unemployed white high school drop-outs in Southern US scapegoat both blacks AND immigrants for taking their jobs. The reality is that these drop-outs wouldn't consider doing the food and farm work, thinking themselves above these jobs that blacks and browns are willing to accept in the marketplace. But that doesn't stop the scapegoating.

Why? Because they have been infected by Groupthink and now collectively believe that they are being taken advantage of by immigrants and blacks. In this case, the 'leaders' of the group, historically the KKK, but more recently, Fox News Opinion Hosts, and guests invited to their shows, lead them down the rosy path.

Scapegoating requires some level of heated action. To keep the group together, with a common 'enemy', this action must occur regularly to keep them focused on their reason for being a group. Their actions are often used against them, being called difficult or irrational, so they blame the scapegoat. We wouldn't have to get agitated if the damn immigrants would go back to Mexico; thus, blaming the scapegoat for their aggressive behavior. It was also the justification used by the KKK and local officials for lynching blacks in the early 1900s.

In my private practice as a sexual health coach, I am often scapegoated for creating 'issues' between couples when my job is to highlight possible 'issues' and start the dialog. These 'issues' are often difficult, and when neither party wants to accept responsibility, they blame the messenger. At times during body-work sessions, clients can experience negative and unwanted emotions. I am held responsible for these, even though the emotions had been held for years or decades. I accept this role as the scapegoat to help the couple or clients make progress with their issues. Thankfully, their stance changes when they see the result (but being at the receiving end is not an easy process to deal with, I guess, it is part of the job). No wonder politicians and leaders generally appear thick-skinned.

Scapegoating and family

Scapegoating is experienced at an early age within families, where the children often bear the brunt. In a harmonious family, such feelings are simplistic, mostly giving a sense of 'black sheep' that doesn't impact that child's attitude and personality. In a dysfunctional family with one or both parents abusive, psychologically unstable, or depicting narcissistic tendencies, or in families where mental disorders, addictions, or illnesses exist, the scapegoated child can be affected mentally and emotionally, often developing symptoms or syndromes (anxiety, depression, suicidal and self-harm tendencies) that can have lifelong effects. These experiences result in traumas and stored emotional pain, which gets played out in politics. When someone shows such tendencies in conversations, instead of replying in a similar manner, we need to learn how to stay grounded, calm, and respond from a place of curiosity, love, and compassion (more on this later in Chapter Fifteen).

- As a coach, from the stories that clients share, I see patterns repeatedly emerging, some of which are mentioned below. My primary coaching is in personal and sexual relations, individually and between couples.

- Someone in the family being a control freak, accusing others of terrible things which might not be true, *"Was there anything said I should know about that you haven't told me yet"*?

- Childhood trauma, feelings of loneliness, or being blamed by parents can lead to self-blame, self-hatred, or hatred towards others.

- Giving ultimatums and saying untrue things about someone. Thus, turning other family members against them makes them unwelcome at family gatherings or

Figure 78: Scapegoating in politics is a common problem happening all over the world.

events.

- Viewing someone as a threat, starting a smear campaign, speaking ill behind someone's back. While feeling threatened is mostly due to one being in a vulnerable position (and possibly feeling fearful about it), the others are due to sinking bad feelings, which lead to narcissistic tendencies.
- Being scapegoated and living with that person out of desperation, pandemic, finances, or other circumstances.
- When scapegoated, perhaps being physically beaten, mentally abused, called the crazy one, lacking empathy, or called a loser.
- Your wrongdoings are scorned and brought up repeatedly even after several years, especially if you highlight others' wrong or how they have hurt you. When defending yourself, you are always being shut down. Living with narcissistic parents, relatives, or siblings.
- Sometimes, it might take decades to realize the extent of the nightmare, lack of sensitivity, and narcissistic tendencies in a family.

Scapegoating and politics

Political scapegoating is a common tactic used by politicians to distract the general population, especially during election times. Trump's attacks on Biden's son and the Democrats' attack on Trump's son or wife. Blaming someone with no involvement does impact the person involved. William Barr, the US Attorney General, says all protesters are "left-wing radicals". It is a statement he can't prove, but it detracts from the fact that the Administration can do little and has done less to stop the rioting in multiple major cities.

Figure 79: No matter how beneficial or effective a policy may be, it may often be declined for political reasons.

Scapegoating and nationalism often find similar cognitive processes. Marine Le Pen in France, Nigel Farage in the UK, and Geert Wilders in the Netherlands have blamed the loss of sovereignty, employment, pride, and setbacks in their countries on immigrants and refugees.

During Brexit, many Remainers denied Brexiters the right to express freedom of choice and labeled them as racist, xenophobic, and stupid. While that might have been true, simply scapegoating them into one 'deplorable bucket' had an impact.

Are Liberals really that liberal? Is Labour really about universal love and openness? Are Conservatives really that conservative? For Greens, everything is about Green, which is delusional, and why they tend to do poorly in the polls, even though the environment is one of the critical aspects to consider in our planet's future.

Trump's 2016 victory was substantially based on fictitious Mexican immigration and Clinton's supposed illegal activities. Using these wedges, votes from the Midwest, and a few suburban women angered by Clinton, collected just barely enough southern whites to make the Electoral College swing his way. Be reminded that Trump lost the popular vote by well over three million. Ahead of the UK's Brexit vote, immi-

Figure 80: Ignorance, real love for leaves, or scapegoat? You can scapegoat anything. Image source: Meme Generator.

grants were also scapegoated for many social problems, from violent crime to funding. It was just enough, a percentage point or so, to tilt the table in favor.

What is abhorrently interesting in both countries since these 'mandate' votes is that violence against immigrants and other right-wing targets has increased exponentially. The scapegoating in both countries has taken hold as a message that hating and being violent towards the scapegoated groups is perfectly fine. The governments will turn a blind eye.

Manipulation – an art, but so is reading between the lines

❖ *US arrests British traders over forex manipulation*
❖ *Volkswagen's chief executive and chairman are charged with 'market manipulation' in Germany over the diesel emissions scandal*
❖ *Switzerland rejects U.S. allegations of currency manipulation*
❖ *Facebook launches 'war room' to combat manipulation*
❖ *Venezuela prosecutors open probe into vote manipulation*
❖ *Putin accuses France of manipulation in UN Syria resolution vote*
❖ *NATO researchers: Social media failing to stop manipulation*
❖ *From sarcastic and humiliating comments to manipulation: The red flags that your relationship has turned toxic*
❖ *Facebook to hire 1,000 human monitors to work alongside its AI to try and stamp out election manipulation*

Manipulation works in much the same way (more on this in Chapter Twelve). It is directed to achieve many of the same goals as Groupthink and Gaslighting:
• Implicit threats

- Dishonesty
- Withholding information
- Isolating a person from loved ones
- Gaslighting
- Use of sex to achieve goals

Gaslighting is a form of manipulation, consciously designed to take advantage of the other person in one way or another.

Gaslighting – a provocation, sowing the seeds of doubt

❖ *Patel: Labour MPs who accused me of gaslighting hold racist view of ethnic women*
❖ *Heartbroken mother tells how her daughter, 28, committed suicide while in a 'toxic' relationship and blasts 'gaslighting' social media trend of psychological manipulation*
❖ *Does your man tell you you're crazy and irrational? He could be 'gaslighting' you! New novel explores this emotional abuse*
❖ *Taylor Swift: America is being gaslighted by Trump's autocratic politics*

The term Gaslighting originated from a play and movie back in 1938. The premise was that a man was manipulating his wife to make her believe things that he told her were happening when they weren't. Somethings that did happen in reality didn't happen in the gaslight world. Today, the concept of fake news would fall into gaslighting the public.

Gaslighting can be done consciously to a specific end, theft, fraud, or the manipulation and dominance of another. Or unconsciously, by repeating political tweets from one particular source, which unknowingly is completely unreliable, and yet, they do it.

Gaslighting, a cultural phenomenon. How do you know if you are being gaslighted?

You won't be gaslighted if you don't allow the gaslighter to confuse you. And you can't be confused unless you permit yourself to be misled, overcomplimented, or any other odd behavior towards you. From those mentioned below, notice if you can identify or have experienced any such behaviors:

Withholding & Causing Confusing–someone who pretends not to understand your questions or inquiries as though you are crazy to even ask. They will also withhold affection or attention and drive you crazy until you 'agree' with their insanities.

Ridiculing & Belittling –an endless stream of inconsiderate words and deeds, one line at a time, until you feel you have gone insane. The person will make fun of everything you do, even though, initially, whatever you did was funny, sexy, and appealing. The gaslighter will find things that upset you and do them as often as possible. Whatever they can do to knock you off your thinking self.

Dismissing & Diminishing –when something bothers you, and you mention it, their comeback is dismissive. "It can't be that upsetting." "Can't you take a joke?" If you pursue, they will seem to apologize for the moment. Very often, the perpetrator will simply say, "I never said that to you," making you believe you are hearing things.

Challenging & Rejecting – discussing and agreeing to do something and then denying the ownership of implementing the actions, or that the discussion and agreement ever took place. The idea is that the perpetrator would rewrite history daily, completely confusing even the best thinking victim. E.g., both partners might discuss and agree on remediation in a relationship. The following day, one of the partners would deny that agreement. On other days, the same partner would even deny that this discussion and agreement ever took place.

Patronizing & Assumption of Authority –being punished for making the wrong choice, second-guessing every decision, and questioning the autonomy. These all lead to a state of fear preventing the other person from making any decisions of their own. Generally, boundaries are ill-defined, fluid, not maintained firmly, and often lead to entanglement. Back-stabbing and involving multiple people in the scenario before creating conflict with half-truths are common tactics.

Why Gaslighting Is So Effective?

The quick and simple is that Gaslighting is often between two people. When the victim brings family or friends into the fray, the abuser is just as cunning with them. The abuser is a pro, and everyone else in the game is an amateur. Gaslighting is one of the premier 'cons' of the world because it is so simple, requiring no one else to be complicit, no tools, and little artifice.

Gaslighting and Politics

In light of the horrific mass shooting in El Paso, President Trump remarked, "mental illness and hatred pulls the trigger, not the gun." Trump is a gaslighting master, particularly with his own base. He has often referred to bringing back coal industry jobs, even touting a mine that reopened and hired 300 workers. In 2016 Trump counted on these voters and needed them again in 2020. While waxing lyrical about coal jobs increasing and pointing out this hiring, he failed to say that over 11,000 coal jobs had been lost since his election. When questioned about this number, he knew nothing of it. He wondered out loud if the fake news was trying to diminish his achievements. Feel free to pick out five different gaslighting techniques there.

Figure 81: Many believe him once and then begin believing him all the time, no matter what he says.

Politicians have gaslighted victims of abuse and rape for decades, declaring that the victim intentionally set out to attract more attention or that they "asked for" the abuse or rape. Accusing the victim is an age-old tactic that worked well until recently. Most rapes had gone unreported for this exact reason, with the victim wondering, "who is going to believe me?"

Unfortunately, with the 'Me Too' movement, we have now allowed many women to gaslight innocent men into obscurity and resignation without so much as a charge or trial. Simply verbalizing an accusation has been enough to render a man guilty of sexual crimes, irrespective of the truth. And there have been several cases in the US, particularly within the entertainment industry, where angry women have decided to go public with spurious and unfounded accusations to destroy someone who didn't help in their careers, wasn't a good boyfriend, or kind enough to them. The man is guilty as charged without evidence, only the word of a handful of women to condemn him. Were we all gaslighted in the reports, information, and numbers about the war in Vietnam? It turns out, yes, we were.

Were all the claims, allegations, and numbers clean in the Brexit fight? No, they were not. The question remains, how would that vote have turned out if only the actual facts were permitted to be advertised and promoted?

Collective belief, unconsciousness, and shadows

In politics, people have little incentive to be completely rational but to be rationally irrational and rationally ignorant when together as a collective. This contributes to political failures in both directions: enabling politicians to act on voters' biased views and causing voters to elect politicians who reflect those biases. A collective belief (we looked at belief in Chapter Three) is adopted by the group to realize their goals. It is a set of beliefs that people refer to and speak of compared to what society believes in. Collective behavior refers to the activities of a sizeable number of people. Although it can be organized, it generally tends to be spontaneous, informal, and volatile. It often encompasses people's experiences through a sense of common interest and identity.

Crowds, revolutionary social movements, panics, passion, fads, and movements containing violence are such behavior features. Collective behavior may determine collective beliefs and vice-versa. These often differ from the beliefs held individually and shaped by cultural and historical context shaping the group's identity. The proliferation of collective beliefs has created distrust and weakens the trust in politics, government, international unions, and collaborations. The rise of populism is one of the consequences of the decline in established political ideologies and group beliefs.

Each of us has our own shadow selves, which is often amplified and played out with large intensity in groups, either triggering each other's shadow individually or collectively. Shadow self can be understood as aspects of ourselves, often born of past traumas or pain in our own lives (which we are often unaware of as a result of the inner child and blind spots, residing in deeper parts of consciousness – more on this in Chapter Twelve), that can manifest as damaging subconscious beliefs, addictions, judgments, behaviors, and emotions, particularly guilt, shame, and repressed desires.

Figure 82: We should embrace our shadow self to enable us to work it through.

It is essential to understand that all of us have shadow selves, not only overtly abusive people or those with addiction problems. How intense and destructive we allow them to become is, of course, highly variable. We need to understand that usually, the shadow self emerges first as a protective mechanism; if allowed, it often takes on a life of its own by suppressing emotions and desires, not dealing with fear, feeding addictions, and following compulsions. Acknowledging and addressing our shadow selves is hard work and always emotionally painful. It becomes an incentive to ignore this part of ourselves, precisely the condition it needs to grow in terms of its destructive force on both our own spirit and those whose lives we impact. Abusive people often seek out such positions of power to feed their shadow self's need for control and manipulation. In the collective, in a large collection of human energies, collective shadow and these energies can overwhelm the conscious mind, which leads to projection and scapegoating. As per Von Franz, "Rather than face our defects as revealed by the Shadow, we project them on to others — for instance in political enemies."[29] Shadows projected by Nazis onto Jews, Brexiteers onto immigrants, and anti-Muslim nationalists in Germany resulting in the burka ban are just some examples (the list is never-ending).

Even though we have progressed as humanity, we haven't worked on our shadows as we continue to project onto others. This is when the collective shadow can be very dangerous and spiteful. Since the shadow is always projected onto others (individuals, family, groups, and leaders), Trump is an excellent example as he acts as a mirror of the people's shadow, a reflection of unconsciousness, projecting racism, xenophobia, misogyny, sexism, and bullying onto the other side; the shadow side of the 'American Dream'. As per Carl Jung, if emotions such as fear, frustration, anger, and pain remain unprocessed and accumulate over many years in the collective unconscious, they can become all-powerful and control a country if channeled by the "right" person.[30]

Jung said, "The psychology of the individual is reflected in the psychology of the nation. What the nation does is also done by each individual. As long as the individual continues to do it, the nation will do likewise. Only a change in the attitude of the individual can initiate a change in the psychology of the nation." And for this, recognition of trauma and healing at both individual and collective levels needs to occur (more on this in Chapter Fourteen).

Conclusion

This chapter, unfortunately, shows us the dark side of people in groups. The reason they join, what they expect, how the group protects them, and the techniques the group uses to maintain members and control them, including manipulation and gaslighting. More often than not, we become so overwhelmed by being in the group and what appears to be working for a similar goal; hence, looking at these shadows and the darker sides does not come into the picture. This chapter is critical reading to protect yourself from others' tactics and the subtle but dangerous play of shadows.

CHAPTER EIGHT

THE GROWING DIVIDE AND THE COMPLEX WORLD

Life can be enjoyed in simplicity but we, as humans, love running after complex things to make it complicated. Human and societal complexities are best dealt with in the right frame of mind and a sense of calmness, both of which can be difficult to find. If all else fails, at least use a checklist to get to the essence of each.

Michael Charming

Introduction

The world we live in is much bigger than just us and our own concerns. The world goes beyond us, our family, our neighborhood, or our country. It encompasses multiple countries (195 to be precise), thousands of societies, possibly tens of thousands of cultures, that all come together to make one world; making it fully interconnected, diverse, complex, and interesting at the same time.

I often come across people who have narrowly focused views that are so self-centered or community-focused that they ignore the macro view. The others have a broad focus on a global scale but ignore the micro view of individualism and the self-centeredness of family and community. The views are often biased; they don't consider multi-faceted dimensions, or the matrix within this interconnected, deeply cob-web like structure of the world. Touching any one aspect will have a ripple effect felt elsewhere and possibly (indirectly) everywhere. No wonder everyone either refrains from politics or gets heated up too quickly. In this chapter, we look at some of society's aspects to increase our awareness. We define the term success and the complexity surrounding every policy, every country, and every person.

Society – composition, challenges and resources

❖ *Big Society agenda 'has failed'*
❖ *Pope allows schismatic society to celebrate marriages*
❖ *Egypt filmmakers defy taboos of conservative society*
❖ *Child abuse is 'woven, covertly, into the fabric in every level of society'*
❖ *Tories are 'dismantling civilised society', says Corbyn*
❖ *Hungary's premier rejects immigration, multicultural society*
❖ *Saudi society will decide if women can drive: prince*
❖ *Theresa May sets out vision for a 'shared society'*

When we talk about society, what are the first thoughts that come to mind? If I were to ask you to name the challenges, lack of resources, and constraints faced by your family, neighborhood, city, and country, what would you say? How do these challenges feature on the global stage? Or do they? While one can say that specific issues, like climate change, Covid-19, terrorism, are faced by each and every country, other issues are country-specific. In fact, many times, most issues are local or country-specific than 'world' issues. Like any individual, we all have the basic needs of food, shelter, and clothing (as seen in chapter Four). Our core needs, belief systems, desires, life experiences, and unresolved traumas tend to differ at a deeper level. It is these differences that impact the way we see and approach things in life.

Figure 83: Today's society... 'I will definitely remain safe and won't drown no matter what!!'. This kind of attitude and thinking amplifies the problems and creates even more division. Should it not be, 'I'm safe. Let me see how I can help someone (or whether I can help someone).'

What is good for your city may not be good for you as an individual. You must decide based on relative importance. Is a priority of the whole country more important than a priority of your town or neighborhood? This helps define the complexity and the greater world.

The problem with 'society' is that too many people can't (won't or don't) think beyond themselves.

Bringing awareness to what a society is and the variables that play into it, as people often forget that and get skewed. The society that I am using here starts from family, local council, groups (religious, specific purpose) to forming a country. Beyond countries, we consider international, global, and the world. People often view things as binary, looking for answers as simple as yes or no, or arguing, believing there is only one right or one wrong answer. Is it really climate change or world destruction? Is it really universal healthcare or millions of people dying from lack of it? Is it really nationalism or globalism?

Society, region, national, country: When we look at these issues, the hierarchy seems to be personal, family, group, neighborhood, society, city, region, ethnic group, country, international, global, world, and universe.

We understand **personal** and **family** and how and why we support these decisions over all others. It is also pretty easy to recognize that **group** and **neighborhood** issues and needs would be prioritized ahead of the others. Our **society**, **city**, and **region** fall somewhere in the middle of our needs structure. We care, but not as much as the needs in our homes or on our own streets.

Country: We certainly must support our **country**, but at this end of the 'complex' list, we, personally, don't care much about what happens and how it happens, as long as there is not too much personal impact. Feelings of nationalism will always be there (think of FIFA, Olympics, World cup matches, and war).

International: The rules governing at a **societal** and **country**-level don't necessarily govern at an **international** level. The world consists of over 190 countries. Each has its own agendas and hierarchies to deal with before dealing with any International needs.

Global: Global co-operation is essential. More than **international**, which suggests how countries interact with each other, **global** requires interaction to maintain one globe and one planet on which we all survive. Internationally, countries can fight, better to say limited war or

Figure 84: Among us, we have several differences but live on the same planet. While we cannot help everyone, we can definitely have good intentions for everyone, including other species.

skirmish, but globally, they cannot use nuclear weapons as that would disturb the entire planet.

Self-interest, national vs. international interest: In conflict, which interests should prevail and why? What are the costs and benefits? When determining which policies are to be defended or discarded on a national level, these critical questions should be asked by individuals.

Indicators and success: What is success, and how do we determine it, especially at society and international levels? Why awareness and analysis are vital, beyond the emotional rhetoric portrayed in the media.

Complexity: The world and the seven billion+ humans on it are complex. How can we reduce this complexity? Are there some basics we can agree on like nuclear war is a no-no? Like all war is a no-no, or is that one too far to grasp? We agree that pandemics must be eliminated quickly, worldwide, regardless of investment or cost. But who bears this cost, and if the country who is to bear it can't, do we help them? Decisions, decisions, this chapter will attempt to help us understand how complex our societies and world are, how to become a bit simpler, and how to make complex decisions when there are over seven billion disparate opinions on almost everything.

What is society?

Society is a large number of people living as a community or having social interactions for a common purpose. Society can encompass a neighborhood, a city, a physical boundary, and be extended to the whole country and its ethnic, religious, and political subdivisions of thought.

Qualities of societies

What comes to mind when we talk about society? What are its qualities, and the qualities of people you want to see in that society? How well do you personally align with those qualities? What are the qualities of people others want to see, and how well do you align with those?

Some attributes of a cohesive society:

- People have shared values and interests and feel a sense of unity and solidarity.
- Members realize that differences exist in terms of values, thinking, and diversity, but similarities exist.
- Tolerance, respect, and appreciation towards each other.
- Right to influence authority, success based on merit.
- Principles of fairness, equality, free access to opportunities, and equal justice.
- Incentive and motivation to work towards harmony.

- Self-interest, self-preservation – national defense and law enforcement to combat crime, diseases, terrorism, and accidents.
- Harmony includes basic respect, shared values, agreement, tolerance, cooperative spirit, and goodwill. It also encompasses:
  Benevolence, a feeling of wanting to do good for others irrespective of whether they have similar reciprocal feelings, is missing in our society. We have become so selfish. How often do you engage in doing something that contributes to society, not for self-interest, but as a volunteer act?
  Fairness, being just and equitable. We know that life is not fair, not for us or for others, so how do you contribute towards creating that fairness?
  Humanity, a feeling of compassion and care towards all society, including the neighbors you dislike the most. We are not even embodying ourselves as humans; how can we think of embodying humanity with all these traits.

Model of society

The model of society consists of several variables, some of which are listed below. I often encounter people deciding in favor or against a policy or a leader, taking a stand for or against an issue, based on one tweet, one headline, or a short two-minute clip. Society is vast and includes multi-facets and so many variables that feed into each other or are part of the whole equation, which, if ignored, will have an impact not forgetting the unknown variables due to the uncertainty of life. The major problem is that once they have taken a stance and formed an opinion about an issue or a leader, they often hold onto that opinion with no room for openness, flexibility, or space for maneuvering. When society consists of so many variables and uncertainties, should we not assess and approach each issue and tweet on a case-by-case basis?

The biggest goal of society is to cater to its people's well-being. Still, people don't exist in a vacuum and are more than just the physical body we see in front of us (as seen in detail in Chapter Three). Some of the variables that define the models relating to society include:

- **People** - individuals, citizens, naturalized and acquired citizens, permanent residents, businesses, and tourists. Within each person, we have already seen further consists of five bodies (mental, physical, spiritual, emotional, and energetics).
- **Government** - governance, constitution, social contracts, law, regulation, rules, and rights – constitutional, civil, human, natural, or unalienable rights.
- **Attributes** - entitlement, deserve, obligation, responsibility and duty, success based on merits, principles of fairness, and equality.
- **Business** - commerce, goods, services, stakeholders, marketing, finance, and Illegal businesses – drug dealers, hackers, and prostitution.
- **Groups and organizations** - cooperate in pursuing a common purpose – sharing information and goals, joint activity – churches, schools, trade un-

ions, non-profit organizations, cooperatives, charity, and allies. Dysfunctional organizations - gangs, mobs, mafias, and cults.

- **Rights** - civil law, civil rights, civic engagement at a community or a national level other than matters of only personal interest – civic events, civic affairs, civic duty.
- **Institutions** - government bodies and agencies, organized religions, marriage, property rights, contract law, and freedoms.
- **Beliefs, customs, and practices** - Monday-Friday, five-day workweek, shaking hands, namaste, volunteering, worship, congregations, festivals, and picnics.
- **Crowds** - people getting together spontaneously due to a common interest or activity, concerts, festivals, sporting events, tourist hot spots, rallies (constitutional and unconstitutional), and protests.
- **Cultures** - ethics, conventions, norms and the violation thereof – admonition, ridiculing, shunning, symbols – flags, values, customs, traditions, practices, fringes of norms and acceptable behaviors, opportunities, expectations, what is expected of individuals, and what individuals expect.
- **Public opinions** - polling, surveys, consultations, samples, and social media.
- **Basic goods and services** - food, water, housing, clothing, education, health care, banking, safety, and justice.
- **Abundance and scarcity of our natural and man-made environment** – shared, public or private- land, water, air, sunlight, gardens, flora, fauna, mineral resources, and trees.
- **Natural and man-made phenomena** - earthquakes, floods, fires, severe weather, the spread of disease, and war and conflict.
- **Natural and man-made Infrastructure** - roads, hills, bridges, buildings, sewers, electricity, power grids, dams, highways, jails, hospitals, theatres, and other leisure centers.
- **Knowledge** - learned, self-guided, intuition, facts, conclusion, ideas, opinions, essence, virtues, meaning, and know-how.
- **Functions performed** - raising self, family, children, government, providing security, providing education, and engaging in social welfare.
- **Philosophy** - science, mathematics, theology, law, politics, ethics, and aesthetics.
- **Peace of mind** - without constant and nagging worries and fears about safety, having mental well-being, confidence, spirituality, and religion.
- **Freedom and liberties** - risk and consequences, majority vs. minority.
- **Diversion and relaxation** - rest, sleep, exercise, dance, sex, memorials, and comedy. Dysfunctional diversion - gambling, wild parties, and pornography. Dysfunctional humor – ridicule and defamation.
- **Escaping mentality** - various dysfunctions in our society often result in people trying to escape facing these using – retreats, yoga, traveling, and detoxing—dysfunctional methods - addiction to drugs, substances, alcohol, porn, or criminal behavior.

- **Symbols** - convey and reinforce values, identity, and solidarity - flags, systems, establishments, and institutional authority - local, regional, state, and national government, and multi-media.
- **Demographics** - youth, middle life, and elders. This affects resistance to change and blind acceptance vs. reluctant acceptance.

Figure 85-86: (Left image) Some values and ethics of modern society. (Right image) Some apparently don't have any. Which values and ethics are important to you, those you can identify within yourself?

Examples of Complex Conflicts

Different societies have different kinds of challenges and conflicts that are hard-wired into their specific culture. Without understanding the depth and history of these issues, forming opinions or expressing a wish list of answers is merely going off tangent. Without this depth of knowledge and understanding of the short, mid, and long-term issues, the solutions would be unrealistic or impractical.

- India: Hindu/Muslim conflict – no wonder anything to do with beef vs. cow escalates quickly. And while it is hardly the basis of the issues, it has been a springboard to further and broader issues between these religions trying to coexist within one country.

Figure 87-88: The same animal is viewed differently by groups due to their religious beliefs. I wonder whether a cow ever distinguishes humans based on them being a Hindu, a Muslim, or a Christian. Humans are undoubtedly the most advanced, developed, and sophisticated animals, but they are also the most disturbed. What is the use of such growth and evolution if we can't live amicably as part of the same species?

- US: African American (Black)/White conflict – History of Black repression vs. White privilege. Clearly not this shallow, as it has been simmering for a few hundred years. The Blacks did not immigrate to the US voluntarily and have been slaves to the Whites for 250 years BEFORE the Civil War emancipated them. And in the 150 years since, there has been precious little movement toward an equal and just society. It is only within the last fifty years that any progress toward equality has been made. From the events of this year, that may not even be the case.
- Israel/Palestine conflict: Relating to Jewish and Muslim (and Christian for that matter) claims on land in the Holy Land area. Each of the warring groups believes the land the other sits on is theirs and will not negotiate for any reason. The battle has gotten to war level several times, but the losing side never seems to stop fighting. Often the world community weighs in with their opinions, and yet, the battle continues, even with peace agreements in place.
- North Korea/US: North Korea's lack of trust in the US after seeing what happened to Saddam Hussein two decades ago. Name-calling and escalation on both sides between two leaders with a combined IQ of under 100. While we can't prove that statement, one would agree if one reads the exchange of tweets.

International – a peek beyond your borders

❖ *World Health Organization delays call on coronavirus international emergency*
❖ *International labor organization criticizes 2020 Olympics working conditions*
❖ *Organization of Islamic Cooperation concerned over Kashmir violence and wants the international community to act*

Rules of international complexities and governance are very different than the rules we use at a national level.

Dealing with society at a national level is already complicated, which becomes even more so when we start looking at inter-country and international levels. The rules that applied to peace, harmony, prosperity, and success of our household are quite different from those applied to the family next-door. Likewise, these rules will vary when we reach a national level, but here we are still tied by the spirit of nationalism. Nationalism, in this context, meaning pride in country, not a deep exclusionary nationalism.

At an international level, we do not have any such spirit. The only things that hold us together at the international level are the desire for safety, smooth functioning, and possibly humanity if still prevalent in individuals. One of the biggest problems I notice when people express opinions or views about issues relating to other countries; they tend to disregard any rules, norms, and cultures existing in those countries and view everything from their own perspective, which by nature is bound to be flawed.

E.g., comparing the UK/US to Sweden/New Zealand in terms of Covid-19 scenarios, and how the latter did so much better. They began criticizing the former's leadership without realizing that both groups' factors and variables are entirely different. People often forget to do like for like comparison (relativity is important).

A political example could be the view of some British and Europeans who consider Modi of India to be authoritarian and totalitarian. They have not considered that in countries like India, with hundreds of political parties ruling over 1.5 billion people, they need leadership and government that acts with full power. They cannot be people-pleasing, as they need to take the reins and stand up to the leadership of neighboring countries of Pakistan and China.

Governance – a costly and complicated but essential mechanism

- *Obama advocates for civic engagement, self-governance*
- *Sheila Dikshit 'praise' over Modi good governance*
- *China's Xi calls for strengthening of reform and governance*
- *US cites global governance crisis for declining human rights*
- *Britain is pro-business, but firms need better governance – minister*
- *Japan's 'good governance' index underperforms stocks it expelled*

If it weren't for governance and various world organizations being set up, we would have witnessed wars at the slightest disagreement. Whether be it UN, NATO, International Criminal Courts, World Bank, or even regional organizations like ASEAN, Pacific Alliance, or Gulf Cooperation Council. There is a reason these organizations have been set up.

A country can be caught between fulfilling national objectives vs. meeting international commitments.

Figure 89: It is not easy or of general public interest to understand governance and why it exists.

EU countries like Greece, with a tourism-based economy, suffered by adopting the same currency as Germany, with their manufacturing-based economy. No wonder European countries with their own currencies did better during the financial crisis than those tied within the Euro mechanism, like Greece and Italy. A good example is the EU's bailout for Greece, which came from Germany's taxpayers' pockets. Understandable why the Germans were not in favor of this bailout.

Self-interest (and greed), national interest, and international interest

Governments have a sizeable task to find a balance between national interest vs. international interest. When these clash, national interest usually takes precedence. Just like when there is a clash between your societal interest and familial interest, the familial will take precedence. The problem arises when we put familial interest ahead without caring about the consequences or impact on others on a larger scale. People in different countries are people like us, but just in different countries, with different cultures, faiths, religions, and colors; they are all still human.

Success and Indicators

As we see it and experience it, life happens within and outside of you as an individual. As seen above, living in a society means we all are connected and influence each other, directly or indirectly. We measure progress by determining our success, but this cannot be one dimensional, just as society is not one dimensional. Success as a person, success as a family member, success as an employee, success as an entrepreneur, and success as a citizen are significant as these form part of your life experience. Success in one aspect with failure in another will have unwanted and negative consequences.

Figure 90: Success is relative. Would you declare writing the first word; or having the book in the reader's hands as success?

Whatever we do in life is generally based on a want, need, or desire. We tend to measure the outcome in terms of success, which is very subjective and depends on each scenario. Achieving a college degree, getting a job, winning the elections, reaching an agreement involving two or even several countries in the eleventh hour, protesting, getting a message heard by the lawmakers, and finding 'the one' and getting married are all indicators of success. When the outcome is defined beforehand, it is easy to measure success. While it is easy to measure success at the individual, group, or organizational levels, how do we measure success at society, regional, and country levels since the needs, desires, interests, and wants of every person vary? At this moment, what criteria are you using to measure success for yourself relating to life? How about your family?

Happiness, contentment, personal growth, more money, being able to stick to a commitment, developing healthier habits, finding the love of your life, and freeing yourself of judgment are all some of the indicators of success at the individual level. At the society level, how do we determine something inclusive of all that is just and sustainable, catering to the needs and welfare of every single person?

Figure 91: Success means different things to different people at different times.

A competitive spirit is an essential part of life to continue progressing either as individuals or in society. Given that success is subjective, the indicators in quantifiable terms help to provide a comparison. In business, the phrase 'what gets measured, gets managed' is often used. Critics counter this with, 'not everything that matters can be measured and not everything that we can measure matters.'

I find that people mostly focus on misleading headlines and sometimes only on the areas they support. E.g., climate change activists will only be concerned about emissions and carbon reduction. Democrat supporters are mostly concerned about women's rights, social welfare, and free Medicare. Conservative supporters are mostly concerned about economic growth and security. In my view, we can support a specific cause or aspect without negating the other variables that exist in our society. Even though these might not be of any interest to us, it doesn't mean they are not of any interest to others who live in the same society.

There are numerous indicators used to determine the success of society, some of which are listed below. Each of these indicators has pros and cons, which are beyond the scope of this book. I believe we should be focusing on the combination of these rather than just one or two. How often have you brought these up during political conversations?

Gross Domestic Product (GDP) – measures the value of all goods and services produced by the country but is often crudely interpreted based on its movement up or down against the previous timeframe.

Genuine Progress Indicator considers GDP and additional factors like volunteer work, income distribution, costs of crime, pollution, and long-term environmental damage, a bit more esoteric and less calculable.

Gross National Happiness – similar to GPI and measures the nation's spiritual well-being, community, cultural engagements by nationals, and environmental concerns.

Figure 92: The domains of Bhutan's Gross National Happiness Index.

Ecological Footprint & Human Development Index (HDI) –represents bio-capacity vs. demand and accounts for health, education, and standard of living. Again, a narrow calculation for such broad results.

Social Progress Index – measures the extent to which countries provide for their citizens' social and environmental needs.

Better Life Index (also known as Regional Well-Being) – developed by OECD to help governments design better policies to improve lives and consists of variables like housing, income, jobs, and education.

Thriving Places Index – was developed by the UK charity Happy City to give local organizers and politicians a better view of the people's welfare and primarily focuses on sustainability, equality, and local conditions.

My suggestions: In addition to the indicators mentioned or already existing, I suggest the following should be included:

Figure 93: The Better Life Index seems great but does anyone really show any interest in these, although everyone desires governments to have better policies?

- Some other important attributes that should be added or considered are courage, faithfulness, generosity, graciousness, contentment, and personality. These indicators mostly miss one's own personal growth, including dealing with emotional and mental triggers and sensitive spots.
- I believe that unless an indicator considers the progress in terms of these triggers and sensitive spots, we will continue to lag behind in creating the humanity we all desire. We can then use this indicator's aggregate to develop one societal number to determine success – a personal growth aimed at nationals. We as a society have made tremendous progress in terms of almost every field (technological innovations, medicine, science, etc.), but we have lagged behind in making proportional progress considering the human aspect.
- Another indicator could be the measuring in terms of fulfillment of everyone's basic and/or core needs.

Trend analysis has shown that countries with a higher GDP do not necessarily equate to a lower unemployment rate or a higher standard of living. Hence, various reports are created looking at several metrics to determine the countries ranking in the world, some of which are listed below:

World Justice Project's Rule of Law Index – examines 'the rule of law fundamentals' like government accountability, the protection of human rights, and fair legal processes, but it ignores wealth.

Best countries report and rankings determine countries' global perception regarding several qualitative characteristics, trade facilitation and potentiality, and travel, investments.

Global Financial Centers Index: ranks the competitiveness of financial centers based on over 29,000 assessments and over 100 indices from organizations such as the World Bank, the Organization for Economic Co-operation and Development, and the Economist Intelligence Unit.

Centre	GFCI 26		GFCI 25		Change In	Change In
	Rank	Rating	Rank	Rating	Rank	Rating
New York	1	790	1	794	0	▼4
London	2	773	2	787	0	▼14
Hong Kong	3	771	3	783	0	▼12
Singapore	4	762	4	772	0	▼10
Shanghai	5	761	5	770	0	▼9
Tokyo	6	757	6	756	0	▲1
Beijing	7	748	9	738	▲2	▲10
Dubai	8	740	12	733	▲4	▲7
Shenzhen	9	739	14	730	▲5	▲9
Sydney	10	738	11	736	▲1	▲2
Toronto	11	737	7	755	▼4	▼18
San Francisco	12	736	16	727	▲4	▲9
Los Angeles	13	735	17	724	▲4	▲11
Zurich	14	734	8	739	▼6	▼5
Frankfurt	15	733	10	737	▼5	▼4
Chicago	16	732	20	717	▲4	▲15
Paris	17	728	27	699	▲10	▲29
Boston	18	727	13	732	▼5	▼5
Melbourne	19	720	15	729	▼4	▼9
Montreal	20	716	18	722	▼2	▼6

Figure 94: Maths, numbers, and statistics might not be your thing. Without a good understanding or at least a bit of statistical analysis knowledge, your conversations relating to politics misses a fundamental attribute. Source: GFCI 26 Report September 2019 Report published by Z/Yen.

Likewise, several other indices give information on how each country has been performing compared to its previous years and other countries. I wonder how many actually pay attention to these, rather than getting overwhelmed and triggered by the news, say, conservatives have passed the law relating to fracking or that Trump has stressed on bringing miners back to avoid them suffering because of technological advancement and reliance on a renewable source of energy, yet, these jobs will never be coming back, as the statistics have indicated.

Complexity – a necessity or created for the intensity?

- *Russian entry adds to Syria complexity*
- *Trump laments complexity of modern airlines in wake of crash*
- *Scale and complexity of terror threat to Southeast Asia growing – ASEAN*
- *Science begins to explain why we act the way we do politically and socially: Human beings are wired to belong, are social animals.....*
- *AI and human perception are too complex to be compared*

The world has become more complex; life has become more stretched; humans spend more time in anxiety and stress than pleasure. A single issue far away can suddenly escalate and lead to uncertainty, whether it be Kim Jung Un's ballistic missiles test or Iran exercising control on the Strait of Hormuz. In such cases, it is not easy to make policy reforms and goals that would continue to serve all the world's societies and countries' best interests. Different policies are tried and tested by various leaders considering what could be best for their country – but people often don't consider each society's dynamics before judging whether the policy is workable or not.

Rhetorics like Sweden/New Zealand's did better than US/UK during Covid-19 gets continuously shared, not realizing that it's not just leadership at play but also the demographics, the size of the population, the logistics, the technology and other systems and coping mechanism and most importantly the ability of people to listen and adhere. A reason that the UK/US suffered the most is also that these are the same countries where nationals created multiple conspiracy theories, vandalism, protests and intensified the mistrust on the government, leading to a merry go round phenomena (i.e., more protests resulting in an increase in spread, causing the government to enforce stricter rules and extend lockdown, which resulted in increased protest, etc.)

In a fast-changing world, development and progress are complex, and solutions are neither simple nor obvious. The more adaptable the government is, the more chances it has to quickly deal with situations and challenges. It is one reason why the EU has not attained some of its core goals despite more than three or four decades. Having 28 (soon 27) members within an organization and the need to cater to each country's needs, goals, and objectives efficiently and strategically also means that it slows down the whole process resulting in bureaucracy and delays when getting 27, or the majority, to agree on anything. Likewise, for some decisions to be made in Congress, because of Democrats and Republicans' involvement and their death battle political conflicts, many vital decisions take years, if ever, to accomplish. In such instances, having someone like Trump, who goes by his instincts, can be beneficial and very risky since his approval base is well under 50%.

Why complexity exists (or should I say, what makes things more complicated than it already is)

- We, as humans, make things more complex than they are. This has already been discussed and needs no further explanation. The crux is that we can't manage ourselves well and add to the chaos (ego, power, greed, and lust). When you return after traveling, you feel so energized, with clarity of mind, very passionate, but what happens when you live the day-to-day life without travel? Do we really need to use travel as an escape mechanism, or should we grow up and behave as responsible adults taking the

Figure 95: Complex problems require discussion, dialog, and the emergence of solutions.

responsibility of managing ourselves, our emotions, our feelings, our energies, and our thoughts in the very place we operate, our home, office, in the tube, on the street, in the shop or even online?

- Most of us tend to determine (or desire) everything in life be simple, Yes or No solutions, a binary choice of In or Out of the EU, favor or against Trump, without realizing some situations will be simple and others will not. Using binary choices to deal with complex situations is incorrect, misleading, and results in more chaos. The world is not binary.

- Artificial intelligence, concepts, choices, distractions, bombardments, and life struggles have been growing, making us push our limits. Do we want to come from a place of power, or do we want to resort to the victim mentality?

- Polarization, collective beliefs, shadows, and consciousness could be very useful tools, but they sometimes play more into creating complexity than resolving it—more on this in later chapters.

Conclusion

- The world is complex, consisting of trillions upon trillions of molecules, policies dependent on hundreds of variables, our brain processes trillions of connections day in and day out. But we often create confusion by mixing things instead of looking at one piece at a time. The way we associate facts clouded by our own perception is mind-boggling. When we are discussing one issue, why do we bring another into the discussion? We often do this to prove our point and lack awareness of doing so (more on this in Chapter Twelve).

- Sometimes we come up with solutions or are only focused on finding solutions from one angle, not realizing that if we sit back, ponder, and allow creative ideas, we will recognize multiple ways of assessing and dealing with situations. Government has different departments that deal with various scenarios to come up with the most feasible and workable solution (it might not be the most appropriate, but at least that's what the study would have shown at that time). With individuals, such discussions hardly take place.

- When having a conversation with others, which part are we having a conversation with? As mentioned in Chapter Three, humans are more than just physical, so are we having a conversation with their spiritual self, emotional self, or mental self? Depending on that part, our conversation would need to change and adapt. E.g., suppose someone is feeling fear. In that case, there is no point in having a mental argument with that person because currently, the triggered emotional state of fear is speaking. Likewise, if the conversation is happening at the mind level, at a cognitive level. In that case, we should present with facts, figures, and not emotional states. It is essential to note that all body layers are important; just mental conversations with no emotional involvement or reflection will result in setbacks, misalignments, and lack of human emotional connection. Even then, within each of these parts, there are many subparts. E.g., a husband comes home from work and sits on a couch to watch the game. What does this tell us? He is physically exhausted, but mentally not, or maybe vice-versa.

- As a society with so much knowledge sharing, internet availability, and social media, there is no doubt that we are more educated (or have more tools to increase awareness) than previously available. It has resulted in too much fake news, incorrect information being shared, and worse. Don't you think it is our responsibility to cut through the noise and see the reality? And if we have not managed to do so, we need to up our game, change the way we look at and dissect the information.

CHAPTER NINE

VOTERS, DIVERSITY, AND ELECTIONS

I matter, and so do other voters.

As voters, we are funny. We elect representatives to govern us. Then we complain about them to our family and friends, often losing them or the peace between them and us. The cycle continues election after election. The real winners are the representatives, donors, and big companies. Voters never get applause, not even for bearing the brunt, which includes depression, anxiety, headaches, and correctly making the incorrect choice.

Michael Charming

Introduction

I often hear people comment that the system doesn't work and that leaders are so fucked up. But, aren't we the ones who selected the system long ago and continue selecting it by agreeing to elect leaders and representatives to the government? When we vote, we complain that we are choosing the lesser of two evils. Seriously, neither Clinton nor Trump had 50% approval of the vote in 2016. In fact, they had the two highest "dislike" polling numbers in modern political history. Higher than Boris and Jeremy, for that matter. This happens over and over again and not just in the US but in several countries. So, we are choosing the best of the worst or the lesser worst of the worst. How did we end up in this position? Should an election not be about making a choice between the best of the best? Since we select these leaders, it means there must be something wrong with us, the voters, don't you think?

Until now, this book has highlighted the point that we all have issues, trauma, and pain within ourselves. Despite trying our best as a society, we still cannot find a solution or a leader who works for everyone. Okay, how about a leader who works for more than 50% of the voters? Bribery to elicit votes in countries like India, where voters are paid to make the system 'work'. Leaders know our pain points and how to target them. Why does it seem to work? Because we react and, in that reaction, we vote and elect. Leaders know this and have different strategies for different kinds of voters. But we, the voters, have the same strategy to measure all leaders. Huh, who is smart here?

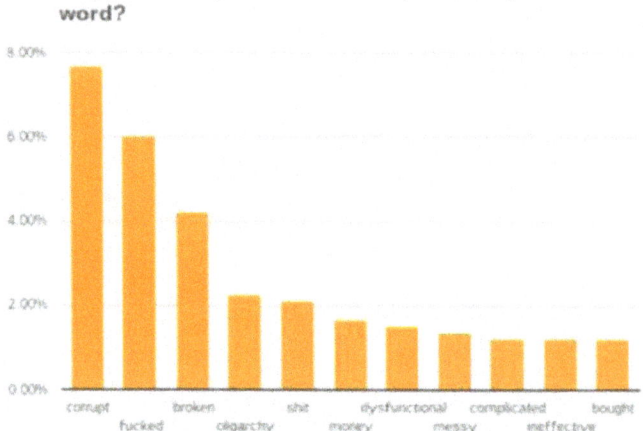

Can you sum up the state of the political system in one word?

Figure 96: 'Corrupt, Fucked, and Broken' will be the first three words that one will get by looking at this graph. (For illustration purposes only). Image source: meme, me.me.

People are not sick of politics; in fact, one of the most significant changes of the Trump and Brexit effect is that people have become more engaged, more outspoken, and opinionated on politics. People are sick of the never-ending problems with no solutions, needing to catch up on fast-changing news, and being unable to distinguish between correct and incorrect information, which makes them feel that the stakes are high. Simply, voters don't trust the leaders to do what they say or to do anything at all. So, the media and pollsters misinterpret this anger as apathy, which they then convert to disengagement. In 2000, voting was at 59%. In 2010 it was at 66%. And in 2016, because of Brexit, voting rose to 72%. The US 2020 election saw the most extensive total voter turnout in US history. So, people are engaged and voting more than before.

Figure 97: As a topic that enlightens, energizes, and motivates us, shouldn't politics have these kinds of effects? There is something that we aren't doing right.

Voters – who are we?

- *Voters would love Boris round for dinner - but even his biggest fans would pick Hunt to babysit their children*
- *How Democrats are disgusted by Trump's p**** tape, but Republicans say he DOES respect women revealed in new poll*
- *Britons vote in favour of same-sex marriage: Public backs PM on gay marriage but says he's doing it to be trendy*
- *Nearly a third of Americans think an armed revolution will be necessary soon*
- *Rory Stewart: Tories would lose four million voters with tougher Brexit stance*
- *Landslide or loss? Pollsters can't agree on the UK election*
- *New party aims to persuade voters to `reconsider' Brexit*

Many voters feel passionate about things currently existing in our society that need to change. Hence, these need to change – poverty, climate, elitists, long working hours, and the capitalist nature. We all believe that real change is necessary, not only from politicians, businessmen, and other social leaders but from each one of us too. The current environment is not sustainable; the sooner we recognize this, are willing to work towards changing this, the sooner we will take steps that will lead us onto the transformation path at a global level. But that change needs to come from each one of us. It should come as no surprise as to why politics and political decisions are complex and complicated. As voters, we don't make it any easier.

Different types of voters and the factors that influence them

Everyone has a place in our society, and some will overlap. We have covered this in preceding chapters, but here we go with some highlights since some like to see it in more concrete terms. Can you identify any categories you fall into?

- Occupation: Police officers, bankers, dance teachers, instructors, leaders, or entrepreneurs.
- Hobbies and interests: Yoga, Tantra, swimming, speaking, or writing.
- Party allegiance: loyalists, undecided, or party identity.
- Age: Youth or elderly, (youth are mostly socialist, the elderly are mostly conservative, youth focus on education and youth unemployment.)
- Change: anger, resentment, resistance to change, or status quo.
- Needs: wants, desires, perspectives, and priorities.
- Traits: hospitable, money-minded, opportunists, sense of duty, or habit. People are likely to vote to avoid the effect of an unfavorable policy or leader rather than supporting a favorable policy or leader.

- Perceptions vs. realities: perception we form of leaders, realities vs. how far are those perceptions from realities. For me, body language and manner of talking play a vital role. No wonder when given a choice among Cameron, May, Boris, and Jeremy, Cameron was always my preferred candidate if only based on his delivery, body language, and looks, followed by Boris due to his ability to bring some humor. Jeremy would be at the bottom because of his shabby appearance. Our brain trusts candidates whom we see more like us, Cameron with a smart suit, and even Trump, for that matter.
- Wouldn't it be great to play a card game like this without the grief?
- Emotions, emotional sensitive spots or triggers, thought processes, feelings, and genetics. If anger persists towards a candidate, one will be less likely to remain open to any good news about this candidate or review favorable policies that this candidate proposes. Anxiety – if one feels anxiety towards a candidate, they are more likely to vote for the opposition. Pride – one is more likely to vote than not. The effect of the topic of politics creates stress, which is likely to be higher days before and on election day.
- Individual, family, society, group, national, global, and universe.

WHICH TYPE OF TRUMP SUPPORTER ARE YOU?

JACK

Says immigrants are taking all our jobs, economically & mentally anxious around them, has a trust overseas to evade all the taxes

AMERICAN SCARLETT

Believes in vitamin & sunshine for immune. Will never get her kids vaccinated even though 2 of them died because she wouldn't vaccinate them.

BENJAMIN

Single, hates feminism, is a macho type. Sends dick pis to women to gain their attention. Gets blocked or friend-zoned easily. Believes that he is not misogynist as he loves all women

OL FRANKLIN

Full of American Patriotism. Fucked & burnt a flag at least once in his life. He's half Italian & half Greek. Hates immigrants. Believes Democrats have fucked America

SAINTTRUMPSTER007

Refuses to use his real name & photo online. Spies on hot girls & sends private messages. Thinks everyone is lunatic & snowflake. Gets offended by literally everything

SUNNY MISS SUNSHINE

Loves getting attention. Admires Trump for 'grab them by pu**y'. Believes women should serve men when told to do so. Cannot stand Crooked Hillary or Sleepy Biden.

Figure 98: Every leader will have supporters with many similarities yet with several distinguishing attributes. As this image shows, the variations, combinations, and similarities are far too many.

- Gender: male, female, or LGTBQ. Women are more attracted to Labour's support for welfare and families. In contrast, men (who are higher earners than women on average) might favor conservative policies of lower taxation.
- Conspiracy theories, propaganda, and a sense of fear.
- Social class – individual income, occupation, education, and wealth. As the income level increases, people become more interested in party cadres, candidates, and local problems. As the education level increases, focus increases on the candidate's former activities.
- Employed vs. unemployed: Managerial or professional workers are more likely to vote. The unemployed are the least likely group to vote.
- Media: newspaper, online platforms, radio, television, apps, websites, blogs, and podcasts.
- Country specific: culture, traditions, and leadership style.
- Actual voting turnout.
- Leaders: leadership and political parties. Canadian PM's Trudeau's gentle, empathetic, and diplomatic approach compared with US President Trump's harsh, blunt, and tactless approach to energize and affect the voter turnout. Corbyn and Sanders can energize but cannot convert as well as Trump.
- Individual vs. Group – collective thinking and group dynamics, vs. the ability to maintain independence while still having the openness towards the group and individuals, family, and lover.
- Open mind vs. closed mind, rigid, how deep the belief systems are ingrained, living experiences in different countries, and taking an interest in their political system and economy.
- Abode: city, town, urban, or rural. The challenges faced by each would vary.
- Voting laws and polling booths: Voter registration and identification laws, early voting, polling booth accessibility, online, and mail.
- Demographics, diversity, race and ethnicity. Black and white tend to have a higher voter turnout than Latinos or Asians.
- Election day itself: facing being rational vs. being emotional, with family and social networks.
- Social factors and issues: housing, infrastructure, employment, childbirth and abortion, war, and healthcare.
- Scenario analysis and reflection on the results and outcome: I run multiple scenarios of what could happen – coalition, hung, pact (UKIP dropping candidates, May + DUP coalition possible, but in case of Labour it would involve coalition with SNP +Lib Dems + Greens + Others which is not possible) and consider the impact it will create. I don't see many others doing this. Doing this is perhaps why I have been mostly correct about the outcomes, whether it relates to Brexit, Trump, Boris Johnson, or Jeremy Corbyn. Time and again, running multiple scenarios allow me to consider different possibilities of what could happen. Taking the case of Brexit, when forming an opinion, I considered that the worst outcome could be that the UK might lose few points in terms of its overall status at an international level, Scotland might leave the UK, and we might deteriorate to that of Greece, but this is

the worst-case scenario. It would be a long road before any of this could happen. Am I prepared to face this outcome?

As shown, the varying reasons someone picks a particular party or leader are so in-depth that it would take months to have one-to-one conversations. I find it really surprising when people judge someone who expresses interest or support towards a particular leader. My question to you is, do you consider the pros and cons with regards to every policy you support or don't support, every decision you make, every opinion you form, and most importantly, do you display an open-minded attitude when others show or decline their support? The latter might be a massive ask, but the least I would expect from you as a voter is to do the former.

Every action, every policy, no matter how good it may sound, will have a consequence. Even planting a tree has a consequence. The nearby area cannot be used for housing, building infrastructure, or other purposes. The questions raised would be; what kind of tree, and why? How would logistics work in terms of watering, maintenance, and upkeep? Unless the goal is to plant a tree in the jungle where nature will sort out itself amongst other trees.

Climate change has been one of the biggest issues recently. While the demand for cutting carbon footprints by 2025 sounds amazing, it is far easier said than done. For any individual to change just one habit over which we have full control takes weeks and sometimes months. How can one imagine that we will cope with changing the whole infrastructure and relying on existing resources in such a short period? People don't think it through or imagine far enough ahead in concrete terms. Bringing an idea out of fantasyland is one thing; making it workable in the real world is quite another. When I ask such people to show me how or put it down on paper, all I hear is pin-drop silence. Why? Imagination as fantasy is good for poems, fiction stories, and movies, but real life is more than just stories played by fictional characters.

Figure 99: Undoubtedly, climate change is caused by several natural phenomena, mainly human action and inaction. Is climate change real to the extent that everything will be destroyed in the near future? Is it a hoax used by the wealthy opportunists serving their own agenda?

While we cannot have in-depth knowledge about every issue surrounding us, we should know about as many as possible. When I say us, I don't mean us as individuals, but us as a society, us as a country, and us as a Global planet. Time and again, I see people not having enough basic information or interest in issues that don't affect them personally. Why?

We might vote based on healthcare, the economy, or equality issues, but just as often, or maybe more often, we vote based on anything from our fear level, our bank balance, to the weather on voting day. Voting is an altruistic act done to pursue and perpetuate the common good. In many countries, it is almost obligatory. Yet, in the United States, the supposed paragon of free speech, often 40-50%
of the nation do not vote at all. In some elections, the non-voters outnumber the voters. The good news is, this has been changing rapidly in recent years.

Elections – we have the power in this process

- *By-elections postponed and triggered complaints*
- *Jeremy Corbyn pushes for general election to 'resolve' national problems*
- *US election systems more secure, but voting problems persist*
- *Conservatives and Labour playing politics as economy holds its breath*
- *No time to bask in re-election glory: Obama faces problems including mass unemployment and Iran's nuclear ambitions in second term*
- *Labor leader Bill Shorten says the close election is just the first of Malcolm Turnbull's problems - as latest vote count shows a Coalition majority*

Elections allow us to make different decisions, change and become better, or aim to bring transformation that we couldn't bring in prior elections.

Despite its current place as being the only way to select leaders rationally, the concept of elections has only been around for 200 years or so. And why has it become the sole method for selecting leaders? Because in the minds of the majority, it has produced a fair result and thus continues to be supported. And only as long as we all support this method will it continue. But recently, the elections themselves have created huge issues that threaten democracy.

What happened? Is what we see now or a result of past outcomes? For a solution, do we go back to how we did elections 50 years ago? Or do we start from where we are today and try something new? I ask myself the same questions regarding sexuality especially considering how it was in India (birth of Kamasutra, the first treatise on sexuality and erotic temples showing eroticism, etc.) and what it has become today (unsafe for women, domestic issues, rape, kissing prohibited on streets, etc.).

- Sometimes I wonder whether having leaders for five years is a good thing in such a fast-paced world. But the need for stable leadership that lasts more than five years is necessary to bring any noticeable and impactful change.
- It is an opportunity for voters to really express themselves for the change they have been longing for. Still, elections should not be the only means to achieve political goals. There are many other ways to do this: contacting your local leader, creating petitions, engaging in activities that support your cause.
- Elections allow leaders and politicians to display their personalities and share their message. It is their chance to show how much they are in or out of touch with ordinary people's problems or constituency issues.
- To form a sensible and well-rounded judgment, it is essential to understand how the whole election process works. It will give more awareness as these vary from country to country – e.g., it involves primaries (open and closed), caucuses, and general elections in the US, but it is a much simpler and more straightforward process in the UK.
- Candidates often use diversions from the main issues, creating a smokescreen to keep voters from remembering. E.g., they may use a terrorist attack to divert awareness from their vote against the care of the homeless.
- Everyone who is a citizen gets to vote, but I think this is a deep flaw in our political system and society. In my view, I don't think everyone should be automatically allowed to vote; there should be a basic eligibility test conducted to determine who qualifies to vote. This test should be based on the country's fundamentals, including questions from many aspects of society (as mentioned in various chapters). Anyone who passes the minimum threshold should be allowed to vote. Because in the current system, people who have no idea or interest in society or political know-how are entitled to vote, meaning the lives of educated professionals or those with some degree of sensibility are also determined by the former category of voters. There are pros and cons, but I firmly believe in not giving everyone a chance to vote. I have heard countless times that voting is my birthright, okay, but what does it say

But I don't wanna vote !!!

I don't like any of these people! Why do we end up selecting the same kinds, again and again and again :(

Figure 100: Whether we like it or not, even if the options are terrible, we will still need to vote (perhaps voting for other parties like Green, Independents, etc.) Deciding not to vote is a terrible strategy, don't you think?

about being an ideal citizen? Is that not our birth obligation?

There is an opposing position that indicates the rules are one person, one vote, and we, as a society, have no right to decide that only the informed may vote. Who prepares the test? Biased against Democrats, Republicans, uneducated, or racially discriminatory? The ability to rig the test means the ability to rig who wins elections. The concept is flawed in many ways. Those uneducated in the South (US) fifty years ago had to produce a driver's license and sign their name to vote. After doing this, they had to pay a fee (a poll tax), and after all, if they were still determined to vote, they had to guess how many jellybeans were in a jar; failing meant they couldn't vote. Period. Many blacks could do none of these but had a fair idea of who they wanted as their leaders. So, the concept of a test to vote has been proven in some instances to be exclusionary.

- Types of elections: Local, officeholders, by-elections, recall elections, and referenda.
- Forgery of ballots or miscounts during tallying, voting boxes with marked ballots lost, violation of secret ballot, tampering or hacking software of voting machines, and destroying legitimately cast ballots.
- Fixed timelines for elections, no-confidence motions, results in early polls
- Election rules on who can contest and who can vote, and candidates' requirements.
- Campaign rules.
- Foreign interference: China in Taiwan, Russia in Latvia, Russia in the US.
- Voters suppression tactics used: stricter voter ID laws, reduction of early votes, elimination or reduction of same-day registration, cuts to polling booths and hours.

Voters psychology – time to make a decision

- ❖ *British voters didn't understand how complex Brexit was, says Macron as he insists UK should 'for sure' be allowed to reverse the decision*
- ❖ *Tell voters who is REALLY to blame: MP calls for Britons to be able to find out who is behind a decision in any public sector body - and why it was made*
- ❖ *Your biggest decision in a generation: Cameron issues rallying cry to voters as Tories take a three-point lead... but one in six are STILL undecided*
- ❖ *Making a choice: Voters talk of decision and of tensions*
- ❖ *Undecided voters see Brexit making them worse off – survey*

Making voting decisions are not easy because:

- The world is not static nor binary. Today's world is fast-moving and sometimes more than we can cope with. Important decisions need to be given much thought, as they are not only for today, tomorrow, or five years down the line. We need to consider the impact our decisions will create for the coming generations. Brexit is a perfect example of a "today" vote that impacts future generations.
- The volume of issues, situations, circumstances, challenges are ever-increasing. One would have thought that technology would ease our lives, but it has brought its own set of complexities and problems. Individuals are stretched beyond the limit, and trying to exercise control is like grabbing air.
- The factors, issues, and challenges that we were considering yesterday or our society is facing today might not be that important for our society tomorrow. New shadows, new issues, and new problems continuously appear; hence our decision making must be pro-active. I often see people reacting to issues and leaders, but only considering current situations or what those leaders said in the past.

Figure 101: Reasons will vary from person to person for voting or not voting. Not exercising one's right to vote shows one's unwillingness to be a good citizen.

- Of course, the past matters; history repeats itself, but let's not get lost in the past. E.g., many thought Trump to be Hitler, but it is yet to be historically determined if this will be so or not. I am of the view that while history is repeated, it is also created.
- What is our decision-making process? What are our sources of information: experiences, friends, news, or media, most of which are manipulative, misleading, and/or full of projections. Or, do we base our decisions on past information gathered? Suppose we gathered information on an issue five years ago. Do we ever go back and check if progress was made? Although we may not be checking, our government or relevant authority might be, thus making most of our information stale.
- Collectiveness plays a part in decision making; please refer to Groupthink in Chapter Seven.
- Do we consider the macro and micro impact (individual, societal, national, and global) as everything is interlinked?
- We cannot know and support everything, but what are our priorities? Do we pursue climate change? Do we pursue equality for minorities? What about capitalism; is it time for another form of economics? I would certainly hope not, but others have different priorities.
- Emotional, mental, and other sensitive spots and triggers. It is an emotional matter if we choose, but often we are not aware that we are acting on emotion; this requires in-depth introspection.
  - Negative campaigning or ads with a negative connotation often drive voters to the other candidate. People remember negative information far more than anything positive. No wonder we see more negative news, headlines, and articles than anything positive the candidate may have achieved. Would it not be much easier to praise one's self more? Trump does both very well.
  - Emotional triggers impact one's opinions. Once the mental association about an issue or aspect is formed due to logic, it is difficult to change these opinions or beliefs. Hence, it is crucial to introspect and look at the logic and belief formations to identify if these were formed due to emotional sensitive spots or triggers being triggered at every stage and continuously. Using my personal case study: Before becoming a UK permanent resident, my attention was focused continuously on the news relating to the government's immigration policies. Immigration was my emotional trigger, fear of what would happen if I had to leave the country. For many reasons, I didn't want to go back to India permanently. Once I became a permanent resident and later a citizen, the government's immigration policies were no longer my emotional trigger. In politics, politicians press on our pain points, generally triggering our emotions of anger and fear. If we remain grounded or less triggered, they will have to change their game. Are we ready to change ours, thus forcing them to change theirs?

Figure 102: We can condemn negative campaign political strategies as much as we like. These will remain because they produce the desired results.

- o Like emotional triggers, there will be mental, physical, and spiritual triggers. E.g., challenging one's belief (voter fraud exists), religious beliefs (heaven, sin, and witch-hunts), handicaps, African-American, gay-lesbian, etc.
- o Balanced people will take facts, policies, and manifestos into account. I always compare the manifestos of various parties to consider what's on offer. Those who generally support Labour believe that climate change is not a Conservative policy, but on checking the manifestos, I saw that all parties had policies relating to climate change listed. The amount of money to be spent, the timeline, and methods of achieving them varied.

Figure 103: Sometimes we lack the proper perspective to view positions.

- ○ Politicians also play towards the voters' exhaustion. 'I'm so bored of Brexit. Just pass the damn fucking deal and move on', 'Can we revoke article 50 and go back' – with this attitude, no wonder 'Get Brexit Done' or 'Drain the Swamp' appeals to many.

Why people still don't vote

- Lack of interest and finding it too complicated to understand politics, government processes, and policies.
- The social media algorithm doesn't create the necessary awareness and know-how relating to elections or are often found to be biased. Many people consume news through social media within their echo chambers rather than a diverse range of online newspapers, TV channels, etc.
- A belief that their party will win (safe seated) as they continue to see social feeds filled only with like-minded people, or they live within a constituency with safe-seated candidates and consider their vote to be a waste: a Tory stronghold or a Democrats stronghold.
- Dissatisfaction because they believe that nothing will change, that their voices are not (or never) seen or heard.
- Distrust towards the elites, establishment, political parties, and leaders being all talk, no action. U-turns and changes of stance by leaders.
- Not seeing the results they wanted and expected to see after previous elections. Negative past experience of being turned away from the voting booth or delays in receiving the voting card.
- Lack of education, knowledge, and awareness.
- Life and election fatigue – mental, physical, and emotional. Whose responsibility is it to manage election fatigue? If you ever have been married, the actual wedding day is tiring, but you start preparing well in advance. What about preparing for school exams? Suppose you struggled to prepare and manage yourself well during school exams or your wedding day. In that case, you will likely struggle to manage yourself on election day, too (repeated pattern perhaps, unless life awakenings and transformations have changed

How to increase voter turnout....

I heard my favorite American Idol is running for President... I have come to vote for him...

Figure 104: There have been numerous recommendations for increasing voter turnout. The one that works is compulsory voting and a national holiday. It doesn't get any easier. Alternatively, bring a candidate like Trump, who energizes his voter base and the opponent's base who would vote for anyone but Trump.

you).

- Issues at polling booths, no timely registration, or many not eligible to vote: prisoners, foreign citizens, dead people voting or under 18 years of age.
- Other reasons may include just not being able to: work commitment, life commitment, based overseas, technological, and other interruptions (tube failure, rain, snow, hot weather, football matches), not feeling well, or unhealthy.

If we don't get the result we want, someone on the other side has achieved the result they wanted. And that person is not an alien, but a human, just like yourself, with their own needs, desires, family, and interests.

Polarization – why we can't tolerate each other or each other's views

- *Germany worried by "polarisation" in Turkey's political debate*
- *India's media is 'scripting the narrative of polarisation' in its coverage of religion*
- *'It's more purple than blue and red': Americans' political views are closer than you think*
- *No Labels movement launches in the U.S. demanding less polarisation in politics... with the help of an achingly trendy theme song penned by Akon*

Why do people believe that someone with a different opinion is misguided, irrational, non-sensical, or even stupid, to the extent that it takes society and the world in the wrong direction?

We hardly see a day without being exposed to political dysfunctions, movements, or causes having opposing views (black lives vs. all lives, Gates pandemic or real pandemic). Our society has never been polarized to this extent. It is not that people have not disagreed in the past. They have, but now politics, leaders, and social media have increased the intensity of those differences, have stirred the underlying unexpressed or stuck emotions, and have provided a platform for everyone to express themselves, thus resulting in a supercharged domino effect.

I often experience people blaming Trump and Brexit for this polarization issue. May I ask the same people; did Trump decide overnight to be the man in charge, and did the UK decided by itself to walk out of the EU? No, both were led by the people, with a proper legislative process, and were the outcome of their expression. People expressed that way because of events that have been building up for years and decades – think of failed healthcare reforms, the Iraq War, the ever-expanding EU and its immigration policy, Obamacare, the financial crisis, the rise of Tea parties, etc. These events had been a long time in the making, so more like the symptoms of existing issues rather than causes of them.

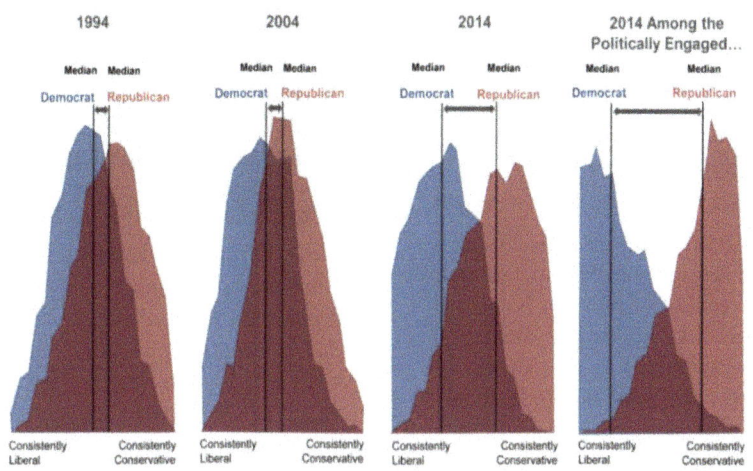

Figure 105: Increasing polarization in the US over the past three decades. Source: Political Polarization in the American Public, Pew Research Center. Source: Survey of US adults conducted Jan 9-14, 2019, Pew Research Center

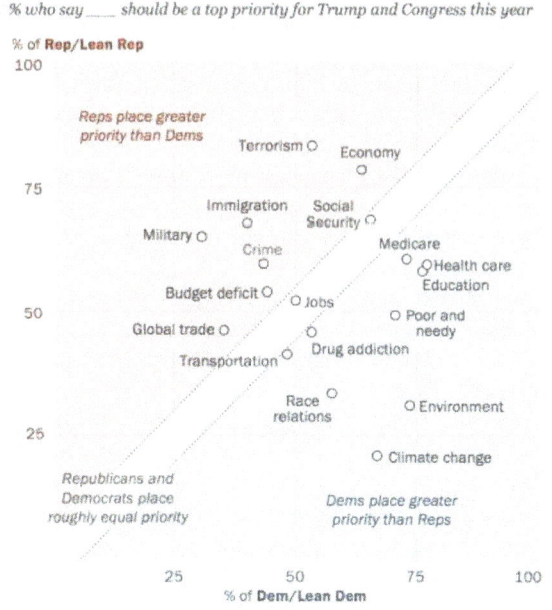

Figure 106: Republicans and Democrats differed over key priorities for the president and Congress in 2019. Source: Survey of US adults conducted Jan 9-14, 2019, Pew Research Center

People have been longing for Trump to be removed as POTUS and Brexit to be canceled because they believe that this will resolve the issues. Well, Brexit can't be canceled, and with regards to Trump, we know what happened in Nov '20. The other side of this coin is that there were extenuating circumstances in Trump's election in 2016 that might have swung the election into Trump's favor, e.g., foreign interference, an outsider, an overdose of outright lying, fed up with existing political system and establishment, etc. Greater doses of each we had never seen before from any previous leader.

Figure 107: With both candidates as our ruling leaders, I wonder what the next issue would be? Perhaps more chaos, more delays, and nothing would ever get done. We may dislike the democratic process, but the other options aren't that exciting or feasible or better. Denying democracy completely vs. admitting faults in the process are two different things.

Causes of polarization

+ Partisan Polarization has increased tremendously in recent decades (i.e., party prioritizes stance that is most aligned with political platform and ideology. Democrats moving to the left, Republicans to the right). Main conceptual frameworks shifted from unifying values to group identities. Left views right as bigots, racists, and nationalists, while right believes left to be lunatics, snowflakes, and politically correct. Each views the other as responsible for tearing the country down.
+ Polarized Electorates: Partisan polarization results in polarization for elites and electorates.
+ Geographic Polarization: supporters of one or the other party cluster together in homogeneous enclaves.
+ A New Type of Political Donor: Historically, donors supported parties and people. Today, the big money, PACs, and such, now aim at specific issues and ideologies. So, obviously, there are now more ways to be divided than to be inclusive.
+ Religious, ethnic, and cultural divides: Democrats are more moderate in religious views; Republicans are more traditionalist and represent most of the evangelical groups.
+ Economic inequality: Clearly, those of the lowest economic classes have many reasons, real and imagined, to be polarized against those who have all the capital and privilege.
+ The decline of responsibility and accountability of journalism and media: There are no longer any standards for the 'opinion' networks, Fox and MSNBC, in the US. Fox, speaking for Trump, will say anything, true or not, to support his positions. MSNBC loves to find every last detail to beat Trump over the head with his own words and deeds.

+ Our way of thinking (or not thinking), feeling (or not feeling), expressing (or not expressing), aligning of soul, mind, and heart (or not aligning), healthy (and unhealthy) habits, empowering (or limiting) beliefs, open mind (or closed) which results in:

  o Binary thinking, i.e., a Yes or a No.
  o Lack of attention or presence to allow for sensible and in-depth conversations.
  o Indulging in motivated reasoning (looking for evidence supporting one's side and viewpoint, rather than providing information for a balanced view).
  o Absolutizing one's preferred values.
  o Failure to recognize that people with different opinions have good intentions and likely good opinions.
  o Seeking validation and approval from 'my side' of the group's thinking. Groupthink.
  o Relying on deductive logic (believing that general premises justify specific conclusions).
  o Not being able or willing to agree on basic facts that do not require any evidence. The sky is blue…or for some reason, it is no longer blue according to one side.

Effects of polarization

One significant negative effect of polarization is in the US Congress. Republicans decided for the eight years of the opposing party being in power that they would pass zero legislation, causing eight years of gridlock. Unfortunately, the price of that position is likely to be, if Democrats seize the Senate in 2020, that Republicans will have zero voice in anything that goes on for the next four years or longer if they cannot seize any power of their own.

Some would argue that polarization stifles public interest in politics, positions, elections, voting turnout, and all that bullshit flying around. Others would argue that polarization makes a party's or candidate's positions more unified and easier to identify for voters of the same interest.

And finally, polarization provides foreign powers the opportunity to play parties against each other on foreign policy, which undercuts a country's foreign policy position and standing in the world.

How to reduce polarization

• Practice curiosity rather than advocacy or an 'I know it all' attitude.
• Cultivate the ability to listen, see, read, and decipher the underlying message of what is being said, shown, or expressed.
• Instead of bringing biased assumptions, judgment, or distrust, bring an attitude of openness and trust.
• Create an environment of discussion rather than debate; create space that allows for more open conversations than closed and restricted conversations.

- Don't aim to control the conversation or ideas in a specific direction but rather let them flow. Set a time limit or intention of discussion beforehand.
- Be honest and transparent about your stance and communication, and act out of integrity.

Results and the days after the elections

Elections are far more unpredictable than before. We have all seen how polls and various predictive models have found it difficult to predict the past few elections' outcomes accurately with too many instances of 'being too close to call' or completely incorrect by more points than the reasonable margin of error.

- Announcements night – anxiety, hopelessness, and fear of the candidate losing. I hardly see people congratulating the opposition candidate and supporters of that candidate. I always do.
- Ballots forgery, double counting, misplaced, corruption, and scandals.
- Five Stages of Grief – In 1969, Elisabeth Kübler-Ross suggested that anyone experiencing grief goes through a series of five emotions popularly referred to as DABDA. Parties and leaders generally get over this quickly, but the voters get stuck in one or more stages for years, often repeating the pattern repeatedly. I strongly support people to go through the five stages to allow the full release of expressions and emotions; otherwise, they will be stuck for years. No wonder people exhibit similar emotions and behavior time and again, and we often find ourselves asking the same question, 'Have we learned anything from the past?'

  o **Denial and isolation** – *'that didn't just happen,' 'how could it be, my candidate was winning,' 'everyone in my newsfeed was talking about this,' 'can't take it anymore,' 'He cannot win,' 'I don't believe people in the UK really wanted to leave the EU,' 'why have it in the first place.'*
  o **Anger** – which also follows protests. *'if only our candidate had done this,' 'I had been saying focus on this issue instead,' 'why is this happening? What did I ever do to America?' 'He should be executed,' 'I'm angry at the result of the referendum,' 'I'm angry at the Brexiteers.'*
  o **Bargaining** – *'I'll do anything. Please don't let him be the President', 'Can we not do anything to change the constitution,' 'Brexit can still be avoided if Remain continues to put its case to the public.'*
  o **Depression** – *'I don't care anymore,' 'We are fucked,' 'I don't want to live in this country which is going to be fucked up,' 'The UK will end up a lonely island sinking of its own,' 'I want to move to the EU, any EU friends know anyone who wants to marry me.'*
  o **Acceptance** – *'Either way, we are screwed, so come fuck me,' 'I realize I can't stop or change anything, and we all are dying anyway. Bring on*

WWIII', 'I have finally accepted that the UK is finally leaving the EU,'
'Sorry, European friends, we tried our best to remain, but alas, we are
leaving now,' 'The UK has exited, but I hope Brexiteers are now cor-
rect and that we don't end up collapsing.'

Figure 108: Our reactions during the five stages of grief.

Conclusion

Well, there you have it. Understanding who votes, why we vote (don't vote), the way we vote (don't vote), the point of it all, the ever-increasing polarization, anxiety, temper, restlessness, aggression, and other mental and emotional turbulences that haunts many during the election cycle and how to deal with grief after the election result. Given now we have a glimpse and a bit of understanding of how difficult it is for various voters to come together, next we will take a look at why it is even more difficult for leaders to do or not do what they do or don't do, the path toward leadership and why leaders are considered failures.

CHAPTER TEN

LEADERSHIP

While it is okay to have high expectations of our leaders, don't you think we should, in turn, offer our support to help meet those expectations? Never-ending criticism has does not motivate anyone. Are you ready to appear before this world as the best version of yourself?

Michael Charming

Introduction

Making a decision as a voter might be easy if simply based on one policy like immigration, social welfare, or dislike towards a particular leader. But suppose you are a voter like me, who is not tied to a particular party or a leader. In that case, you will then realize that making decisions about which party or leader to support is not that easy. I am not a party or leader loyalist; I prefer to focus on policies, national and global circumstances, and leaderships available before deciding which leader to support. Before deciding, I spend much time consider-

ing the multiple variables involved, as seen in previous chapters, considering the pros and cons, not only of an individual leader but also towards the party, country, internationally, and the overall impact for generations to come.

As voters, when we struggle with so much, can you imagine the leader's difficulty deciding on supporting or not supporting a policy or another member of their party. I stood in student union elections at college. It wasn't until then I realized how much it takes to win an election, any election. My view was

"Here we have what I think is a brilliant idea."

Figure 109: Everyone wants their leaders to implement the best of the best policies. Given society's complexity, we know that a policy that works for everyone doesn't exist.

that candidates come, do speeches, run campaigns, vote, and boom, the leader is elected. After that experience, I realized how many strategies, hundreds of never-ending meetings with people ranging from locals to party members to other contestants, energy, time, money, and a hundred other factors are needed to win an election, even a simple election in the college.

In this chapter, we look at the struggles leaders go through, including the role the government plays, the different categories of leadership styles, the context and comparison of situations, why leaders are often considered failures, and lastly, some important recommendations to consider when making your decision next time.

We will learn how difficult it is to be a (political) leader and realize that every leader has strengths and weaknesses. Many do not want to acknowledge the strengths of the leaders they dislike. In terms of their opinion, they are too fixated, mostly with no room to consider anything beyond their fixed belief about the party or leadership they support. The aim is to bring into their awareness how leaders emerge, what it takes to stay as a leader, and how voters contribute towards seeing leaders as failures, even when they are or not.

Government – is big brother watching us, or are we watching him?

- *Belgium PM reshuffles government after government crisis*
- *Estonian government collapses: economic issues were key*
- *China hopes new S. Korean government will correct problems*
- *Government failing to address safety problems in prison – report*
- *Sir John Timpson appointed to lead panel set up by Government to look at problems facing UK High Streets*
- *Apple urges government to form commission on encryption issues*

When we talk about politics, you will often hear people blaming the leader and the government, even when they have no role to play in their misery. Government, good or bad, is the term universally used to describe a country's leadership and how it continues to exist and run on a day-to-day basis. It is up to the government to secure the national safety, support the national currency (with the help of Central Banks), raise an army, make economic and social policies, take care of those who cannot care for themselves, and keep domestic peace. The selected government or organizations created for specific purposes help achieve this.

That elected leader we see, talk about, and show our resentment or support is actually the puzzle's final piece in this process. Though at the forefront once nominated, the leader is often not selected until the last minute in the whole election process. Are you aware of the entire process before any candidate is elected as the leader? It is easier to point one, two, or even ten fingers at someone while

calling them deplorable, shitty, idiot, or lunatic; try sitting your emotions and consider the struggles that each leader has overcome before being elected as the leader of the party, and if successful, leader of the country. I am not saying that we should support every leader; I am saying that the path to leadership and then maintaining the same is far more difficult than any of us can even imagine. Otherwise, everyone would want to be a leader or fight with fists and elbows for that seat. That, of course, has also happened.

Figure 110: Political correctness, a lack of tolerance, or getting offended too easily happens far too often.

Each country's government has different processes relating to how they function, how they conduct their election system, how a leader is elected in each party, how long an elected government remains in power, at what stage are new elections called, and what are the rules of engagement. Are you aware of these processes within your own country? I often hear people in the UK, the US, and elsewhere criticizing the Russian, Saudi Arabian, or Chinese government. Why, because they view the leadership from their lens before making suggestions based on what they would like to see in their country. But why? Aren't these countries completely different, with their own history, culture, and norms?

Yes, while it is great to support freedom of expression, women's rights, equality, and less oppression, every country has its own well-established culture, which in some cases is deeply rooted and has lasted centuries. Merely removing their leader or government will not necessarily achieve what you may anticipate. If Putin was replaced with someone like Merkel as the leader in Russia, you might feel great achievement because you will be focus-

Figure 111: We judge people based on their ethnicity. We don't judge their country's policies or their governments' way of functioning, campaigning, governing based on that country's culture and constitution. Interesting, isn't it?

ing on it at face value of Merkel being humanitarian and Putin being a communist leader. You may not realize there will be far deeper wounds that will be created, not only for Putin's supporters but also for Merkel's supporters in that country. To become less divided and more unified, the shift would need to be gradual (rather than revolutionary), including education, awareness, and preparation.

E.g., the UK government is led by the prime minister, who once elected, selects all other ministers. The senior ministers belong to the supreme decision-making committee known as the Cabinet.

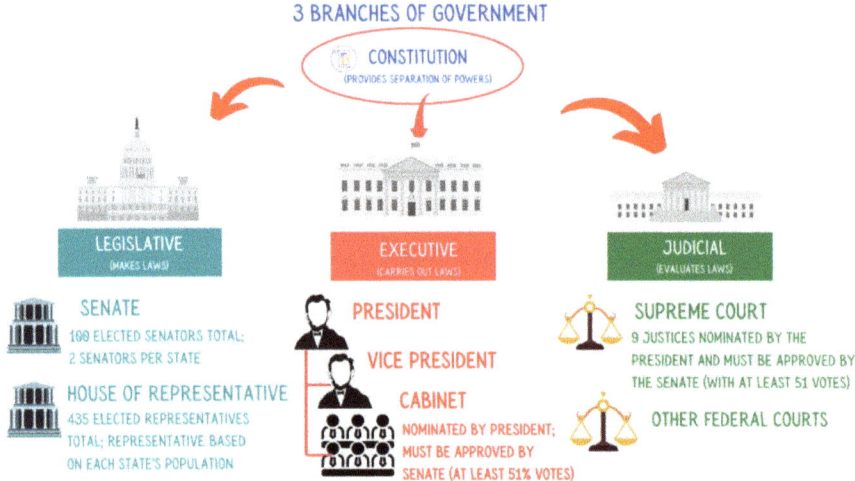

Figure 112: Three branches of government. Honestly speaking, are you aware of the structure within your country (and the countries you have conversations about) and the roles that each performs.

In the US, it is comprised of three branches: the legislative, executive, and judicial. Each branch works together, or not, to set the laws. The legislative branch, the Congress, Senate, and House of Representatives, makes the laws while the President, Vice President, and the Cabinet fall under the executive branch, which carries out the laws. The judicial branch consists of the Supreme Court and other federal courts that evaluate the laws' legitimacy.

Three branches of the US government, I wonder, what percentage of American voters (and people in the rest of the world who express opinions on US elections) know this?

People are generally not aware of this process. They often don't think about the policy-making hurdles and start arguing or reacting emotionally to any kind of proposals that a leader or party suggests, which media tweaks in their favor to create the necessary hype. Every leader's job is to be open to different suggestions, consider different proposals, and have their team perform detailed analysis (pros, cons, feasibility, budgets) on the credible ones before the government selects which they think is worth pursuing.

Take the case of vaccines being mandatory. Many started associating theories and became anti-vaxxers during the pandemic, and then anti-government because they don't want to be forced to be vaccinated. I asked the question, 'Do you know the process for a vaccine to become mandatory?' I hear nothing but silence and rhetoric that they don't want a vaccine because they don't want to be vaccinated... period. No answer.

Figure 113: The problem with using a narrative to match our opinion is that it leads to jumping to conclusions.

Citizens blame the government for all their miseries and problems. The train is disrupted; there is a housing crisis, a corona crisis, tensions due to North Korea firing ballistic missiles, and inflation... blame the government. At times we are ready to blame the government, even for the weather. The rich are making more money, there is an increase in terrorism, someone lost their job...we know what to do, blame the government. There is hardly anything we do not hold the government responsible for.

We seldom realize that government has far more critical things to look at than to cater to each and every person's needs and happiness, to worry about how you might be feeling on a nice sunny day, or how you might be coping because of an unwanted Facebook post, Twitter feed or TikTok video. You probably already know this, but might not have it in your awareness when you are discussing politics, so to give you an idea, here are a few aspects to consider that government actually focuses on:

- Social security plans, welfare plans, investment plans
- Law and order, terrorism, war (including cyber and proxy), commitments (like NATO), immigration and customs
- National, State, and international co-operation, foreign policy, various kinds of spending and aids
- Various laws and international protection of rights
- Demographics of different voters (refer to the previous chapter) – farmers, climate change supporters, bankers, entrepreneurs, pensioners, veterans, working-class, elites

- Economy, budgets, corruption, scandals, monetary, and fiscal and legislative policies
- Various forces – navy, air, military, police, fire, border patrol
- Taxes – income, corporation, sales, value-added, environmental
- Preservation (and integration where applicable) - Ethnicities, culture, history, tourism, environment
- Education, school, universities, research organizations, sports
- Medical facilities, housing, parks, recreational, monuments
- Regulatory bodies, agencies, enforcement officers, insurance agencies
- Social justice and empowerment, bodies and embassies in their own country and abroad
- Negotiations (including Brexit case of the UK), press conferences, media, and public backlash
- Peace with neighboring countries (e.g., India, China, Pakistan), international relations and diplomacy
- Uncertainties – weather, storms, events in other countries, and pandemics
- Equality or/and fairness: residents, citizens, migrants, immigrants, minorities, the disabled
- Minister holidays, electoral cycle, transitions, ethics
- Stability of the country, peace, harmony, equality, gender equality, staying abreast of new technological innovations, smooth running of administration, illegal drug use and trafficking

As individuals, what do we have to consider? Oneself and perhaps, immediate family? When PM (or President) faces PMQs (briefings), they can be asked questions on any topic and need to provide answers. In politics, how many things do you have an interest in (climate change, Black Lives Matter or All Lives Matter, your taxes, immigration) that you can remember and have the know-how or detailed knowledge of? One of the most significant points I hear from many is that the government should spend more money on social causes or provide helicopter money.

Tell me about your current financial position and why it has anything to do with taxing the rich? Do you think you will get some of that money? Perhaps something should be done about companies, especially giants, who earn substantially and evade taxes by having offshore operations. They pay peanuts in tax, mainly due to loopholes in tax laws that allow this to happen. But the situation is much more complicated.

Many don't realize is that taxes are calculated according to income brackets, which means that higher incomes are taxed at a much higher rate than lower incomes. Comparing yourself to the rich and feeling inferior that you cannot afford to spend lavishly is drawing the wrong comparison. Everyone's situation is different. People who started with nothing didn't compare themselves to the rich, but to what they had last week, and felt gratified to be doing better. The following week, and the one after, they did the same until they were part of the rich. They felt inspired by the rich and decided to be like them by learning and implementing habits and strategies.

Government works on budgets that are released by Treasury or the Chancellor. Have you ever read the budget to understand what it includes? Finding the changes that have been made compared to the previous period? Do you know why spending on certain things has been included or excluded? Have you questioned and spent time finding out before sharing your conclusions that the government isn't doing much about climate change or not spending on X, Y, and Z?

Government debt (also known as public debt) is money owed to lenders (both internally and externally). The government sources funding by issuing bonds and bills. An investor will only be interested in buying these government instruments if the country's government has a good rating. The lower the rating, the riskier the debt, hence the more costly it will be for that government to borrow. No, the government cannot just print the money it requires, but this explanation is beyond this book's scope; you can do a simple search to determine why.

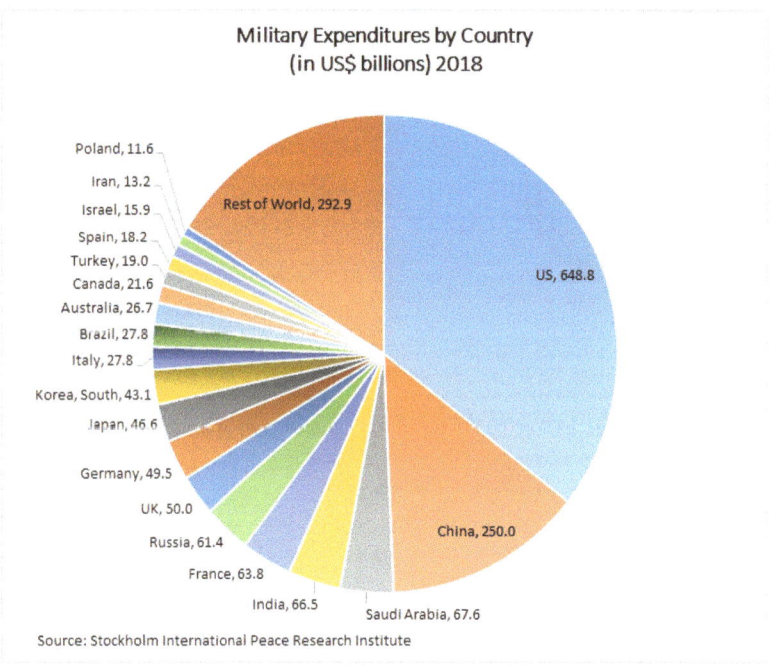

Figure 114: Military expenditure is a sizeable and necessary piece of every country's budget. It will remain so unless each and every country of the world agree to disarmament.

Suppose you don't know how all of this works. In that case, it is essential to get the knowledge or ask someone who can educate you, or at least keep you updated, before you form your opinion.

In the UK, the finance bill, presented by the Chancellor, is debated line-by-line extensively in parliament before being presented to the Commons Treasury

Select Committee for close scrutiny before final approval. Even once approved, close scrutiny is paid on the elements of everything that is discussed by various departments and committees. You can see how it is such a thorough and rigorous process. The same applies to the passing of any law, especially if critical and impact society's well-being or functioning. It is not and will never be possible to meet every section of society's needs. Like us, the government is limited by resources, time, money, manpower, and technology. It is so easy to say, 'Why didn't the government or leader do this?' It is so much more difficult to truly consider the reasoning as to why they didn't, what they decided instead, and why they did? Once you realize the importance of this last sentence, welcome, you are on your way to a massive mind shift and growth.

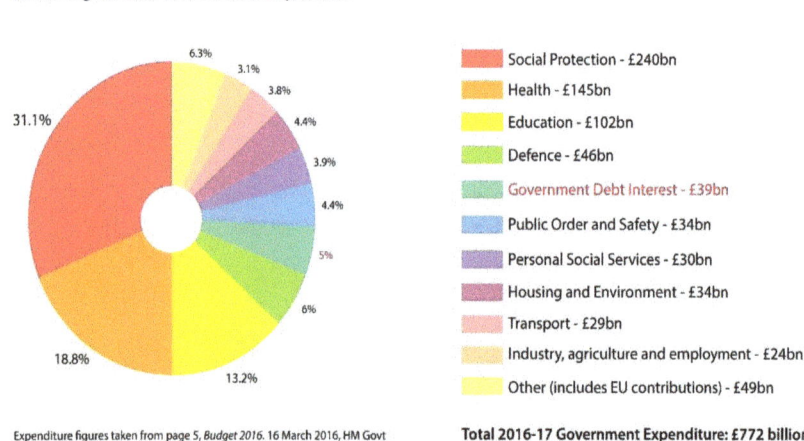

United Kingdom 2016-17 Government Expenditure

- Social Protection - £240bn
- Health - £145bn
- Education - £102bn
- Defence - £46bn
- Government Debt Interest - £39bn
- Public Order and Safety - £34bn
- Personal Social Services - £30bn
- Housing and Environment - £34bn
- Transport - £29bn
- Industry, agriculture and employment - £24bn
- Other (includes EU contributions) - £49bn

Expenditure figures taken from page 5, *Budget 2016*. 16 March 2016, HM Govt

Total 2016-17 Government Expenditure: £772 billion

Figure 115: Have you ever looked at the Government announced budget vs. the actual spending incurred and questioned why it spends the way it does? Do you only question and draw conclusions on one type of spending, or do you consider an overall perspective? On a side note, how are your finances? Do you keep your incomings and outgoings in check and still achieve your savings target every month?

Why People Don't Trust or Have Lost Trust in Government

Historically, trust in most governments is low. It stems from elections not producing the leaders everyone wants and elections not helping them fulfill their promises. Much of this process resides with us and not with the government. We favor policies that enhance our well-being and are seldom willing to make compromises or offer any consideration for people with whom we disagree. How often do we draw a list of needs and wants which align with global interests, growth, and needs? E.g., let's consider climate change. Some might argue that it is real (not the extremes), so the question is, what are YOU doing in this regard; reducing the use of plastics, reducing air travel, reducing consumption and consumerism, playing your part in increasing the breeds of other species through various animal welfare programs, etc.?

You can disagree. Working towards a better environment should still be a positive factor for your well-being. However, it might not be your priority. What are you doing about it, and are you willing to compromise on something so fundamental to everyone?

When was the last time you said, 'okay, I'm willing to support you in this matter, even though it goes against my own principles and priorities'? We all understand that we need policing, but at times police do act inappropriately. We simply

Figure 116: Let's try to work towards creating more trust and supporting one another.

can't agree on what has to happen next. So, even though you might be 100% pro-police, could you agree to ban chokeholds and other methods that could result in victim deaths? Yes, likely you can.

Figure 117: Trust. What does it actually mean? What does it take for someone to trust? Understandably, many don't trust the government, but do we trust one another? Do we trust ourselves? Do we act with integrity and authenticity all the time?

171

Reasons why the government find it difficult to have good governance:

- Short electoral cycles: frequent elections in democratic nations put too much energy and resources into trying to contest, fight, and win, making politicians focus on quick fixes and short-term goals, thus undermining any long-term growth.

- Interest group lobbying and large donors: These both have a significant impact on which policy or agenda gets priority; hence wealth and power are used to influence political outcomes resulting in the creation of further inequality. Politicians have to respond to these people's demands or risk losing their funding during the next contest. Neither the voter nor the leader wants to be one-timers. And when a person like Trump enters the stage intending to drain the swamp, we get triggered by the way he does and responds to things. Equally as critical, when he fails and does the opposite, there is substantial noise in objection.

Figure 118: We don't need the government to state the obvious.

- Voters ignorance, disinformation, emotional reactions, and outbursts: Too many people live in their own bubble, only listening to like-minded people, with little interest in those they disagree with. Thus, making conspiracy theories and fake news viral, creating a loop of misinformation and distrust.

Incompetent political leaders and party support: Generally, in a democracy, anyone can run for office after meeting the basic criteria, opening the door to having more incompetent leaders (Luigi Di Maio (Five Star Movement in Italy), and Trump are examples). Party members not forcefully removing or asking their leaders to resign even when the incompetency is clearly visible; e.g., Jeremy Corbyn not resigning, even when he lost his MPs' support.

- Use of referendum and voting rights: Having a referendum on a topic like Brexit or every citizen having the right to vote is flawed because these tend to create new problems more than resolving the existing ones. How will giving someone with zero know-how about the election process or any basic knowledge of society the same right to vote serve society's well-being? On the other hand, one person, one vote!

Suggestions to improve these issues:
- Public sector salaries to be aligned to private sector, strict rules
- Stricter and tighter rules to avoid lobbying
- The policies, laws, and commitments (critical ones at least) of past governments should be mandatory to be continued by new governments (seems difficult to think in feasible terms, but we need to be open to the idea of more recent suggestions rather than dismissing them outright), so that incoming leader knows what they are getting into
- Research and develop a non-discriminatory system to prequalify voters
- Stricter rules on criteria to qualify to run for the office

Political Parties and Oppositions

❖ *Syrian opposition says government obstructing peace talks*
❖ *Venezuela government, opposition conclude talks without agreement*
❖ *Opposition pressures UK government to act on climate change*
❖ *Madagascar opposition calls for government to resign after court ruling*
❖ *Swedish opposition party launches budget bid to bring down government*
❖ *More parties are splitting leadership positions between men and women.*

In a democratic economy, just like the budget, there are rigorous and established processes, including meeting various contingencies and scenario planning in selecting a leader for the party. I saw people show their dissent at Theresa May and Boris Johnson for not being elected via the election process, just because they were unhappy with them. The selection from the Conservative Party is a process, just like Trump winning the US presidential election via the electoral vote instead of the popular vote. Suppose you want to express your frustration at an existing process. Why do you do it only when the leader you don't support is elected, and not when your choice of leader is elected? Why do you have such double standards? We can't change the rules in the middle of the game; if you are interested in bringing change, work on it before or after.

The opposition and other parties play a crucial role in keeping the elected government accountable. But suppose the opposition party is in disarray (be it Labour due to a leader like Corbyn or be it the Indian Congress due to a leader like Rahul Gandhi). In that case, it provides a free pass to the ruling party to act to the detriment of society. Would Brexit really have taken three years, after the vote, without an opposition leader like Corbyn?. On the other hand, if there is too much opposition, it can stall the entire system. In the 2000s, the Republicans decided not to pass any bill, a tactic they are currently repeating, other than for small things they want.

Communist countries, like China, really gain from stability. They benefit from long-term direction and focus of resources, time, and energy into the country's progress, rather than infighting between parties every five years. Dislike Communism as much as you want to, but it comes as no surprise why China has made such progress. At the same time, countries like the US and India lag far behind in terms of overall progress.

Manifesto

- ❖ *Nationalisation of key industries `in leaked draft of Labour manifesto'*
- ❖ *`Tens of thousands' migration target will be Tory manifesto pledge*
- ❖ *Jeremy Corbyn sets out Labour manifesto promising a `better future'*
- ❖ *Turkish PM puts new constitution at heart of election manifesto*
- ❖ *`Tens of thousands' migration target will be Tory manifesto pledge*
- ❖ *Single market protection and devolved immigration control key to SNP manifesto*
- ❖ *Johnson remains opposed to Heathrow expansion despite Tory manifesto pledge*

Honestly speaking, have you ever looked at each party's manifesto to understand their main focus points and the differences between them? Headlines or two minutes clips can never show what a party really stands for or all the areas they will be focusing on. Agreed, each party might focus on a few critical issues like immigration or Brexit for the upcoming period, but that doesn't mean other issues are thrown into the garbage. The headlines above demonstrate that the government needs to focus on many issues, which means appropriate resources need to be allocated to each. Just because the Conservative Party focuses and talks more about Brexit or fracking, it doesn't mean the environment is not one of their priorities. Many people support Labour because climate change was mentioned as their priority. This does not mean that other areas were not present in their manifesto – arms, oil deals, etc. There is a reason the Green Party hasn't progressed much even though that party's intention is good. If I can think out loud, "all green is so boring, no matter how deeply refreshing green trees are."

Let's understand a manifesto. In simple terms, it is the published 'paper' defining a party's position on various issues. Some parties have a paper for each, others for only the critical issues. Even though a party may recognize that implementing all items is impossible, it becomes their list of objectives.

When deciding which party I should support, this was my summary:

'Get Brexit Done,' 'Make America Great Again,' 'It's Time for Real Change,' 'Stop Brexit. Build a Brighter Future', 'For the Many. Not the Few',

'Forward Together,' I'm With Her.' Slogans tell a story. They indicate a direction, but we shouldn't get swept up in slogans; instead, we should focus on overall objectives as laid down in manifestos.

When manifestos become irrelevant:
- Impractical or unpopular suggestions
- A coalition government, hung parliaments, or government with a very minimal majority
- Constantly changing governments
- Conflicting promises or incompatible policy commitments, e.g. - increased spending, reduced tax
- Not adopted to reflect the diverse needs of society or misses the most critical issues the country faces
- Voters are not paying attention to them; instead, taking short cut measures to determine the party's core values and leadership direction by focusing only on media and news
- Parties launching manifestos purely to turn the against voters in favor of them, knowing that the core policies are deeply and fundamentally flawed

In their manifesto, all the parties include policies relating to dealing with the environment and climate change. Some have it as a priority, and others merely as an essential aspect.

Figure 119: There is no such thing as the Golden Bible of Manifestos; each involves give and take.

Area	Conservative	Labour	Lib Dem	SNP
Brexit	Pro. Leave the EU in Jan 2020	Can't make up their mind. Largely, renegotiate a deal & hold 2nd referendum	Remain but then made U-turn. Generally Revoke A-50	Anti
Immigration	Points based. Prevent foreign offenders from entering country	End hostile policy, close immigration detention centers, automatic rights of EU nationals. Pro-immigration (but no focus on control)	End hostile policy. Replace Tier 2 work visas with flexible merit based system. Abolish income requirements for partner visas	Oppose hostile policy. Support Scottish visa. Oppose min. salary threshold
Trade	10 freeports around the UK. FTA especially, with US, NZ, Japan & Australia	Custom Union with EU	Support international rules based system	Press UK Govt. to fund promotion for Scottish products. Avoid dodgy trade deals with environmental impact
NHS	Increase funding 3.1%. Build 40 hospitals in 10yrs. 50k more nurses, 6k more GPs. Introduce NHS visa	Increase funding by 4.3%. Free NHS Dental check up. £1.6bn for mental health. Reverse privatization	Increase funding 3.8%. 1p income tax for mental health.	Trade deals will not undermine NHS principles. UK govt to match Scottish per capital NHS spending
Police	Tough sentences for offenders, 20k new police officers, increase stop and search	22k new officers	16.5k new officers	Demand refund of £175m in VAT paid by emergency services
Tax	Raise National insurance to £9.5k & up to £12.5k. Corporation tax to stay at 19% instead of 17%. Cut taxes for hard working families	Reduce income threshold for 45% rate from £150k to £80k and introduce 50% from 125k. Increase corporation tax to 26% overtime. New taxes on MNCs. Annual tax on second homes	Increase income tax all rates by 1%. Increase corporation tax to 20%.	Abolition of bedroom tax
Climate change	Reduce net zero carbon by 2050. £1bn on marine pollution & in nature. £4bn on flood defences. £2.5bn on energy efficiency, de-carbonising. Ban export of plastic waste	Reduce net zero carbon by 2030. Change LSE de-listing for company that fails to contribute to tackle climate emergency. Establish £250bn Green Transformation Fund	Reduce net zero carbon by 2045. Plant 60 million trees. £16bn Green Investment bank, flood prevention, zero carbon heating etc.	Demand acceleration on net zero carbon by 2035. Propose Green Energy deal, support reforms for Greener choices etc.
Transport	£100bn investment in infrastructure	Public ownership of railways, cut rail fares by 33%, free bus travel for under 25s, etc	£130bn in infrastructure	
Scottish referendum	Oppose	No agreement	Oppose	Demand

Table 1: Prior to the 2019 UK Parliamentary election, my table of the highlights of different parties' manifestos.

Leadership – are we better or worse off?

Nelson Mandela: "A leader is like a shepherd. He stays behind the flock, letting the most nimble go out ahead, whereupon the others follow, not realizing that all along that they are being directed from behind."

What is the definition of a leader and great leadership? Given the variables involved, how do we define whether a leader has been a success or not? As individuals or families, we can determine success even though, at times, we will still struggle. As a society, we can evaluate success based on different indicators, as mentioned in Chapter Eight. But how do we determine whether a leader is/was successful for the society or not? Is it based on higher GDP, better satisfaction levels, less polarization, fewer conflicts, more regulations, more globalization, fewer wars, or less of their own country first? Do we use the country's relative progress from prior years as a comparison, or do we also compare to other countries? Let us consider Trump; just because he is triggering people by pressing on their emotional sensitive spots, does that make him a bad leader? Or, do we thank him for actually giving us a chance to introspect and grow as individuals and society? Or do we look at his performance, compared to previous Presidents, before deciding good and bad? Or do we look at his accomplishments and failures and compare them in some way?

Notice the dramatic changes to society in the past decade or two. Understand that it is bound to change more rapidly in the near future. The thoughts of a stable world, a sense of peace, calmness, the ability to relax, and not having to cope with higher demands of the internet just so we can remain seen seem to be far in the distant memory. The slower pace of the past has been replaced by a faster, less predictive, more uncertain, and almost unimaginable future. With rapidly changing realities, whether 500 million animals lost in Australian bush fires or lockdowns due to the virus, our present-day feels like the past of many months ago.

A political leader must manage values, interests, and needs; they must create certainty and manage competition from other countries; they must deal with less tolerant and more self-centered groups and individuals. We haven't even focused on the leader's expectations about themselves and their family expectations as a father, mother, husband, wife, son, or daughter.

With increased knowledge shared on social media and online platforms, leaders can no longer expound at length about what they have achieved or not achieved and what they want people to do for them. Today's voters are different; a little dissent and an online petition is ready. A minor disagreement with one policy causes protests without care for the pandemic at play. A small invitation for engagement and participation, everyone jumps in for online press face to face discussions, but be ready for trolls, a back-

Figure 120: Every day we take on several roles, as does a leader. The many masks are often transparent and not visible to the naked eyes.

lash, and all the nasty stuff that goes with it. Leaders are used to receiving criticisms; hence, their thick skin doesn't allow them to start taking things too personally. Else, they would end up spending their time defending or fighting about themselves, like Trump. Is it good or bad? You decide.

The leadership of yesteryear (old and outdated leadership styles)

In the past, leadership could be categorized into the following styles:
- Authoritarian – Follow me, or else it will be bad
- Autocratic – Do as I say, or it might get pretty bad
- Paternalistic – The concept of a benevolent dictator
- Democratic – What do you all think… let's vote on it
- Delegative (laissez-Faire) - We will have our department heads decide
- Transformational – Let's work on shifting the mindset
- Transactional – Unfortunately, Donald Trump
- Strategic – Democratic with some level of intelligence tossed in
- Bureaucratic – Everything takes forever to get done
- Charismatic – Usually one prophetic person, who eventually becomes pathetic, often suicidal

Qualities of a good leader

As voters, there are many variables present in our decision making; likewise, for leaders – their beliefs, background, experiences, alignment with five body layers (more emotional like Trump, more spiritual like Marianne Williamson, or more humanistic like Nelson Mandela), and other attributes like their needs, perspectives, and priorities. In short, leaders are no different; they are just on the other side of the spectrum.

It is essential to understand what differentiates leaders and voters. Voters are not generally accountable to anyone (one bad vote or one bad policy support will not cause much impact), but leaders are. Voters are not under constant media scrutiny, with millions of eyes watching and anticipating the next move to be made, but leaders are. And most importantly, voters do not face personal criticism, backlash, blame, and hatred, which every leader has to go through, no matter how much good they might do for society. No leader can fulfill all the needs, wants, and priorities of society and each individual. As we have seen in previous chapters, our society's resources are in limited supply. Our leader has to make the best use of these resources (time, human power, materials, and services offered) and optimize these in the best possible way. There will always be a tug of war, a give and take, a compromise made here, and a compromise made there, leading to more upset, disappointment, hurt, pain, and sorrow than happiness and joy. In the long run, no matter how well-intentioned a leader might be, there is no way they can please even half the people, half the time.

What makes a good politician? What do you focus on; the political party or do you favor a particular leader? Do you focus on the kind of leadership qualities a leader possesses? If you were to ask others about a certain leader's qualities, apart from a few basic similarities, you are bound to get conflicting and mixed responses. The reason is perception; everyone has their individual perception and emotional spots that a leader triggers. Emotional spots are not only negative; these can be positive. Our feelings towards a leader depend on our perceptions, even Hitler - a mediocre artist with a total lack of social skills. Yet, he still managed to rise to power.

In today's rapidly shifting world, full of fast technological innovations, uncertainties, and complexities of life, there has never been a more urgent need to have responsive and responsible leadership. As voters, we all know this, but still, time and again, we find ourselves selecting just the opposite.

No leaders can have or be viewed as having all of these qualities by everyone. If I were to ask you the qualities of being a good citizen, what will you say? Paying taxes, doing something for others, engaging in charitable causes, and saving the environment (group A); or having respect, no criminal offense, and treating others, including your friends and people who disagree with you, with respect and dignity (group B). Which group identifies you more? Should it not be both? If you do not tick all of these personally, how can you expect this of your leaders? What matters to you the most is okay; it matters to you for yourself. A leader has to consider so much more than what matters to them personally.

Do you see the difference? They mostly can't do what they want to do – reason, being bound by parties, manifestos, visions, processes, and national responsibility. What process are you bound by – possibly your commitment towards your family (if you still fulfill them with sincerity), your house rules, and perhaps some rules of society, many of which I am sure you would be happy to avoid if given a chance (think of taxes, skipping a traffic light, less governance or having to pay fines for not wearing masks, etc.). We demand these qualities in a leader, but do you have these qualities in yourself? Practice what you preach!

What qualities should a leader have depends on whom you ask? The answer is mostly based on their human composition and experience.

Why Do Talented Leaders Fail or Why We Consider Them to be Failures?

Why do we consider leaders to be failures, even though they were the most talented people for the job, elected after a thorough and rigorous process, and had been a leader in making for years? Who decides they are a failure, and on what basis? There is not a single factor we can use to determine their success or failure, unlike the GDP for the economy or a person buying two houses for themselves. Would creating more peace at the cost of a slower economy and falling in the global countries ranking be considered a success? Would avoiding war or confrontation with another country, but at the expense of giving up land or territory, be considered a success? What about a reduction in the crime rate with increased spending in this area, but reduced spending in other social welfares; will that be considered a success?

As a politician, one is constantly under public scrutiny, willing to bear insults, be ridiculed, mocked, and take a stance that may alienate them from their friends and families, knock on doors of strangers to ask for support, be willing to say the right thing even if it means having to resign from the job or being evicted from the party, and not being able to see family for days or weeks. So, when we are finger-pointing, blaming them, and listing their failures, it is essential to be aware of all of the above to form a well-rounded list of failures or blames.

Leaders are going to fuck things up. Plain and simple. It is as certain as the sun rising every day. E.g., consider Angela Merkel; her dealing with the virus was considered a success, unlike the humanitarian crisis, which saw her backtrack on her open-door immigration policy. Of course, the response from her party and people to each of these issues played a part. To mention that female leaders are not necessarily favored over male leaders is silliness. The list of successful leaders, both male and female, is lengthy.

Our view of our leader's capability and personality is based on our perception. It is deeply influenced by our needs, priorities, and perspective. There is no issue in that, but we should always view both the negatives and the positives, and most fall short in considering both aspects. Suppose you dislike Trump and Biden and even Marianne Williamson (unless it's someone like Kim Jong-un or Hitler). In that case, you know that it has less to do with them and more to do with you, the broken system, your disgust with the past in general, politics, and your attitude towards politicians.

Why can leaders with two distinctly opposite personalities both be viewed as failures? Modi likes control, personally supervises everyone under him, is a risk-taker, a pro-active thinker, knows how to brand himself, and can inspire youth on a large scale. On the other hand, Sonia Gandhi was a reluctant politician. She enjoyed the privilege of having the Gandhi surname and lacked the charisma and energy needed to inspire voters.

A list of reasons we see politicians as failures:

- Situations beyond their control – financial crisis, COVID-19, tech bubble – automatically culminate the mood of exhaustion, frustration, anger, betrayal, and distrust
- Our (unreasonable) expectations not being met due to lack of awareness or bias 'I voted for Labour because I believe a strong European Union is a fundamental precondition for the UK's economic growth.'
- Not being adaptable or responding to the needs of society
- Constant hindrance by the opposition and other parties
- Being too forceful to get their goal
- Unlucky ones: Cameron following Brexit
- Failure to provide a clear and shared vision
- Media's portrayal, peoples' perception, and false consensus (it's tough to change one's bias or beliefs, no matter how distorted and incorrect they might be)
- Lack of knowledge, awareness, or engagement with other countries at a regional and global scale
- Past legacies that have proven detrimental to the party's image (e.g., Blair and Bush due to Iraq war)
- Losing support of own party members (May, no confidence in their leader)
- Leaders elected on emotions, but then reality and factual reasoning kick in. Also known as buyer's remorse
- Lack of credible options to choose from, hence selection of best from the worst meant that leadership was doomed to fail from the beginning
- People haven't worked on themselves and are still living in one of the five stages of grief as mentioned in the previous chapter, which is going to taint their decision making (denial, stigmatization, hopelessness, helplessness, fear, and avoidance)

If you want to make everybody happy, then don't be a politician. Go and sell ice-creams instead or become a clown in a circus show.

Figure 121: We forget that leaders are human. They also have families, kids, and their own human composition and try to do the best they can.

Suggestions – Future Leaders and Governments

Our world is changing every day, in fact, every minute. The old election systems, selection of leaders, and deciding what a good leader should be, needs to change as old methods get tossed out like last week's rubbish. Voters are angry at putting up with incompetent leadership, irrational spending, pork-barrel programs and policies, and high taxes.

So, what will this new style of leadership and new leader look like:

- Flexible leadership that includes a mix of leadership styles
- Balanced government consisting of a mix of both genders
- Possibly have two roles in each ministry – one being a person with experience and another a younger person with energy, drive, and passion for carrying out the plan
- More engagement of the public and not just at election times, i.e., the bottom-up approach rather than a disconnect of establishment with the general public
- Standardized rating criteria instead of several polls
- Leaders and ministers pay tied in with the overall functioning of the economy and welfare of society

---

Some important points to consider for your next political discussion about leaders, leadership, or anything related

Context Matters

Will Chuck Norris, Elon Musk, or Dwayne Johnson do a great job being a politician? How about the Pope? Okay, how about Jesus Christ? Was Mike Tyson a bad person? Will Trump be a good boxer or lawyer? I often see people drawing this type of comparison:

1. Comparing a leader to someone who is not a leader (Pope to Trump, Oprah to Trump, and concluding that they would be a better President than Trump). Some will support them, and some would want them to be their leader. Why haven't these personalities become the President yet if some support them so deeply? Just because they are well-known personalities, it doesn't mean their path to becoming the nation's leader will

Figure 122: Putting things in context is easier said than done, but we know that practice makes perfect.

be any easier. Stop fantasizing, start considering the realities, and accept the results even if it is not who you would have wanted. Context Matters!!!

2. Comparing leaders of different countries. Another pattern is that many compare a leader of one country with the leader of another. Some would wish the PM of New Zealand, Arcenda, to be President of the US or Merkel to be PM of the UK. Again, my question to you is why? Don't you think the US and

the UK have Arcenda or Merkel like leaders in their own countries? I have no problem if someone was to rank Merkel and Arcenda as their favorite leaders and Trump and Boris at the bottom of their table, but I do have a problem when people start fantasizing. The country, culture, people dynamics, demographics, political parties, and circumstances that got these ladies elected in their countries are entirely different from what got Trump and Boris elected. To make a comparison, at least draw a comparison between one country's existing leaderships or from countries that can actually be compared on a like-to-like basis. Avoid comparing with past leaders because the past is past. The circumstances in the world and life were different from the current. What you are experiencing today will be very different from tomorrow. Context Matters!!

Figure 123: I think Donald Trump will struggle with this; so would the cavemen, but not Chuck Norris. Image source: meme generator.

3. Not understanding the rules of the game. There is a reason that Mike Tyson was a good boxer. There is a reason that Chuck Norris and Bruce Lee are considered the best martial artists of all time. There is a reason that Trump can never be a good boxer or even an average martial artist. Why? Because of passion and the rules of the game. The rules of each are completely different from the rules of politics. It's a no brainer, it goes without saying - but still, some will have conversations that defy these logics.

Did that all shed some light; can you walk the end of the tunnel alone without me taking you by the hand? What makes politics far worse than a boxing match is that there are rules in a boxing match, all of which are pre-defined and known by the contenders. Should anyone not adhere to these rules, they will be disqualified. But the rules of the game called 'Politics' are not clearly defined, and those that are clear still tend to be vague with room for grey areas and blurred lines. No wonder, candidates like Trump, can appear to be ruthless, often portraying sociopath or pathological killer behavior but still become the leader of the most powerful nation in the world and that, too, via a fair democratic process. Do you blame Trump for playing this way, or do you blame the voters for supporting him, or do you blame the past leaders who failed to lay down the game's clear rules for everyone and play by? Context Matters!!

Principle of Relativity

In asking the question, how can you support Trump, would you support Hillary instead? The answer generally comes as a BIG NO. So? Who would you pick, considering you are limited to the choice of the best of the worst or worst of the worst? People often forget that relativity matters. Remember, the choices were not Pope vs. Trump or Oprah vs. Trump. Otherwise, it would have been much easier for society to make a better decision. What do you think of the choices for the Nov'20 US elections? Any better than 2016 options? No matter the result, have both sides learned nothing? It was a deeply contested election with more than 74 million votes for each candidate, and I still hear and read the same question, 'How can you support him'? Trump supporters asking Biden supporters and vice-versa. The better question would have been, 'Could you tell me why you support him?'.

SWOT Analysis – time for a business management lesson

I so often find that people criticize the leaders they don't support. When I ask them to tell me a few positive things about that leader, their responses are, *'he/she is an asshole,' 'there is nothing good about him/her,' 'this person should just be killed,' 'are you out of your mind.'*

We know that each individual is unique, and by now, you would have realized in much depth what makes us unique. We also know that no one is perfect and that good and bad exists in each of us. Every person has some good sides (the traits that some find positive) and some bad sides (the traits that some find negative). Why do you think this won't apply to leaders? Remember, politics is a hard game. Leaders have to make sacrifices to reach where they are today, just like you would have made tremendous sacrifices to get to where you are today. Irrespective of whether you like the leader or not because of their policies, we still need to recognize the effort and struggles they have been through to get where they are today. Just because you can't see or don't want to see, because you are too hurt, or your ego is being crushed at the result's announcement, it doesn't mean others can't see the good quali-

Figure 124: *What if you did a SWOT analysis on yourself and your life? You may be so shocked that emergency services would have to respond.*

ties in that leader. Perspectives? Negative information often tends to stick to the voter's mind more than positive. We must work through our minds to form a balanced view rather than maintain our distorted view. No wonder leaders, media, and news channels focus more on negatives than positives. Should we blame them for giving us what we want to hear, or should we take ownership and responsibility for our own behavior and do something about it?

I use SWOT analysis to form a rational analysis and see the individual in full spectrum. My analysis per SWOT may not be in line with other people's or general perspectives; it will allow me to bring into my awareness the picture of full (or near full) and not just the half-empty glass. It will offer me a broader perspective.

SWOT stands for:
- Strength: list the strengths of this person. What can they do well, what positive things have led them to where they are now, what unique traits does this person possess?
- Weaknesses: what are the things this person does not do well, what things do they need to improve, what traits you dislike about them?
- Opportunities: What opportunities can this person bring for you, your society, your country, and the world at large; what trends or shifts will this person bring or start; what strengths will they be able to capitalize on and turn them into opportunities for all of us?
- Threats: What threats does this person bring, what harm, uncertainty, or risk will we become open to should this person's weaknesses materialize?

Likewise, time and again, I have done a similar analysis for other leaders, either individually or in comparisons, such as the elections between Theresa May and Jeremy Corbyn or Boris Johnson and Jeremy Corbyn, comparing policies, Brexit, situations, and other possible outcomes. I hope you get the idea and keep in mind to remain as unbiased and fair as you possibly can.

Strengths	Weaknesses	Opportunities	Threats
Great architect and builder with class - as evidenced from his famous and good looking hotels	Makes outrageous comments - which can be very confronting but truthful	Great possibility to tackle terrorism be it ISIS, or in Pakistan or anywhere as it has been one of his top priorities	US-Russia can join hands which can be dangerous to the world
Always inspires - his speeches leave us with more energy, more positivity... Great starter of new American Revolution, largest turnout for speeches	Lacks diplomacy	Possibility of forging good US - Russia relationship which can bring peace in the world	His outrageous statements have resulted in crimes, racism etc (not his intention). People listen & act on what is being heard
Charismatic & entertaining leader. Great marketer. Has the capability to keep the audience engaged	One man show - there is a great team behind him, but in the end it is a one man show - uses different tactics (bullying, nasty) to achieve what he wants	Bringing change in the world and in terms of how people think	Devastation to the American society instead of making policies good for the American society, might end up making policies good for his businesses
Unique & smart thinking - evidenced by destroying other established candidates	Lack of political experience especially in international relations & foreign policy	Possibility of reducing crime through law and order enforcement	Dollar collapse or may default US payment resulting in financial shocks and catastrophe
Quick learner & willing to try new things to win: script, without script. Different businesses (Trump university, bottled water, card game etc.) Or evidenced from his different U turn decisions (anti-abortion, LGBT etc)	Lacks emotional touch and empathy in his speeches which is very much needed by leaders	Possibility of sorting out North Korea, bringing stability in Middle East	He could be all talk and no action - (although his history and so far the election history points to the contrary)
Never afraid of calling a spade a spade - be it Saudi Arabia, China or against Pakistan for terrorism, or even Putin	Makes friends but also makes equal or more enemies because of being abrupt and calling other person out loudly and brashly	Reduction of number of existing legislations as he is against having unnecessary numerous legislations	Robotics and automation technology will pose different challenges in future - he will need to be pragmatic
Understand politics is a dirty business and that media is corrupt so tackles both very well - shows know how to convert the disadvantages into advantages	Considered as sexist and misogynist by many. Grab them by p***y does him no favor. Numerous allegations by women	Possibility of bringing the complete overhaul to infrastructure, transport, buildings, airport, etc as being a real estate mogul this is his speciality	White supremacy could be a residual by-product as a result of this election (opportunist using his rashness to their advantage)
Being a one man show but he has the ability to pressurize and get things done	Not releasing tax returns – not required but it results in creating suspicion	Reduction to illegal immigration even more	US-China can end up in confrontation with each other, which won't be good for business due to trade wars, etc.
Appreciates and encourages others when it feels right – whether it be police officers, ex-army officials etc. Receptive of others' admiration for him - always says 'Thank you' when he feels it right	Doesn't admit his mistakes even when being at fault or wrong	Possibility of closing more loop holes in taxes should he wish, as a businessmen he knows where the loop holes exist, but doubt he would	End up creating more instability in the world with possibility of nukes being used elsewhere

Table 2: My SWOT analysis was conducted in 2016 after Donald Trump showed his intention to stand for Presidential elections and before being elected as the Republican candidate. This exercise aims to consider all possibilities based on the given knowledge and awareness one has at the time.

Strengths	Weaknesses	Opportunities	Threats
30 years experience - knows everything inside out including foreign relations	30 years of experience - means know too much and for too long to really bring about any change. Run by elites, media, big corporations so will most likely to act as a puppet	Continue strengthening relationships with Allies (ir particular EU)	Continue conflict with Russia thus resulting in much bigger War
Her experience gives her the advantage of knowing how to contest main states, hold grassroots positions, gain early momentum	Despite being in Politics for 30 years, she is considered to be one of the most unfavourable candidate by Americans in US history (and there are reasons for it)	Avoid conflict with Russia and China, thus avoid any scrt of big wars	Unable to control the growing dominance of China
Strong support from Wallstreet and big corporations, Woman card (in my opinion this is her biggest advantage)	Full of scandals and bad judgements e.g. Benghazi, email scandals, private servers, Clinton Foundation, Foreign donors	Although if she wins, most of the things will remain status quo (but there is a possibility of her bringing America together, although I doubt that she can)	Problems continues as it is (trillion dollar debt, shootings, fall in standards of living)
Unique & smart thinking, great marketer - as evidenced by destroying other established candidates.	She used to be a great inspirer as a leader but I haven't felt that from her in ages	Sigh of relief for US and rest of the world necessarily means a good and positive th ng)	In favor of opening borders - threat to safety and security of America, its nationals and its culture (it is not a catastrophic threat but still can pose a serious challenge if allowed in big numbers)
She is very private (unlike Trump, she doesn't says things openly which can be both strength and weakness)	Health issues (although not fully sure on this but media does point out towards that)		Continue supporting arms and ammunition sales in Saudi Arabia (and we know what's happening in Middle East)
Has the capacity to go to any means to match the opponent i.e. will not be afraid of getting hands as dirty as required	Has lost elections many times against different opponents (which tells a lot about her)		America will be very divided after this election so it might not be possible for her to bring everyone together
Can maintain calm composure even in heated debates and discussion. Doesn't bite upfront like Trump so doesn't trigger people (although will most likely hit it from the back)			Regulations will continue making it much more difficult and complex from a trade perspective
Has support of big and famous celebrities, leaders, CEOs and most importantly of Michelle Obama that lets her play her woman card (at emotional level) very easily			ME instability continues and can become even more instable

Table 3: My Hillary Clinton SWOT analysis as conducted in 2016.

Scenario Analysis

Leaders can't just do anything they want. They are bound by many things: constitution, donors, political party rules and manifestos, domestic vs. international policies, and more. This makes it vital to run various scenario analyses to bring into your awareness all possible outcomes and then draw the possibilities of them happening, including your tolerance or lack of tolerance should any of these occur.

Figure 125: Even the worst outcome can be pretty good. Image source: memecenter.

Rankings – who is on top?

What if Trump or Obama or Boris or Modi were footballers, and the political parties were cricket or football teams?

Have you ever been interested in football, cricket, or horse racing, for that matter? Points are allocated to each player, team, or horse based on their performance in a particular match, season, or race? Players, teams, and horses move up and down the ranking table all the time.

Why do we not apply the same mindset to politics, political parties, and leaders? Why do we take things so personally, knowing that we are 1 in 66 million and 1 in 328 million people living in the UK and USA, respectively? Even if every person in these nations were to vote, each would have made a 0.0000015% and 0.0000003% change in the UK and USA's overall result. If your contribution towards something other than politics would be that negligible, would you even care? My guess would be NO. Of course, as responsible citizens, we should care, but do we need to get personal, start having fists fights, becoming verbally abusive, and disrupt our family dinner, especially knowing that the person in front of us would have made a similarly insignificant impact on the result. Even an entire family consisting of 100 members would not have made any significant impact either.

Of course, there is a sidebar here. Only about 70% of the population is qualified to vote for whatever rules and reasons. Considering that only 30% to 75% actually vote depending on whether it is a national or a local election, here you could actually make a difference. History shows that a single percentage vote could have turned Presidential elections, at least in the United States. E.g., in 1960, a change of less than a percentage point in a few states would have meant Nixon becoming President eight years sooner, and Mr. Kennedy might still be alive. Might.

My suggestion would be to start ranking the leaders on their performance throughout their time in office, just like you would rank them based on their performance in debates before elections. Don't get fixated on the leader or party; judge them based on their performance per policy, per statement, per season, per year, and per election, and then rank them using merits and demerits. E.g., Trump was perhaps -10 in your ranking, but based on his performance with North Korea, he should be getting at least +1. Perhaps a -1 for pulling out of the Paris Agreement if

Football Specials Betting Odds

| Football Specials | Enhanced Multiples | Manager Specials | |

FIFA Mens Player Of The Year Winner — View all odds >

| Robert Lewandowski | 1/33 | Cristiano Ronaldo | 12/1 |
| Lionel Messi | 20/1 | Mo Salah | 28/1 |

Jack Wilshere Next Permanent Club — View all odds >

| Arsenal | 9/5 | Rangers | 7/2 |
| Aston Villa | 5/1 | Any MLS club | 9/1 |

Christian Eriksen Club After January Transfer Window — View all odds >

| Inter Milan | 1/2 | Borussia Dortmund | 4/1 |
| Arsenal | 9/1 | Man Utd | 12/1 |

Figure 126: Football betting odds.

you believe in climate change and that accord, a +1 for calling out on China on intellectual property thefts that China has been doing for decades. You rank the policies that matter to you the most, allocate them a weighted percentage before ranking each leader based on that percentage without bias. Repeat this process for all leaders in contention. **To play our part in bringing change in our society and having the right kind of leadership, we must move away from our closed-mindedness towards having an open mind and tolerant approach, including the opposition and any leaders we may dislike.**

Figure 127: Cristiano Ronaldo trends in odds based on his performance.

Gender in Politics

There is no evidence that women perform differently in politics. Still, there are clearly many reasons why it is harder for women to enter the political arena and progress once in position.

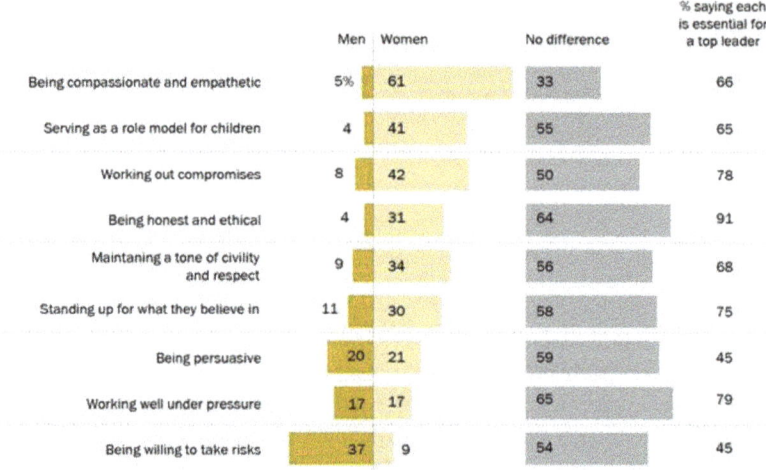

% saying men/women in high political offices are better at each of the following

	Men	Women	No difference	% saying each is essential for a top leader
Being compassionate and empathetic	5%	61	33	66
Serving as a role model for children	4	41	55	65
Working out compromises	8	42	50	78
Being honest and ethical	4	31	64	91
Maintaning a tone of civility and respect	9	34	56	68
Standing up for what they believe in	11	30	58	75
Being persuasive	20	21	59	45
Working well under pressure	17	17	65	79
Being willing to take risks	37	9	54	45

Figure 128: Men see no gap between male and female political leaders on key leadership qualities; among those who see a difference, women have the edge on most. Source: Survey of US adults conducted June 9-July 2, 2018. "Women and Leadership, 2018". Pew Research Center.

Women politicians often hear from male counterparts, 'I am all for equality, but politics is a dirty game.' It is, but that is what the experienced political and campaign managers and advisors are for.

It is evident in studies and polls that female leaders are considered more compassionate and empathetic than men. It has also been said that women have many other qualities superior to their male counterparts. In politics, compared to men, women are more likely to be viewed as better role models; in business, more see them as better able to create a safe and respectful workplace.

As a final point on this subject, in modern history, name a woman who started a war?

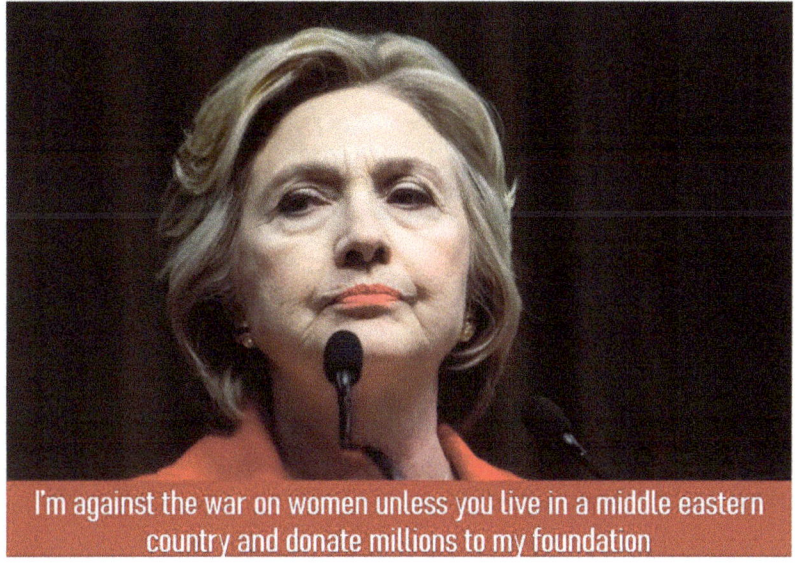

I'm against the war on women unless you live in a middle eastern country and donate millions to my foundation

Figure 129: What candidates say will depend on who is behind them to keep them in power.

Conclusion

Now that we have talked about leaders and leadership, it is time to go one step further and discuss relationships. As we keep getting deeper into this, in a few chapters, we will hopefully come out on the other side with some reasonable answers and suggestions for a better way of dealing with political conversations without having a bloodbath or banging heads (and perhaps with better politics as well).

CHAPTER ELEVEN

RELATIONSHIP

Without relationships, we would all become hermits and very cranky. With relationships, we don't do much better, but for some reason, we keep trying.

Michael Charming

Introduction

Relationships have been discussed in almost every chapter, but now we go a bit deeper, delving into more aspects of relationships. We will look at the most important relationship, the one with yourself, before observing your interaction with others. Many considerations drive these interactions, including your childhood and adult history, needs, wants, and internal and external realities.

Relationship with Self

In Chapter Three, though we covered the human body composition, we will now discuss this in more detail. It shouldn't surprise us that we don't really spend enough time with ourselves to get to know who we are, what we need and desire in life, and our relationships - from every policymaker, every leader, and in every aspect of life. What things trigger us at different times during political discussions? How would we want others to behave towards us when triggered?

Due to a lack of this awareness, we often react rather than respond. We have become accustomed to the hard and fast life, often forgetting to pause, reflect, and realize why it is essential to fully understand, acknowledge, and appreciate who we truly are. Each of us is an individual who not only just shows up in the physical body we see but is also an individual who comes up with mental arguments, who feels emotionally, who aspires towards creating a better life for self or many by bringing spiritual well-being. Would you agree? It is not easy to see human beings beyond the physical or interact with them beyond what happens on the surface level. Some might consider all of this strange. I also felt that way a few years ago, and if you had said this to me, while it would have made sense, my immediate reaction would have been saying something like, 'have you gone out of your mind, are you high on something, or are you playing a prank'.

My seven-year journey has led me to dive deeper into each of these, giving me a felt sense experience and made me realize that mediocre is the only way to describe how we really live in this human body. Motivational coaches constantly use the term, **'we are not realizing our full human potential'** to achieve our life goals. The journey towards self-understanding and self-awareness begins by diving inwards (though external realities do play a part. More on this later).

Figure 130: Some researchers say we only use 2% of the brain; others say 10%. But what we do know for sure is that there is always room to increase our human potential.

We need to become less reactive during interactions with others, meaning less automatic action based on our set of values and beliefs, and more responsive, meaning thoughtful action based on what we are being told by the other person. We will then stop this knee jerk and mostly negative and vituperative reaction to others' opinions.

Don't you think it is our duty and responsibility to present the world with the best version of ourselves? Before driving our car, we ensure it is fully functional. If we are aware it is faulty, we become extra cautious. If we are unaware that our car is faulty, we could have an accident. Yes, an accident may cause someone else to suffer because of us and our faulty car. We tend to treat our car so well, but we treat our body, the most fascinating machine that we have ever driven, in a shitty way. No wonder there are accidents everywhere – physically, we might avoid bumping into each other, but our energies are colliding, be it in the tube, in the supermarket, at the fair, or in political conversations.

Anger experienced across the road can affect our mood and alter our state. Suppose our partner is upset; for us to really relate, we will find ourselves having to shift our mood, even though we might not have anything to do with the experience causing their upset. I hope you get my point. So, let's learn to drive this human car well and teach others to drive it well, too. In doing so, we will have less physical, energetic, mental, emotional, and spiritual collisions, giving everyone more breathing space, a safe space, a space that would allow each of us to expand rather than contract. This space would allow us to authentically connect with each other rather than running away or giving the other person the cold shoulder.

So, being the driver of this vital human car, don't you believe we should know which parts are perfect and which are faulty – allowing us to exercise caution. Not only for ourselves, but for the other drivers sharing the same road of life? We have seen how every aspect of society is intertwined. Every aspect affects who we are, making this human body not only an incredible and complex machine but an overly complicated one due to a lack of self-awareness. We talked about emotional sensitive spots or triggers that exist in every person. The question is, are you aware of your own sensitive spots or triggers?

Figure 131: Resistance to illegal immigration has been an American policy for decades. I cannot ever remember a leader saying, 'illegal immigrants are welcome.'. Many do not understand the difference between 'illegal immigrant' and 'legal immigrant'.

Do you find yourself getting agitated or nervous at the immigration bill being passed? Do you find yourself full of joy when social benefits are announced? Do you find yourself frustrated when Brexit gets delayed for another six months? Do you find yourself fuming with anger when Trump supporters say they believe he is sent by God to save America? Do you find yourself disappointed when a policy relating to gender for LGBTQ is made that makes it mandatory for them to classify themselves either as male or female?

More importantly, if these affect you, do you know how others can help and support you in this condition? On the road, if we see an accident, we either stop and help, or we stop and observe, or we ignore it and keep driving. What we don't do is to intentionally smash our car into the accident, increasing the impact. I do not drive a car, and I have never driven a car, but I know a bit about it because I can relate. This is what relationships are like. We don't need to have any experience to see if we can understand the situation completely, but we do need to know how to relate. We will discuss this again in the last chapter, but let's work on the basic ABC of relationships. No one gives us lessons in this area, not our parents, not society, and not the media in a way that helps us experience it from the perspective of being part of the accident in a safe manner rather than a passer-by or being someone who has been amplified and becomes part of the accident bringing in more danger to everyone.

Here is another analogy before we really start the first section. The vast majority of us know how a phone works, what to do when the battery is flat, and how to operate a few basic features. Wouldn't it be amazing to spend some time really learning some cool features so we can enjoy our phone entirely and not just a tiny portion of it? The manufacturers make it so easy for us by providing the guide. I wonder how many users actually read that from front to the back?

Would it not be easier if we had a user guide for our human car to give to others when we meet? Suppose we are developing deeper friendships, and most importantly, having conversations on confronting topics like politics, sexuality, and religion. Wouldn't this be a useful tool for all to have? A phone is an inanimate object, designed for experiences and makes our lives smoother and more interesting. What does this say about this human car? Does it not deserve more attention, more focus, and more awareness, especially given that no matter how we engage or relate with someone, it will impact them, one way or another, whether mildly or intensely?

Knowing about politics is important, but knowing about self is far more critical and something we hardly pay attention to. When you are angry, how do you behave? How does your body respond? People experience a reaction, but we often are unaware of that experience in our bodies.

If I were to ask you, "can you list everything relating to political conversations that makes you angry," will you be able to do so? If I were to ask you, "how and where do you feel in your body when different issues are discussed," will you be able to do so? Can you list this with specificity, in concrete form, in an understandable language to give a real and tangible sense of where, how, which intensity, how much pressure, and the impact it creates (hint: recall sensations from Chapter One)?

If you can identify what makes you angry and where you feel it in your body. In that case, you are more prone to deal with responding rather than reacting to others. Reacting is automatic, visceral, and almost Pavlovian. Responding requires a step back, some thought, some reflection to emotional, mental, physical, and other states before giving a reasoned and controlled reply.

Without knowing ourselves, how can we expect our family, friends, or even strangers, who are in similar situations, to understand us, know our feelings, and expect them to relate with us amicably and harmoniously? The first step of relating is relating to self. But in life, even this is back to front. We appear before others, without knowing who we truly are, and then expect them to figure us out in a few milliseconds about our tastes, our needs, our history, our political stance, and that they should know the impact their relating will cause on us. If we find ourselves not being heard, seen, or understood, we come with defenses leading to full-blown confrontation, as seen in Chapter One.

Sometimes this is visible, but most of the time, all of this happens in the subconscious mind and energetic body, in our psyche, without us being aware of it. It is so simple to point fingers at someone else, but it is challenging to look back to see whether our behavior is in line with what we are preaching.

The next section might not be an easy read, so if you find yourself getting triggered or overwhelmed, take a rest and slow down your breathing. While looking at each of these bodies/layers, this time, focus on self. Understanding yourself in this way is the hardest part. It might sound strange, but the good news is that once you get the hang of this, not only will relating with yourself but also with others becomes easy and natural. Notice and see whether you relate with any or all of these.

The Emotional Body: What are the political issues that make you happy and joyful (let's list them under Group A)? What are the issues that make you angry, hurt, and disappointed (Group B)? Where do you feel them in your body? Which of your needs are being fulfilled in the issues relating to Group A, and what is your history of the needs not being fulfilled under Group B? Here is an example we will use throughout this section. Trump is separating kids from parents who are illegal immigrants. Does this make you feel upset? Most likely, you might feel heaviness in the heart or contraction in the belly. You feel the need for care and love for children taken away from their parents. A few questions to ask here would be: do you feel the same way every time you see this news irrespective of who the leader is, or is it more related explicitly to Trump's act? Had this news not been brought to your attention, would you willfully do the research on where else are such acts and laws passed, and if so, what would you do (or have done) about them? What is your point of view of someone doing things illegally? Do you consider it okay, or do you believe that people should follow the law?

Figure 132: It is definitely not fair to separate kids from parents. Is it okay for parents to take the risk despite being aware of the repercussions? If someone (a homeless person with a kid) barged into your home without your consent, will you welcome them in with a cup of tea, or will you show them the way out?

The Mental Body: Using the same example. What are your beliefs relating to a couple, whether they should have children or not, considering that they are not well-off financially or emotionally stable? If you are married with kids, how is this showing up for you in your situation? How do you think it would show up for you if you were to have kids in the future? What are your beliefs relating to parents engaging in acts that could affect their kids' safety? Should they indulge in or refrain from those acts? How many children besides your own, if any, have you supported or sponsored in the past? Are you aware that a legal process exists allowing immigrants to take shelter in the country? What are your core values surrounding immigration, immigration laws, border force officers, relevant policymakers, and people who do not adhere to such laws? What are your past experiences, whether as a traveler, an immigrant, or someone who has witnessed immigrants joining your society?

The Energetic Body: While it is easy to place blame out of anger or hurt for putting illegal immigrants in cages, but what would you say regarding your feelings towards someone who cares more for his country and his country's people than people from other countries? Understandably, you need to show your feelings for the illegal immigrants because you feel sympathy for them, relating to their countries' poor conditions. Still, how many homeless people or orphaned kids have you helped or allowed into your own home with the offer of the best treatment? Have you perhaps offered permanent shelter to at least one of them in your home? Considering that the physical human body only needs up to seven or eight feet above the ground, a three-by-six-foot area to sleep, surely your home could easily accommodate someone. Is your heart is big and full of enough unconditional love to create such space for someone? Have you thought about it and done something in this regard?

We often project our unhappiness about things happening elsewhere; it becomes a hard stance, an outlet based on habits and daily practices. What are the ways you connect with yourself, especially energetically? Why is it important? Are you ready to take a closer look at internal vs. external realities?

The Physical Body: Have you considered the financial, human logistics, and resources required to cater to all such immigrants? Aspects to carefully consider are the decade-long cultural integration process, education, language barriers, and welfare conducive to them and society. How does this impact the mindset of those who have not yet immigrated but would now be willing to take the risk? Integration is not only for immigrants; it also affects everyone already living in that society. Have you considered this impact? Will it create more safety or less safety for them, more or fewer employment opportunities, and will it make their lives easier or more difficult?

The Spiritual Body: What do you really want in terms of immigration? What are your desires and fears around this issue? Is doing something about immigrants' core to you and your needs? Because we can't have every need fulfilled (hint: Chapter Four), we need to know which core needs would need to be fulfilled and which we could be okay with if not fulfilled. One can't expect to fall in love and not feel hurt or pain because love and hurt are part of the same package. Suppose you care for immigrants because it is your overall life purpose. In that case, you should also care for the people in the

Figure 133: Someone, human or icon, has to be the country's 'voice' to do the right thing.

communities where the immigrants are being placed. If it is not your life purpose, then be willing to care less and compromise.

The journey with self begins with knowing each of these layers of the body. Know your pain points, triggers, beliefs, fears, and be willing to leave your comfort zone. Develop a sense of self-control and life purpose, and understand how supporting particular causes align with your life purpose.

As a bodyworker, I am always surprised at what people withhold and don't discuss or let out in any way. They, too, are surprised. Rage towards a dad who was controlling during their childhood, anger and pain over a relationship breakup that occurred years before, childhood trauma and abuse that they had no recollection or memory of, various healing modalities used after a miscarriage without realizing that pain was still held in the womb, becoming resentful at themselves for spending half of their life running after wants instead of desires, seeking attention in covert ways to hide their insecurities, not giving themselves permission to experience pleasure, always putting others needs before their own, doing something from a sense obligation because of a fear of abandonment rather than from deep core place of desire and intent, developing addictions due to dismissing their own emotions, feelings and desire for connection, and repeating the same pattern in a relationship with a partner often taken due to a lack of love and other issues from their mother; the list is endless.

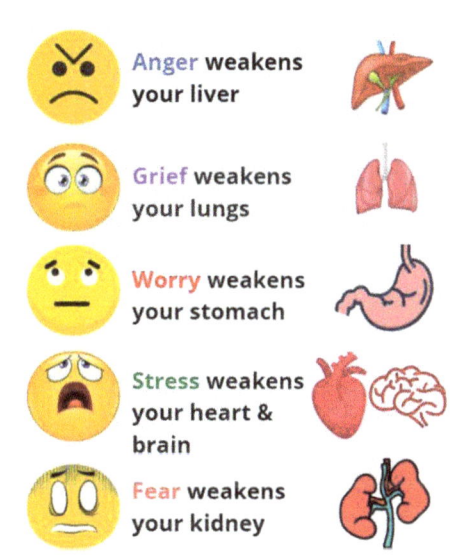

Figure 134: How emotions harm your body

To know about yourself at a basic level, ask these simple questions. Are you an introvert or an extrovert? Are you organized or disorganized? Which laws and rules do you embrace, and which do your rebel against? Are you patient or impatient? Do you generally have a lot of energy or do you lack energy? Do you take responsibility for your mistakes or dodge and blame someone else? To know about yourself at the next level, ask these questions: what are your beliefs relating to specific policies, leaders, and government? Where did you pick up the habits that you do not want to associate with anymore? What kind of painful experiences have you been in your life, and have you dealt with that pain completely? Likewise, to know about yourself even further, a new set of questions would need to be asked.

Relationships with Others

My personal belief is that we should not even think about connecting or relating with others unless we know ourselves well enough to create our human car guide to be given to others as a handout.

As a sexuality and relationship coach, I say to my clients, *'Relationships go beyond you but start with you. Relationships are not as complicated as we make them out to be, but we are. Keep it simple.'*

Figure 135: An easy but unhealthy relationship ploy is blaming your partner for something you don't want to do.

The human species has made so much progress, from Ice Age to the Industrial Revolution, from technological innovations to artificial intelligence, from finding our way to the Moon to the deepest parts of the Earth. We have created clones and connected everyone worldwide. Still, it feels like we have regressed, especially in recent times when relating with other human beings.

Political conversations within a family, with friends, or with strangers, can quickly create an 'us against them' or 'us against the whole world' or 'me against you' (as seen in Chapter Six). If we are conversing with underlying intentions, you will find that there is really no such distinction.

% of single-and-looking **Republicans/Democrats** who say they would/would NOT consider being in a committed relationship with someone who ...

	AMONG REP/LEAN REP		AMONG DEM/LEAN DEM	
	Voted for Clinton	Is a Democrat	Voted for Trump	Is a Republican
		74		57
Net	51	12		8
Already have Definitely would	4 12	21	28	16
Probably would	35	40	4 8 16	33
Probably would NOT	29	12 12 24	27	24 19
Definitely would NOT	19		45	43
Net	47		71	

Note: "Single-and-looking" refers to those who are not in a committed romantic relationship but are looking for one. Figures may not add to subtotals due to rounding.

Figure 136: A survey showed that about seven in ten Democratic daters would not consider a relationship with a Trump supporter. Source: Survey of US adults conducted Oct. 16-18, 2019. Pew Research Center.

A study showed that over 50% of those interviewed either have had or would consider having a relationship with someone who supports another political party.[31] The percentages in the very young and very old were substantially lower. Yet only 5% of interviewees confirmed a relationship breakdown over politics.

Almost 60% refused to share their family's political views. When it came to climate change, one in six would not have a relationship with someone who didn't share their views, and four in ten said it would be hard but not a deal-breaker.

We carry pain from our childhood and upbringing, often displaying narcissistic tendencies in one form or another. We like to believe that time has healed us, and we are perfect or nearly perfect, but others are not.

More than we care to admit, we actually live in denial with shame, guilt, and regrets. No wonder we continuously aspire to and externally seek happiness, joy, positivity, and pleasure. Since childhood, we have been carrying these, like a rucksack; hence, it doesn't feel heavy because we cannot remember the experience of not carrying such a heavy load.

In my line as a bodyworker, I work on removing this (invisible) rucksack; only then do people begin to realize what life should actually feel like without this load. They get to experience something tangible to compare, no wonder many want more sessions after their first, and no wonder they start feeling orgasmic. (But let's keep it to politics). As a child, most of us have actually experienced life without the rucksack. As adults, it hard to even imagine or recall what it might have felt like. No wonder people say, 'children are the best, childhood is the best.' More on what causes this change later in this chapter.

Do you desire to be with someone of similar views or different views in a friendship or a relationship?

Figure 137: Our mind and trapped emotions fuck with us far more than we realize.

'It's just politics', 'I don't want politics to come between us', 'I don't ever want to discuss politics with you because it spoils our mood and has an effect on our relationship', 'Oh no, not again. Now, you will get upset, groan, moan, and want to sleep alone', 'why did you have to mention it in the first instance'.

THIS IS A DUCK BUTT.

NO POLITICS. NO VIRUS. JUST A DUCK BUTT.

Figure 138: On social media, people argue about anything. Some will argue that this is not a duck; it is definitely not white; it cannot be a butt because two cheeks are missing. Or, this duck has ulterior motives. Why is the head not straight? And the list goes on and on.... Freedom of expression. Stating your point of view is one thing but making a fool of yourself is quite another. Image source: meme generator.

These phrases are so common between couples. With the minimal adjustment, they could refer to friendships. Before I started the orgasm (or self-development) journey, these were ubiquitous phrases between my then partner and me. We would often find ourselves taking different stances, having an argument which would escalate to a bigger conflict and almost towards the point of breaking the relationship (sex, what sex? when this happens, no sex for sure; hence, one more reason not to talk about politics between us).

A few years back, I was three or four years into the orgasm journey and found my experiences to be very different with my partner at that time. We often found ourselves on opposite sides of the political spectrum, but this brought a lot of chemistry between us, causing both to want to engage in more political conversations. (Hint: without any conflict or hardly any). So, the question is, what made this dynamic shift? Wouldn't we all want to be in such a position? How amazing would it feel to be like this, not only with our partner, our parents, and our friends but also with strangers? Hence, me, writing this book, shouldn't come as a surprise 😊. Most of what I have already shared should have given you the insights into these tips, but I will mention some again as reminders.

While the tips refer to a relationship with a lover, they could be applied to anyone you want to converse with. My partner played a significant role in having me understand how to have conversations. I was eager to learn for many reasons and on many levels.

- Begin with knowing more about yourself and then share with each other continuously. Each will have the clues of what to do when the other is triggered, what support to provide, and what signs to look for. These include body language, rolling of eyes, body feeling fatigued, voice getting louder, and energetically feeling intense or heavy.
- Zero tolerance for abusive and passive-aggressive communication. Follow protocols of matured conversation with no stereotyping, labeling, belittling, disrespecting, insulting, dismissing, cutting them off, or jumping topics.

- The intention should not be on changing the other person's opinion, but of sharing perspectives, ideas, education, know-how, and then let them decide what they want to do with this enhanced knowledge and awareness.
- Communication is a two-way street, and roles need to be switched and inter-changed, perhaps not during the same conversation, especially if it feels heavy, but at other times. Rotation of roles is essential even if the other person knows far less or nothing because one can always give an opinion or share their viewpoints based on what they know.
- Focusing on dialog and discussion rather than a debate (more on this in the next chapter).
- Decide on the timeframe. How long do you want to have this conversation and set a timer beforehand? Know when either or both of you have had enough or if you wish to continue discussing. Agree and adjust the timer accordingly.
- It is not about lecturing but about sharing. It is not about trusting or not trusting what you say. Without trust, the person wouldn't be with you or having this conversation, so avoid unnecessary jargon.
- Agree beforehand on the issues and topics you want to talk about. Political conversations are intertwined, so discussing one issue will open the pandora's box of issues. Suppose you are unable to agree on the issues you want to discuss. In that case, each of you can pick the one that matters most to you and discuss that, ensuring the other person shows interest and is genuinely present.
- Share well-researched information. Keep your relationship out of the discussion. The other person needs to be respected and should be provided the best of your best knowledge. Treat them as you would like to be treated by them in every single aspect of this conversation. If you are unsure about any information, communicate that you do not know, rather than pretending or making something up.
- Agree on the intention of the conversation beforehand. Is it to exchange knowledge and ideas, prove yourself, listen to the other person, find a solution, think out loud, or come up with various scenarios? Conversations can quickly deviate from the original intention, making it important to be aware of both parties' original intentions. If you find it shifting, it is important to mention that and agree before proceeding further or adjust accordingly.
- Have pen and paper handy to note down points that come up during the conversation. Some of these you might want to discuss later, another time, or some you may want to reflect on for yourself. Taking notes will help us stay present and relaxed, allowing us not to interrupt the other person. We often show this tendency to interrupt the other person because we feel we may forget this point or will not get a chance to express our view. Keep in mind that political conversations will bring up old wounds (non-supporting beliefs, past bad experiences), so it is crucial to notice when these show up and agree to discuss these later as part of relating to each other.

Remember, a relationship is about relating with one another and growing together. Having political conversations is one of the best ways because it provides excellent ammunition but needs to be handled with care and diligence. Follow these guidelines, and you will be able to run through the landmines. These days, I see many in relationships that are shallow, as deep as a small puddle. Do we want to dive deeper into the oceans' depths, or do we want to keep splashing in the puddle and shallowness? Given a choice, I would always prefer to date women with opposing views. It will allow us to learn more through shared conversations without doing the work relating to the other side. I love such friends (i.e., those with opposing views) as long as they follow the protocols of mutual respect, matured conversations, and can talk in the sense of positives, negatives, and SWOT, for each candidate. Natural-

Figure 139: There are times when your silence says it best. Inquire before speaking. When it is so easy for anyone to feel offended in today's days, we should even ask permission to sneeze or cough. Would requesting permission to breathe in their space be considered a violation of their constitutional rights?

ly, I am not keen to talk with people who can't see the positives of candidates they dislike. We should thank our friends with opposing views as they make our lives easier by saving us the time we may have spent researching the opposing side. Be careful to note whether they are sharing biased or factual information.

Issues will arise time and again, whether you talk with your partner or not. In orgasm, my work as a coach helps clients talk through things that they have generally not discussed. At times we feel discomfort, so what do we do then, and who do we ask for support? Growth lies in moving out of your comfort zone and listening to others, especially those with opposing views.

A Few Important Concepts to Consider When Relating with Anyone

Connecting with Your Inner Child

Have you ever wondered why some adults behave like children or have childish thoughts? Ignoring the absence of proper communication, why do some adults display some terrible patterns even though they initially seem intelligent, well-mannered, and worthy? The modality of the inner child, which is very popular in psychology, might help answer some questions. The inner child technique allows one to go into the deepest recess of the mind (subconscious and unconscious) to uncover the negative or unwanted adult behaviors (self-sabotage, passive hostility, self-destructive symptoms) that existed during childhood.

You might be wondering what this has to do with politics? Well, not directly; it has to do with relationships. With a wounded or neglected inner child, people often exhibit these behaviors in relationships with others. These become more pronounced in

Figure 140: Isn't that the truth?

confrontational topics like politics. Have you been accused of being immature, petulant, incorrigible, and stubborn in a political argument? Well, there is a plateful of inner child words. So, the question to ask is, how was your childhood? Experiences relating to the loss of someone close, any kind of abuse (physical, emotional, sexual, mental, or substance), bullying, serious illnesses, a victim of violence, feeling isolated, and anxiety are some examples.

A wounded inner child often manifests in distrust in people, mood swings, inability to maintain relationships, difficulty sleeping, feeling stressed, developing an addiction, or other similar forms of mental and emotional symptoms, thus impacting our choices, our response to challenges, and our behaviors.

Everyone experiences various kinds of traumas throughout their lives (more on this in Chapter Fourteen). If we have experienced trauma during childhood, which we, or our body, has been unable to deal or cope with. In that case, it will be carried into our adulthood, impacting our behaviors.

Figure 141: When an adult has a tantrum or outburst, it generally indicates that their inner child needs attention, validation, comfort, and healing.

If this concept sounds strange or unfamiliar, my invitation would be to remain open and curious. There is a reason professionals working in neuro-linguistic programming (NLP), hypnotherapy, support groups, and more focus on this therapy.

What is this inner child? First things first, it doesn't mean a physical child within us; it is a figurative and metaphorical term. In psychology, the inner child refers to an individual's childlike aspect, often conceived as a semi-independent persona in the deep conscious parts (the unconscious) of the mind during childhood.[32] Any unmet need and suppression of emotions during childhood (anger, hurt, sadness, trauma) continues to be held by this inner child as we grow up. *'You'd better not say what you really think', 'you are not smart enough', 'do as you are told', 'You aren't allowed to be spontaneous', 'punished for speaking up or acting differently', 'shamed, criticized, held responsible for sufferings of the family regularly', 'you end up becoming people pleaser', 'a hoarder, an inadequate, unable to express your emotions', 'fear of abandonment'.*

Connecting with the inner child helps access these fragmented parts of self to uncover the deeply rooted phobias, fears, insecurities, and other destructive patterns. Quite often in politics, I see many people expressing their opinions based on these deep-seated emotions and not being aware of it. Inner child work allows one to contact, understand, embrace, and heal the inner child, allowing one to experience positivity, joy, playfulness, innocence, and exercise curiosity more often. According to the Cambridge Dictionary, "Your inner child is the part of your personality that still reacts and feels like a child." During my sessions as a bodyworker, I focus on connecting with the person's inner child and understanding this child's needs.

"It sounds corny, but I've promised my inner child that never again will I abandon myself for anything or anyone else." - Wynonna Judd
"Caring for your inner child has a powerful and surprisingly quick result: Do it and the child heals." - Martha Beck

Dealing with the inner child is often difficult and uncomfortable, as it brings pain, hurt, and upset, but it is important to note that these experiences are only temporary. Once the inner child is liberated, one begins to experience joy, happiness, and pleasure in life, impacting one's attitude towards life positively, including political decisions and opinions. **Globally, we should have and celebrate Inner-Child Day. Everyone can connect with and bring their inner child out.**

Instead of only focusing on leaders' weaknesses, one might start focusing on their strengths, including looking at positive sides more than negative attributes of the leaders they dislike. Just because this child has been ignored doesn't mean it doesn't exist. This child has always been there and is often craving attention, seeking love, care, and compassion. Since people are unaware, they cannot meet the needs of this child. The pain and hurt suffered during childhood (or even during the rest of the life), can you tell me where that goes? Surely it doesn't just leave the body and walk away? It should now come as no surprise why we often see such a tremendous change in many people's behaviors during political conversations. Some may show their true colors or their true (or deeply hidden) personalities make an appearance. One may wonder, *'what has happened to this person, all of a sudden?'*

Notice which of the tendencies you show or your friend shows when you have political conversations, and then inquire about their childhood, should they be willing to share.

The Karpman Drama Triangle

When considering relating with others, talking about politics wouldn't be complete without focusing on the Karpman Drama Triangle. Stephen Karpman developed this forty years ago, but it is still very relevant today. Why? Because people exhibit such behaviors. The Karpman Drama Triangle is a dynamic model that many people play out unconsciously or manipulate other people to play during social interactions and conflicts. There are three roles within this triangle:

- **Victim:** stance is *'poor me';* they see themselves as victimized, oppressed, powerless, dejected, ashamed, hopeless, and helpless; they deny ownership of their actions for their current circumstances and hold others responsible for them. They will always be looking for someone else to rescue them (the rescuer). If that person doesn't meet their expectations, they will perceive them as the persecutor. They will often have difficulties making decisions, understanding self-destructive and self-perpetuating behaviors, finding solutions to resolve problems, and denying any potential for self-generated power. *'The world is collapsing', 'your decision on selecting XYZ leader has caused all my agony'.*
- **Rescuer** (the fixers, the saviors, the nice guy/girl who hooks into the victim): stance is *'let me help you'.* They see themselves as someone who needs to help other people feel good about themselves while often neglecting their own needs and fulfillment. They need victims to feel good about themselves and feel guilty when they are not rescuing someone. They often feel exhausted, tired, overworked, and stretched but carry a lot of underlying resentment, which they might not be aware of. Their belief is, *'If I take care of them, sooner or later, they will take care of me or give me respect', 'if Trump really loves the country, he wouldn't be doing this', 'If you need me, you will not leave me'.*
- **Persecutors**: stance is *'it's all your fault'* and see themselves as someone *who needs* someone to be blamed for the victims. They have strict and rigid limits, can be controlling, authoritative, and often use threats, attacks, and bullying behaviors to control and dominate. They are rigid but never vulnerable, often complain and criticize but offer no solutions, and take no action in resolving the issues; neither do they help anyone solve the problems. Their behavior is most likely based on shame, perhaps, some sort of abuse received during childhood. They tend to deny their vulnerabilities and inadequacies but tend to continually fight to survive. *'Life is tough. And you are no exception to this equation', 'Many countries have been ripping America. It is all your fault', 'Had you not supported the BLM movement, we wouldn't have had chaos, thuggery, and loss of life and property'.*

During political conversations, we will often encounter people who play versions of each of these roles at some point, without actually getting out of the triangle, seeing the bigger picture, or taking responsibility for the part they are playing. The characters are stuck in yet constantly feeding the loop. The victim depends on the rescuer. The rescuer needs the victim to feel good. The persecutor needs a scapegoat, either the victim or the rescuer, to feel superior. This creates dysfunctional social dynamics with unhealthy and toxic relationship behavior, which impacts us directly or indirectly. Having studied about society in Chapter Seven, it should come as no surprise that every single person, whether we know them or not, whether we like them or not, with ten homes or without a single home, plays a part in the matrix of the very society we found ourselves in.

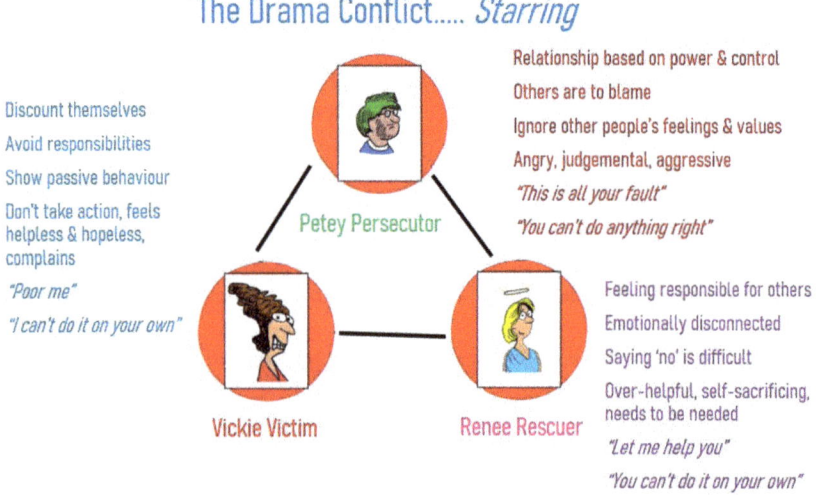

The Drama Conflict..... *Starring*

Discount themselves

Avoid responsibilities

Show passive behaviour

Don't take action, feels helpless & hopeless, complains

"Poor me"

"I can't do it on your own"

Petey Persecutor

Relationship based on power & control

Others are to blame

Ignore other people's feelings & values

Angry, judgemental, aggressive

"This is all your fault"

"You can't do anything right"

Vickie Victim

Renee Rescuer

Feeling responsible for others

Emotionally disconnected

Saying 'no' is difficult

Over-helpful, self-sacrificing, needs to be needed

"Let me help you"

"You can't do it on your own"

Figure 142: Watching the unfolding Drama from a Triangular view!

Any of the people involved (or someone from outside) would need to become conscious of and show the repeated pattern played out for anyone to change this dynamic. Victims must take responsibility for their actions rather than looking for saviors, challenge their deep core beliefs, and develop leadership and decision-making abilities. Rescuers should focus on their needs and only help others (preferably when asked) without reciprocity expectations. And persecutors should focus on self-accountability, be willing to become vulnerable, and work towards relinquishing control. If you take a moment, will you be able to identify your friends or family members who would fit in any of these categories? It is important to note that these are roles and not the characteristics of the person. Your friend might not be any of these in reality, but as soon as political conversations start, they are triggered and start acting out these roles unconsciously.

Relationship and Interplay between Internal vs. External Realities

❖ *Budget realities confront McDaniel's rhetoric*
❖ *Sanders campaign plans clash with political realities*
❖ *Italian campaign promises gloss over grim economic realities*
❖ *EU to adapt its foreign policy to new realities, crises*
❖ *Analysis: Trump's old ways colliding with new realities*
❖ *African start-ups aim high, harsh realities temper hopes*

We are affected by the interplay between our internal and external realities. Internal realities would be composed of everything relating to human composition (as per Chapter Three), being our belief systems and fantasies, the conscious, subconscious, and deeply conscious (unconscious), our physical body make up (the eleven body systems, the erratic impulses sent by neurons, the chemical interactions), our energy pathways, our spiritual path and life purpose, our ideas, our thoughts and behavior patterns, and our dreams, sensations, breath, and imaginations.

The external realities consist of everything that is outside of us but still within our radar – the news and media around the world that we see or hear, the society we live in, the energies of other people interacting, especially those coming towards us, our home and family members or housemates, the government, the pandemic, this book, the movies we have an option to choose, the leader and policies that we are currently listening to or reading about, and several different circumstances.

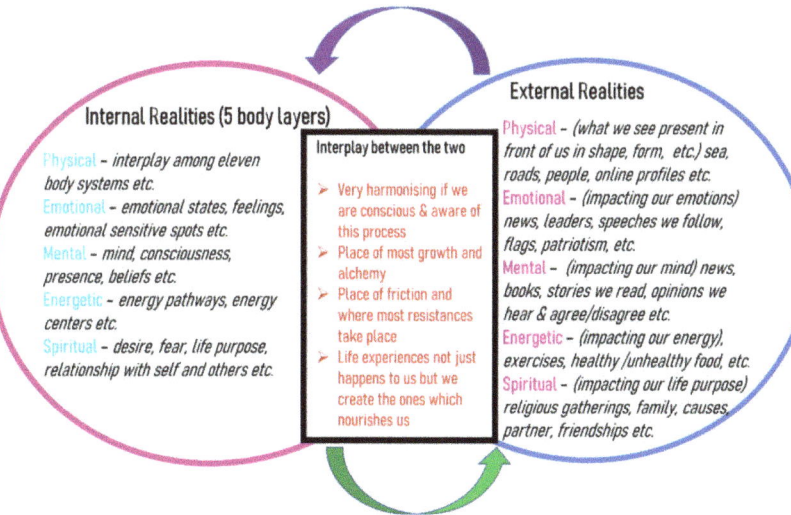

Figure 143: The interrelationship between internal and ex-ternal realities.

The meaning we give to what we see externally depends on the associations we make about the information coming towards us internally. Hence, talking about the interrelationship between internal and external realities encompasses perception in a much broader and deeper sense. Perception, per psychology and the cognitive sciences, is the process of getting, interpreting, selecting, and organizing sensory information. While perception is an active process, the interplay between internal and external realities is a dynamic process.

As a human, if we are to have better, clearer, and harmonious relationships between our internal and external realities, we would need to work on clearing and detoxing our human system allowing the information perceived by us to be accepted neutrally, so that we can put enough initial unbiased attention on anything we aim to conceive before internalizing that information. These internal and external experiences become part of our memories, affecting how we behave, relate with ourselves and others, and show up in the world. Being conscious of this process lets us impact this interplay and become more well-rounded individuals, allowing us to have political or any other conversations in a way that feels healthier not only for us but also for others, no matter what their viewpoints might be. *'The reality of situation or policy or his tweet is A, B, or C'*. Well, my question would be, *'Your reality or mine'*.

A few tips on how to make the most from this interplay:

+ Be conscious of the volume and type of information you are consuming from your external reality.
+ Be conscious of how you feel internally. Be mindful of all layers of your body (perhaps via body scanning throughout the day).
+ Work on clearing and detoxing your unwanted sensitive spots (triggers).
+ Engage in activities that bring more awareness, presence, and consciousness to whatever you do. Activities like yoga, drawing, dance, and meditation would be suitable.
+ Pay attention to subtleties.
+ Reflect on your internal realities from time to time.
+ Be willing to change the external realities and work on altering the internal realities if they no longer feel right.

Blind Spots – visible to others but not to self

❖ *Terror threat 'blind spots' warning*
❖ *Shooters sometimes exploit limited weapons laws, blind spots*
❖ *Accused of racism, renowned museum confronts its blind spots*
❖ *Insurance blind spots: 5 coverage gaps that could cost you*

We discussed triggers in Chapter Three (and ever since). These spots are so sensitive for us if touched, they are bound to cause some sort of reaction. When these spots are not known, or in our awareness, they become our blind spots. In relating with each other, especially having confrontational conversations like politics, we express our perspective from these blind spots more often than not.

Our sensitive spots and blind spots, although connected, are not the same. A blind spot is in our unconscious; we are blind to them and don't see them. While triggers or sensitive spots are reactions to something external, reminding us of past trauma or challenging a belief system in our blind spot. These are, however, visceral, physical, and chemical responses that come from our neuroception.

Triggers are like the signposts to blind spots. Having conversations full of contempt, conveying disgust, harsh judgment, and sarcasm are some of the signs that could mean one is operating from a blind spot. These sensitive spots or triggers have been triggered/touched. The interesting thing about these spots is that they could be totally obvious to others but not to the person reacting. Being controlling and demanding, not being able to own one's mistake, being critical, and making decisions alone when working in a group are examples.

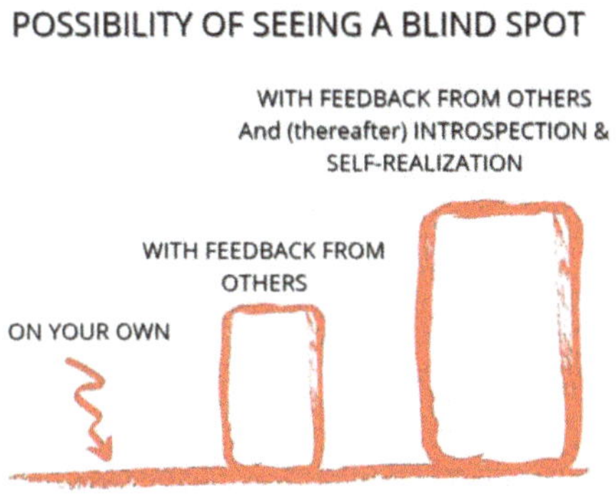

POSSIBILITY OF SEEING A BLIND SPOT

WITH FEEDBACK FROM OTHERS
And (thereafter) INTROSPECTION &
SELF-REALIZATION

WITH FEEDBACK FROM OTHERS

ON YOUR OWN

Figure 144: I ask my very good friends to let me know what habits they would prefer me to change.

How to recognize these blind spots

- Become aware: If you are reacting, and others are not, then most likely, these sensitive spots, which are not known to you, have been triggered. We all have blind spots, aspects of our personalities that we don't know exist but affect how we operate and show up in the world.
- Reflect rather than react: If something doesn't feel good only to you (or to people who display similar behavior), it is better to ponder why it doesn't feel right.
- Pay attention: to how others are reacting and draw a comparison with your behavior. Be willing to be open-minded, take yourself out of the context so that you can see the bigger picture or other perspectives. What do I want? What do I need? Are there other ways of achieving

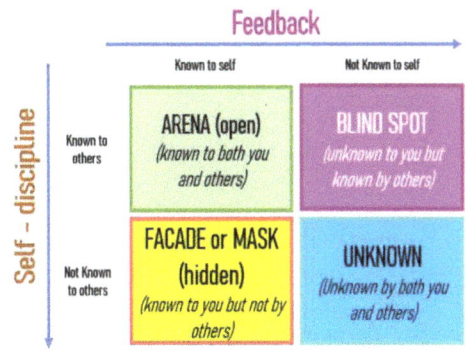

Figure 145: Another matrix, known as The Johari Window, helps people better understand their relationship with themselves and others. Credits: Luft, J. & Ingham, H. (1955).

the same? What are others trying to achieve, and how is that different from mine?

- Be willing to work on yourself: Growth happens outside of your comfort zone, so realize that working on these sensitive spots, which until now were blind spots, would make you uncomfortable and require real work. One of the exercises I have used is to get feedback from people (whom I can trust and know will be honest) about how they see me and what areas they believe I should be working on to improve myself. It wasn't easy, but it was worth doing this exercise. For years, I did this, focusing only on the areas that resonated with me. I ignored the feedback that I felt came from their own projection about self rather than the reality. I remained focussed on the points that reflected a common pattern in those feedbacks.

Conclusion

I hope after reading this chapter, you will now have a more in-depth insight and tips on how to introspect your relationship with self and how to manage the relationship with others. What I find so ironic and pathetic at the same time is that we are taught science, engineering, mathematics and all kinds of subjects at school but the most fundamental piece to every person living on this planet, so crucial for every society existing in this world, is hardly mentioned or part of any curriculum. Imagine if we were given this kind of education that teaches us how to manage ourselves and relate with others from an early age; what kind of person would we become, and how our human potential would transpire.

CHAPTER TWELVE

COMMUNICATION

Communication is key to the development of civilization. Without it, not only do we achieve nothing with others, but we create the conditions for conflict. With it, we may still experience conflict, but we also have the opportunity to achieve harmony, peace, and, most of all, our ability to express love.

Michael Charming

Introduction

Have you ever wondered why sometimes we have conflicts about things that are not worthy of the conflict? While the reasons are understandable during political conversations, how often have you experienced these in your relationships with family, friends, partner, and then partner again, grandparents (okay, not so much with them), neighbors, and strangers?

Because we generally don't have a good way of communicating, our political conversations tend to show our worst side, similar to our conflicts with a partner. This is due to our lack of awareness, our inner child wounds, our underlying intention to prove someone wrong or prove to others that we know better. At times this is done with a lack of awareness, and other times, it is actually done intentionally and knowingly. The intention of wanting to share information so that the other person can gain more knowledge about the issue (not so much). Fighting like cats and dogs, topping over

There are more posts on my social media feeds that tell me how tired everyone is from political posts..... than actual political posts

Figure 146: So many people are tired of either posting or having to explain their views on their political posts. There is also a lot of enthusiasm about sharing opinions and bringing change, especially on how the political system works.

each other, raising voices, expressing frustration, agitation, dismay, and then leading to full-blown arguments. Regularly seen on the news at the Trump/anti-Trump demonstrations?

'People may not remember what you did or what you said, but they will always remember how you made them feel.' --- Maya Angelou

No wonder the pre-Trump leaders in America focused more on how they made people feel rather than what they said. Do you recall utterly despising this political correctness? Why? Because we were upset at things that were happening; never-ending wars, the dire state of healthcare, endless troubles of the common man, and the untaxing of the rich. Then came Trump, who cared not an inch for political correctness, and while some felt happy and loved him for that, others despised him for his rashness, his manner of spewing whatever he thought from his mouth, and saying things that simply were not factual, no matter how many times he repeated them. Something must have made people feel good about what he said and how he said it, that got him elected as President even though the odds were stacked against him.

Interestingly, I feel I am one of the exceptions in which I really didn't care about how he made me feel but instead what he said. While I don't support his way of speaking, but considering the overall picture, I realized it was a strategy he used to win, so I focused my attention on deciding what he was capable of doing.

In this chapter, we look at communication, something that goes beyond just the words uttered. It includes the subtle nuances – the body language, the facial expression, the tonality, and the context.

Communication with Self

"Watch your thoughts, they become your words; watch your words, they become your actions; watch your actions, they become your habits; watch your habits, they become your character; watch your character, it becomes your destiny." ...... Lao Tzu

Just like relationships begin with oneself, so does communication. Waking up in the morning, deciding whether or not to snooze the alarm for another 20 minutes, which coffee to choose, and what to wear for the day are all signs of communication with oneself.

There is always the element of mental process, cognitive thinking, the automatic mind-body response. If we dissect this process, you will notice these are all kinds of communication, including the never-ending or often wandering mind-chatter and internal dialogues that are happening at much faster speeds than we can even track. I am not sure if you will believe me, but when we can master our communication, have a level of self-control to stop our tongue mid-sentence, then we have actually won 90% of our verbal battles (not literally but metaphorically). A wise man once said, 'words are like arrows, which once released, can never be stopped.' We can't undo the impact our words have on someone's feelings or emotions, but the good thing is we have the option to make amends retroactively (more on this in Chapter Fifteen).

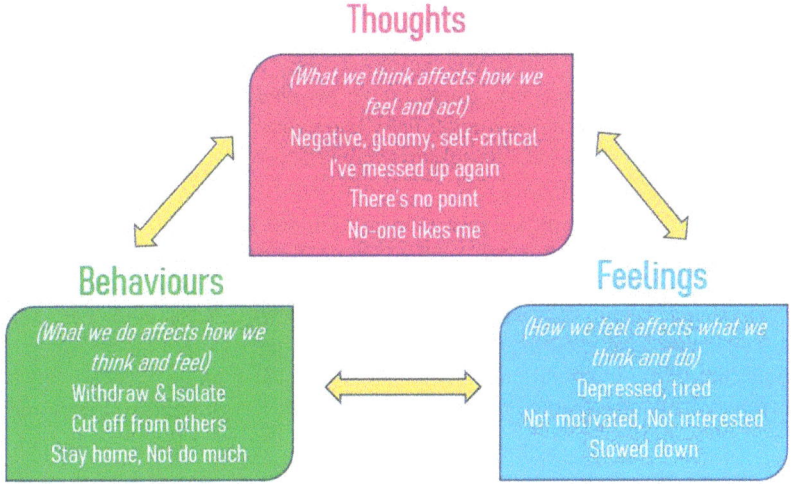

Figure 147: The Cognitive Triangle is a therapeutic model used in Cognitive Behavior Therapy (CBT) in the mental health field (treating mental disorders, depression, anxiety, phobias, PTSD, etc.). It emphasizes the relationship between our thoughts, feelings, and behaviors, and without intervention, the process continues. Credit: Dr Aaron T. Beck.

Mind-Chatter

Physical control is a skill that needs to be mastered. Our mind-body has conscious control of our reflexes. Otherwise, we will be coming to blows and kicking those around us and not being able to stop it. But, thankfully, this part is taken care of anatomically. We can also have mental control to stop ourselves from overthinking by engaging in various activities like mindfulness, yoga, or at worst, stop overthinking after mental fatigue.

We either have far too much control at an emotional level (we repress, dismiss or disown) or express far too much resulting in emotional outbursts. Hence, we have an imbalance.

When it comes to politics, we have a much bigger emotional outburst than is really necessary, mainly due to a lack of verbal control. Have you ever thought about tongue or mouth mastery (yeah, you ask me what the heck is that)? It merely means mastering your tongue or mouth. Well, if I can answer for you, I guess your answer would be NO. Mine was, too, until a few years ago.

A few years ago, I realized that I had developed great mastery in ejaculation control as a guy. I had developed emotional, physical, and all sorts of control, but I never focused on tongue mastery, stopping it mid-sentence, mid-syllable, or being aware of my speaking. I made this my next challenge (yes, I love challenges. Suppose you are on the path of personal growth. In that case, you will get used to finding new challenges because growth only happens outside your comfort zone, and anything there will feel challenging at first). At that moment, I realized that with this mastery, I could have avoided so many arguments. Some breakups with past lovers may never have happened (and might have resulted in me getting married with kids, and perhaps this book would never have been written... but I'm not complaining 😊).

Political conversations are like being on an ice ramp. If one doesn't know how to stop, one is bound to fall, causing chaos for others, often leading them to fall, too. When one's communication level drops, the others tend to fall even lower. Do you recall yourself doing that on numerous occasions? Yes, numerous. For the next six months, I focused on every aspect to gain this mastery – my beliefs, thoughts, imaginations, and inner dialogues. Finally, I was happy with the results. This transformed my connection with others through conversations.

Inner Dialog

We are used to having internal dialogues from an early age, leading to unnecessary mental fatigue due to never-ending thoughts. Are you aware of these dialogues; when do you have them, and what are they about? Do I like that classmate? Should I speak to that girl at school? What will I tell my parents about having failed the exam? Self-control. It's not just about speaking out or verbally vomiting whatever one is thinking.

Why don't we pause for a few seconds before speaking? Hello, how are you? How was your weekend? What did you do? This kind of interaction happens more in the western world than in developing countries.

Positive inner chatter leaves us feeling happy, vibrant, and empowered. Sadly, we don't always have a positive inner chatter; instead, we lean towards a very negative, depressing, melancholy chatter. How often have you said to yourself, oh wow, this leader is really amazing vs. what a fucking asshole? Be aware and see it for yourself.

Think of a scenario. You offer your partner a cup of coffee, and they reply, "I don't fucking want a coffee." Your immediate reaction could be one of these – "okay, you don't have to shout at me," "Why are you reacting in this way?" "I am never going to offer coffee again." These are all internal dialogues. What if, in this situation, if you were to simply say, "okay, is there anything you would like," or "should I leave you alone for now?" This is awareness. This is self-control. Imagine if we could just agree that wearing masks saves lives instead of making it a political issue (isn't prevention better than cure?). Then we could all live a better life sooner.

Inner dialog, or self-talk, gives us a chance to reconsider, think pros and cons, allowing us to internalize the knowledge and awareness gained so that we can arrive at a justifiable conclusion.

- Positive self-talk: results in empowering us, often overriding our negative and limiting beliefs.
- Negative self-talk: results in inner critic, makes us view things through a biased and filtered lens, often leading to negativity. "I am worthless", "I am a failure", "I am unlovable," when applied to dislike towards leaders end up becoming, 'he/she is a failure', 'he/she is an idiot'.

We have what we call a monkey mind. Monkey mind is a metaphor based on Buddhism, denoting a monkey as uncontrollable, chattering, and always on the lookout for mental distraction. (Completing this book would have never been possible if I had allowed monkey mind to take over the show.) If it weren't for this monkey mind, you would be happy right now, just realizing that you are breathing and alive (150,000 people die every day). Untamed monkey mind has a neg-

Figure 148: It is better to be aware of your inner critique and your inner committees' dialog than not.

ative impact on our behavior, which also impacts how we view everything relating to politics.

We have the power to shift our thoughts and move through our emotions. When driving a car, we have the power to shift our car using the steering wheel; after all, we are driving. We spend time and energy blaming the media for showing negative news (playing the victim card), but if we have the power to shift, does it really matter what anyone shows us?

Before the election relating to Brexit, I spent three full weeks researching everything on this topic. I felt the decision was important to me. I wanted to consider all the pros and cons before deciding – what is the EU? Why was it formed? Why did the UK join? Why did Denmark hold various referendums relating to membership? After the voting day, I heard that people felt misled by both sides. There were fear-mongering strategies implemented that many things were exaggerated. It was all new to me because I had no idea what either side had been propagating and campaigning for. So, the question to ask is, do we hold the media and leaders responsible for misleading us, or do we move away from the state of being the victims, take control, and operate from a place of power? The job of steering is to move the car; there is no hidden science. The job of a light bulb, if still working, is to give light as soon as it is switched on. The job of the mind is to fire thoughts erratically, aimlessly, and numerously unless tamed.

INNER CRITIC	VS	INNER GUIDANCE
❖ Focuses on problems, negative, depressing thoughts ❖ Thinks situations in binary terms: blank/white, either/or; this/that ❖ No or less sense of gratitude ❖ Scarcity/lack/never enough mindset ❖ Hold others responsible for their problems ❖ Uses shame, fear, guilt to motivate ❖ Generally devoid of love & compassion		❖ Focuses on solutions, positive, inspiring thoughts ❖ Recognizes complexities/gray areas ❖ Filled with or express gratitude ❖ Abundance, creation mindset ❖ Take responsibility for their problems ❖ Uses pride, desires, innocence to motivate ❖ Generally filled with love & compassion

Figure 149: Just like we have an inner critic, we also have our inner guidance. Which one do you use the most? Or in other words, which one controls and directs you the most?

Communication at All Layers of the Body

While we all are familiar with inner dialog, monkey mind, and inner chatter, what if I were to tell you that communication is actually happening across all layers of your body (within your internal and external realities simultaneously). How often do you have an awareness of your emotions, mental thoughts, feelings, sensations, desires, state of your physical body, all at once? When people feel emotional, there is no point in communicating with them mentally or asking them for their point of view. It is essential to talk about feelings and create space for more feelings to emerge.

As mentioned in previous chapters, we live in a polarized society, but the way we actually communicate and relate with each other has a lot to do with it. (Reminder: basic needs of all humans are mostly the same). Suppose a person is talking about their desire or need. In that case, it is essential to create space where they can go deeper into the body sensations and express the felt-sense impact of this desire or need rather than talking about whether a particular policy is good or bad for the economy (taking them from spiritual to mental layer abruptly).

If our body wants to feel and express, let it be, rather than shutting it down with mental thoughts. If our mind is in thinking or doing mode, then pay attention to emotions or feelings that are coming up, but don't let them take over at that moment. When each of us realizes this and starts integrating and embodying ourselves entirely in this human machine, we start living and experiencing the full potential it has to offer. We will begin to make a tremendous shift that will impact the world, politics, and leaders (remember, we elect leaders, and leaders share messages based on what appeals most to their supporters). Only then will we truly create the planet we aspire to, or else we will continue fighting with each other over things as trivial as toilet paper, no matter how educated and smart we might be.

Figure 150: Our monkey mind comes up with all kinds of random thoughts. Do you accept these as-is, dismiss them, or question where they come from?

Other important relationship dynamics with self and others

Echo Chambers and Epistemic Bubbles

* *Pro-painkiller echo chamber shaped policy amid drug epidemic*
* *White House BRAGS about how it tricked reporters into cheerleading for Obama's Iran nuclear deal by creating a media 'echo chamber'*
* *Facebook's 'echo chamber' really DOES make you narrow minded: People use the site to seek out opinions that confirm what they already believe*

Epistemic bubble is a bubble where insiders aren't exposed to people from the opposite side. When people rely on one social media platform, say Facebook, because they live in this bubble, they would hear arguments only from one side of the political spectrum without exposure to the other side's views.

Echo chamber: is an environment in which a person only encounters information or opinions that reflect and reinforce their own, resulting in a distorted perspective, creating misinformation, and often resulting in significant resistance to consider opposing views and discussing complicated topics. It leads members to distrust everyone outside their chamber, thus putting an unquestioned reliance and trust on everyone inside this chamber (which can often feel like a cult). This is very much akin to Groupthink discussed in Chapter Seven.

We know multiple variables result in different perspectives. Suppose you are constantly seeing the same perspective over and over again, online or in real life; it means you are living in an echo chamber. You can easily find like-minded people on social media, making many fall prey to living in an echo chamber. During and just after Brexit and the US election, I saw many friends complaining and not understanding how Brexit and Trump could win. In their feeds, they only saw posts supporting Remain and Hillary. They were shocked at the results.

Every day, there are millions of blogs, tweets, Instagram photos, and videos because people love propagating information and sharing opinions, thus giving a sense of self-worth and creating change (yes, there is entertainment, insecurity, and what-else-to-do-with-my-life, too).

Once trust has been broken, people tend to put their trust elsewhere. They seek alternative sources to place their trust. Sadly, it may not be the most trustworthy, but it offers them an alternative view to the one where their trust was broken.

With many social media platforms available, a person is likely to come across opposing views whether they like it or not. A study found that 8% of people with media diversity lived in echo chambers.[33] However, for those who rely on one source of information, this figure is then much higher.

'Motivated reasoning' makes people only search for arguments leading to conclusions they want to believe, resulting in false beliefs. The tendency of confirmation bias makes it worse as people cherry-pick information that supports their beliefs, ignoring the rest of the available information that doesn't support their beliefs.

Many have created a feeling-based rather than a factually

Figure 151: There you go! Now 99% of philosophical de-bates and rational thinking can be skipped. The problem with some opinions is that they have already been formed. Shouldn't it be the other way around? I.e., we should research first, with an open and curious mind, and then develop our opinion.

based society or follows an imbalanced approach (i.e., feelings over facts). Many opt to believe information that feels good to them, irrespective of whether it is a fact or not. The rise of conspiracy theories, the spread of misinformation, and fake news create information chaos that goes against the internet's objectives to spread knowledge and awareness.

Multi-media helps to break through these chambers
The complex media environment consisting of print media, television, online media, and various social platforms (Twitter, Facebook) allows us to break through these echo chambers. Many are bound to stumble upon opposing views, news, and articles. The problem is those who tend not to listen or not be open to other perspectives, as this is when echo chambers can exist, making them dangerous to those living in them.

Three D's – Debate, Dialog, or Discussion

❖ *Debate commission: Democrats didn't rig debate schedule*
❖ *Government reignites citizenship debate*
❖ *Debate Takeaways: Clinton gets under Trump's skin in debate*
❖ *Japan's Abe says poll result shows voters want debate on charter revision*
❖ *UK condemns Hong Kong violence, urges dialogue*
❖ *Lebanese President Aoun invites protesters to dialogue*

Are we debating, discussing, or having a dialog when conversing with our friends, family, or strangers? Each of these has different protocols, which gives different results. Do you know the difference and how to move from one form to another, especially when you realize that a debate is turning into an argument? It would be an amazing and useful skill, especially being able to leave on common ground, fostering depth of conversation and depth of relationship. Our friends and families are not our foes. Our objective is not to defeat them or become victorious, as often happens in a debate. Still, we are not willing to let go of our viewpoints either. We end up talking AT each other rather than WITH one another.

Figure 152: This is what is happening subtlety (energetically) as we debate.

Debate

Most of us are familiar with debates as we see the Presidential and Ministerial debates and often engage with each other using this form of communication. We do not follow the rules and end up following half the format that doesn't serve us well, often resulting in full-blown arguments. Sadly, we fail to utilize the benefits that this amazing form of communication offers.

Discussion

Discussion is a slightly better version of a debate. The participants still focus on advocating their viewpoints, challenging others, and pushing for a winning idea, but discussions also tend to be fast-paced and persuasive conversations with one person aiming to convince others of their point of view or solution. While these appear to be polite and respectful, the bang in the head in the form of clashing of perspectives and opinions is often found, especially if participants are unwilling to move towards finding resolutions where differences exist.

Dialog

Dialog aims to find a shared connection, listen to each other more deeply, build on shared points of view, and better understand each other. Instead of winning or losing, it aims for mediation and resolution. If everyone involved has an open and curious mind and heart, leaves ego aside, there will be less chance of taking things personally or feeling threatened.

Approaching conversation or confrontation with a sense of dialog gives everyone a learning opportunity. It works together to find strengths and solutions, leaving all involved with a win-win satisfaction. If it gets heated, the mediator will turn it around, keeping everyone engaged, focusing on finding the middle ground. The only downside is that it requires far more time to get to the core of an issue, unlike debates, which tend to ping pong among several issues with no resolution. Dialog can be uncomfortable, but it is not from a place of having to defend, but instead of vulnerability, the vulnerability of our own limitations and contributions.

Media – without it, we could be ourselves

Media plays with us big time, in far more ways than we realize. In recent years, most of the media doesn't focus on actual facts as much as on what the audience wants to hear, echoing their confirmation bias. Numerous times I have seen the same newspapers publishing different arguments in parallel (one in favor and one against) depending on the voter demographics in specific constituencies, for the same date and time. Could there be any other better proof showing how we are being misled? How do you determine what is correct and what isn't, what is fake and what isn't, which media to rely on and which you shouldn't? Are you attached to a particular news channel, or media, tailored towards a particular party or a leader? If so, it goes without saying that whatever information you are consuming is already biased, showing half or even a quarter of the perspective. In this case, your decisions are also only considering half or even a quarter of the overall scenario.

To ensure that I see all sides of the story, I read articles and watch clips produced by companies that present the facts, with no editorial or journalist opinion. I then do the same from sources that show me the extremes of both sides of the arguments (the one that tells that Trump is an idiot, and the other that tells me how great he is). In doing so, I get to know the actual story and both extreme versions of the same event or incident, allowing me to gather the full picture. One could ask why I need to consider both sides when I have factual information from unbiased sources.

Figure 153: In the words of Malcolm X, 'The media is the most powerful entity on Earth. They have the power to make the innocent guilty and the guilty innocent, and that's power. Because they control the minds of the masses.'

The reason being SWOT. Remember this term? It allows me to gather information, which will help me complete this model in the most realistic way possible, giving me a chance to input best-case and worst-case scenarios. The downside is that instead of getting through three issues at a time, I only manage one. But that one is bulletproof, filled with concrete facts that will allow me to confidently form my opinions. It is already given that we cannot know about every single issue or policy, so it is better to consider a few in detail than many with only half the perspectives.

Social Media – a place to rant and share your frustrations

Social media, supposed to be an online place of socializing, has become a place of frustration, annoyance, complication, and not so great where political discussions are concerned. Outside the groups of echo chambers, there are going to be opposing voices on almost every issue. Suppose we continue to defriend and disengage from those who don't resonate with our views. In that case, we may soon have a connection with only three people – Me, Myself, and I. Because, at some

"I haven't taken a day off since old media was new media."

Figure 154: Is it social media or an anti-social media?

point, we will also disagree with people with whom we currently agree.

A gentle reminder that if you get physically, mentally, energetically, emotionally, or spiritually affected by others' news feeds, posts, shares, and comments, you need to decide when to take a break, when to snooze, and when to disconnect— your well-being is in your hands.

Memes – should I laugh, or should I cry?

❖ *Spain proposes a BAN on memes... and its government is immediately mocked with memes*

❖ *Fake news 'spreading to young people through Instagram memes'*

❖ *'Cool' candidate Bloomberg adds memes to campaign arsenal*

❖ *Election candidate is slammed for posting memes praising Adolf Hitler and joking about school shootings*

❖ *'Black and the new orange!' Memes mock Donald Trump's meeting with Kanye West*

Memes, a term first developed by Richard Dawkins in 1976, which used to contain words and phrases with intentional misspellings and incorrect grammar, has now evolved to a more elaborate (and sort of shorthand) form of communication with GIFs, emojis, catchphrases, and viral sensations. Every meme goes through a process of assimilation (noticing it, understanding it, and accepting it will depend on our perception), retention (uniqueness, consistency with the norm, presentation format), expression (into a form that transmits the message, an idea into a form for others to imitate) and transmission.

What makes memes so appealing and one of the most used forms of communication is their emotional contagion appeal, whether positive or negative (mostly humor, anger, or disgust), and psychological arousal making them spread like wildfire.

When seen with repetition, images presented in a meme often skip the users' critical thinking, making it easier for them to get the message and lead them to believe the story being presented. Adding satire, irony, or mockery into that mix makes it humorous. It then starts feeding our hormones, making us feel good about the meme, irrespective of whether the information shared is correct. There is no harm in having a laugh about anything, but the problem is that the ideas presented are often in extremes making people believe that even '*pigs can fly.*'

Memes can deliver powerful messages and make a complex topic like politics much easier to understand. They capture the fundamental aspects of collective imagination or deeper reflections on society's issues, evoke powerful emotions, and cultivate a sense of cultural belonging; however, they are based on their creator's perception.

There is more to memes than meets the eye. Gone are the days when they were considered harmless entertainment, as they are now used as weapons. Most are filled with mockery, snarky comments relating to leaders, their personality, physical appearance, which can then be tied with unrelated and highly provocative issues like coronavirus to magnify the impact. Since information on memes is rarely questioned, these cannot be fact-checked. Because they are taken at face value, it is difficult to hold the creators accountable for the misinformation being spread. Politicians also use memes to support their own agenda.

Petition – I signed what?

❖ Iran celebs launch petition against US sanctions
❖ UK petition calls for Guantanamo detainee's release
❖ Commons to debate 1.6m petition over Trump state visit
❖ Revoke Article 50 petition hits five million signatures

A petition is a formal request for action written to a governmental authority or individual public office holder. Depending on the country, petitions are used by both the government (in the US to qualify candidates for public office to appear on a ballot) and by people petitioning the government regarding a specific issue. Depending on the number of signatures gained, petitions can have a massive impact on movements (millions of signatures helped free Nelson Mandela, but 4.1 million signatures couldn't stop Brexit or implement a second referendum).

Rules for petitions vary from country to country. In the UK, 10,000 signatures make it mandatory for the government to respond, and 100,000 signatures pave the way for a Parliamentary debate. When signing petitions, people often don't check whether it has already been debated by the government, whether there is already a similar petition open, or whether it asks for explicit action. Petitions containing false statements, jokes, advertisements, defamatory remarks, refer to an active court case, or contain material protected by an injunction order are often dismissed. Millions

Figure 155: Signing your name is the beginning of losing your mind.

signed the petition relating to a second referendum, Brexit stalemate, and EU citizens missing out on the EU elections vote – because people don't really understand the petition process.

Though real petitions do have a chance of enhanced engagement in Parliament, allowing voters to express themselves, most petitions don't really achieve anything apart from raising awareness, which can still be beneficial in the long term. People often express support with a mere click or input of few details online, but hardly any follow it through.

Here's a list of some of the ridiculous petitions, but hey, I am not judging

- ❖ *Petition to humans to abolish the word Ma'am*
- ❖ *Petition on behalf of Blue Ivy to comb her hair*
- ❖ *Fans go crazy over Ben Affleck as Batman and petition Obama to make it illegal*
- ❖ *Petition to make the Eurovision Song Contest a national holiday*
- ❖ *Petition to make it compulsory for train conductors to say 'all aboard' before people embark*
- ❖ *Petition to make Snapchat downgrade to version 10.24.5.0*
- ❖ *Petition to only have World Cup matches on the BBC because we tend to lose when the match is shown on ITV*

I am curious that if people want to exercise support, why would they not make it part of their goal or life purpose, something they can regularly work on? Many will hardly remember what they signed for if you ask them a few days or weeks later. No wonder online petitions are often seen as a form of 'slacktivism.' This is a small act performed via the internet to support a political or social cause that doesn't require any commitment from the person signing it. However, it makes them feel good about doing something meaningful for society and demonstrating this by sharing it on social media platforms. Most often, it has just become a way for people to vent their anger and resentment before passing the responsibility of actually doing something to someone else.

We need to realize, while online petitions are easier to start, especially if they are related to topics or issues highlighted by current headlines, but if we really want a petition to work, especially over a shorter timeframe, then we need to do more than just signing. Achieving real change requires hard work sustained for an extended period consistently and persistently (more on change in Chapter Thirteen).

Sometimes before blindly signing petitions, ask yourselves, does this really have to do with the issue? There was a petition relating to banning Trump from visiting the UK. I wondered what the purpose was – to show that we do not welcome a person filled with hate speech to our country. Taking that stance, aren't we showing hate towards hate? Where is love in that action? Would it not have been better to have a petition to show him what love actually feels like? Why do we choose to fall to someone's level instead of keeping high standards? Of course, the other side of that argument is that we accept his behavior and rhetoric by inviting him. That signal is equally wrong.

Protests – are we fighting, or are we expressing?

❖ *Thousands of British Muslims gathered to protest against cartoons showing the Prophet Mohammed today*
❖ *Morocco protest leader arrested: officials*
❖ *Students swell Lebanon protest movement*
❖ *Kuwaitis protest against government corruption*

A protest is peoples' expression of dissent, resentment, and disapproval towards a political leader, policy, or a cause. Protest can take many forms – individual statements, demonstrations, Black Lives Matter. There is a protest on every issue. Protests that are systematic, peaceful, well-executed, and non-violent to exercise pressure or persuasion go beyond protests and may be called civil resistance or non-violent resistance.

A protest is an umbrella term and includes many different forms of expression, rallies or demonstrations, marches, vigils, photobombing, disrupting live broadcasts, or other non-violent movements like silent protests. As per the Global Nonviolent Action Database, Gene Sharp classifies 198 methods of non-violent action that fall under protest.

Figure 156: There are times we aren't exactly sure of the point of our actions.

For a protest to lead to change, it depends on several factors – attention and coverage it receives from media and online platforms, the intensity with which it is being shared, etc. When emotions are high, people make fast decisions. Things to consider regarding protests: the overall purpose of the protest (asking for policy change vs. bringing awareness), efficiency or the contagion effect, group dynamics and behavior (groups with hidden agendas can turn protests violent), duration of the protests (more prolonged protests require much longer survival mode, power, energy, resources), who is the protest against, whether peaceful, non-violent, or violent (vandalism, looting), willingness or flexibility to compromise, collective beliefs of protestors, time, day and month of protest.

Reasons for protests include grievances (experience of inequality, feelings of injustice), efficacy (expectation to change circumstances or policies), identity (sense of belonging to the group, shared emotions, obligation as part of a member of a group), emotions (mostly anger together with the desire to do something, to take action) and network functions (mobilization, recruitment of people to carry the movement).

Violent protests, especially those involving disregard for safety, purpose, and looting, lead to negative opinions. In contrast, peaceful protests generally tend to have positive opinions, but the impact could be inversely correlated. Have you participated in a protest, and if so, what was your behavior and attitude throughout the process? Were you aware of why you participated in a specific protest, or was it a case of not having anything else exciting to do, making your participation feel appropriate? Did you think through the cause, impact, and rationale behind all that was being done? Your behavior had an impact. Did you turn angry at police and lawmakers exercising force, or did you continue to follow the rules of peaceful protest? As we discussed in Chapters Three and Seven, the human body is more than just the physical body. Due to collectives, there is a large clashing of energies subtlety taking place. It is no wonder so many protests turn violent, no matter how well-intended, because of high emotions and the mixing and clashing of energies.

Propaganda – who did what, and how did I end up getting involved?

- *I'm all Reich! Propaganda footage emerges of Hitler visiting wounded soldiers in hospital shortly after an assassination attempt on his life*
- *Facebook takes down first covert propaganda campaign tied to Saudi Government which places the kingdom in good light, while disparaging its enemies*
- *Disney Channel accused of feeding children 'anti-communist propaganda' in resurfaced Girl Meets World clip*

Figure 157: Let us not forget that memes are just modern-day propaganda.

Propaganda uses manipulative tactics, distorted messages, and fake news delivered through wide sources ranging from media, multi-media, social platforms, radio, tv shows, websites, bots, music, and others, like sporting events, books, and libraries. Why people believe propaganda depends on the communicator's ability to persuade them using various kinds of manipulative tricks. Given the fast-paced and complex world we live in, we are all looking for shortcuts in our lives –

shortcuts to making money, short cuts to becoming multi-orgasmic, and short cuts to finding news that resonates and serves our purpose. Since we cannot know everything, rationalize and analyze different aspects of issues, and do not have time or energy and focus, we often believe in what is in front of our eyes feels or most appealing to us. Any tactic used in persuasion follows the four criteria: to be seen, understood, remembered, and acted upon.

Conspiracy Theories (CT) – are you feeling entertained, or are you really doing your research?

❖ *Bill Gates denies conspiracy theories he created virus outbreak*
❖ *Conspiracy theories flourish after Turkey's failed coup*
❖ *Andrew Breitbart's unexpected death sparks wild conspiracy theories*
❖ *Conspiracy theories fill Italy media over pope brain tumour story*

With the ever-increasing use of social media, blogs, and YouTube, in current situations like the pandemic, CT could be related to events (9/11, Kennedy assassination), systemic (securing control of country or region), and super conspiracy theories (multiple alleged conspiracies together). CT often claims what institutional analysis does not, thus giving a sense of chaotic and confusing scenarios, playing on collective anxieties and obsessions; it often appeals and is presented as secret knowledge or something unique that aims to fill the knowledge gap (ambiguous plane crashes, coronavirus_19).

As per political psychologist Dr. Joanne Miller, *"All of these conspiracy theories are positively correlated. Meaning that people who believe one often believe the others as they hang together as a belief system."*[34] Uncertainty, conspiratorial thinking, denialism, and partisan-

Figure 158: Considering oneself 'woke' or 'intelligent' and the masses as 'sheeple' or 'dumb as fuck', I don't believe this to be the best way to create awareness and wake the other group.

motivation are some of the factors that support and perpetuate such theories.

When people have mistrust or a negative attitude toward the government or anything in life, it is easy to believe in something that provides trust, emotional satisfaction, and answers to mysteries. Considering that government inquiries and other legitimate forms of information and data collection, analysis, and research can be prolonged and the world and political views are deeply polarized. Have you ever believed in any such theories? Do you remain open or shut from the get-go when a CT is mentioned, and how far do you go in supporting the theory? If you are a believer, do any of the statements previously mentioned resonate with you (emotional pleasure, getting answers when, in reality, there are none, emotions relating to anxiety or fear)? CT can be entertaining, but they are also very dangerous, speculative (rather than firm evidence), as shared in Chapter Three. Once we start believing and giving our own narrative, it is hard to disown those beliefs. We will then fight to prove them right and defend them rather than dismantle them.

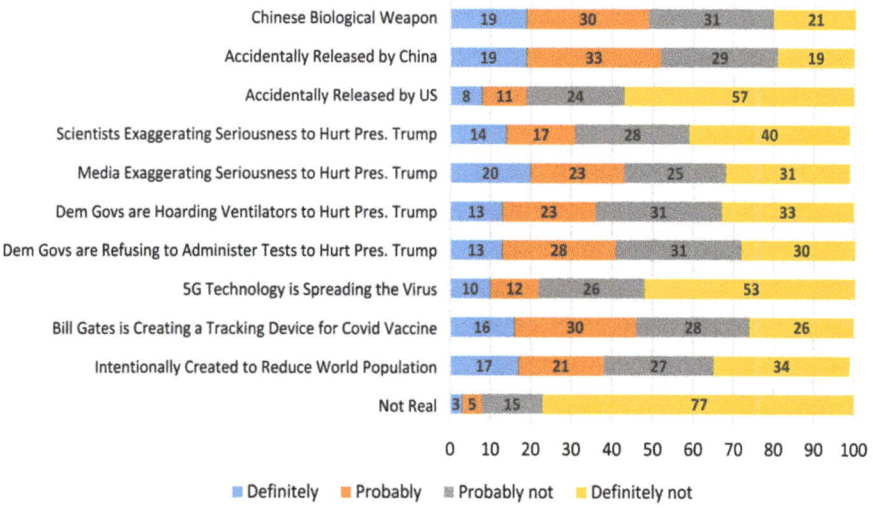

Figure 159: Distribution of COVID-19 Conspiracy Theories. Source: Miller, J. (2020). Do COVID-19 Conspiracy Theory Beliefs Form a Monological Belief System? Canadian Journal of Political Science, 53(2), 319-326. doi:10.1017/S0008423920000517.

Freedom of Speech (FoS) – your constitutional values vs. your own values relating to integrity

❖ *Singapore contempt of court bill seen suppressing freedom of speech*
❖ *Facebook says EU court opinion undermines freedom of speech*
❖ *Transgender tweets were freedom of speech, British judge rules*

What is your interpretation of the term Freedom of Speech? Do you believe it is okay to share your views online, knowing they can go viral with positive or negative consequences? The massive expansion of social media, causing the reduction in traditional media, means that now it is no longer possible to hold anyone accurately responsible for unwanted actions in society. Anyone can mold and manipulate the news or information in one's favor before spreading it like wildfire.

We have freedom of the press, but given the internet crisis currently faced by most democratic countries, one wonders if the press and free speech restriction in countries like Russia and China is a good thing. It allows the government to focus on things they want to do rather than spending energy and resources defending and explaining themselves for something that exists. Are censorship and restriction really that bad? How do we set the bar in the current environment? The bar of threshold, tolerance, staying within limits, and true to reality. I don't expect laws being passed to shut down free press or speech, so most likely, we are stuck with them, which means the onus falls on social media giants to become more stringent. These platforms struggle with a carrot and stick dilemma (AI and algorithms allowing the news users like to be shared vs. restricting fake news).

Looking at behavior and the support of Freedom of Speech, I sometimes wonder where common sense went. When will we grow up? Why do we blindly follow the crowd? Why don't we look, pause, and understand what is happening, why and who is behind it, ask sensible questions, deal with our emotions, and avoid reacting so that we can respond and take actions which are genuinely focused on society's well-being?

I have found that people are open to express all kinds of views in the name of FoS, but when it comes to owning the responsibility, they fall short or don't care. Consider the case of 5G causing COVID-19. During the early days of Mar/Apr'20, those who believed it to be true shared the articles, news, and views extensively supporting their argument. Once confirmed that 5G doesn't cause COVID-19, don't you think everyone who shared their views should apologize? But you will not find that happening (talk about integrity).

The pattern is that these things are just swept under the carpet; the subject is changed or a covert change of opinion by such people. As part of development and growth, we often say that 'this is where I was then,' which is fine. We all learn, and we all grow, and it is okay; we are humans, after all. Don't you think that after having grown or moved away from where they were, they need to reflect on their actions and apologize?

My thoughts, *'Well, you were there then. You are not there now. So, should you not be owning your shit and acting with integrity. If you used Freedom of Speech to share whatever your views were, why is the same Freedom of Speech not being used to own your actions and those views? I personally think this is a double standard.'*

Projection, perception, associations, assumptions, and communication

❖ *The Conservative Party has a "perception problem" with ethnic minority voters, Sajid Javid has admitted.*
❖ *Politicians should worry about public perception*
❖ *Turkey's role in Libya adds to pro-Islamist perception*
❖ *Kelly pushes back against perception of White House chaos*
❖ *'He's projecting his own unruliness': Pelosi hits back at Trump on his claim of congressional 'harassment' as Democratic investigators dig in on his finances*

When we talk about communication, especially politics, it is essential to look at the psychological processes of perception, projection, associations, and assumptions. These contribute massively to confrontations and full-blown arguments, ultimately leading to disconnection, disassociations, and loss of friendships.

Projection: Has anyone ever asked you to stop projecting your feelings onto them? As the name suggests, psychological projection is seeing qualities that we unknowingly possess (feelings, emotions, beliefs, and internal realities) showing up in other people. It allows difficult qualities to be attributed to someone else without fully recognizing them in oneself. We seem more comfortable pointing out the negative and unwanted parts of others rather than looking and confronting them within ourselves (pointing one finger at someone, rather than looking at three fingers pointing back at us). Projection can be positive or negative, and it is often these differences that lead to clashes.

According to Karen R. Koenig, *"projection does what all defense mechanisms are meant to do: keep discomfort about ourselves at bay and outside our awareness."*[35] Here are some examples: *'Trump is racist. No, he is not', 'I can't stand her, she is so controlling', 'he is xenophobic', 'he hates me', 'if I can do it, other people can as well', 'the house I live in is terrible; hence no one would want to date me', 'married man attracted to another female can accuse her of flirting with him', 'someone keeps talking, and if you interrupt, you are accused of not being a good listener", "I didn't want to argue but just that what you said earlier, I found it to be unethical"*. People who don't really know themselves (even if they think otherwise) are more prone to project. The opposite for people who self-reflect and are willing to accept their faults, weaknesses, and failures tend not to project. As per Koenig, *"They have no need, as they can tolerate recognizing or experiencing the negatives about themselves"*.

Emotions repressed and held within for years make people project. They want to cut off parts they don't accept or approve of – more like a shadow, resulting in creating blind spots. Can you imagine the kind of things (feelings, emotions, beliefs) my clients project onto me when I work with them either as a coach or as a bodyworker? Active projection is positive. It allows us to feel ourselves in others' shoes (empathy, more on this in the final chapter). On a collective level, projection can result in scapegoating, protest, violence, and confrontations between different groups.

Figure 160: When someone highlights our projecting, we should thank them rather than being defensive and disconnecting.

Perception is our sensory experience of the world, which depends on how each of our body layers feels (emotional, mental, physical, etc.) at that moment. It refers to the way sensory information is organized, identified, interpreted, and understood by us. As such, perception is a subjective experience of surroundings (external realities) that are objectively present around us. We constantly perceive everything around us, but we also project our own self-formed narratives on what we perceive. Why do some consider Trump to be sexist, but others don't? Why do some consider policy XYZ to be beneficial, but others don't? Why do some believe Trump will win while others think Biden will?

Our natural tendency is to recognize, hear, and see images and words in how we have perceived them before – people, views about them, situations, and interactions. The question remains: Are we perceiving reality or projecting what we want (or don't want) to see, hear, and read? The answer is we are doing both. Perception is projection, and vice-versa; we need to be aware of the fine line between the two. Perception and projection, if far away from reality (or reality of the other person), will result in misunderstandings, miscommunications, and conflicts. If we have fear within us, we will project fear onto others. Our perceptions are limited because there is always more to what we perceive. Psychological projection is generally an unconscious or subconscious act of one's thoughts, feelings, weaknesses, and failures, thus blaming the external realities for sensory experiences felt inside the body.

Associations: From birth and throughout our life, our brain takes every piece of information and stimulation from every experience and processes it. It then organizes this information in a very structured way, creating and maintaining associations between memories and experiences. It picks specific chunks of sensory experiences and associates them with other stimuli. We assign meaning to information coming to us from this stored information (hence perception). Thus, creating cause and effect.

In a remarkable discovery, scientists found that the hippocampus, a part of the brain, fires neurons that at first seem random but are made up of complex patterns that help the brain build associations. Dr. Fusi said, *"We were happy to see that the brain doesn't maintain ongoing activity over all these seconds because, metabolically, that's not the most efficient way to store information. The brain seems to have a more efficient way to build this bridge, which we suspect may involve changing the strength of the synapses."[36]*

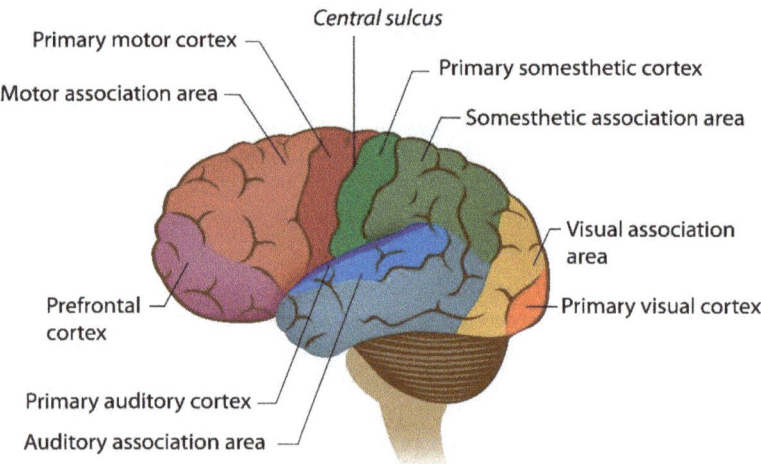

Consider the following examples relating to Trump:

- *'Grab her by the pussy'. When* a few women accuse him of rape, our brain makes associations and allows us to believe that he is a rapist.
- *'When Mexico is sending its people, they are not sending their best... they are bringing drugs. They are bringing crime. They're rapists'. When* he talks

about illegal immigrants and Muslims, many associate him with being a racist.

- *'Trump businesses filed for bankruptcy multiple times.* O*ur* mind associates with him being a terrible businessman, without considering the bankruptcy's underlying reasons.

Awareness and wisdom would mean being able to intercept information coming at us, disassociate with the stored information, and look at each piece of information piece by piece.

Assumptions: Has anyone ever said anything about you, which wasn't true or made inaccurate assumptions about you? We are fast at firing and making quick assumptions about everyone and everything. Instead, we should hold our guns, take a pause, come with an open and inquisitive mind, and a willingness to find out more before drawing conclusions. 'she collects food *stamp means she is lazy'*, *'he supports Tories means he doesn't value social welfare'*, *'he looks happy in all her Instagram posts means he must have everything she desires'*, *'she can't be the American President because she is not white'*, *'she looks beautiful means she knows everything she is talking about or can help serve me as my coach better'*.

As per Jack Colwell and Chip Huth, *"We automatically tend to assume the following: The way I see something is the way it is. The way I feel about someone is the way he or she is. The way I remember an event is the way it was. If you disagree with me, you are stupid, a liar, or psychotic (disconnected from reality)."*[37] Our brain maintains connections and fills the gaps by making up information (assumptions) using what is stored within the brain files and human body (emotions, feelings, beliefs, past experiences). This allows the brain to save a great deal of energy by making assumptions based on past experiences patterns rather than drawing conclusions from ten thousand connections made from information received within brain cells.

Assumptions can be both beneficial and harmful but become problematic when we believe them to be accurate and real (can be for others or for ourselves) and add judgment and begin labeling. When we are questioned and need to validate, we protect ourselves using our defense mechanisms. We take things personally and have emotional and mental outbursts because our ego does not want to confess that we have been wrong.

When we are communicating, all of these psychological processes are playing out. When you have a conversation, notice how someone might be projecting, become curious about what they are perceiving, and the kind of assumptions and associations their minds are making. Suppose you can do this well. In that case, you will realize the person may be unknowingly trapped by these processes. If conveyed in the right manner, you might help them break through some of their old patterns. Beware that more triggers and defense mechanisms like denial, distortion, passive aggression and repression might emerge.

Manipulation – an art, but so is reading between the lines

❖ *Top Madagascar presidential hopeful alleges vote 'manipulation'*
❖ *Sonic attack allegations are 'political manipulation': Cuba*
❖ *Switzerland rejects U.S. allegations of currency manipulation*
❖ *Volkswagen bosses charged with market manipulation*

When does decent (or not so decent) communication become manipulation? In communication, we are either expressing ourselves to be seen and heard, or we are aiming to influence the others directly or indirectly (us speaking to our lovers, leaders exercising their influence on voters, convince someone of untrue claims, entrepreneurs on investors, teachers on students, writers on readers).

The dictionary defines manipulation as: "To manage or influence skillfully, especially in an unfair manner: to manipulate people's feelings."

How often do you find yourself being manipulated? Left-wing media? Right-wing media? Your partner? A Facebook connection? Political and sales speeches and advertisements are all about manipulation. The difference between a motivational conversation that we love to hear vs. a conversation that feels off is the intention behind the words and whether they are acting in the interest of listeners or themselves only. Some forms of manipulation are considered socially acceptable, like using smiles, making eye contact, or back-patting to increase human connection. Here are some tricks used by manipulators. Can you identify any or all of these in leaders, political parties, and even the person you engage and have political conversations with?

- Always suggesting a place of their choice, which gives them more control and dominance, disregarding safety.
- Asking questions with a hidden agenda allows them to gain more information about you before realize you are providing this information. It also gives them time to find your weak points and prepare their arguments
- Exaggerating the facts, using confirmed or one-sided bias. Withholding key information to tilt towards their version of the truth.
- Taking advantage of your vulnerability by using your mental, physical, emotional exhaustion to their advantage, overwhelming you with facts, giving irrelevant or too much information, and asking you to make decisions when you are not in the position to do so.
- Overwhelming with bureaucracy, paperwork, procedures, and the power of authority – this happens a lot in the Indian culture – the aim is to delay seeking the truth, hide flaws, and prolong the process.
- Emotional blackmail or loud voice and assertive body language (standing too close) to exercise pressure.
- Using negative information to kill your morale and cause intellectual harassment to gain a psychological advantage and influence your opinion or decision before presenting the offer.

- Using time pressure or ultimatums giving you little or no adequate time to decide. *'if you don't accept what I say, it's all over,'* *'you have one day to decide.'*
- Using criticisms, cutting remarks, sarcasm, humor, or ridicule to disempower you and make you feel insecure, inadequate, and inferior. *'You are weak',* *'You are impossible to talk to'.*
- Giving the silent treatment (stonewalling) thus creating doubts and uncertainty in your mind, *'Now is not the good time', 'I don't want to talk about it', 'I don't have time', 'why are you bringing this up now?'*
- Pretending ignorance and playing dumb, thus playing with another person's mind, *'I don't understand what you mean'.* Lying and denial or changing the subject are also used.
- Touching sensitive spots (triggers, the soft or pain points) makes you feel vulnerable, often repeating your name, thus using a clever control mechanism. Using fear to control.
- Playing the victim by exaggerating personal issues, health issues, playing weak or powerless to exploit benefits and concessions.
- Using other forms of passive aggression behavior (voicing displeasure or anger without directly expressing the emotions) like guilt-tripping and giving back-handed compliments.
- Gaslighting, as seen in an earlier chapter.
- Sometimes people might engage in manipulation without knowing that they are doing so—poor communication skills or defensiveness, without knowing that they are being defensive.
- Love bombing or intermittent flattery and attention (whether in the form of text, calls, emojis, or in-person).

Basic Styles of Communication

We all are unique, with our own level of understanding, mindset, set of emotions. We should not be surprised to know that we have our own way of communicating, our own way and speed of listening and digesting the information, but we are not aware of this. Not all five fingers are of an equal shape or size; hence, when we have a conversation with someone, we should judge what level, speed, and mode of communication they understand. Of course, they should take the responsibility to ask you to slow down if it is too fast or for repetition if something is not clear. Still, we should have this awareness. The problem is we are too often consumed by our thoughts within our bubble that we hardly have any attention span left for the others.

When Trump called Kim Jong-Un, Little Man, many mocked him for his language, but hardly anyone noticed when he gave him respect. Why is that? When Trump mocked Merkel for her bad immigration policy, many called Trump stupid, but when he showed her respect for her good policy decisions, we did not offer any positive affirmation. Double standards? Something I have learned about Trump is that he is one of the few political figures to call a spade a spade, but we get triggered because we are not familiar with this style of communication. I will not convince you to believe whether it is correct or not; I want you to be aware.

We know how Trump communicates; we have seen him communicating this way for years now (Twitter rants, name-calling, belittling, then acknowledging when things are done or good). Yet we still expect him to be Presidential. What is being Presidential anyway? We want him to change his communication style, to become more decent, and when this does not happen, we refer to him as childish and an idiot. Given that we know how he communicates, don't you think we should change how we understand and listen (not suggesting approving but to acknowledge)? But we don't. We still expect him to be Presidential. I wonder who is really stupid or foolish here – Trump who communicates in this way or us, who knows how he communicates, but still expect him to be decent or disregard him because his communication style doesn't align with ours.

The five basic styles of communication often used are:

- Passive communication: Developing a pattern of avoidance in expressing their feelings or opinions. Protecting their rights, needs, and thus avoiding hurtful or anger-induced situations. Emotional outbursts are bound to happen once the boundaries and threshold of high tolerance are reached. Outbursts often lead to feelings of shame, guilt, and confusion, bringing them back to being passive.
- Aggressive communication: Feelings and opinions are expressed, and needs are advocated in a way that violates others' rights. Will often dominate, humiliate, criticize, blame, or attack others.
- Passive-aggressive: These individuals appear passive on the surface but are acting out of anger and resentment directly or indirectly in subtle ways. Will feel powerless, stuck, resentful, and will express their anger by subtly undermining the object of their resentment.
- Assertive: Feelings and opinions are expressed, and rights and needs are advocated in a way that doesn't violate others' rights.
- Manipulative: – as seen earlier in this chapter.

Just like relationships, communication requires work. Can you identify which of the above communication styles you most often use? How often have you

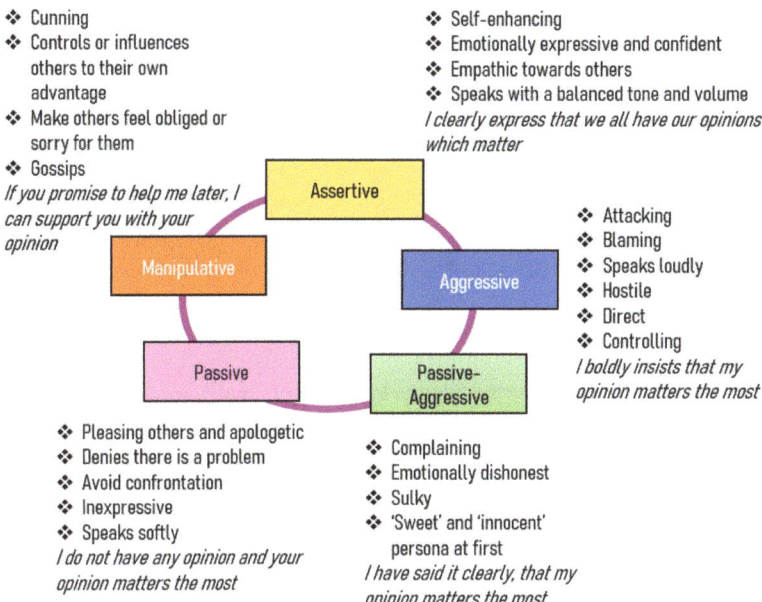

- Cunning
- Controls or influences others to their own advantage
- Make others feel obliged or sorry for them
- Gossips

If you promise to help me later, I can support you with your opinion

Manipulative

Assertive

- Self-enhancing
- Emotionally expressive and confident
- Empathic towards others
- Speaks with a balanced tone and volume

I clearly express that we all have our opinions which matter

Aggressive

- Attacking
- Blaming
- Speaks loudly
- Hostile
- Direct
- Controlling

I boldly insists that my opinion matters the most

Passive

- Pleasing others and apologetic
- Denies there is a problem
- Avoid confrontation
- Inexpressive
- Speaks softly

I do not have any opinion and your opinion matters the most

Passive-Aggressive

- Complaining
- Emotionally dishonest
- Sulky
- 'Sweet' and 'innocent' persona at first

I have said it clearly, that my opinion matters the most

Figure 162: Five basic styles of communication. Which one do you use with whom and under what circumstances?

walked away from a conversation feeling angry, upset, disappointed, triggered, and misunderstood? How often have you found yourself switching from being assertive to becoming passive-aggressive, aggressive, or even manipulative during your conversations? We don't often realize how we fall into and switch between these categories, but we can point at others who do. They lack the tongue control, we get triggered, we lack the tongue control, we go low, they go lower, the voice becomes loud, your tempo escalates. Boom! Everyone involved is done with that conversation, done with that kind of relationship dynamic at least for a reasonable period, or an oath gets taken 'never to discuss politics again with you, ever' or maybe never to speak to that person again.

When we have a level of awareness of these communication styles, not only can we pause and reflect, but we can also bring this to the attention of the other person and help each other grow while keeping the passion for political conversation alive. The success of political conversation is not the responsibility of others but of everyone involved, including yourself.

Nonviolent Communication (NVC)

I used to have (and to some extent still have) passive and active aggression in my communication (who doesn't unless one is willing to work on it), and never realized that. Growing up in India, where, barring Bollywood romance, my communication style was very aggressive because of the society I grew up in. Indian society, in terms of conversations, can be very aggressive, not because of culture per se, but because of external circumstances - people struggling for basic necessities, pollution, large population, and extremely hot and humid weather. When I realized this, I decided to change. It took me a good six months to move away from this unhealthy style to something more decent and assertive. During that time, I came across NVC. I would recommend this as a good start for anyone wanting to engage in political conversations in a civil way. Learning NVC may feel like learning a second language, but it is really worth it.

NVC is based on the principle of nonviolence. The assumption that human beings have the capacity for compassion and empathy and that violent strategies are learned and supported by prevailing cultures. When we do not recognize more effective strategies for meeting our same universal needs of being heard, understood, valued, and respected, we resort to violence.

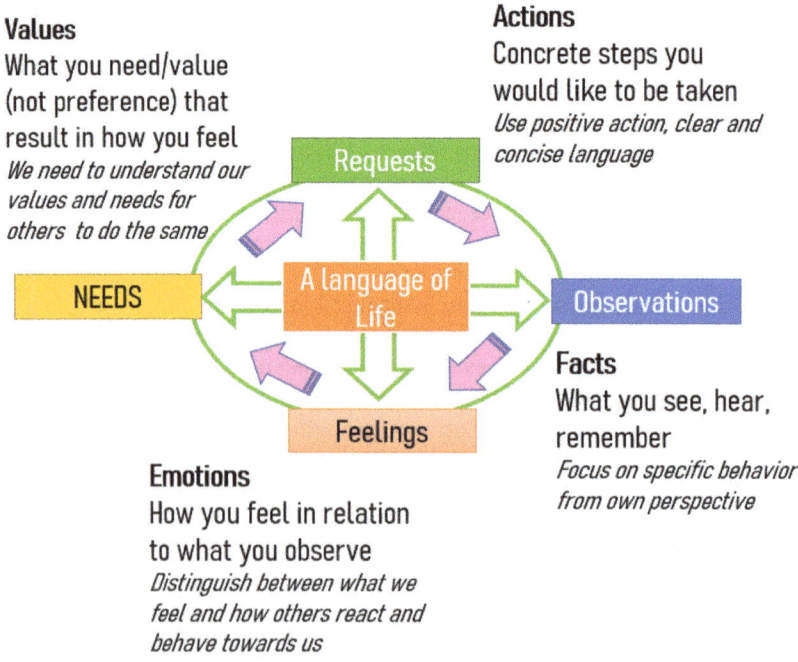

Values
What you need/value (not preference) that result in how you feel
We need to understand our values and needs for others to do the same

Actions
Concrete steps you would like to be taken
Use positive action, clear and concise language

Requests

NEEDS

A language of Life

Observations

Feelings

Facts
What you see, hear, remember
Focus on specific behavior from own perspective

Emotions
How you feel in relation to what you observe
Distinguish between what we feel and how others react and behave towards us

Figure 163: The Four Components of the Nonviolent Communication model

Non-Violent Communication focuses on three aspects of awareness and communication:

- Self-empathy: Involves identification and connection with body sensations, feelings, emotions, values, and needs without judgment, blame, or criticism.
- Empathy for others: Involves listening with attention, presence, and compassion to the feelings and needs of others.
- Honest self-expression: An authentic way relating to your experience of engagement and shares.

Rosenberg suggested a four-step approach (OFNR) to meaningful conversations to connect with everyone's needs:

- Observe and recap. It's a bit like reflective listening, without adding any judgment, analysis, interpretations, story, or emotional input to your response. Thus making neutral statements of what one actually and objectively sees or hears with no subjective filters.
- Describe emotions, feelings, body sensations, and not issues. If you intend to be heard, it is essential to talk about emotions and feelings without perceptions or victim verbs (attack, blame, disrespect, dismissive) or without talking about points relating to policies.
- Identify unmet needs. Needs relating to connection, honesty, play, physical well-being, sense of autonomy, and peace.
- Making requests. Instead of demands, which often use fear, guilt, shame, and reward that aim to ask for concrete actions, which often arise organically if people are connected with each other, would help satisfy that need. The request needs to be made once it is ensured that all parties engaged have a good understanding and have space to hear everyone out. A request can be a connection request (request for reflection) or a solution request (targeted towards action, finding resolution)

Context – fuck context, out of context is so much more interesting!

We talked about context in the Leadership Chapter. Well, guess what? Context is also essential when it comes to communication. We often have the tendency not to pay attention to the context of the topic, time, and relevance when a particular statement, opinion, or viewpoint is expressed. This happens far too often in terms of what different leaders have expressed. Trump said, 'grab them by the pussy.' Fine, it is disgusting, but, in all honesty, all men, at least once in their life, would have objectified women, whether in their teenage, adult youth, or going through heartbreak, and feeling desire for revenge. I shook my head when everyone started criticizing him for what he said, rather than really thinking about the context in which it was spoken. What was he involved in? Has he said anything like that since becoming a candidate or during his Presidency?

We forget that leaders are being watched for every move, every word, and people find clips and opinions from the time when that leader had nothing to do with leadership. We often forget that the media has been manipulating the information, combining statements of leaders they dislike out of context to serve their purpose and make a particular leader look terrible. When the media fails to do their job correctly, it is our responsibility as individuals and citizens to do our job properly rather than getting played like puppets in the media's hands. As time moves, everything evolves.

Have you not evolved as a person and become a better version of yourself? Some policies or opinions which are core to candidates (Bernie has been talking about welfare for 40+ yrs.) in that case, it is important to pay attention, but Bernie has been in politics for those years, too. Likewise, take the case of Corbyn, who has always been anti-EU, but people voted Labour just because they knew that Conservatives are a Brexit party, not realizing that the opposition leader has been a Brexit supporter ever since the UK came into the EU. Hence, context is important, especially in the current climate, where events, news, and dialogues move faster and where everything changes before one even has a chance to blink. Leadership is about making decisions according to society's needs and requirements at present (with a pro-active estimation of the future), but not based on what was happening 5, 10, or 30 years ago. Likewise, when expressing our opinions, we need to consider context and be willing to change our views. The more open-minded and less rigid we are, the more it would be possible for us to truly reflect and play a part in catering to society's needs.

Subtle Nuances

Subtle nuances will include the non-verbal responses; a person's receptivity to our opinions and views during conversation reflected in their facial expression, tonality, and body language. Suppose you are not familiar with how all these subtle nuances play a part in communicating. You will most likely miss the initial warnings leading up to full-blown arguments. Rolling of eyes, nodding of the head, expansion of the chest, and biting of lips are all nuances that can decipher someone's feelings, which they might not be aware of themselves. Consider these as the milestones of the marathon—little things boiling underneath but giving you hints.

I've been in drama, so I can have a good understanding of how body language conveys messages. Trudeau has a very calm presence, so whatever he says will appear confident. Still, we need to go beyond what he is saying. At times, Trump's body language expresses a lot more than his words; hence, it is important to pay attention to this. I find it surprising that people do not realize that when Trump is at his rallies, he energizes his voters by including entertainment, even if it means making gestures relating to a handicap. However, that doesn't make it right.

But, when Trump addresses press conferences, especially in other countries, his body language is entirely different. Have you ever noticed that? What does this tell us about his character, and if you haven't noticed this and fail to understand and read them, what does this make of your character? A bad reader, a person who takes everything in the literal sense and cannot put things in perspective, context, or pull apart the meaning to read the depths. Next time, you have a conversation with family and friends, pay attention, and see if you can pre-empt how someone might be feeling inside before it becomes obvious at the surface.

Tips for having more graceful political conversations

- Respect the opinions of others. No one has all the right answers or knows everything, but one can definitely form opinions based on what one knows.
- Avoid rejecting any new piece of information outright, even if it challenges your beliefs and thinking.

Oh, so you use lol, upside-down face and shruggie emoticons to convey sarcasm and goofiness. Please tell me more about the subtle complexities and ironic words of your nuanced diction... lol

Figure 164: Every emoji, word, and phrase used has a hidden meaning we try to convey but are seldom aware of. Let's stick to memes for now, shall we?

- Don't aim at changing other people's minds. There is no one perfect solution for any specific issue, but instead multiple options. Each has its own pros, cons, and consequences impacting everyone in society, one way or another, since we are all intertwined. Remember, most will suffer from confirmation bias and motivated reasoning. If your friends are arguing, interrupt, and check-in about their intention of the conversation.
- Avoid coming from a place of assumptions, but use openness and curiosity. What are the reasons for them forming a particular? Does it resonate with you or not? Even if it doesn't resonate with you, it doesn't mean it won't resonate with others.
- Hard feelings can come up, so allow them to emerge rather than discuss the issue further. Focus on feelings and providing support when that happens.
- Ask questions genuinely to expand your knowledge. Listen carefully, even if you disagree with what is being said. Learn to disagree gracefully.

- Follow normal protocols of conversations, avoid interjecting, using aggressive language, sarcastic tones, or name-calling.
- Share information that you've thoroughly checked on multiple credible sources and full of facts rather than scams, rumors, hoaxes, or someone else's opinion. Validate the person who has produced that information as fake news, which looks exactly like real news.
- Stay connected with your feelings and avoid sharing any information based on knee-jerk reactions.
- Don't form opinions based on headlines or few second or minute clips but rather read the entire article. Read two instead of four if you don't have time; address one issue instead of several if you don't have time; watch one clip in full instead of many mini clips if you don't have time.
- Practice reflective listening, paying attention, and understanding what is being shared. Reflect back to the other person to feel heard, understood, and ensure that their information is received in the way they want to communicate, thus free of the listener's bias and assumptions.

Conclusion

It is critical to understand that communication takes place at many levels. As a human being, we are more than just the physical body we see; likewise, spoken or written words or expression through body language is only a tiny portion of communication taking place within a person and with other people. The sooner we get this, the sooner we will be able to avoid misunderstandings not only in the political aspect but in any part of our lives, including relationships (who wouldn't love that? 😊). I have always wished our parents, schools, and society had provided this kind of information during our upbringings rather than us having to learn this as adults. Dismantling old patterns and integrating new ones is much more difficult than adopting great patterns from the beginning, especially when we are so naïve. The past is the past, and we can't change it. Let's make an effort from this moment and look forward to a future with great aspirations and hope. Most importantly, let's teach others to do the same, not by using aggressive or forceful tactics but by inspiring them and leading by example. In the next chapter, we move onto one of the most dreaded aspects of life. Change!

CHAPTER THIRTEEN

CHANGE

I come across many who say they want to change the world. I come across very few who say I am ready to change myself. When we change, our world changes. If you love yourself deeply enough, be willing to change. If you want to grow, be ready for change. If you want to inspire someone, be the change.

Michael Charming

Introduction

The only constant in life is change, so the question to ask is how do you deal with change? We elect leaders to bring the change. We implement policies to bring the change. We have conversations to find resolutions that bring the change. Our conversations often end up going nowhere; some things need to be verbally vomited, which, if handled well, avoids confrontation; if not, we have war among us. What if, from the get-go, we agree that no matter what, we will all share one thing that this conversation has resulted in bringing a change within us, within our thinking, and within our perspective? What do you think those conversations would be like, and most importantly, what would the wrap-up discussion be like? No fists and blows but hugs, handshakes, and maybe kisses (whether on the cheek, lips or forehead will depend on the people and intimacy between them).

When asked the question, what is leadership, you will hear many different answers – it is about service, it is about keeping cool, it is about finding the best solutions relating to intense situations, it is about uniting the country, it is about draining the swamp, and it is about X, Y and Z. In my view, leadership is more about being able to guide us through change, change that circumstances require, as swiftly as possible. Be it coming out of the pandemic victoriously, preparing to face the AI world, or just about anything else that we want, based on our needs, the needs of society, and the world at large.

Change – our part of life

❖ Carney demands 'fundamental change' including further curbs on pay after a succession of major scandals

❖ NHS faces a 'full-blown crisis without big change': Toxic mix of cuts and privatisation puts the future of NHS at risk

❖ Pope demands urgent need to tackle "extraordinary climate change and an unprecedented destruction of ecosystems"

❖ Scottish Government denies flag change

❖ Chile's constitutional conundrum: To change or not to change?

❖ U.S. says Zimbabwe failed to make needed political, economic changes

❖ Egyptian inquiry into political violence seeks changes to protest law

❖ 'They've got a problem': Obama mocks Republicans for committing political 'suicide' by opposing broad changes to immigration laws

Change in bus and train timetables or change in children's school opening and closing times are some of the changes we experience in our lives that are easily dealt with or at least more familiar with. Many struggle to cope with these changes to such an extent that they blame the government if their dentist changes their appointment (oh hello, dentist definitely not your fault). Then we have the change in government (after 4 or 5 years), change in leaders and ministers bringing in different sets of knowledge, thinking, and management style, change in policies impacting some in positive and others in negative ways, and change in inter-relations and cooperations (US-China, OPEC Cartel + Russia, EU-Turkey, US-NATO). And then we have the once in a lifetime change – change in EU-UK relations due to Brexit, change in the US-rest of the world due to withdrawing from the Paris Climate Accord, or the US-rest of the countries withdrawing from the treaty with Iran, change of house, and change of life-time partner (i.e., divorce or death). At times change happens out of necessity, but in some cases, due to something else. Human nature wants to keep things status quo due to uncertainty, stress, extra work, time, and energy required to deal with change. But then, as human beings, we are used to change; in fact, we strive for it. Brexit was a lifetime opportunity

Figure 165: Not everyone can use cognitive functions to think through issues and aspects in great detail.

for change for some; it was a nightmare of uncertainty for others. As an outsider, Trump meant a newer perspective for some. In contrast, it meant a lack of experience in dealing with social and political affairs for others.

So, change is the only constant aspect of life; leadership is about change; we have been experiencing change since childhood - so the question that arises is why we are so resistant to it? Why do we have a defense wall that doesn't want to even consider the benefits that a particular change may bring? Most importantly, how do we deal with it effectively that it becomes not only acceptable to all but something that we all look forward to with passion. Recognizing the need for change and then working towards making it successful is a process, but before that, we need to understand what causes us to resist change.

Why people resist change

From time immemorial, world political systems have been changing. From the disintegration of great empires to the emergence and vanishing of nation-states. From world wars to innumerable revolutions. The shifting of domestic and international policies, various financial and humanitarian crises, political landscape changes with women's rights, gender equality, multiple ideologies, and never-ending social, economic, technological, and AI developments. Each of these have demanded one thing – change. Whether we like it or not, whether we were ready for it or not, whether many would have lived to see that change through or not.

Figure 166: The change curve

Change in one area is going to cause a change in other areas. This is a given. Building a new station means the landscape will be changed; perhaps you will no longer have that free space or sunshine you are used to. A change in Medicare implies a change in your lifestyle relating to finances, health, and eating habits. A change in government indications relating to the pandemic requires you to maintain social distance, wear masks, stay indoors, or only meet in a group of ten or less. Sometimes, change is necessary due to circumstances. Sometimes, change is self-driven as part of our society, necessity, or need. When change is self-driven, it motivates us, often empowering others to join us for the cause (even though some might feel deaf to our passion), while in other cases, we might have huge resistance or attitude of indifference towards it. Resistance to change shows in our behavior – anger, self-sabotage, hostility, passive-aggressive, lethargic, resentment, unhappiness, lack of participation, and *some things will never change—same old, same old.*

"One reason people resist change is because they focus on what they have to give up instead of what they have to gain."   **--- Anony-mous**

Why leaders could resist change

While leaders are elected for change, even they are sometimes resistant. Although the problem relating to resistance has more to do with people than with leaders, here are some of the reasons leaders could resist change:

- Fear of losing control and authority
- Lack of time
- Cons weigh more than pros
- It doesn't serve the greater needs of society
- It is not urgent or high on the priority list
- The impact is not worth the time, energy, resources, or money to be spent on it
- Comfort with the status quo
- Party over society and vice-versa depending on leadership
- Politics over humanity and vice-versa
- Effectiveness
- Their tenure in that role
- The rules, laws, and legal complications that prevents them from exercising the change

Figure 167: We all want the change to happen, but are we willing to work for it?

Types of resistances

Kurdistan conflict in Turkey and Iran; Palestinian militants (ongoing); Green Resistance (ongoing); Insurgency in Jammu and Kashmir (ongoing); Black

Guerrilla Family (ongoing); Charles de Gaulle Civil rights movement; Nonviolent resistance; Opposition to the Iraq War.

When it comes to change, people fall into the following categories:
- Ones who will initiate change
- Ones who will accept the proposed change
- Ones who will be indifferent
- Ones who will not accept change
- Ones who will not accept change and create resistance movements such as protests

Political uncertainty is challenging and can affect us in many ways, no matter our beliefs and attitudes towards that uncertainty.

Figure 168: Change is constant; nothing stays the same.

When we have resistance towards something, it undergoes a process at one or many layers of the body and the association and attachment outside. This can be categorized as:

Micro Factors:
- Mental layer resistance: relating to logical and cognitive resistance due to beliefs, mental health, bias, *anything not meeting the norm, is automatically resisted*
- Emotional layer resistance: relating to emotional upset and reactions to change such as anger, confusion, *anything that doesn't bring happiness and joy, is automatically resisted*
- Physical layer resistance: relating to effects on the physical such as headaches, insomnia, anxiety, *anything that brings tension is automatically resisted*
- Energetic layer resistance: relating to exhaustion, feelings of suffocation, *anything which feels tiring, drains energy, or disharmonizing is automatically resisted*
- Spiritual layer resistance: relating to not per religious beliefs, purpose, not meeting everyone's desires or due to fear *anything that results in fear, is automatically resisted*

There could be a possibility of misalignment at the macro level, where one or more layers support it, but others reject it.

Macro Factors:
- Psychological resistance; resistance of our body in relation to external factors
- Sociological resistance; resistance relating to customs, groups, and cultures
- Family and relationships resistance; just because our partner or parents don't like it; hence we do not like it either and resist change

- Economic factors resistances; due to a negative impact or no impact on our finances
- Safety and security resistances; resistance relating to our job and our safety
- Group resistances; resistance relating to trade unions protection, self-interest, and ethnicities & minorities, don't always serve the country nor are in the self-interest of the country
- Global resistances; resistance relating to policies requiring co-operation, and sometimes compromise leading to peace and harmony

Figure 169: The forces of resistance at the micro and macro levels. This diagram may feel repetitive considering the similar messages I have shared in text and images throughout this book. It is being mentioned again because while it may seem a simple concept to understand and agree with, it is challenging to recognize and integrate these concepts in life. But rest assured, life would feel better once these are comprehended and integrated.

How to manage resistance and bring change

'It is not the strongest of the species that survives, nor the most intelligent that survives. It is the one that is most adaptable to change.' --- Charles Darwin.

At an individual level

If we want to change something, we first should focus on changing ourselves. You want peace in the country, but how peaceful are you with everyone (and with yourself)? You want environmental protection, but how much effort do you put into not using or reusing plastic or into other things that are conducive to the environment? How much effort have you put in to get yourself educated about how you can take actions to bring the change you want to see? You want to support Black Lives Matter, but how often do you do something for them? You want to save the animals, but then are you a meat-eater?

Be the change that you wish to see in the world. - Mahatma Gandhi.

By leadership

The question then arises of how leaders should deal with the necessary change. Do they ensure that they have enough support to remain in office, or do they ensure that the economy remains competitive in the world?

Should we as individuals make our leader's job easier or more difficult, irrespective of whether we like them or not. Because we dislike them does not mean they are disliked by the majority, as to a large extent, leaders win through fair and square elections. Country leaders use their resistances, some in taking their country further and others mostly trying to take their country further.

What can we do, individually, to support the leader of our country? Are you opposed to your ruling leader, or are you pro? Just because the change that leader is about to bring doesn't meet your needs doesn't mean it is not meeting others' needs. Of course, it doesn't mean that every policy and action needs to be supported. It merely means to have the awareness that other people are demanding the change, and if that size is big enough, then it is worth reconsidering your stance, and if it resonates even a tiny bit, be willing to support the change. And most importantly, ask yourself how you can have a healthier attitude towards the current ruling leader, no matter how much you might dislike them? In the next election cycle, you can take your frustration out all over again.

"The announcement of the changes really went well."

Figure 170: Leaders generally have a tough job bringing about any change.

Types of change

Here are a few examples of changes that take place:
- Happened Change: is unpredictable in nature and usually caused by the impact of external factors.
- Reactive Change: takes place in response to an event or a chain of events.
- Anticipatory Change: is implemented with prior anticipation of an event or a chain of events.
- Planned Change: is implemented to improve current operational processes and for achieving a pre-defined goal.
- Incremental Change: happens in small increments and is implemented at the micro-level, units, or subunits.

- Strategic Change: is implemented to bring changes in components or strategies of a unit or organization.
- Fundamental Change: involves the redefinition of a vision or mission.
- Likewise, other changes also exist; technological change, evolutionary and revolutionary change, developmental change, transformational change, etc.

"What if we don't change at all ... and something magical just happens?"

Figure 171: Wishful thinking vs. realistic thinking. These are very different unless you live in airy-fairy land. Focus on concrete and tangible measures.

Managing political change

How do great leaders like Mahatma Gandhi (nonviolent resistance), Nelson Mandela (abolishing apartheid), Martin Luther King (equality), and Dalai Lama (peaceful coexistence) manage to get people to support their call for change?

How does one person bring change with such a significant shift, while other leaders struggle to bring a tiny or any change at all? How did a skinny semi-clad person, who supported racial segregation, made derogatory remarks about blacks, opposed contraception, end up being called 'Father of India', and an 80-year-old won the hearts of not only Africa but of the entire world?

People see Trump as an enemy or dislike him without realizing that he has been the change leader based on the ugliness and hard realities, rage, delusions of America's greatness, inequalities created by the predatory capitalist society, which have been existing in American society (and many other societies) for decades. Trump just didn't magically get into power through the wave of a magic wand. He was chosen, by the people, to bring the change, just like Obama was chosen to bring the change most needed at that time. And no, socialism is not the answer either.

Ways to deal with resistance and change

Listed below are few ways to deal with resistance and change:
- Recognizing that they exist, being willing to listen, and then trying to have an open dialog.
- Repression is an option, but it should not be used from the get-go. Modern democracies do show this pattern of not using repression from the onset.
- Having the awareness that resistance happens at all layers of the body and then finding ways to deal with them. Support groups to deal with emotional outbursts or overwhelm, dialog groups for mental cognitive functions or mental disorders.
- Great communication, better orator, as most of the time, people are actually open about resistance if the speaker can make a case.

- Engagement throughout the process with regular updates (no wonder Arcinda won support; the way she communicated and kept everyone engaged).
- People don't resist change per se, but they do resist being changed. Put them in charge of the change process, help them develop solutions, have surveys, and show the surveys' results.
- Participation isn't what you would like to do (there can be some element), but rather your need to feel part of something, so hopefully, you can find a good balance. If you want to implement ten policy changes, have people voice out and engage on two, explain in simple terms why the remaining eight are being changed.

Figure 172: To achieve something different, you have to be willing to do something different.

Some Models – Time for some management lessons

Many famous psychologists, professors, academics, professionals, and scholars have various change models consistently applied in organizations. Most of these models are successful and have helped organizations grow, but I wonder why it is difficult for governments to carry out their plans effectively and efficiently. When these changes are proposed, do we understand how the whole change process works? We often say *Government planning was shit. There were not enough ballot booths. There wasn't enough security, or that there was a technological failure.*

If we understood the whole change process or have it in our awareness that there are project managers who work at bringing change in every project that runs, then it will help us stop pointing fingers at the government. I am not saying we shouldn't be criticizing, but let's not make it a blanket rule. Should you deem the whole initiative a failure, do you consider the entire government to be ineffective? We need to look at different aspects of the project to ascertain which weren't implemented correctly. A vital question is, what did we do to support the project, especially the one that might have failed because of our actions or inactions. Here are some of the models to give an idea of how projects and change are implemented.

Kurt Lewin's Change Management Model

- Unfreeze: ensuring readiness for change by preparing to understand and accept the criticality of change (ascertain the need for change, gather support, develop strategy, and plan to communicate, manage for uncertainties)
- Change (transition): making the required changes (communicating methodologically, dismiss hearsay, encourage action, engagement)
- Freeze (or refreezing): reinforcing and institutionalizing the desired changes and incorporating them into the organizational culture (embed the change, plan to sustain, support, and celebrate success)

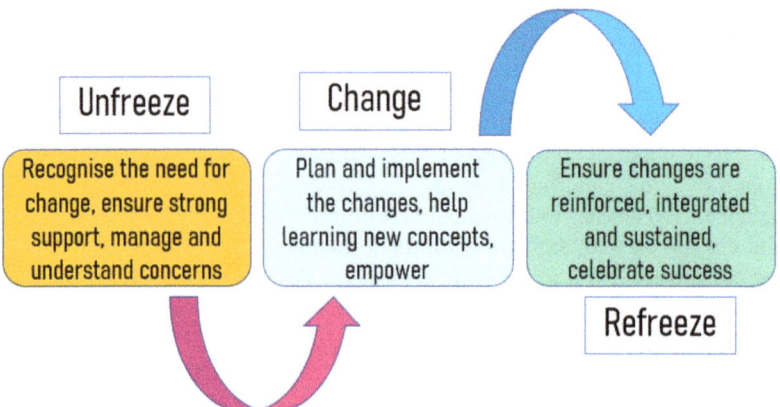

Figure 173: Kurt Lewin's Change Management Model

Kotter's Eight-Step Model of Change

- Create a sense of urgency: Help others understand the need for change through an inspiring, courageous statement or dialog that emphasizes the importance of acting immediately.
- Powerful coalition: Convince and identify a group of volunteers, who once fully bought-into the need for change, to work as a team to guide, coordinate, and communicate the activities.
- Forming strategic vision: Formulate a clear vision and coordinate so that individuals can understand the project's depth and link initiatives directly to the vision so that the change of direction makes more sense.
- Communicate the vision: Communicating with the wider community helps to encourage cooperation and support throughout. Consider appropriate channels and ways of communication.
- Removing obstacles: Identify any resistance, continuously check for barriers, and work on eliminating these obstacles as quickly as possible.
- Generating short-term wins: Quick short-term wins keep the motivation. Create short-term achievable targets with little room for failure.

- Sustaining change: Avoid declaring victory too early, rather focus on feedback from each step of the process to identify improvement areas.
- Integrating and anchoring: For any change to stay, it must become part of the culture. Hence, continuous efforts should be spent to ensure that change is seen in every aspect.

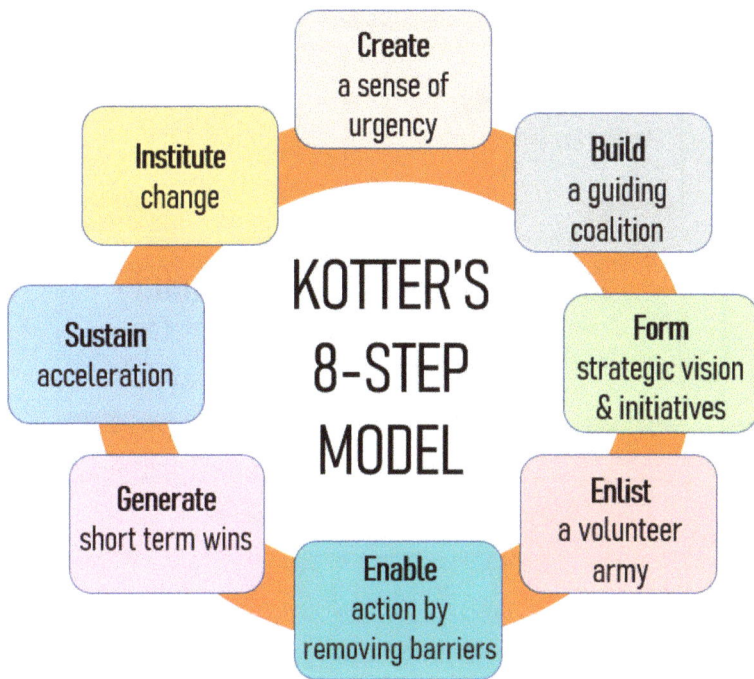

Figure 174: Kotter's model provides clear steps and guidance for the change process.

Driving Organizational Change by Embracing Agile and Facing the VUCA World

This focuses on risk-taking and managing uncertainties and turbulence. The United States Army War College was one of the first organizations to use the VUCA acronym, which stands for:

- Volatility – the world is constantly changing, becoming more unstable and unpredictable in its nature and extent. It becomes impossible to determine cause and effect.
- Uncertainty – becomes difficult to anticipate results or predict how they will unfold. Historical forecasts and past experiences are losing relevance. Planning for investment, growth, and development is becoming extremely difficult and uncertain.
- Complexity – the world is more complex than ever before, with many different, interconnected factors coming into play. Getting an overview with

accuracy is difficult. Reactions and counter-reactions impact decision making with the potential to cause chaos and confusion.

- Ambiguity – Not everything is black and white. One size fits all doesn't work anymore. Demands are contradictory and absurd, challenging our values and beliefs to the core. There is a lack of clarity or awareness about situations.

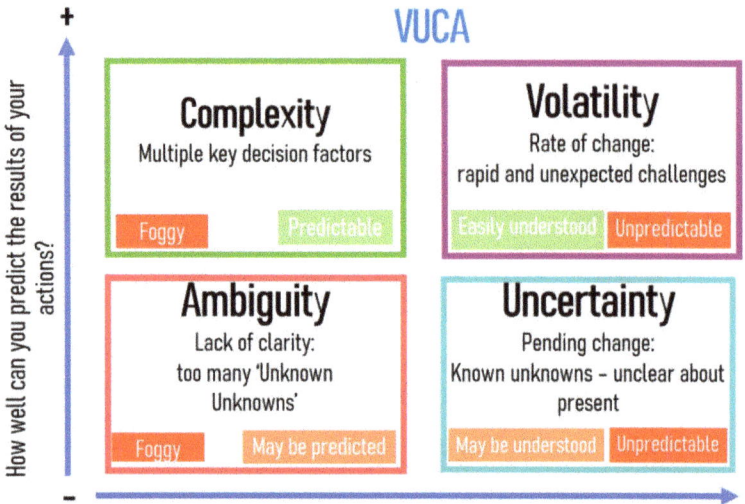

Figure 175: Driving Organizational Change by Embracing Agile and Facing the VUCA World.

There are several other models like Mintzberg and Quinn's model of change, McKinsey 7S change model, Anderson & Anderson's change model, transformational change and change management, models of transformational change, that you can look into to understand how the project works, how various stages are implemented, obstacles faced, and resolutions and remediations put in place. It is worth highlighting that an extensive study is generally conducted before implementing a project (the bigger the project, the more extensive the study).

Detecting problems and finding solutions

- ❖ *Can identifying mental illness stop terrorism? Researchers link psychological problems to 'lone wolf' attacks*
- ❖ *All 2017's terrorist attacks in UK had online element, says Home Secretary*
- ❖ *Russia hosts North Korean diplomat for talks on new tensions*
- ❖ *US body fines Credit Suisse $16.5 mn for lax controls*

'Complaining is finding fault. Wisdom is finding solutions.'
-- Anonymous.

How we can help. As humanity, we have been amazing, evolving from apes, gorillas, cavemen, and hunters to enhancing consciousness, developing speech, creating rituals and globally connected communities, and facing the adversity of time, come what may. The evolution of man was part of an evolutionary process demanded by external factors. We aspire to make progress with our desire to grow, dedication to creating better, more comfortable, and interesting lives for ourselves (survival of the fittest and desire to rule). No other animal species has made this kind of progress.

What does this say about us – that humans are geniuses? We have tremendous capabilities and potentials, many of which remain unexplored, untapped, and undreamt throughout our lives. The reason being, we spend so much time fighting with each other. We move from one toxic relationship to another, keep creating and reliving the repeated unhealthy patterns passed to us through generations, often living a lifestyle that isn't conducive to our body layers until something hits home, making us realize, introspect, and contemplate and perhaps, then we are ready for change. This blow in the face can happen sooner, during a mid-life crisis, or in later years and for some souls, it never happens. We come, we survive and somehow manage to live, and we die. It doesn't need to be this way.

Our human body is made in this way for us to experience more pleasure, more happiness, and bliss rather than pain, but it happens quite to the contrary. It makes me recall what my dad used to say, '*Humans are the most advanced, most developed, and most disturbed animals on this planet.*' I think his words are so true. Well, he was a man of great experience and wisdom, after all.

One of our greatest assets that has allowed humanity to survive, prosper, and rule over other beasty animals is our ability to find solutions to problems. Problems will be part of life, part of relating with each other, and part of developing or altering policies, no matter how hard we try not to face them. We need to develop a positive and embracing attitude towards resolving problems. When we talk

The more I learn, the more I realize how much I don't know
.... Einstein

I'm like, really smart and a very stable genius... probably the smartest, intelligent, and most genius person in the world
... Trump

Figure 176: Can you pick the real genius? E=mc2 or I'm the best President the United States of America has ever had...

of change, it is done with the intention of solving problems. Are we focusing our resources on solving existing problems, creating more problems, or solving a problem that did not exist to start with? These are often portrayed in readers' minds by the media for political motivation, creating hype around nonexistent problems, and making mountains out of molehills. How can we solve a problem that doesn't exist?

Some of the issues in finding solutions relating to existing problems:
- Many are too fixed in the way things are and not even open to considering alternatives, forget about actually implementing them.
- We place too much focus on 'what's in it for me', then 'what's in it for us', 'what's in it for you', or 'how is this going to help my family or me and if so, when and how?
- We focus too heavily on monetary terms, which is important, but the pros and cons must be considered, from cognitive thinking, feelings and emotions attached to the people who will be impacted. Having ten people make more money is far worse than having 100 people feeling genuinely unhappy about it.

- Sometimes politicians focus on problems that can easily be sold to the public, authority, media, and various groups to have their buy-in to continue to remain in power. Focus is driven by agenda rather than focusing on real issues. Different groups will have varying interests, which will hardly be aligned.
- Some problems are hard to solve because of the imbalance in trade-offs between the winners and losers and nonexistent solutions currently. Most problems have solutions as long as we are all willing to work towards them, including compromises. Being willing to make sacrifices for others should be a self-driven initiative rather than government forced.
- We need to move away from only serving elites' interests or making policies behind closed doors where broader populations' interests are involved.
- Political leaders, media, and the press should be held accountable for the lies, manipulation, and hype they tell and create. How can leaders not be held accountable for disrupting entire nations (Iraq, Libya) or get away with telling lies (leaders on both sides of the Brexit campaign)? No wonder the trust between rulers and those being ruled tends to suffer – who is to blame? Can you consider – how can the most educat-

Figure 177: *It is truly that simple.*

ed leaders make such a bad decision relating to Iraq? How can the EU continue to make mistakes like unlimited open-door immigration policies impacting the immigrants and the people living in those communities? How can they forget about cultural integration? How can we continue to allow Italy to continue living in debt with substantial non-performing loans? How can a city like London continue to have a housing crisis where getting a home becomes unaffordable? I am not suggesting that we have an easy or quick fix; I am implying that even with the best of the best experts and the sharpest of the sharpest minds available, some problems continue to exist. What are we not doing right? Why do we run under a broken political system (and the irony is that we all know it is broken) where the economically efficient and most obvious solutions and policies are not or seldom implemented? Why do private companies tend to oust government departments in many aspects? Why?

+ Why do we continue to have the same voting method? We have no choices for the least preferred candidate or the second and third-best choice. We don't have eligibility criteria for voting, nor an emotional, psychological, and aptitude test for politicians and voters.

+ To find solutions that better serve us in the current century, we need to start being open to other possibilities in our present circumstances and considering things not considered before. These solutions will potentially cause resistance initially, but we have to recognize what we have currently hasn't worked in the best interest of everyone's well-being. While politics might be broken, how broken are we as individuals, especially towards each other, as human beings living in one society? Challenges are that historical circumstances and mindsets were different from what they are now and what present circumstances demand.

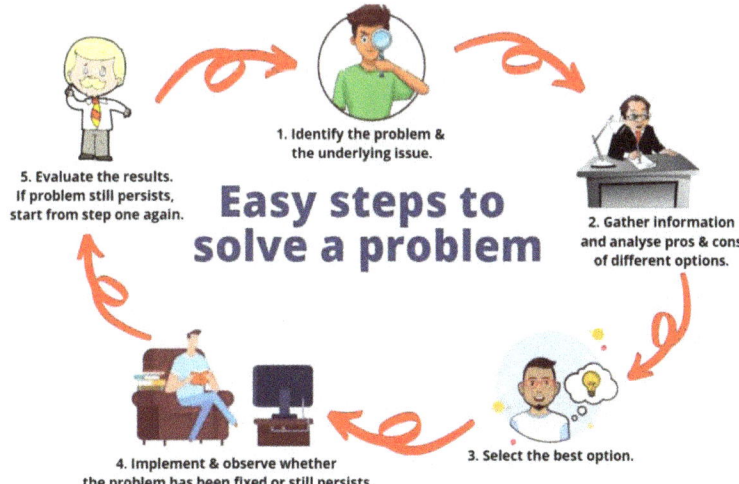

Figure 178: Simple steps to finding solutions.

+ Political jargons need to be done away with. Instead, the focus should be on connection – human to human connection, rather than delivering a well-prepared script. When Trump shows up, he does precisely that. We need to be ready to hear the unheard, untrigger the triggered, and underwhelm the overwhelm. Like him or not, when he speaks, he speaks directly to people about their issues, in a simple and understandable language as someone who cares more about the American people than the rest of the world. No wonder continued to remain in the Presidency throughout his tenure despite everything portrayed about him.

- As voters, we should be more focused on help and support than criticizing and blaming and never being happy with the government. We need to avoid having double standards.
- Start by identifying who or what is holding us back – the voters, the agencies, or the government departments?

Ask the right questions – are we asking out of interest or to genuinely find a solution?

We know the world, the society we live in, and our lives are full of complexities with numerous problems that arise from time to time. We cannot consider solving all in one go, especially considering our finite resources; hence we need to prioritize and find solutions that work for most from the start. The best way to find solutions is to take a step back and consider things from the micro and macro level (which is what this book aims to do). Doing this will widen our perspective, clear our internal turbulence or messiness to avoid having strong judgments about anyone or anything, and view the problem from a place of curiosity rather than perceptions and strongly held beliefs. We can then consider various scenarios and possible options by asking the right questions and staying open to having open dialogues.

Figure 179: By asking the right questions at the right time, we might be able to take our friendships and connections deeper and come up with workable solutions to complex problems.

Quite often, I've found that people have strong judgments or assumptions about someone's political views. Asking the right questions would allow us to find more information about why they hold those views, which will help us understand and provide deeper insights into their minds, emotions, and life histories. E.g., during Brexit, I was labeled a racist and closed-minded person who disliked immigrants. Many commented, *'just a reminder, Michael, you are an immigrant yourself.'*

Hardly anyone asked about my reasons for supporting Brexit. Those who know and are familiar with me know that I'm one of the most loving, open-minded, and intelligent people they could meet, but this is forgotten when one is triggered. I did not grow up in the UK/EU. I spent ten years of my life getting visas, paying money, booking never-ending visa appointments while enduring the frustration of consolidating the documents for submission and then keeping my fingers crossed, hoping to get the visa for the country I wish to travel or immigrate to. This was the life I was used to instead of someone who had the privilege to move across borders by merely taking a passport or driving license or even none at all. My life experience in this immigration aspect had been different. I saw both the merit and disadvantages from the perspective of an immigrant like me and someone as an EU or UK national with the advantage of moving across borders at their will.

While deciding, I did make sure not to do this from deep hurt and pain or wanting other immigrants to suffer the same difficulties because it is what happens. We operate from a place of revenge, hurt, and pain, often wanting, without us knowing, the same for others. My decision was based on pros and cons relating to the mental body and cognitive functions as I can't see how having an open-border policy, with no checks, is good for any country, especially a country like the UK, which many want to immigrate to as they consider this heaven in comparison to the place they are now. (I did the same). No wonder Merkel took a U-turn on her open-door policy, even though she strongly supported it from the beginning, which I wasn't happy about.

So, in my case, I wish that people had asked me questions from a place of openness and curiosity. Apart from one Italian friend who asked the right questions, no other friend asked me the right questions that would have allowed me to share my perspective and decision-making process, giving more room for more open discussion. She got to understand my reasons for supporting Brexit relating to immigration and said, '*ah, so you are not familiar with the benefits of having the freedom to travel without worrying about visas. I'm sorry about the experiences you had and that our world operates this way*'. She and I are still best friends. Some of the appropriate questions should have been:

+ Could you let us know why you have these views (including your mental and emotional states, if possible)?
+ Michael, what is your view on open-door immigration vs. restricted immigration?
+ Tell me about your experiences that led you to this decision?
+ What would your life have been like had you lived in the EU or UK with that level of freedom to travel?
+ Would your opinion and decision have been the same?
+ What would it take for you to support open-immigration or not support Brexit, if at all?

It is impossible to have a preset list of questions to ask. Each case, situation, issue, and scenario would vary, so there are endless permutations and combinations that could be created. Here are some suggestions that can help in asking the appropriate questions:

- Have an open mind. In my book, Amplify Your Orgasm, I share the differences between the brain and the mind. The brain is more of an anatomical structure made up of lobes and neurons, which are visible and lead to the creation of habits, neural pathways, and conditioning. The mind encompasses the world of feelings, thoughts, attitudes, desires, beliefs, consciousness, and imagination. An open mind results in broader and deeper consciousness, more awareness, better presence, more attention at all layers of the body, and the right set of intentions can allow a better exchange and flow of energy, ideas, and thoughts.
- Ask questions that lead to understanding the different elements of SWOT analysis. Sometimes people might not have considered these; in such a case, you can ask them, what are the opportunities resulting from this, or what are the threats posed as a result of XYZ?
- Stay connected with your emotions and feelings, and ask questions to understand the other person's feelings and emotions. Sometimes, they might not be aware of this, so asking the question will help focus on these. If someone is feeling fear, then no matter what might be happening on the outside, their state is currently that of fear, so their expressions, opinions, and judgments would be mostly clouded with this emotion.
- Ask them questions relating to their priorities and which needs are getting fulfilled and which are not.
- Ask them questions relating to other aspects of society that a particular decision or policy might impact (remember, everything is connected directly or indirectly, so it will affect other areas of society).
- When you are asking questions, where are you operating from at that moment? In my previous book, I asked my readers, 'where do you live?' And I would like to ask you the same question, where are you living when you have these conversations? In Chapter Three, we discussed our different energy centers at an energetic level. Are you asking questions from headspace or by dropping into your heart or combining both? The impact of these would be different. If you are using the headspace, the questions are more analytical, along the lines of wanting to find an immediate solution, counter-argue, go into the mode of who is right and who is wrong. If we are operating from heart, it is more about hearing the other person, staying connected to your own love energy (more on this in the next chapter) no matter how different or triggering the other person's opinion.
- Ensure that you are not jumping from one issue to another, ping-ponging back and forth, or bringing in other points to prove your point. Stay on track with the question. If you ask someone about women's rights, do not bring up the topic of immigration, gun control, financial crisis, or what you cooked for dinner last night. Close the discussion relating to one issue first, before moving to the next topic. Women's rights might be connected to immigration or what your dad wore last night, but have it in your awareness that a new topic is being brought up and ensure everyone knows this. It is better to discuss one topic thoroughly or enough to get the juice than to discuss ten topics with hardly any possibility of increasing one's perspective.

- Most importantly, ask the questions that open the other person rather than having them closed and shut down. In my example of supporting Brexit, the topics were related to immigration. When you are having a conversation, remember, you are not on a podium trying to convince the masses to gather more votes, but with a friend, family member, or even a stranger, with whom you want to enjoy the experience, connect as humans, and to relate and share.
- Sometimes, you might want to ask questions that would prove that you know better or the ones that will boost your ego. It is okay, as long as you are aware of doing this and conscious of its impact on others. To take this one step further, let others know what you are doing and why. It would be very uncomfortable and vulnerable to say this, but see what happens afterward.
- This might be a stretch, but if possible, ask how the conversation went and close by sharing how it can be improved the next time and what each can do to make this topic more engaging for everyone.
- Sometimes we might not be able to find solutions for a topic, and it is okay. Remember, politics is complicated, and we might not find a fix there and then. We have this attitude of finding the fix, not knowing that finding a solution should happen over time to find something that beneficially works for most. There needs to be an expansion of perspectives, integration of thought processes and ideas, reflection on conversations exchanged, and possibly further research based on the new knowledge gained.
- Remember, questions relating to both micro and macro are essential; it's not one or the other. It can be one or the other at that moment, depending on a person's states (emotional, mental, physical), but the focus should be on both. Suppose the person is worried about their child's security or needs to be seen and heard. In that case, there is no point in asking their view about NATO or China, but to keep it to the micro-level first, something that affects their children's safety or something that affects them.
- Avoid asking questions just for the sake of asking. If you feel like you have not been given a chance to express yourself, let everyone know and then ask for the time for that expression.
- Open-ended questions will provide deeper insights, but closed-ended questions can keep things short, depending on the scenario. When asking questions, stay focused on what your underlying intention is. Is there any bias or confirmation bias that you aim to skirt someone to, or are you genuinely asking the question to know more about the person and their views?
- Keep your questions short, clear, and precise to avoid ambiguity or fogging everyone else. Terribly formulated questions will lead to more confusion and chaos. They might cause you to lose credibility in asking questions and sharing your opinions. Keep them simple. The most complicated things can be discussed by having simple conversations.

Conclusion

Change is an integral part of life. Let's be willing to dive deeper and understand the rationale and the pros and cons of the change being proposed or implemented before jumping to conclusions and resorting to protests or dismay at the government. When needed, consider the right method of expressing resistance and do this with awareness rather than emotional or mental reactions. Treat other humans with as much love and warmth as possible. Be willing to ask the right questions at the right time, especially when engaging in political conversations. And lastly, do ask questions. I see people that don't ask questions and accept the status quo. You might ask me, how can one still convey love and warmth to someone we disagree with or who supports policies that go against the fulfillment of our needs. The next chapter will answer precisely these questions.

CHAPTER FOURTEEN

COMING TOGETHER

When you strip away politics, wars, bluster, poverty, sickness, pandemics, skirmishes, disagreements, and everything else, both good and bad, the only thing you have left in your life, is love.

Michael Charming

Introduction

What is love? Love for ourselves? Love for others? Platonic love, familial love, romantic love, love for a pet, love for a city, or love for country? On the macro level, how can we love our world better? We can express the kind of love we have for family or a partner, so why can't we find a piece of that love to express for people when we discuss essential subjects, like politics, which includes the direction of our shared lives, country, and world?

> ❖ *Pope gives tough love to Mexico's political, church elite*
> ❖ *When Boris and Jo Johnson's brotherly love is tested by political differences*
> ❖ *`We love your country,' Trump tells May*
> ❖ *Dominic Sandbrook: We love our country. Jeremy Corbyn never understood that. Boris Johnson did. And THAT is why he won*

I have traveled to over 45 countries and more than 100 cities in the world. I have found that while problems relating to various cities, countries, and societies may vary, people, in general, are not bad. They all tend to have good intentions for themselves, their family, their city, and their country. But with everyone being caught up in the hullaballoo of life, forgetting to take a pause, not being in tune with their emotional and other bodily responses; add the complexities of politics, not been clear about their needs, desires, and wants, is what make people react in the way they do. If you were to sit down and have an open and honest conversation, you would find that people do have the capacity to love each other.

At our deepest core, love is what we seek. Why do we then deflect from this natural desire? Why does this innate quality get buried deep down in the dungeon of our human body, often feeling like an unfamiliar territory? Love should be available to us at a mere snap of a finger but ends up becoming a longing, a deep craving, an unmet desire. Why?

Figure 180: One wonders how many times this plays out in real life.

This brings us to the question of what love means for you? If you were to ask others, you would find multiple variations of what this means. Is it a feeling, words of expression, act of care, spending quality time, craving of doing something good for others, a combination of emotions, or perhaps a drive or sudden adrenaline or oxytocin rush at the mere thought of someone? What is it? Is it a choice? Do we even have a choice to love someone or not?

When something as simple as love becomes so complex, then how does politics even stand a chance at being that simple? I hope this book has shown you the multiple layers involved and has brought clarity to make this overly complicated topic much simpler

We spend our lives experiencing, feeling, and trying to understand love. Yet, we still find it difficult to relate to others with the feeling of love, even though we have done this on dozens of occasions before.

When we are filled with love, we have less need to be defensive and a greater need to stay positive and have amicable relationships. When the feeling of love does this to us, don't you think we should be spending more time engaging in doing things that give us more love? When was the last time you hugged someone for longer than fifteen seconds, cuddled with your partner, or connected with someone from the heart?

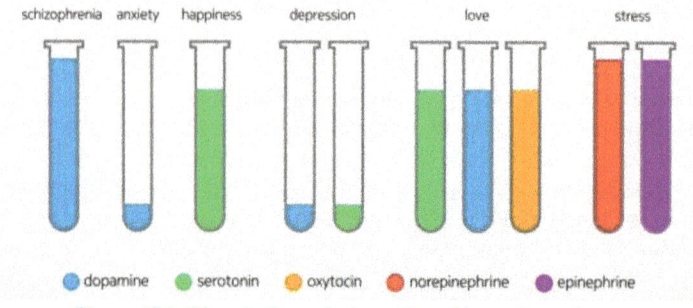

Figure 181: Chemicals control our thoughts and emotions.

How amazing would it be to have political conversations when we are filled with various love hormones and pleasure-giving chemicals?

Do you think we would still be prone to fistfights, or would it be more of an attitude of let's hug and find a resolution together, or agree to disagree amicably? Loving others begins with loving ourselves, but we are mostly running devoid of love; our human car is running out of love fuel. We live a life of scarcity – scarcity mindset, scarcity of money, scarcity of connection, and scarcity of love. Humans are the most advanced, most sophisticated, and most disturbed animals on this planet. We should be setting idealism for other species to be proud of us, rather than having them running scared.

No wonder conversations around confrontational topics like politics become a home ground battlefield where two people are ready to fight like bulls in a china shop. Time and again, we engage just to prove ourselves right, even when the best thing would be to stop and avoid any further mental or physical drain on the body. Can we really say that we love ourselves if we put ourselves through so much pain and torture, or is it more of an unconscious, habitual pattern, where our mind chatter, internal dialog, and most importantly, our ego takes over? We might not have fallen in love with politics, but we do seem to fall in love with the idea of wanting to be right or getting pleasure from hurting ourselves (unconsciously)?

EGO – friend or foe?

❖ *No wonder we laugh at them! From Ed Miliband and Wallace to Mayor Boris and Barney Rubble... the politicians and their cartoon alter egos*
❖ *'Humility is the most important virtue': Defence Minister tells scientists to learn from rishis*
❖ *For Trump, it's about America's ego _ and his own*
❖ *'We have a Napoleon in the making': Democrats rain on Trump's military parade idea as they claim he only wants to stroke his own ego*
❖ *Chicago Jeweler Pens Letter to Lightfoot After Looting: 'Put Politics and Ego Aside'*

When love for self, love for family, love for the city, love for your country is all we seek, and all that matters to everyone — then the question to ask is what stops us from seeing and realizing this? The answer is ego. Most of us are unfamiliar with it, but ego involves processes or reactions that have connotations to I, me, and mine. Ego is the false reality created before we are born into this world and are still breathing life through umbilical cords. It is a survival and defense mechanism that has always existed within us. Yet, though it has always existed, we are not familiar with its existence. Our task is to recognize its existence, differentiate from the 'I' that exists without the ego, and then work towards having love overcome it. This might sound like Zen, and might very well be. There is no harm in learning and adapting good philosophies and teachings from various studies to create better versions of humans and society.

We know that everyone has their own perspective. Yet, we find it challenging to step out of our own shoes and into someone else's to possibly see their perspective. Just like love, ego exists in all of us. It is hard to describe as it comprises of beliefs, opinions, and attachment to identity. Possibly the best way to experience ego is by looking at the symptoms, the emotional reaction one would feel when the ego is touched – the person would generally feel charged, angry, wanting to be right, overreacting, and then feeling regret. *I know better; you are a stupid idiot.* If you have ever said, *I don't know what just came over me or why I reacted that way,* it is likely either the trauma (more on this a bit later) or the ego's work. Feeling the need for constant admiration, behaving arrogantly, occupied in your own self-bubble and self-identity, and lacking empathy, ego has many meanings in modern English.

Figure 182-183: Ego can be useful, but first, we need to be-come familiar with it and then know where, when, and how to use it for our own benefit.

Ego can be healthy and unhealthy. If we want to operate from a place of love, we have to stop our unhealthy ego from overpowering us. We need to become conscious of its presence and take steps to let love overcome it. Feeling insecure, worthless, inadequate, and lacking confidence are some of the symptoms of ego presence. A healthy ego is good as it empowers us. It drives us. It gives us the fuel to compete, thrive, and succeed, but an unhealthy ego is an enemy, an enemy living within us.

Unhealthy ego results in:

- It keeps us out of touch with reality, making it difficult for us to connect with others.

- It creates unrealistic expectations and entitlement. Giving the feeling of this is mine because I deserve it, thus creating unrealistic and ridiculous expectations.
- Becoming dependent on external validation makes us want to engage in activities that enable more likes, follows, and external validation to feel satisfied.

One of the best ways to manage one's own ego is by focusing on providing support to others, genuinely caring about their needs and desires. This includes listening to their perspective, their opinion, and remaining open to them no matter what. You will be surprised that the resulting feeling, the nourishment, and the level of satisfaction will be far greater than the pleasure you would feel if you were right. Have you ever tried doing something for others with no reward or obligation, something of will, something of your heart's desire, and if so, what has been your experience relating to that? How did that really make you feel?

Arrogance, bigheadedness, self-image, and loss of self-concept, always talking about yourself, are symptoms of living with ego. Here are some of the ways ego works:

- Creates strong emotional reactivity
- Results in black and white or rigid thinking
- Feeling insecure and constantly comparing with others
- Judging others (mocking, ridiculing, insulting)
- Not listening to others or rejecting their perspective from the start
- Constant thinking and obsession with one's own thoughts

We cannot kill our ego or deny its existence, but should rather become aware of its presence and work through to have love overtake it. Only then will we make substantial progress towards creating a really loving, tolerant, and open society that we all aspire to.

Figure 184: As Zen as it may sound, the ego is part of one's identity, which can be malicious and harm self and our relation-ship with others if not controlled.

HATE – does hating the hate mean love?

❖ *PM Modi won't tolerate politics of hate*
❖ *People don't hate me anymore! Back with a follow-up to his Trump series, Ed Balls says his popularity's rocketed since he left politics - and he won't be returning*
❖ *New map shows the booming number of hate groups that have sprung up since Trump ran for president after his candidacy 'energized the radical right'*
❖ *'If I had my time again, I wouldn't go into politics': Thatcher regretted becoming PM because of effect it had on her family*

Figure 185: I genuinely believe hate is a strong word.

Love vs. hate has become the norm in describing the current political environment. Research shows that hate can destroy relationships, leave scars on both the person who is hating and the person who is hated, create divisions, and results in unintended consequences in a society in the form of racism, misogyny, xenophobia, homophobia, Islamophobia, and transphobia, all leading to further divisions.

When others go low, do we go low, or we continue to set the bar high. If one is willing to get dirty, we need to ask ourselves, do we need to do the same?

Show of palm, finger, or opening of arms. Have we lost the capacity of love? Imagine that if you were angry on a particular day and met with anger from another person, what would that result in? But imagine another scenario. You were angry, but the other person listened to you and continued giving you space to express your anger and love. Sooner or later, your anger would subside, you would feel guilty, and most likely apologize to that person for your behavior. This is the power of love.

If love is all that really matters for everyone, then what is really needed is to move away from politics and political conversations that lead to disconnection and towards politics and political conversations that foster harmony, love, and connectedness. These seem to be the crossroad where we see more division, hate, and violence. Our conversations should be filled with love, sympathy, compassion, and empathy, both at individual and collective levels. I regularly see posts on social media platforms saying, *'if you voted for XYZ, unfriend me,"* or *"don't ever talk to me again."* Over the past four or five years, I have experienced many people defriending me due to my political views, and I wondered why? I've never defriended anyone because of their political views because I remind myself that their perspective is just like mine and that they have love for themselves, their family, and their country, just like I have.

In the early days, when I started sharing about politics, I would often come across the difference of opinion by friends, which would result in breathlessness, a feeling of suffocation, and agitation within me. But through regular practice and daily reminders, I began to shift these emotional, mental, and physical bodily re-

This is Jessica. She voted for Trump. This is Jessica's friend Andrew. Andrew voted for Biden. Jessica & Andrew are still friends and have political conversations at great length because both of them are adults. Be like Jessica & Andrew.

Figure 186: I love you, but I hate your politics. Or, I love you, I disagree with your politics, but I love you anyway, and the fact that you have your views is fine.

sponses by directing my attention, energy, and focus away from my head and dropping it into my body, into my feelings, into my spiritual heart (the place from which unconditional love emerges). Now, I don't even need to remember because it has now become part of my personality, ingrained and embodied into my being.

Let's consider an example. Should we blame and show all our cruelty towards a person who becomes a terrorist, or should we show all our cruelty towards the circumstances that make them become one? As far as I know, no person is born a terrorist, and science has yet to find the genes that make someone a terrorist.

Let's go back to the example of Trump deciding to visit the UK, and many protest to stop him from coming to the country. The reason being hatred is not welcome in the UK, but if we protest by showing hatred towards this person, are we not engaging in tit for tat? Is that the best we can do to convey our message? Can we welcome him and show him that we welcome him with love despite the hatred he has aimed at creating. We don't want to stoop low because we want to show that we are far beyond hate. Is removing a slave trader statue and throwing it in the river the best way to convey our message against hatred, especially for something that took place many centuries ago? Or could there be a better option of expressing love by surrounding the statue with something that denotes compassion and love? Should we blame the government with less than necessary targets of reducing carbon emissions on the agenda, or blame the activists concerned and have their targets because of their fear of climate change effects?

What does this tell about each of these regarding love for future generations? Who has more and who has less? How about hating vegans because of their love for animals? Where do we draw the line between choosing who to love, who to hate? Suppose we are going to hate everyone we dislike. In that case, we would, over the years, find ourselves loving only a handful of people; the majority would consist of me, myself, and I.

Taking the case of Trump, while it is easy to say that he is causing hate, my question to you is, is he really forcefully feeding you doses of hate capsules, or is it more a case of being triggered due to hate being your emotional sensitive spot as mentioned in Chapter Three? And what do we say to the fact that he is doing this for the love of his country? Is his love, not love, but your love is love? Can we agree that people show love in different ways, as shown in five love languages and that each of those ways can vary from person to person? If Obama was all about love and compassion, then why do so many people not like him?

Figure 187: What do you see in this image? People protesting against Trump? What about at the energetic level – how much anger, hate, hurt, pain, etc., is being created, amplified, and shared?

I do believe that everything we do in life should be done from love. Love should be of paramount importance to every action we take. As humans, we have different emotions bound to come up repeatedly as we relate with each other, as we relate with internal and external realities. For me, the greatest love is to accept the person the way they are and then be willing to come from a place of curiosity to understand who they are, what their experiences have been, what their desires and needs are, and then see how we can help in fulfilling them or providing support in one way or the another, at least some sort of human comfort. Responding to negative or unwanted emotions, whether in politics or not, is by not shutting down such emotions but creating the space for them to surface to be worked through. Repressing them creates toxic chemicals in the body, impacting behavior that will show up at a later stage in the form of rage, anger, hate, and resentment.

There should be a love-embracing test for every politician before they are allowed to take office, like a drunk driving test. There should be regular reviews to see how much love they have been spreading. It sounds cynical, doesn't it? We have to think outside the box; we have to think beyond what we have been used to, try new measures, and open new ideas and possibilities if we really want to bring change.

CONNECTION – we are all connected; we've got hashtags!

❖ *US voices concern over Chinese money in Australian politics*

❖ *Obama's brother running for seat in Kenyan government saying that he has been 'inspired and challenged' by the U.S. President*

❖ *Ukraine president appoints lawyer linked to PrivatBank tycoon as administration chief*

❖ *Camilla Duchess of Cornwall's family tree shows she is related to Madonna, Celine Dion - and even Prince Charles*

What does connection mean to you, and why do you think connection is essential for opening ourselves to the possibilities of experiencing love with one another? Do you feel alienated from others, or do you alienate others? Do you feel being nit-picked, ripped apart, and disconnected from others?

Why do we limit connections to our families, to our loved ones, and to our friends? What would happen if we were to operate in a life full of warmth, compassion, and love towards anyone irrespective of whether we know them or not? (It is likely we would get arrested!) Why is there a time frame to get to know someone before building a deeper connection with them? Would it not hasten this friendliness process if we were to operate with our walls down, guards down, and curiosity and desire to connect with human beings? I am not saying that one doesn't need boundaries or become an open book straightaway because those are important, but what I am talking about is carrying the feeling of warmth in your aura, in your personality, so that everyone feels welcomed from the get-go.

How connected are you to different parts of the human body, and where do you live within your body? You might find this question a bit strange but bear with me. We discussed the different energy centers in the body in Chapter Three. How connected are you to your heart, intuition, and sexual energy (yes, sexual energy because it plays a part in whichever way

Figure 188: The network of connection. The center person can't know the people at the far end as closely as people in the immediate inner circle.

we operate in the world, but that is a topic in my book on orgasms)?

So, where do you live? Just like different rooms of the house have different functions, in the same way, different energy centers in our body have different functions. Due to our lives' demands, we are often required to use our cognitive processes so much that we spend too much time in our body's mental layer and stay completely disconnected from our heart, crown, and other energy centers. Suppose you don't work on activating these centers. You are not making the most of your capacity to operate from these vital sources of energy and wisdom, which offer essential advantages in the right context. If you had asked me a few years ago how it feels like to live in the heart or root energy center all the time, I wouldn't have understood the question. However, over the years, I have embodied more of myself into my whole energetic body and worked on activating and strengthening my energy centers. I now have the option to choose whether I want to live in my third eye energy center or my heart energy center or my sacral energy center or alternate among any combination of different energy centers throughout various parts of the day.

A story: On my way to work one morning, as I left the station, I experienced severe pain in the center of my chest. The pain was severe yet not harmful, noticeable, yet I could continue working. After a few hours, the pain had subsided. A few days later, I felt so much love emanating from the center of my chest. I didn't have a teacher to guide me, so I researched to find out exactly what happened. The symptoms were very similar to having the heart center opened. It felt like petals opening, but since energy was making its way through this area, it tended to impact the physical body, and pain was felt on the physical plane. I remember those moments very well. Since then, my feeling of love towards myself and others has changed, and I have come to understand what real love, compassion, and care means, which goes beyond one's own selfish love and care. Now whatever I do in life, I am filled with this love. I do not have to consciously put my attention into it, look for five hugs a day, or cuddle to feel the oxytocin running through the body. If I am filled with love, I can ooze love and if I am not, then love just remains the words rather than actual tangible feelings that can be felt by another person.

Figure 189: Next time you are at the beach with sun rays falling onto your body, pay attention to these energy centers and see if you experience anything different.

Figure 190-191: Heart energy is experienced in the form of incredible electric sensations, warm and loving energy.

It is vital to connect with your body as much as possible. Connecting with the different energy centers will help you stay grounded (more on this a bit later). When we are fully connected with ourselves and grounded, we can connect with others and deal with their turbulence without being impacted. Here are a few ways to connect with another human being, which becomes easier:

- Being present and able to hear, listen, understand, and relate with each other
- Have sympathy, empathy, and exercise emotional intelligence
- Be willing to help others out, if possible, unconditionally or without obligation
- Smile at strangers and see them as human beings, in this world, doing their own things just like you
- Create shared experiences that one would love to cherish, enjoy, and remember

POLITICAL CONNECTIONS – many wish that they had some

Have you ever favored someone you knew more than someone you didn't? Why? Have you ever discriminated against someone because someone else was more closely connected with you than others? If the answer to any of these has been yes, why would you think it will be different in a political context? A few points to note about political connections:

We may not have any political connection, but let me spoil you with my love and kindness.

- Firms, elites, corporations, organizations, establishments, and donors (let's call them Group B) use various methods to promote their own agenda and impact political negotiations, laws, rules, and policies.
- Creates a conflict of interest, although some rules and laws forbid leaders from taking such benefits nonetheless, there are many loopholes in laws
- Political connections are more plateau, looking at meeting worldly wants rather than deeper human needs
- Politicians and political parties need money, lots of cash for campaigns to get elected (Group A). Group B provides them with the finances, backing

Figure 192: On a deeper level, I wish that everything around us be filled with love. People express love and warmth towards each other. Our politics be full of love, compassion, kindness, and respect that winning or losing wouldn't matter. Image source: meme generator.

in lieu of benefit for themselves, assurances that policies will not be made which will be economically damaging to them, receiving subsidies or grants, and other benefits. Who should we blame here ......Group A or Group B? Hence, political connections are made to escape the harmful effects of regulations, policies, and laws or take advantage of them. Still, at times, it can favor society. Politicians can compel organizations to invest more in infrastructure and societal projects. It's easy to say don't take money, but then how do political parties succeed? And If they don't win, they are not even in the game. Where does moral responsibility take precedence over profits? However, things are not really that bad when various environmentally friendly regulations are made that companies have to adhere to or end up facing large fines.

- When our connections with other humans are superficial, mostly worldly, does it come as a surprise that political connections between political parties and others (Group B) tend to primarily focus on profit motive (it is important to remind you that while Group B might be providing cash and financing, it is ultimately us who vote and choose our leaders, at least in democratic nations)?

TRAUMA – whether we like it or not, we all have our share

❖ *Post-war reconciliation can open wounds, deepen trauma – researchers*
❖ *Pakistanis mourn after election rally bombing kills 128*
❖ *It caused him tremendous depression and anxiety': Lawyer says trauma of Iraq set off Sgt Bales propelling the soldier into depression prior to the killings of 17 Afghan civilians.*
❖ *'The day I was raped': Author and model Tara Moss speaks for the first time about terrifying sex attack 20 years ago*

Most of the behavior we see in people is generally due to experiencing trauma, which many are not even aware of. It is no wonder that topics like sexuality, politics, and relationships become the battleground where various traumas are repeatedly brought to the surface. So, what is trauma? Trauma can be confusing and complex if the other party in the conversation has not experienced it or is not familiar with it.

Trauma can be defined as disturbing or distressing experiences at one or all of the bodies: the physical, emotional, mental, energetic, and spiritual bodies. An injury from an accident or an assault would be experienced at the physical level. An unwanted psychological experience could adversely affect our emotional, mental, energetic, or spiritual bodies. Accident, injury, violent attack, whether experienced or witnessed, bullying (online, in-person), domestic violence, rejection, kidnapped or being held hostage can all cause trauma.

Figure 193: It is really painful to hear what people go through as part of trauma, especially when it hasn't been their fault.

Peter Levine, a well-known psychological trauma theorist, characterizes trauma not by the event but by one's reaction to it and symptoms. He explains that "any overwhelming and distressing experience can cause trauma and that trauma is only recognizable by its symptoms."

"Human beings have been designed over millennia, through natural selection and evolution, to live with and to move through extreme events and loss, and to process feelings of helplessness and terror without becoming stuck or traumatized." Peter Levine, *Unspoken Voice*

Our bodies are designed to have the capacity to overcome trauma and heal. Just as well because traumatic events and losses are a part of everyone's life. The impact and intensity of the trauma, the nature and timeframe of support, and healing provided to a survivor of trauma may cause them not to recognize themselves and their identity. They may say things like, *I'm not the same person I was before. I don't exist. I'm nobody. I don't recognize you. I've lost myself. I am losing my mind.* Some survivors are overtly aware of the resulting symptoms;

however, memory loss or memory blocking may cause them to have no recollection of the actual traumatic event.

Traumatic events affect those directly involved and those who witness something traumatic happening to someone else. In an attempt to shut out the trauma or painful memories, survivors may seem to shut down, feel distant, sad, numbed, and isolated. As they struggle to find their way out of the after-effects of trauma, they may need ongoing help and support.

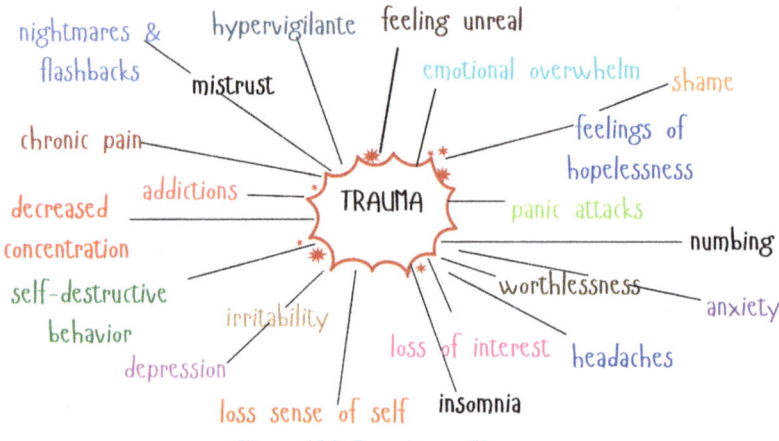

Figure 194: Symptoms of trauma

Suppose trauma from childhood is not resolved; it can create a sense of fear, anxiety, and helplessness later in life and set the stage for further trauma. I have worked with several clients who seem to have forgotten entirely about abuse, bullying, or traumatic events they experienced during their childhood. After working with me, those memories, which had been stored in the cellular body and deeper parts of the subconscious brain, emerged to the surface. This allowed them to recall the experiences after which we worked to get the impact of those events released from the body. A lady who experienced trauma at the age of eight or nine; throughout her 35+ years of life, she had been very distant from everyone, often living in fear but couldn't understand why. Her fear of confrontation forces her to avoid any kind of political conversation as these leave her feeling stressed. After the body de-armoring session, when trauma came to the surface, we worked on releasing it. She soon began to experience positive changes in her body, attitude towards the world, and life in general. She also became more open to having political conversations though exercised caution.

Figure 195: When we have political conversations, we don't realize that these can easily (and do) trigger traumas stored in everyone.

Another lady client, who was sexually abused during childhood, at the age of eight, and throughout her life, struggled to express herself, make sounds, and felt shame for who she had been. After working together, she recalled the whole incident and worked on bringing her voice back, which boosted her self-confidence, raised her self-esteem, and allowed her to have a positive attitude about herself and life in general. Being unable to express herself negatively impacted her relationships in a sexual context and in any difficult conversations, including politics. After the bodywork session, she found herself able to voice her opinions with confidence. Another example is a male client who carried a lot of anger and rigidity in life as the family's caretaker.

He was supposed to be macho, provide for the family, and take care of their emotional needs; he never expressed himself emotionally or mentally. This created a lot of resentment in him, which was stuck in his body without him realizing it. After a few sessions, not only did he have an emotional release, but he was filled with gratitude and immense love for himself, his family, towards me, and for everyone at large. He felt he had become softer in his approach as a man, wanting to give hugs rather than staying distant and remaining stiff and rigid. His change of attitude was also felt in his relationships and political conversations.

These examples bear testimony to how bodywork sessions impact a person 360 degrees. These are powerful and holistic sessions. If one session can have this effect, I will leave for you to imagine the transformation two or three sessions can create and how interactions during political conversations will change. Personally, I believe that every single person on this planet will benefit from bodywork sessions.

People react to trauma differently, including confusion, mood swings, anxiety, fear, irritability, inability to focus, aches and pains in the body, muscle tension, and fatigue. Some of these can result in PTSD (post-traumatic stress disorder), which can shock the nervous system, making it difficult for the person to make sense of anything that is happening around them and process their emotions. There are so many variations of how one can feel if a traumatic event has been experienced in life.

In context to politics, situations, issues, and incidents often get repeated, again and again. Hence it becomes all the more important that we really pay attention to our responses and work towards releasing the trauma stored in the body. The daily news, a debate or confrontation between two leaders, or strangers on someone else's social media feed can trigger the trauma. Sometimes, the leaders' confrontation would be resolved (as we have seen time again between Trump and Kim Jong Un). However, the impact of that confrontation would still continue to exist within peoples' bodies.

- Painful childhood or past memories can be triggered, reminding someone of an unhealthy relationship with their parents
- Trigger and reactivate long-buried memories related to an assault or inappropriate dealing by authorities
- Trigger memories relating to past abusive relationships or memories relating to discrimination or being bullied in school

The memes, phrases, images, and jokes relating to political leaders or issues that get shared on the internet often convey a psychological message that triggers us. If one is not aware of this, then one continues to keep falling within a never-ending loop and keep repeating the same pattern over and over again.

Suppose we know that immigrants, minorities, and others have undergone so much trauma. Should we have a hostile attitude towards them? Or should we have an attitude of love? I am not saying that we need to tolerate their behavior or embrace them despite them crossing the border illegally, but the least we can do is:

- Not judge and treat every immigrant or minority in the same way (recall context)
- Still have an attitude of warmth towards the immigrant who crossed illegally. We can put them behind bars for breaking the law. We can restrict them from coming to certain areas. Yet, all of this can be done with compassion (possible?).

How to deal with trauma

When trauma gets triggered or when people even start reacting from triggers, it is essential to note that triggers have nothing to do with you but will often be directed at you. This can be petrifying for the person at the receiving end; hence, our defense mechanism comes out without us knowing. We become defensive, argue, dismiss their point of view, often using abusive language, not realizing that the real issue is actually happening under the radar.

Instead of getting up caught up with words or on the surface, we need to develop the skills that allow us to read things happening subtly if we really want to help each other. As an orgasm coach, relationship expert, and bodyworker, I work with clients on very intimate levels, especially when giving bodywork sessions. I work with many clients who have undergone some trauma, especially sexual trauma. Past hurt, anger, and resentment come to the surface. Many women hold me responsible for all their experiences with men. My role is not to take things personally but to stay grounded and continue doing what I am doing.

Once these unexpressed emotions or traumas are released, clients feel happy, positive, energized, and orgasmic. Many apologize for things that were said during the sessions, to which I politely smile and say, 'no worries.' It is all part of the healing process. I'm not asking you to get intimate with people you are having conversations with, but I am trying to show that humans carry scars, pain, and trauma due to our life experiences. We need to stay firm, grounded, hold, and support each other, if we want to grow together in society and create the world we really all aspire to create. When negativity leaves the body, space becomes free. If such space is filled with positive emotions, it starts bringing change, an overall feeling of well-being, and a positive attitude towards life.

Here are some of the ways to deal with trauma and help each other:

- Patience: Healing through trauma will not necessarily take place overnight. It can take months, years, or even a decade for trauma to be worked through and released. Hence, it is normal for people to continue repeating the same pattern over and over again.
- Support system: All parties must have a support system that helps everyone to provide guidance, understanding, and tips on how to navigate the conflicting situations that emerge during conversations. We will need to work through it, which means being willing to get messy and getting dirty, but have support available for guidance.
- Communication: Effective communication is key to developing trust and fostering the bond in a relationship. Learn and engage as much as possible through nonviolent communication. Learn how to create a safe space so that feelings can be expressed. You need to learn how to respond when feelings are expressed and understand that it is not about fixing the person but being with the person. Feelings are not to be repressed but to be expressed.
- Acknowledge and reconnect with emotions and feelings: Everyone must pay attention to their emotions and feelings as and when they arise. All emotions and feelings would need to be acknowledged and felt rather than to repress or deny them. This will allow the person to help them release these through their body and avoid creating resentment and numbness that can develop over time.
- Engage in doing nicer things later on when everything has subsided. Recollect positive and happy memories of the connection you had together as friends, family members, or partners.
- Get emotional detox or bodywork de-armoring sessions: It is highly recommended that a person who has undergone trauma enroll themselves for emotional detox or body de-armoring sessions. In such sessions, we look at the blockages, pain, and trauma stored in the cellular memory and then help clear them by using breathwork, massage techniques, sound, and body movement. I have worked with several clients who have had traumatic experiences in their life, and every client has found these sessions to be powerful and life-changing. The sessions are designed based on the client's needs after a thorough consultation.

HEALING – a painful but very liberating process

❖ *David Miliband says he can 'never erase' Labour leadership loss to his brother... but adds the rift is finally healing*

❖ *After blistering campaign, Americans wonder how to heal*
❖ *Surfing brings healing for wounded US veterans*
❖ *Venezuelans seek strength, healing from mythical goddess*
❖ *25 years after genocide, Rwanda's president praises healing*
❖ *Julianne Hough opens up about being shamed for holistic healing: 'Trust me, I got all the comments'*

Let's heal ourselves, heal the political divide, and heal our fractured society.

Given the crossroads, a deeply divided and polarized society, it has become all the more critical for us to really look at deeply carried wounds and trauma and be open to healing. While we have survived and returned victorious from many battles, we have repeatedly made our human species proud. We have progressed in marvelous ways, but we have not gone through the process of healing. We have often progressed rapidly without providing full emotional, mental, and spiritual support, which has been very much required. The way that the Universe, God, Allah, Jesus, or whomever you believe in, made us with such a great sophistication, such an amazing machine; we are supposed to be living a life of pleasure, not pain.

Pain is the part of the experience we accumulate throughout our life. Have you ever had political conversations when you are deeply filled with love? In such a scenario, when someone disagrees with you, you would not get angry with them but rather reply with love, something like *I hear you. You have made interesting arguments. I beg to differ.* You will not be in an angry state. I'm sure all of us would desire to maintain this state all the time when engaging in political conversations.

Figure 196: *Be extra careful when it comes to healing. Greed knows no ifs and bounds. Majority of people are ruled by greed and majority of people also need healing including the ones ruled by greed.*

We, the People, will need to work together to help heal our ailing democracy—and if we do not, who will? Recall through Chapter Seven, you will realize that we are all in this together. Leaders, economists, teachers, businessmen, shop owners, everyone, every single one of us. Millennials are confused, fearful, anxious, and deprived of love. We need to do something for them while also doing something for ourselves.

Healing is an ongoing journey rather than a one-stop destination. It crosses many stations ranging from hurt to pain and happiness to sorrow. We have to be willing to go to such dark places and get ourselves worked up not only for ourselves but for our future generations.

Healing needs to take place at each level of human layers within ourselves, in relation to others we know and the society we live in, especially after the Brexit and Trump divide. There are ample tools and modalities available to go through the healing journey – therapies, journaling, religious and worship places, body-work, meditations, retreats, and medicinal herbs.

At an individual level, we need to inquire within. Still, before we do that, we will first need to learn how to inquire within as we are so disconnected from our-selves, from our body. The healing process can be uncomfortable at first (perhaps that is why many run away from it or don't want to engage in it), but it becomes such an amazing process after a while.

Staying Grounded, Centered, and having a positive reference point is the least we can do.

Understandably, we might not have time to improve ourselves, take various personal development courses, or go away to different retreats. The least we can do is stay grounded and centered not only for yourself but also for your partner, for your family member, and if you are really the one with a big heart, for socie-ty.

Being grounded is possessing the ability to be utterly aware of emotions, feelings, and sensations arising in the body, being conscious of the reactions they can cause, but having enough presence and control over ourselves that instead of reacting, we experience it, we observe, we alchemize, before responding in a way that feels more appropriate, supportive, welcoming to the other person.

Being grounded allows us to control all layers of our body, including this human car used in the physical sense. So, how would this appear in practice?

Being centered means staying present in the heart, so consciously putting your attention at the heart level until you really develop this as a way of your living.

Conclusion

Having a reference point relating to a memory, an experience, relating with your friend, your family member, and your social media connection, you can refer to when things get edgy. Quite often, when things get heated, we blow out. In the future, we start disconnecting because we tend to remember this worst interac-tion. What if we were to shift our minds to remember the positive interactions we have had with them in the past? This suggestion is not to meet them with open arms if the differences are too much and too many, but at least have com-passion. Let go of things, memories that don't serve, and build on to the moments that help spread more love. If something feels off or edgy and needs to be expressed or discussed, then be willing to initiate the conversation and use the tips mentioned in Chapter One (confrontation) and Chapter Twelve (communica-tion).

CHAPTER FIFTEEN

EMOTIONAL INTELLIGENCE

Having knowledge doesn't make someone intelligent. It only makes someone knowledgeable. Intelligence is using that knowledge at the right place, in the right proportion, and at the right time. As one of my partners used to say, "It's the intelligence, especially emotional intelligence, that she finds it sexy in a man."

Michael Charming

Introduction

There is no shortage of mental intelligence in the world. Everyone considers themselves to be intelligent (and often sees the other one as stupid). I can see how misguided and ill-informed people are about themselves. Really? Can anyone be sufficiently intelligent to know everything? Given the kind of information, issues, and complexities of society, I am in awe when I read comments like, '*He is stupid*', '*I know everything, what do you know about it?*'. At a government level, some experts have in-depth knowledge of a particular subject, yet they only focus on one or two aspects. How can someone else, on the opposite side of the social platform, or the other side of the dining table, know everything about the country's issues?

It would be different if we said, '*I believe I have sufficient information to form some reasonable judgments*' rather than considering the other person stupid. They might not have as much or the same information as we do. In the former scenario, shouldn't we come from a place of support, giving them the information they are missing? In the latter scenario, listen carefully to consider the information they have, fill

Figure 197: While calling others stupid is indeed easy but do note that that other person can think the same about you. Image source: meme, me.me.

the knowledge gap, expand on what they don't know, or perhaps help us understand what we don't know?

So, while we might not be missing mental intelligence, what we are definitely missing in the world is empathy and emotional intelligence (EI). How can we expect to have EI when there is hardly any mention of emotions in our academic studies, society, or elsewhere? From our school days, we are given textbooks to study, learn, cram, and then appear for the exams. Seldom are we offered any knowledge on how to relate with each other in terms of emotions. A student did something that made another student cry. The teacher will ask the student to say *'sorry'*; an elder sibling hit the younger one that made them feel hurt. Their parents will ask the elder one to apologize. *'Why are you upset'*, *'Don't be upset, don't cry'*, *'are you always going to be a cry baby'*, *'don't be angry at him'*, these are our lessons in relating with emotions.

So how is one supposed to gain emotional intelligence? We should also have energetic and spiritual intelligence, but society would have already made significant progress with only emotional intelligence. With emotional intelligence, we can navigate where we are in terms of our emotions and alter our conversations accordingly.

Forgiveness and reconciliation are essential aspects of relating. Differences are bound to creep up, and distances will be formed, especially when conversational topics are controversial. Things will be said that are painful to hear, especially with a lack of emotional intelligence and empathy, so the question to ask is what we can do to reconcile, not only with one another but with ourselves? The minimum is to forgive so that grudges towards each other are not held. Life is too short for this.

Sympathy – let's not let it die within us

> ❖ *Brexit: sympathy without support from Europe's right.*
> ❖ *Imprisoned academic Kylie Moore-Gilbert deserves more sympathy than Assange, Sharma says.*
> ❖ *Seoul mayor's death prompts sympathy and questions of his acts.*
> ❖ *No, we should not feel sympathy for Theresa May. Her policies have ruined lives.*
> ❖ *Left wing radicalism linked to sympathy for violent extremism.*

Sympathy is feeling bad for someone because something unwanted happened to them. *'Give them my sympathy'*, *'I really feel for him'*.

Per dictionary, sympathy: power of entering into another's feelings or mind. Our perception of someone's need determines the amount of sympathy we give them.

We reflect sympathy:

- when we pay attention to the person (although not in the way we should be paying, by being physically, emotionally and mentally present.)
- the closer or more ingroup the person is, the more sympathetic we can be with them
- if we have been through a similar experience, it will make us more sympathetic towards the other person
- our ability to sympathize with others is one of the things that enable us to connect, support, and help each other, especially during difficult times (but we don't do that well or enough as well)
- ways to show sympathy can be verbal, giving a hug, patting the shoulder, lending a shoulder to cry on or for support, or sending a sympathy message

At a political level, we will hear, read, and watch leaders giving a salute to soldiers who have died, victims of hurricanes or other natural disasters, consoling the victims and relatives of mass shootings, and speaking out against violent events around the world. Albeit many of these displays are politically motivated, some actually mean it.

As individuals, it is not easy for us to sympathize with people of opposing views. I wonder why? When Boris Johnson contracted coronavirus, some people wanted him to die. Why? Many want Trump to contract the virus and die, too. My question remains, why? Are we really at the level where we fail to recognize that they are leaders doing their job to the best of their ability (which is different from your expectation, hence the resentment)? Most importantly, the people elected them to be leaders; they did not elect themselves.

Figure 198: Sympathy or KPI? Sympathy or scapegoating? Sympathy or pretense? No one shows sympathy to me.

Before leaders sympathize with victims, they do not first consider if the person or area is Democrat or Republican; this is furthest from their mind (it would be very rare). What does this tell us about the people who wish ill of such leaders? I wonder if they would wish the same for all people with opposing views? Your guess is as good as mine in this case.

Growing up, my father told me a story. Upon completing his art studies, a teacher said to a student, 'You are excellent and the best student I've had. I wish you great success.' A few months later, one of the student's paintings, 'the portrait of a man' was part of an exhibition. Many people criticized his work. Some said, '*I wish he could have made the nose a bit smaller*', '*If only he could have added more expression in the eyes*', '*the face should be slightly more pointed*'. *On h*earing the reviews, the artist was distraught and went to have a conversation

Figure 199: Actually, this is a good start. If we can just do that... our society would have already made tremendous progress.

with his teacher. The teacher studied the painting and found no problem whatsoever. He felt the painting was a masterpiece. When the student told him of the reviews, the teacher smiled and said, *'Ah, I see. Exhibit the painting again but this time, offer a monetary reward to anyone who draws a better picture.'* A few months later, the student's painting was exhibited again, but this time with the reward on offer. Many people complained, like before, but when they started making their corrections, they struggled. They realized that other areas of the painting wouldn't look right if they were to do as they wanted. Finally, everyone left saying that this was a great painting, and no one could do it better. The student learned what he needed to know and went back to thank the teacher for the insight.

It is easy for us to say things from where we are, but it gets more difficult when we put ourselves into someone else's shoes. Consider this before commenting on whether what is being done is reasonable, the best, or could be done better. This is what we will learn when discussing sympathy and empathy (more about empathy in the next section), putting ourselves into someone else's shoes.

Theresa May did the best she could given the delicate position she was in; she never had the ruling majority and was often met with conflicting demands from coalition DUP, backbenchers, hard Brexiters, other party members, opposition, the general public, and the EU. Of course, her dealing with some issues such as Grenfell tower, immigration policy, and Windrush were terrible, and she came across as less sympathetic than we would expect of a leader. Do we really need to have a tit for tat and become less sympathetic towards her? Suppose we consider that she has always been a person to express less sympathy. How could we expect her to suddenly be different? She had always been considered the toughest member during the Cameron government.

But it is because of this toughness that she accused the Police Federation of budget cuts, she created a hostile environment for illegal immigrants, she took matters away from the EU on issues relating to the deportation of high profile terrorists, she was the force seen as the cornerstone of the Conservative Party dur-

Figure 200: Unfortunately, it isn't that easy...

ing the coalition which compromised of liberals following elections in 2010, and she took charge of the reins of Brexit when Brexit was suffering from a political leadership vacuum following Cameron's resignation and Boris stepping down from contending in leadership. She initially backed Remain, but after a call from the country, she moved to support exit. Does that not call for more sympathy towards her? We don't know what made her the way she is. Her upbringing, parental and British culture and etiquettes, her own life struggles, who knows?

Her own words, *'I have done my best and that it wasn't enough,'* was an emotional speech. I never expected her to be sympathetic with Corbyn; I did wish her to be a little more sympathetic in general. Her apparent lack of sympathy did not change me remaining sympathetic towards her. I didn't like some of her decisions or how she handled some of the issues, especially Grenfell tower and Windrush.

It is easier to say that the ability to feel sympathy towards her will depend on which side one is on and whether they have been impacted by her policies or not. If we consider the human element, would we say the same? I am not asking you to support her, as her legacy will be defined by failures, miscalculations, and humiliations. Still, I am asking for us to have a bit of tolerance and be sympathetic considering everything, even though the other person might not be. When we open up to others, it gives them an invitation to open up to us too, even though they might have been closed throughout (try opening your arms and giving a hug to someone and see whether their reaction and attitude changes). In Theresa May's case, some things were out of her hands. Some resulted from her cabinet's poor advice and others due to unprecedented political crises due to daunting and once in a history uncertain events like Brexit.

Can we disagree and still sympathize with the leader? Is that a possibility? Let us consider opposition; Remainers felt that being part of the EU, they were part of a family, and leaving would cause them to miss out on all the amazing things that come by being part of the family. Brexiteers felt that being in the family was detrimental. They felt ripped off by other countries, not having the freedom to make more beneficial laws for their country. In reality, deep down, people on both sides actually cared for their country; doesn't that speak volumes about each other? Consider this rather than calling the other side xenophobic, racist, or snowflakes?

Empathy – easy to receive but difficult to give

- ❖ *Michelle Obama, in DNC speech, rips Trump White House for 'chaos' and 'lack of empathy'*
- ❖ *Rush Limbaugh slams Michelle Obama's DNC speech as more 'phony' empathy from left*
- ❖ *'Empathy makes me a stronger leader'- Ardern*

Per the dictionary, empathy: the power of entering into another's personality and imaginatively experiencing their experiences.

Empathy goes a few steps further because we try to feel what the other person is feeling emotionally. When we empathize, we aim to see their point of view, imagine ourselves to be in their place, and the experiences that we might be going through then. To empathize, we have to come out of our heads and drop into our feelings and emotions.

Political examples may include stoning in many countries. Because not everyone is affected by it, many cannot drop into emotions, have the awareness to take a pause, and relate with what the person being stoned might be feeling or would be going through due to this torturous punishment. Likewise, think of Female Genital Mutilation. People in certain tribes are so blinded by culture, traditions, and ideological beliefs that they don't question whether it is correct, how the affected person is impacted, and whether the beliefs on which such practices were established still hold true in the light of newer information and better and enhanced understanding.

Five types of empathy concerning the five layers of our existence:

- Emotional (affective) empathy: being able to relate to another person's emotions and feelings and respond accordingly. If someone is feeling sad, then instead of cheering them up, we need to relate with them from the place of sadness, loss of someone close, grieving the EU exit.
- Physical (somatic) empathy: bodily reaction, physical response to someone's experience, hunger, upset stomach.
- Mental (cognitive) empathy (perspective taking): Understanding another person's mental state and having the ability to think what they might be thinking in that situation.
- Energetic (auric) empathy: the ability to tap into another person's energy levels and 'vibe'.
- Spiritual (divine) empathy: fear, religion, desire, purpose. To consider another person's spiritual or religious beliefs, innate desires, life purpose, and fear making them foggy.

Barriers to empathy are:

- Cognitive bias. Blaming failure on one's shortcomings but not looking at the external factors contributing to it.
- Clouded with one's own perception. When Trump says, 'people coming from Mexico or Mexicans,' he is considered being racist. That is not racist but per dictionary and geography. Mexico is a neighboring country to the US, and the people of Mexico are called Mexicans.
- Unable to connect with one's feelings and emotions and lacking awareness of how energy works.

- Not taking a pause to think during a conversation impacts listening, paying attention, and remaining present.
- Behaviors that exhibit scapegoating, gaslighting, and playing the victim mode.

Back to the example of Boris Johnson. People who believed that he had been unfair and held a negative opinion about him were less empathetic towards him when he caught the virus. Now question to ask is, should experiences of empathy really be determined by ingroup vs. outgroup. A pain is a pain, and if we are to relate with someone and put ourselves in their shoes, we should be able to feel their pain, no? Whether we would want to do something to help them ease their pain or not is different.

Here are a few steps that can help to practice empathy (I am guilty of not practicing this enough but have been making a constant effort. I still have a long way to go):

- Become a better listener. It is less about you and more about the other person. You will be surprised that once you have given them space to speak, and once they have spoken (provided you have heard them), they would be more than willing to listen to you.
- Pay attention to all aspects of human composition, yours and theirs, as much as possible. What kind of beliefs are emerging, and what is happening to their energy levels? What is their body language and other types of nonverbal communication trying to tell you? Be willing to go beyond just the spoken words.
- Ask relevant questions with curiosity that will provide more information about the person, their issue, and things being addressed, not something that will meet your interest. Ask questions that allow the other person to open up.
- Don't offer advice unless specifically asked, and definitely don't aim at fixing them, as there is nothing to be fixed. Take a pause if needed, and avoid jumping the gun.
- While it is about them, you can share your own experiences, making the other person feel that you can relate to them, only if you have similar experiences to share. Being vulnerable in these situations is okay but know when it has started becoming about you and when to stop.

Figure 201: The difference between empathy and sympathy in simple words.

The American Political Science Review found that people behave radically and empathetically differently based on ingroup and outgroup bias.[38] High empathy people view the outgroup more unfavorably than their ingroup. It found:

- people who scored high on the empathy scale showed higher affective polarization levels, giving a more favorable rating to their party than the opposing party.
- People who scored high on empathy were prone to schadenfreude, pleasure, or amusement derived from another person's misfortune.

Like being sympathetic, is it possible for us to still be empathetic towards each other, no matter our differences or political affiliations? We do tend to make friends with those who share our ideologies. If we want to continuously grow and stay connected to our society, should we not have friends with various interests?

Figure 202: If others don't have the time or ability to empathize with us, should we adopt a tit for tat attitude?

Empathy is hard work. Friends of mine, who are empathy coaches, often find themselves exhausted, burnt out, and frustrated at how people operate or take up their energy. They cannot help feeling this way because their nature is empathetic, loving, and caring towards others.

An ex-girlfriend used to make fun of moms with baby carriages. When she became a mom, this stopped. She could now relate to their plight, feel their stress, and understood the problems they had to go through as she was experiencing this herself. We can't understand each other's circumstances unless we go through the same experiences - whether be minority groups fighting for their rights, gays and lesbians fighting for equality and same-sex marriage, or aborigines fighting for their land and freedom that they fear being taken away. Go and live with them for days and weeks and see life from their lens to get a broader perspective. If that is not possible, the least we can do is drop into our feelings, into our emotions, and relate with each other at an empathetic level.

What makes leaders like Franklin, Gandhi, Mandela, Jacinda, and Obama the great leaders? It is not that they have or had answers and solutions to all problems, but they did have empathy. What makes Corbyn and Sanders continue to have peoples' support is that they could relate to their painful experiences. They showed that they cared and, hence, became their voice.

Proposed policies, manifestos, and visions do need to have credibility, an area where Corbyn and Sanders suffered the most. On the other hand, Trump has a good heart and has been doing everything with America and its citizens as his primary focus. Still, he often faces backlash because his speeches don't show empathy. His speeches use a different strategy, focusing on degrading the opponents to create a negative image in his supporters' minds before energizing them by talking about achievements and giving hope.

It's not that people cannot empathize; they get caught up with life situations, triggering sensitive spots, perceptions, and lack of perspectives. In the previous chapter, we discussed love and how love exists in all but is not accessible to everyone all the time. Notice how people point fingers when someone makes a mistake.

When our surroundings do not meet our core needs and are inattentive to our sufferings, it affects our psyche resulting in distress, anger, hurt, pessimism, trauma, and lack of trust. We have so many issues in our society – inequality, injustice, mental health, violence, discrimination, unemployment, and lack of human touch, but one study found that the need for empathy is much higher when inequality exists—inequality results in creating insecurity, bias judgments, and social distancing, resulting in an even larger empathy gap.[39]

Always aim to bring love, kindness, authenticity and empathy with you

Figure 203: Our world is in short supply!

While compassion, care, and love are the basis for both sympathy and empathy, it is possible to feel both. There is a vast difference in the impact these create:

- The ability to listen instead of fix: Empathy involves being in touch with emotions, feelings, and bodily sensations, which can sometimes be uncomfortable. It can include sitting with that discomfort rather than finding solutions or engaging in a happy, cheerful mood with that person. Fixing will come but just not at that moment. Sympathy involves finding solutions or help for that person.
- Validating their feelings and emotions rather than invalidating them with phrases like, *'How can you feel bad, you have always been a cheerful person',* instead of saying, *'I hear you. You feel sad and upset. Let me know how I can support you'.*
- In empathy, you put your viewpoint aside and try to see things from their perspective. In sympathy, one often presents their viewpoint.
- The focus should be on opening further conversations, building trust, enhancing the relating, remaining curious, being observant, staying non-judgmental, asking them what they would like to do next rather than telling them what they should be doing next.
- Sympathy can include focusing on yourself, your story, and your life experiences, while empathy is always about the other person. Sympathy can be patronizing and bring division between you and the other person, while empathy is about companionship, support, and trust.

Tips to improve emotional intelligence

Emotional intelligence (EI) is the ability to understand and act on input guiding, thinking and adjusting your own to the circumstances or environment in which you live, in order to achieve a balanced life and personal goals.

- Perceiving emotions – identifying your own emotions and picking up and understanding others' emotions from expressions, tones, and taking cultural differences into account. Emotional intelligence makes the processing of all other emotional information possible.
- Using emotions – identifying your emotions and finding the key to harnessing these to facilitate cognitive activities, such as thinking and problem-solving. Emotional intelligence allows using the alchemy of mood changes to one's own advantage.
- Understanding emotions – with vast variations in emotions, understanding each individually and comprehending the combinations while being sensitive to even the slightest variations, and how they evolve over time.
- Managing emotions – emotionally intelligent can use both positive and negative emotions to achieve their desired outcomes. To achieve this, they must have the ability to control their emotions and others when needed with the right framework of mind and intention.

"A big part of emotional intelligence is being able to feel an emotion without having to act on it." --- *Anonymous.*

Since empathy is a product of emotional intelligence, the tips discussed earlier are also relevant here. Some additional tips to help grow your emotional intelligence:

- Practice self-awareness, which means understanding and being aware of all five layers of your body. Self-awareness allows stop driving in auto-pilot mode and gives more control of this human car. Know your strengths and weaknesses. Play to your strengths and work on bridging those weaknesses.
- Make speaking about emotions and feelings part of your life, especially relating to your bodily sensation. What are you feeling, where are you feeling it, and what has made you feel that way? Every emotion that we can possibly feel needs to be

Emotional Intelligence

Low	High
Aggressive	Assertive
Bossy	Ambitious
Confrontational	Bold
Demanding	Decisive
Egotistical	Driving
Timid	Strong-willed
Easily Distracted	Charming
Glib	Passionate
Impulsive	Persuasive
Poor Listener	Sociable
Selfish	Warm
Inattentive	Attentive
Passive	Consistent
Resistant to change	Good listener
Slow	Patient
Stubborn	Predictable
Un-responsive	Stable
Critical	Careful
Fussy	Detailed
Hard to please	Meticulous
Perfectionist	Neat
Picky	Systematic

Figure 204: Difference between low and high emotional intelligence.

acknowledged. There is no such thing as a good or bad emotion because it just is. You are getting the promotion, having a baby, getting married, or re-solving conflict. Since emotion is also an energy in motion, we need to learn how to channel that energy to best fit the given scenario. Don't ask how are you doing; instead, consider asking, how are you feeling?

+ Make emotional regulation and clearing part of your daily routine. Just like you clean your teeth, take a shower to clean your physical body, in the same way, have activities that help to cleanse and remove the stagnant and un-wanted emotions accumulated throughout the day.

+ Recognize recurring patterns bringing unwanted emotions and find ways to work through them. I want to feel relaxed when I see Trump speaking; I will focus on my breathing, with a slow and deep inhale, I will move my body by walking or dancing slowly as he speaks, and when I can no longer take it, I will take a break from listening to him.

+ Make vulnerability, empathy, intimacy, hugs, and good values part of your life. The more these are integrated into your life, the more you will be living a life full of or wrapped around emotions. Doing this will help bring more awareness of emotions and the energies surrounding each emotion, allowing you to play, channel, and more with different emotional states.

Reconciliation – making amends – more than just an apology

❖ *New generation delivers message of peace on 75th anniversary of Hiro-shima bomb*

❖ *Queen's message of reconciliation: The Queen has used her Christmas Day broadcast to highlight the importance of reconciliation between op-posing sides - from communities in Northern Ireland to those involved in the Scottish Independence referendum.*

❖ *'Please forgive me': Ousted CBB star Jeremy Jackson makes tearful plea to Chloe Goodman after breast-exposing scandal*

❖ *Now Hispanic Republicans in Congress say they won't back Donald Trump unless he starts 'apologizing to all the people he's offended'*

❖ *'I hope she can forgive me - for her sake': Marla Maples reveals she wants to make amends with Ivana Trump, 25 years after her affair with Donald ended his first marriage*

No matter what our differences might have been, unless someone has caused harm intentionally, whether physical, mental, financial, energetic, or in any form, we should make all efforts to reconcile the differences. Life is not only short; it is very delicate. Given that we live in an environment of uncertainty, we don't honestly know what can happen to any of us at any moment. X number of people die every day, every minute, and just because it is not us, we find it difficult to relate that someday it will be.

Imagine this being your last day on Earth. Do you really want to leave holding grudges? Being distanced from people who were closer to you at one point? All due to differences in political views. I think we should reconcile relating to every aspect of life, but we will stick with politics since this is a political book.

Figure 205-206: (Left image) Some people have outsized expectations for making amends. (Right image) Simple rules for making amends.

Do you really want to carry that unwanted energy stuck within you relating to someone? If you were on your death bed, I am sure you do not wish to hold any grief, but rather enjoy and embrace the life you have lived. One tiny portion of this would be making amends with people, doing your best to reconcile the differences, and living with maximum integrity.

Reconciliation – if only I could balance my love as easily as my bank statement?

Suppose we strive for a deeper connection with someone. In that case, we know that our relationship will go through ups and downs, sometimes becoming challenging, sometimes resulting in hurt and sadness, sometimes staying platonic, and many times being jovial and happy. When the relating goes off-tangent, at the earlier opportunity, make every attempt to reconcile the differences. You will be surprised how relieved you will feel; your body will feel lighter, and your chest more expanded as if some sort of physical burden has been lifted. Like I advocate, sex should be a practice that you are mostly doing for yourself, for your satisfaction, contentment, and as part of your personality. If you do not reconcile, you will often think of the situation when you think of the other person. You will remember more of the moments in which you had differences than the positive ones. Similar to deciding whether you should confront or not, you should ask yourself whether you should make an effort to reconcile or not. Ask yourself what the pain is, the loss of not doing this, and then consider the gain should reconciliation occur.

A few points about reconciliation

+ Reconciliation is different than forgiveness: Forgiveness involves sympathy, which doesn't necessarily involve both parties, but for reconciliation to happen, everyone should be involved.
+ Have a realistic expectation of the result: The goal should be to reconcile and let the relationship unfold from there. Don't be goal-oriented, expecting it to go back to how it was; focus on working through the differences and let the relationship heal.
+ Instead of your ego, make empathy your power tool: Reconciliation would require listening to one another, being willing to consider things from the other person's perspective, and being ready to apologize and make amends.
+ Boundaries: Like houses have walls and doors for protection against invaders and other harmful people, we need boundaries to protect our human car and human composition. Boundaries are barriers that help us know that it will not make us feel good if crossed by us or someone else. These can (and should) exist in all the five layers of the body. It could be not speaking against anyone's religion, not disrespecting anyone at the spiritual layer, and not disregarding anyone's beliefs, calling them stupid, or mentally attacking them at the mental layer. During reconciliation, it is vital to determine what boundaries would need to be in place for this to occur.
+ Vulnerabilities: In today's society, there is a misconception that vulnerability is a weakness. It becomes a weakness when it is manipulated and misused by the person we are vulnerable to. Vulnerability means letting others know how a particular thing has made you feel and the impact it has caused you or your life.
+ Beyond ego: Be sure not to operate from the place of ego and keep your defensiveness out of the conversation. This is about accessing a deeper part of yourself, going beyond ego, diving deeper, and bringing all other emotions that exist but lay hidden beneath the surface.
+ Withholds: Are things that we wanted to say but don't. Withholding what we need to say creates heaviness and a sort of suffocation in our body. When I am in a relationship, I have a daily or weekly practice where I ask for a few minutes of her time to say what I need to say about our interaction, especially things that didn't feel right. Likewise, allow her space to do the same. The sooner you do this, the better it is for you and your relationship.
+ Check-in: With each other's feelings, emotions, mental state, thoughts, and beliefs emerging throughout this process. Take regular breaks when neces-

sary. If additional points are coming up in the conversation, journal them to be discussed later. Notice how your actions, words, and views were perceived differently by others and how you perceived theirs. This will serve as a useful guide to know where someone is emotionally. The point is not to stop expressing what you want to say but to be mindful of how it will be perceived by the other person and where they might be coming from.

- Safe ports, warnings, and common ground: Establish common ground, the ground rules for conversation, and safe places.
- Priorities: There could be several points to discuss but instead prioritize and focus on the most important ones. Every point can have a lot of energetic and emotional overwhelm attached.
- Note down your reflections and key take away points: To ensure that you do not repeat the same behavior or forget what was discussed and reflected upon, it is important to note them down. Some of these points might require a change of behavior and an integration into life, so you will need to put appropriate measures in place for the same.
- An apology is different from making amends: An apology can be sincere or insincere. A sincere apology means one is validating the other person's feelings of hurt and pain. When you apologize, you are not apologizing for who you are but how it contributed to someone's feelings. The apology would generally mean that one regrets what one did, is taking responsibility for their actions, and is willing to do something to ensure that it isn't repeated. 'I'm sorry for what I did. I shouldn't have done this, and it shall never happen again.' While amends are similar, it goes a few steps further. In amends, you invite the person you wronged and hear all they have to say and ask them how they would like you to make it up to them. An apology can be made without a clear heart, but amends should generally be done when one has a clear heart. There are three kinds of amends:

  Direct: One takes responsibility for their actions and confronts the person they would like to reconcile with.

  Indirect: Engaging in activities not necessarily related to the wronged person but in other ways like volunteering, helping others.

  Living: Bringing a lifestyle change and making a life-long promise to ensure that the unwanted patterns and behaviors are not repeated. Examples of this are quitting smoking or drinking or committing oneself to grow.

- Initiate the action: Be willing to make the first move. Ensure that you desire or want the reconciliation and that you are not doing this for its sake or out of obligation.
- Practice reflective listening throughout: Vital, especially if you find yourself struggling to understand the other person or vice-versa or find that there is too much misunderstanding in the interactions.
- Like communication, reconciliation is a two-way process: During, or after, reconciliation, there will not necessarily be equal give and take. It is critical to identify your boundaries and how far you can stretch them, if need be, without triggering something that would need another reconciliation session.

Find out what is acceptable outside your comfort zone, and identify your No-Go area.

+ Reconciliation is a process of letting go: This allows you to focus on the present instead of rehashing old conversations and behaviors. Ask each other what is needed to let go of the past unwanted interactions and experiences.

+ Everyone's unique journey: Accept that not everyone will be able to reconcile at the same time. Reconciliation is a healing and transformative process, and everyone follows their own journey because everyone has their own human composition. Focus on acknowledging where one is and whether one has moved from where they were before this process. It is not about how far but whether or not. The other person might not be ready for reconciliation at all.

Figure 207: Everyone has their own way of reconciliation.

The Reconciliation process itself

+ Beforehand, one should convey and establish the purpose of the discussion and the genuine desire of what is expected. Use phrases like, 'I feel a few things have been off between us, and I would like to work on making things better', 'I realize that what I said might have impacted you, and I would like to hear you and make amends where necessary'.

+ Set the time limit. Reconciliation is a process that might rehash some older issues, some of which might not be related to your interaction, and it is essential to not get lost in these and lose track of time. Using a timer to set the time limit beforehand ensures that you do not run over time, which might make things even worse.

+ Acknowledge all emotions, feelings, and sensations felt and experienced as part of the process. These might not have anything to do with the topic or point that was part of the interaction, but honoring each other's bodily responses is equally important because these responses are happening concerning each other and in relation to those topics.

+ Consider a mediator if you feel you will struggle. The mediator doesn't need to know the entire background of the issue. Their role is simply to hold the space and the group and ensure that all reconciliation protocols are followed, giving each individual time and space.

+ Notice when you are checking out. At times, you might find yourself not being fully present, lost in your own thoughts, or another issue triggered in your mental state; thus, it can take your attention away from the group space. Hence, make a note of instances when you have checked out. Practice more mindfulness and presence to avoid this happening. Confess to the group every time you check-out to trick and tame your mind. If need be, ask others to check-in with you at regular intervals.

+ Take regular breaks. Move your body, your energy, go for a short walk, hug a tree, or hug each other to ensure that you are alchemizing these emotions in a faster way. This will also bring clarity of mind while energizing your body. Take a pause if need be. In that instance, the discussion topic will not be that important. It will need to be addressed once the emotional states are back to normal.

+ Reconciliation is a joint effort. If everything fails and still no reconciliation happens, ensure and know that you tried, and you gave your all. Since everyone is on their own journey, the other person might not be ready for reconciliation. In such a case, you can say what you needed to say so that they can hear or look at it at a later stage and then leave it up to them to see what they would like to do with it.

Reconciliation at the society or political level

Time and again, people have suffered from atrocities, injustice, war, and discrimination, and our society needs a healing and reconciliation process. Take the case of the Israel-Palestine conflict or Pakistan-India conflict. When innocent civilians die, it fills their family members and community with aggression, rage, sufferings, and hurt, resulting in more anger, hostility, hatred, bitterness, and fear for the governments. Some of this can also be directed at international leaders and organizations for letting this happen time and again.

When I work with clients during bodywork, I find that many have been living in denial or suppressed rage and anger as part of their survival strategy. Whether from a past relationship (family, lover, boss, relatives) or other aspects of life, they have not realized that being in these states is unhealthy for them, creating more pain in their bodies.

Sometimes they are not ready to face the emerging emotions in one session for various reasons (fear, discomfort, too much to deal with). Still, they recognize that they will have to go through this painful process to bring the change. Eventually, they become ready. Hence, it is natural for people in society not to be prepared for this whole process, but it is crucial that by engaging in forgiveness and healing, we are all in this to let go of the part of us that wants to mourn, grieve, and make peace with others and society at large.

Rape, molestation, domestic abuse, child abuse

Forgiveness and reconciliation help rebuild broken relationships, repair the damage done to communities, and play a big part in the peace-building process. Ignoring them means ignoring a section of society bound to affect all of us directly or indirectly. Like the body, every single part, every single organ, and every single cell is vital for the body's functioning in the most effective way; in the same way, every single section of the community is important.

At the society level, reconciliation could involve the following steps:

- Creating a shared vision for the whole country and for different sections of society.
- Acknowledging the past's wrongdoings, the impact it might have caused, and being willing to admit.
- Creating safe and supportive places for reflections, forgiveness, empathy, and reconciliation to take place and for healthier relationships to emerge. Starting grassroots initiatives, developing victim-offender support groups, using the power of stories to unite people, helping them learn from each other, cultivating dialogues, and ensuring fairness at all levels. Create opportunities for people to engage with each other, provide platforms for people to develop understanding among families, groups, and communities.
- Working on developing a cultural and attitudinal change by education, awareness, and openness. At an individual level, we will also need to do our part and take on more responsibility. To be compassionate towards each other, learn how to forgive and be willing to reconcile, work through our traumas, and shift our mindset and behaviors. Focus on creating a dialog that allows genuine expression of self and others, address concerns and the root cause of conflicts.
- Bringing change in all aspects of society, economic, political, and social.

Conclusion

As humans, we are really a very intelligent species but let's learn to tap into this intelligence. Let's not allow ourselves to get bogged down and impacted by life circumstances that tend to bring out the worst in us. Sometimes circumstances do this, but let's not make this a regular feature or use them as an excuse. I do an exercise every day (or aim to do it every day). During the day, I take time out to see whether I am operating as the best version of myself on that day or not. If not, I identify the areas that are not performing as the best version and spend time bringing them to the best states possible. Using the analogy of driving the car. You want to make sure that every part is working to optimum capacity. Suppose a particular part is not. It would either need repair, replacement, or a complete overhaul, perhaps not immediately but soon. I apply a similar concept to myself.

On the contrary, if I am working as the best version of myself that day, my focus shifts to making myself better. It doesn't mean making any substantial shift in one go; even a tiny bit would work wonders. Reflection and willingness to make oneself better are what is important. Every day or so, I reflect and give myself an overall ranking out of 10 (10 being the best version of myself), just as I would rank the leaders or football player (think of rankings from Chapter Ten). This may sound strange or stupid, but I firmly believe that if we as humanity wants to rise and realize the best human potential available to each of us, then every human being on this planet will need to develop daily self-accountability and self-responsibility mechanism. It should not be a hotch-potch mix of relationships with other human beings: your mother, partner, daughter, or complete stranger but rather as part of an individual within the human species.

Your world matters for as long as you matter. When you are gone, your world goes with you, collapsed and buried or burnt. When considering something, ask yourself, "If today is my last day on Earth, would it be worth it."

Michael Charming

Hopefully, after hundreds of pages of information and analyses, you have gained enough understanding to feel like a bit of an expert in human psychology, interaction, and relationships.

Whenever you need further analysis or some revision, use this book as a reference. Keep it handy and continue coming back to pieces until the concepts that resonated with you become deeply ingrained into your psyche. Look through the courses and blog on my website, www.michaelcharming.com, from time to time that may offer further insight. If you have any questions or queries, please feel free to reach out to us via email: coach@michaelcharming.com

Focus on NOT losing family or friends just because of political conversations. Initially, it may have been odd to think that your uncle or cousin or partner could possibly support that jackass (whoever that may be at the moment, and yes, they will keep popping up like the moles in whack-a-mole). That jackass will eventually fade away. Moreover, by enquiring, you will realize why they support whom they support (hint: life experiences, priorities, emotional resonance, blinded and bound by (invisibly held) trauma, etc.). Unless they support a carbon copy of Adolf Hitler or Attila the Hun, it really doesn't matter in the universal scheme of things. What matters is that you maintain, develop, and even strengthen your relationships with your family, partner, and friends. If possible, you can even help them by using the tips and tools gained through this book.

In the US, Richard Nixon is but a ghost of a memory. So is Uganda's Idi Amin, though he was substantially more dangerous. Almost every jackass fades away. We just aren't too sure about Trump yet. But he also will eventually fade away.... And even if he comes back in 2024... then by 2028, he is gone, and maybe by then, his whole ideology will have died with him.

So, read carefully and learn to listen, to love, to hug, and to be as open as you can be. Frankly, we have far less influence than we like to think about what is going to play out, so we might as well just move on with our lives and SEE what happens and only then deal with it. It doesn't mean that we shouldn't make efforts for the causes and issues we support, but it merely means that we should be putting our efforts and energy in the right place. Fighting over the comments section of Facebook, news feed, article, or having an argument at the dinner table is not going to be one of them. Instead, write a blog post yourself, create a video, share your views publicly, work or support the movements supporting those causes, etc. Hence, my final thoughts:

"No politician or political party is worth fighting for if it ruins any relationships or your sex life. These cannot go deeper if issues that really concern one or both partners are not discussed together in a grown-up and mature manner. So, a bit like carrot and stick, with balance, awareness, and willingness, everything can be dealt with and navigated through."

And here is a recap of some of the things we learned:

- Confrontations will happen if we interact and have conversations relating to sensitive and seldom discussed topics like politics, sexuality, and challenging someone's beliefs. Calling someone stupid or an asshole is not going to be a positive way of dealing with such confrontations.
- Humans are more than we see, hear, or read about them at face value. Everyone has their own fair share of life experiences. Everyone has traveled their own unique life journeys. If you want to know more about the person and why they held particular views, be willing to inquire about their experiences and journeys.
- The human body is more than just the physical body we see before us. Many things are interplaying at a deeper level: beliefs, ideologies, exhaustion and fatigue, emotions, feelings, triggers, etc. The majority of people on this planet are not aware of these. If you want to up your game and become good at reading people, you must focus on these. You might allow them to discover something about themselves.
- We should be running away from wants towards fulfilling needs and desires; both concepts are generally foreign to many. Hence, if you understand these concepts, you might need to first guide them to understand what these are and why fulfilling them matters for one's well-being before engaging in conversations.
- No perspective is ever wrong because it is one's perspective. A perspective can be selfish or selfless, it can be narrow or broad-minded, focusing on micro or macro or both, but it can never be wrong. Suppose we have to see another person's perspective. In that case, we have to be willing to drop the layers and filters that guide our perception and become open to theirs.
- People who haven't done the work on personal growth, will at every opportunity, scapegoat a leader or political party or even you for the problems they have. Be loving towards them because these scapegoating patterns, gaslighting, etc., run deep in our families, and we all pick these up early in life. We pick up good habits, and we also pick up bad habits. In political conversations, when things start getting hot, the person's worst side will be experienced. It's a given.
- Leaders are far more restricted in terms of what they can and can't do, more so than we voters like to think. When a leader takes (or doesn't take) a particular stance, be willing to look at factors that may have led him to take that stance before expressing your dissent towards them.
- Sometimes aggressive communication may be necessary but use nonviolent communication as much as possible. There will be a long-term payoff during political (and any) conversations, not to mention preventing divorces or

break-ups in personal relationships. If you use the tips mentioned in the communication chapter (or in any chapter) and get more hugs, please drop me a line. I love seeing people happy, positive, and enjoying their relationships full of love and warmth. I would love to hear from you.

- And lastly, work on that ego. It is a little devil who has been sitting within us since birth; hence, it might be difficult to imagine separating. Remember, everyone in this world desires to love and be loved. Keep in mind that love and hugs cannot buy food or be used to sustain life. Money and other things are equally important. There is a place for love, and there is a place for money. Learn to find a balance and help others find a balance too.

I have spent the better part of nine months writing this book. I took this precious time away from my work relating to sexuality, orgasm, and relationships because, given the way things were, with people fighting, arguing, and disconnecting from each other, whenever politics was mentioned, I felt the need. Hence, my goal has been to help everyone understand that politics is not binary. Neither are political decisions taken by leaders or policies implemented by political parties. We should move away from the tendency of finding quick fixes or judging each other at the whim of one's views and definitely avoid categorizing everything into binary, i.e., either 0 or 1.

After reading this book, I hope it will enable people to work together, come together, and drive towards connection no matter whatever opinions or views are held or expressed. SO, read, study, use the techniques in the book, and get together. You will be surprised how good it makes you feel to no longer be 'on guard' all the time.

And just a reminder, if you notice anything incorrect or have anything that may add value in the next edition, please feel free to provide feedback. I strive to learn from those I aim to 'teach' and will always continue on that path. If this book has helped you in any way, I would love to hear from you. So, please drop me a line or two.

I am sending you love, hugs, and best wishes on your further human journey. Until we meet or speak again, adios!!

Be safe, be cool, be loving, and be yourself.

Until next time, with another book, on another topic……

Your very own

Michael Charming
Orgasm Coach, Relationship Expert, Sexual Healer,
Certified Bodyworker, International Speaker, and Best-Selling Author.

Email: *coach@michaelcharming.com*
Website: *michaelcharming.com*

WORKS CITED

1. Resnick B. A new brain study sheds light on why it can be so hard to change someone's political beliefs. Vox.com. https://www.vox.com/science-and-health/2016/12/28/14088992/brain-study-change-minds. Published Jan 23, 2017. Accessed May 15, 2020

2. Kaplan, J., Gimbel, S. & Harris, S. Neural correlates of maintaining one's political beliefs in the face of counterevidence. Sci Rep 6, 39589 (2016). https://doi.org/10.1038/srep39589

3. Hibbing, J. (2013). Ten Misconceptions Concerning Neurobiology and Politics. *Perspectives on Politics, 11*(2), 475-489. Retrieved February 3, 2021, from http://www.jstor.org/stable/43280800

4. Janov, A. (2009). Life before birth: How experience in the womb can affect our lives forever. Journal of Prenatal & Perinatal Psychology & Health, 23(3), 143.

5. Anderson S. Genes and Politics. Magazine.utoronto.ca. https://magazine.utoronto.ca/research-ideas/culture-society/genopolitics-peter-loewen-genetics-and-political-viewpoints. Published December 4, 2009. Accessed June 15, 2020.

6. Edsall T. B. How Much Do Our Genes Influence Our Political Beliefs? Nytimes.com. https://www.nytimes.com/2014/07/09/opinion/thomas-edsall-how-much-do-our-genes-influence-our-political-beliefs.html. Published July 8, 2014. Accessed Jun 15, 2020.

7. Settle JE, Dawes CT, Loewen PJ, Panagopoulos C. Negative Affectivity, Political Contention, and Turnout: A Genopolitics Field Experiment. Onlinelibrary.wiley.com. https://onlinelibrary.wiley.com/doi/abs/10.1111/pops.12379. Published Dec 05, 2016. Accessed May 25, 2020.

8. ALFORD, J., FUNK, C., & HIBBING, J. (2005). Are Political Orientations Genetically Transmitted? American Political Science Review, 99(2), 153-167. doi:10.1017/S0003055405051579

9. Ebstein Richard P., Monakhov Mikhail V., Lu Yunfeng, Jiang Yushi, Lai Poh San and Chew Soo Hong 2015Association between the dopamine D4 receptor

gene exon III variable number of tandem repeats and political attitudes in female Han ChineseProc. R. Soc. B.28220151360

http://doi.org/10.1098/rspb.2015.1360

10. Campbell R, Cowley P. What Voters Want: Reactions to Candidate Characteristics in a Survey Experiment. Political Studies. 2014;62(4):745-765. doi:10.1111/1467-9248.12048

11. James H. Fowler and Christopher T. Dawes. Two Genes Predict Voter Turnout. Journal of Politics, Volume70, Issue 3, July 2008

12. Smith K.N. Your Political Beliefs Are Partly Shaped By Genetics. Discovermagazine.com. https://www.discovermagazine.com/mind/your-political-beliefs-are-partly-shaped-by-genetics. Published August 5, 2015. Accessed June 25, 2020.

13. Settle JE, Dawes CT, Christakis NA, Fowler JH. Friendships Moderate an Association Between a Dopamine Gene Variant and Political Ideology. J Polit. 2010;72(4):1189-1198. doi:10.1017/S0022381610000617

14. Ebstein RP, Monakhov MV, Lu Y, Jiang Y, Lai PS, Chew SH. Association between the dopamine D4 receptor gene exon III variable number of tandem repeats and political attitudes in female Han Chinese. Proc Biol Sci. 2015;282(1813):20151360. doi:10.1098/rspb.2015.1360

15. Warmflash D. Voting genes: Are political views inherited? Geneticliteracyproject.org. https://geneticliteracyproject.org/2016/03/22/voting-genes-are-political-views-inherited. Published March 22, 2016. Accessed July 15, 2020.

16. Dinas, E. (2014). Why Does the Apple Fall Far from the Tree? How Early Political Socialization Prompts Parent-Child Dissimilarity. British Journal of Political Science, 44(4), 827-852. doi:10.1017/S0007123413000033

17. Lyons J. The Family and Partisan Socialization in Red and Blue America. Onlinelibrary.wiley.com. https://onlinelibrary.wiley.com/doi/abs/10.1111/pops.12336. Published Mar 09, 2016. Accessed Jul 26, 2020.

18. Ekman P. Emotions revealed. BMJ. 2004;328(Suppl S5):0405184. doi:10.1136/sbmj.0405184

19. Fone KCF, Porkess MV. Behavioural and neurochemical effects of post-weaning social isolation in rodents-relevance to developmental neuropsychiatric disorders. Neurosci Biobehav Rev. 2008;32(6):1087-1102

20. Pan Y, Liu Y, Young KA, Zhang Z, Wang Z. Post-weaning social isolation alters anxiety-related behavior and neurochemical gene expression in the brain of male prairie voles. Neurosci Lett. 2009;454(1):67-71

21. Fried I. Human Lateral Temporal Cortical Single Neuron Activity during Language, Recent Memory, and Learning. Single Neuron Studies of the Human Brain. 2014:247-272. doi:10.7551/mitpress/9780262027205.003.0014

22. Maslow AH. A theory of human motivation. Psychological Review. 1943;50(4):370-396. doi:10.1037/h0054346

23. Slovic, Paul & Finucane, Melissa & Peters, Ellen & MacGregor, Donald. (2007). The Affect Heuristic. European Journal of Operational Research. 177. 1333-1352. 10.1016/j.ejor.2005.04.006.

24. Ropeik D. Why Changing Somebody's Mind, or Yours, Is Hard to Do. Psychologytoday.com. https://www.psychologytoday.com/us/blog/how-risky-is-it-really/201007/why-changing-somebody-s-mind-or-yours-is-hard-do. Published July 13, 2010. Accessed Aug 12, 2020.

25. Lytwyn, Tracy (2012). The Personality of Policy Preferences: Analyzing the Relationship
between Myers-Briggs Personality Types and Political Views. Res Publica - Journal of
Undergraduate Research: Vol. 17
Available at: http://digitalcommons.iwu.edu/respublica/vol17/iss1/11

26. Daniel Bell, in Bullock A. & Trombley S. 1999. The new Fontana dictionary of modern thought. London: HarperCollins, p414. IBSN 0-00-255871-8

27. Seuss, Dr. *The sneetches*. 1960

28. Groupthink. Psychologytoday.com. https://www.psychologytoday.com/gb/basics/groupthink. Accessed Sep 19, 2020

29. Jung, Carl Gustav, Marie-Luise Von Franz, Joseph Lewis Henderson, Aniela Jaffé, and Jolande Jacobi. Man and his symbols. Vol. 5183. Dell, 1964.

30. Conger, J. P. (2005). Jung & Reich: The body as shadow. North Atlantic Books.

31. Relationships Australia. (2011). Relationships Indicators Survey (p. 11). Retrieved from https://www.relationships.org.au/what-we-do/research/australian-relationships-indicators/relationships-indicator-2011

32. Diamond S.A. Essential Secrets of Psychotherapy: The Inner Child. Psychologytoday.com. https://www.psychologytoday.com/gb/blog/evil-deeds/200806/essential-secrets-psychotherapy-the-inner-child. Published June 07, 2018. Accessed September 12, 2020.

33. Dubois, Elizabeth & Blank, Grant. (2018). The echo chamber is overstated: the moderating effect of political interest and diverse media. Information, Communication & Society. 1-17. 10.1080/1369118X.2018.1428656

34. Miller, J. (2020). Do COVID-19 Conspiracy Theory Beliefs Form a Monological Belief System? *Canadian Journal of Political Science, 53*(2), 319-326. doi:10.1017/S0008423920000517

35. Lindberg S. It's Not Me, It's You: Projection Explained in Human Terms. Healthline.com. https://www.healthline.com/health/projection-psychology#examples. Published Sep 15, 2018. Accessed Oct 20, 2020

36. The Zuckerman Institute at Columbia University. (2020, May 8). How does the brain link events to form a memory? Study reveals unexpected mental processes. *ScienceDaily*. Retrieved January 21, 2021 from www.sciencedaily.com/releases/2020/05/200508112903.htm

37. Colwell, J., & Huth, C. (2010). Integrity: The Basis of Unconditional Respect. In Unleashing the Power of Unconditional Respect (pp. 35-44). CRC Press.

38. SIMAS, E., CLIFFORD, S., & KIRKLAND, J. (2020). How Empathic Concern Fuels Political Polarization. American Political Science Review, 114(1), 258-269. doi:10.1017/S0003055419000534

39. Liebig, S. Richard Wilkinson and Kate Pickett (2009): The Spirit Level. Why More Equal Societies Almost Always Do Better. Allen Lane, London. Soc Just Res 25, 102–107 (2012). https://doi.org/10.1007/s11211-012-0148-9

DESCRIPTION

Orgasm, we know it all. But do we? We all want to have it, no matter who we are or how old we are. No matter how often we've experienced it before, we still crave more.

We live in a world where harder and faster sex is considered better and sex toys and porn are the norms. The belief that erection is proof of men's masculinity creates massive performance pressure. Women are being objectified and shamed for their bodies creating huge confidence issues. Men believe that they know it all when it comes to sex. Women, on the other hand, often don't give themselves the permission to explore their true desires.

We spend a large part of our lives desiring sex and pleasure but very little time enjoying it! It doesn't have to be this way!!!

"Orgasm happens both from within us and from the connection between us. Your partner doesn't give you orgasm. Your partner creates the space for it to happen."
Michael Charming

Amplify Your Orgasm was inspired by my own journey to amplify my own orgasm as a man. In this book, I speak about the hard realities we face in our relationships and sex lives.

This two part book series draws on the latest in neuroscience, biology, and sexology as well as ancient ways of exploring sex through spiritual practices and energetic bodywork to help the reader explore their body and mind in new and profound ways.

The accompanying workbook offers a step by step and practical guide for both women and men on how to lay the foundation for a nourishing connection and deeper, sensational, and intense sex.

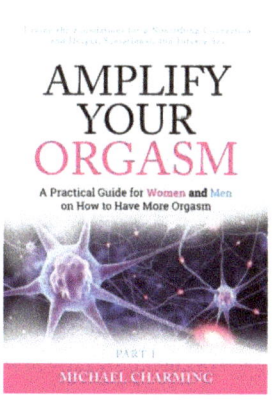

READERS WILL LEARN...

✓ How to explore different dimensions of the human body to experience sex and orgasms that go well beyond the physical realm
✓ A path away from sex that is fast, disconnected, and depleting to developing sex as a practice that feels deeply nourishing, pleasurable, and energizing

- ✓ How to identify harmful beliefs that block our access to sexual pleasure and replace them with healthier and more positive narratives
- ✓ How neuroplasticity offers practical tools to reprogram our mind and body to open up new pathways to experience amplified orgasm and heal from sexual trauma
- ✓ How energy moves through the body and can be harnessed to experience mind blowing orgasms including: mindgasms, whole body orgasms, and becoming multi- orgasmic
- ✓ The deep connection between desire and fear and why these are connected to sex, orgasm, and indeed our higher purpose on our life journey

REVIEWS

I just finished reading Amplify Your Orgasm. It was awesome! I loved that it gave me the language to talk about how my thoughts, emotions, and spiritual wellness affect my experience of orgasm. I can't wait for the workbook to come out so that I can do all of the exercises. Not only does the author explain a lot about how the different aspects of the self affect intimacy and pleasure, but he also gives concrete actions that I can use to actually chart my own course to getting more out of my sex life and relationships. Also...I was really impressed by the care taken to include lots of meaningful images. It is a good balance between theory and practice with tons of examples to explain the main concepts. The book gets into a lot of modern research on neuroscience too with tons of citations from peer-reviewed journals. I really appreciated this comprehensive look at orgasm and I have learned a great deal from this book!

****

Before reading Michael's book, I thought as a 57-year-old man that I knew everything I needed to know about my sexuality, my own body and especially, orgasms, but I now stand corrected. I'm not going to go as far as spelling out the changes his book has made in my life in such a public forum, but what I can share is this... I've never felt so comfortable about applying the new-found knowledge I discovered in,
"Amplify Your Orgasm!" There's a saying in life that says, "You're never too old to learn new things" and that's what you'll experience when you read and implement the learnings in this fantastic book. I highly recommend it, so the 5 stars are well deserved.

****

Ingram Content Group UK Ltd.
Milton Keynes UK
UKHW020604260523
422390UK00007B/26